CHASING SHADOWS

VISIONS OF OUR COMING TRANSPARENT WORLD

CHASING SHADOWS

VISIONS OF OUR COMING TRANSPARENT WORLD

EDITED BY

DAVID BRIN AND
STEPHEN W. POTTS

SPONSORED BY
THE ARTHUR C. CLARKE CENTER
FOR HUMAN IMAGINATION (UCSD)

TOR

A Tom Doherty Associates Book
New York

CHASING SHADOWS: VISIONS OF OUR COMING TRANSPARENT WORLD

Copyright © 2017 by David Brin and Stephen W. Potts

A Tor Book
Published by Tom Doherty Associates
175 Fifth Avenue
New York, NY 10010

www.tor-forge.com

Tor® is a registered trademark of Macmillan Publishing Group, LLC.

The Library of Congress Cataloging-in-Publication Data is available upon request.

ISBN 978-0-7653-8258-0 (hardcover)
ISBN 978-1-4668-8825-8 (e-book)

Our books may be purchased in bulk for promotional, educational, or business use. Please contact your local bookseller or the Macmillan Corporate and Premium Sales Department at 1-800-221-7945, extension 5442, or by e-mail at MacmillanSpecialMarkets@macmillan.com.

First Edition: January 2017

Printed in the United States of America

0 9 8 7 6 5 4 3 2 1

COPYRIGHT ACKNOWLEDGMENTS

CONTENTS

BIG BROTHER, LITTLE BROTHER, VILLAGE

NO PLACE TO HIDE

LOOKING BACK . . . AND LOOKING UP

CHASING SHADOWS

VISIONS OF OUR COMING
TRANSPARENT WORLD

Tsunami of lights
Life is illuminated
Scrutinize the eyes

INTRODUCTION
PRIVATE LIVES
JAMES GUNN

We look upon the current debate between privacy and the various forms of technology-driven surveillance as a contemporary issue, but it seems to be central to the human condition.

Among our hunter/gatherer ancestors privacy must have been a rare commodity, if it was possible at all. In a small group dependent upon every member for mutual survival, secrets are not only hard to protect, they may be dangerous. Once agriculture was introduced and life became more stable, predictable, and attached to a particular place, the issue of privacy—surely a central condition of self-consciousness and the growing possibilities of individualism—could take root along with the grains humans were beginning to plant.

Commerce and the development of early technologies led to larger communities and then to cities, where rural families, attracted to new opportunities, would migrate, leaving behind their social ties and intimacies for the anonymity of urban life. As a personal example, my wife grew up in a rural town of two thousand (which she always remembered as a golden time), and I was astonished by the familiarity she displayed, without considering it unusual, with the details of everybody's life and situation. I, on the other hand, grew up in a city where I knew only the people who lived on the same block, and even then only a few and nothing at all about those who lived across the street. My mother knew more and sometimes enlightened me, so my lack of social knowledge may have been the tunnel vision of youth, but even later, in neighborhoods where my own family was established, personal information was sheltered, and bits of insight came as revelations.

A consequence of urban anonymity was the attempt to replace common small-community intimacy with substitutes that could at least provide the illusion of familiarity: gossip, informal and formal groupings like clubs and organizations, and media, beginning with town criers and progressing to news-papers, radio, television, and finally the return to the self-revelations of today's social media. To be sure, each of these had other purposes—clubs and organizations got people of similar interests together to further social goals, while news-gathering-and-dispensing innovations had public information functions—but they also served the basic human need for connection and even the desire for insights into everyone else's personal histories. How else can we explain the enduring popularity of interviews, feature stories, agony columns, talk shows, and confessionals? Even, perhaps, the autobiography?

So, it seems to me, these two human attributes—the protection from public scrutiny of our inner selves and even of our personal activities that we call privacy, and the desire for intimate knowledge of others and the impulse toward self-revelation that is subsumed under surveillance—have been in conflict from the beginning. It is only in current circumstances, with the society-wide availability of electronic communication devices, that the conflict has come to a head.

WE SAW IT COMING

Science fiction isn't a predictive medium. It is a speculative genre, invested in creating plausible scenarios extrapolated from current developments. John W. Campbell once wrote that it exists between the laboratory and the marketplace, between possibility and availability. But every now and then—like a stopped clock that is right twice a day—perceptive authors come up with scenarios that match future realities. Surveillance was one of them. Shortly after the Second World War, George Orwell began work on his magnum opus, *1984*, which would terrify tens of millions into a lifelong dread of one-way, top-down, universal observation, the most potent tool of any would-be Big Brother.

Orwell wasn't alone. Others were already pondering the notion of transparency—a world not of surveillance, but *omniveillance*. For example, Pulitzer Prize–winning author John Cheever's "The Enormous Radio"—published in the May 17, 1947 issue of *The New Yorker*—takes place in the New York apartment of Cheever's favorite characters, Jim and Irene Westcott, only this time the Westcotts enter a sci-fi warp. (The story would be adapted for *The Twilight Zone*.) As described by critic David Truesdale:

Irene is distraught when their radio quits. Jim buys an expensive new one, which they soon discover has some . . . unusual qualities. This radio picks up the most unusual conversations from their neighbors, and shows that beneath the surface displayed to the public, people argue and fight, showing their true selves and lesser natures behind closed doors. It becomes such a distraction and troubles Irene to the point of depression that she convinces Jim to get rid of the damned machine. Whereupon, several strange twists occur in their own relationship.

Several stories in *Chasing Shadows* take on this theme, portraying potential effects of transparency on relationships—isn't it said that the truth can cleanse, but it can also hurt?

Continuing our scan of classic, transparency-related science fiction, T. L. Sherred's "E for Effort" showed that a device for filming the past could also spy on everyone's secrets, anticipating dozens of paranoia-inducing films. Not many years after Orwell and Cheever, in a 1962 issue of *Analog*, "The Circuit Riders" by R. C. Fitzpatrick envisioned a future when a kind of radar can detect individual emotions at long range—at least those that involve anger, verging on violence. Police use triangulation to zero in and detain potential murderers, in a manner not too dissimilar to Philip K. Dick's later "Minority Report" (still later filmed by Steven Spielberg). Fitzpatrick forgoes the absurd exaggerations of Dick and Spielberg, making clear that such detentions can only be precautionary and nonpunitive—a matter of brief triage and observation and warning—and hence the state's use of this method is portrayed as benign. Though the reader can extrapolate in either direction. Might this paternalistic power coalesce into something Orwellian, if it stays a state monopoly?

Or else, suppose that *everyone* gets access to such emotional radar? That is the notion explored by several stories in this volume.

An Internet search for "surveillance in science fiction" turned up a long list featuring "aerostat monitors" (Neal Stephenson) to "zed-rays" (Ray Cummings in 1936) and including "Invisible Watchers" (Edmond Hamilton, 1938), "Watchbird" (Robert Sheckley) and "Surveillance" (John Brunner, 1975). One of the earliest, surely, was Russia's Yevgeny Zamiatin's *We*. Two of the most recent are David Brin's *Earth* and Cory Doctorow's *Little Brother*, although the last was more reactions to present realities than anticipation.

One of my favorites is "Private Eye" by "Lewis Padgett" (the writing team of Henry Kuttner and C. L. Moore) in their 1949 speculation in *Analog*, 1949, which offered the ultimate surveillance system in the ability to recover images from the imprint of light rays on everyday walls. In the story it is used as a crime-fighting device and a way to prove intent, but it is a remarkable anticipation of the kind of universal surveillance that street, shop and home cameras aim at and toward which, perhaps, the trend is heading. Moreover, it offers an aspect to technological developments that I will return to later—the ability of people to adjust their behavior to accommodate new conditions. In

"Private Eye," it is the ability of a single clever criminal to conceal intent (the story is more concerned with psychological issues than privacy invasions) just as, in William Gibson's *Neuromancer,* the lower levels of society develop their own methods ("street smarts") for surviving, and even eventually prevailing over, seemingly overwhelming technological difficulties—thus earning the "punk" part of "cyberpunk."

Oh, but even such meticulous care will be for naught, if we get the ultimate-transparency future portrayed by Damon Knight in his classic 1972 story "I See You" (included in this volume). When neither law, nor technology nor cleverness can prevent everyone from seeing absolutely everything, human adaptability might mean changing every assumption that our ancestors held. This possibility is also explored thirty years later by Arthur C. Clarke and Stephen Baxter in their novel *The Light of Other Days,* wherein a "WormCam" allows anyone to observe anything through tiny wormholes, even using the technology to link minds.

Again and again, the real question is not whether new technologies will keep expanding humans' ability to see. The core dilemma is *who* will get these powers? Even if they are widely shared—thus preventing Big Brother—will that lead to wise citizenship? Or the opposite?

■ ■ ■

It is this bold tradition of thought-experimentation that *Chasing Shadows* carries forward, exploring possible consequences of what David Brin has called a "tsunami of light." Some authors react to this onrush of new sensory power with dread or loathing, as in Scott Sigler's "Public Domain," Jack McDevitt's "Your Lying Eyes," or Robert Silverberg's classic "To See the Invisible Man" (included in this volume), which contrasts in interesting ways to David Brin's story "Insistence of Vision."

Others take up the point made in Brin's *The Transparent Society,* that freedom and safety and even compassion may augment, if we all share the ability to look back, especially at power—a theme struck in this volume by James Morrow, Nancy Fulda, Brenda Cooper and Vylar Kaftan. Meanwhile, affecting stories by David Ramirez and Cat Rambo stand on a middle ground—aware of benefits, while noting too a poignant sense of passage.

TECHNOLOGY'S DANCE WITH SCIENCE FICTION

Do these stories reveal where we're all heading? The recent development of the smartphone comes at the end of a long line of communication devices intended to lessen the distance—or even the isolation—of people separated by other technological improvements such as roads, railroads, ships and other forms of getting people from one place to another in accessible and affordable ways. First came the handwritten message, the daily mail, the telegraph and eventually the telephone. The fact that these were instruments of basic human intercourse was underscored by a numbered series of standard messages used by families of service personnel during World War II to save the wires for official use. One such message was "I am pregnant," which led one congressman to suggest that a companion message ought to be "I am not pregnant."

The development of the telephone fostered a culture of self-revelation. What was difficult to say face-to-face became easier to talk about into a receiver in the sanctity of one's own home. But it also meant that strangers could intrude into your own private space, and even friends and family members might be induced by this deceptive new device to blurt out unwelcome "truths." In the film *Inherit the Wind*, Spencer Tracy as defense lawyer Clarence Darrow sums up to the jury the way in which technology changes the world, "Sure you can have the telephone—but you'll give up your privacy." Protocols for using such technologies were immediately adopted and then evolved.

So it was with the computer. When I got my first computer, probably about 1980, it was only a machine for creating documents, an upgrade from the electric typewriter, which was itself an upgrade from the standard typewriter, which was itself an upgrade over the portable Smith-Corona with which I started my literary life. My first computer printer was really just a glorified electric typewriter. But then the computer was connected to the Internet, and it became a device that allowed me to communicate with people anywhere, particularly in distant places. And the messages that once took days or even weeks to reach foreign friends and potential students and colleagues now were virtually instantaneous.

I speculated then that the generation that grew up with the world at their fingertips would experience a different concept of distance. People in far-off places would no longer be aliens; they would be as close as the people you see every day. Surely, I thought, violent conflicts between people of different races and different political beliefs would no longer be possible when potential enemies could no longer be dehumanized. I'm not sure it has worked out that way. Maybe the older generation, with all of its misconceptions, is still in charge. Or maybe the younger generation still has time to shape a new world.

Certainly the smartphone, with its unrelenting communication, its textual temptations, and its ability to photograph or film anything, any time, anywhere, has raised the stakes. The concept of the world as a place you can reach out to if you wish is now something that you carry around with you. In fact, for many, it is something they cannot do without. I see students on campus every day walking to their classes with phones held to their ears, oblivious to the scenery or their fellow students or even the traffic, which halts obligingly for them to cross. Not every place is so forgiving. Many years ago I wrote a story about the development of a silencer that shut out noise by broadcasting a wave 180 degrees out of phase. One side effect was that people got struck down by cars they didn't hear. Horace Gold thought it was ridiculous that people would abandon the habits of a lifetime and rejected it. But that's what has happened to the phone-addicted generation—and it will get both worse and better, as they start to wear augmented reality glasses that overlay artificiality upon the real world, complete with noise-canceling earbuds and overlays that cover up whatever they do not wish to see.

Protocols have developed for smartphones as well, though they are still in flux. It turns out that people using smartphones while driving, particularly texting, are distracted. They have accidents and kill other people and themselves. So first we have campaigns urging people to stop, and then we get laws. Eventually, people learn how to live with it rather than die by it. But they'll get the right to text at the wheel back soon, when cars are driving themselves. Meanwhile, those selfsame phones will tap into satellite views of traffic, just ahead, or whether your luncheon date is still waiting for you, by the public fountain. And yes, this too will call on us to adapt.

That brings me to my final point. With every new technological development, there are a series of reactions that vary from individual to individual and from group to group, ranging from joyous acceptance to disdainful rejection. But if the new technology has benefits, if it makes life—for a sufficient number—more efficient or more interesting, it gets adopted and its use becomes broadspread enough to change the nature of society itself.

The rise of social media may not have been as predictable. The ways in which people can interact—orally, textually, and visually—proliferate, and it is difficult to see at this point in the evolution of digital devices and methods of aggregating communications where the advancements will end. Perhaps never as long as there is money—or, at least, the prospect of profits—to be made from providing platforms and as long as there is a hunger, particularly among the young, for intimate interactions at a distance.

All of this has coincided with, or been precipitated by, a growing fascination among the young for self-revelation and a consequent contraction of the need for, or perhaps even the expectation of, privacy. Combine this with the possible anonymity of the Internet and growing political uprisings across the world and the potential for social revolution is high and rising. Protocols for resolving such conflicts are still debated. On one side are the forces of tradition and government, both of which want to set limits and monitor transgressions; on the other, the dynamism of technologies, voiced by spokespeople within science fiction such as Cory Doctorow and preempted by political revolutionary groups like ISIS. Where it will all come out is still, at this time, in doubt.

One outcome is certain, however: technologies will win. The genie is out of the bottle. Hardly ever in the history of invention (with the possible exception, so far, of the thermonuclear bomb) has a powerful technology been invented and not implemented. It is useful to remind ourselves, however, of Isaac Asimov's musings about "futuristics," which ended with his comment that it isn't the prediction that is difficult but the side effect, the unanticipated consequence: not the automobile, he wrote, but the traffic jam; not radio but the soap opera; not the income tax but the expense account.

And a comment that Horace Gold once wrote to me when he was laying out instructions about writing stories for *Galaxy*: "The truest thing that humanity has learned is that you can't fight city hall." So it is with whatever state of affairs science, technology and politics may bring about. Humanity will learn how to live with it. We will learn how to balance our desire for interaction and intimacy against our need to preserve our inner selves against exposure.

That's what science fiction has taught us.

AD JUSTITIAM PER LUCEM

AD JUSTITIAM PER LUCEM

Smaller and smaller
Cameras proliferating
Nothing will stop them

Beware what you sign up for. Those user agreements . . .
. . . can be tough.

MINE, YOURS, OURS

JACK SKILLINGSTEAD

They wanted a piece of her body.

Emily was collating tax documents for a client when an urgent alert flashed red in her Corneal Window where, like so many things, it was impossible to ignore: an exclamation point in the shape of a stylized caduceus with the letters I.O.E beneath it.

Emily's heart fluttered and her breathing went shallow with anxiety. She pushed back from the workstation. Regardless of her exaggerated anxiety level, as Dr. Schafer called it, the alert from I.O.E. triggered an anxiety spike. How foolish she had been ever to submit her profile.

She wouldn't be able to resume work until she responded. Emily closed her eyes. It flashed in the dark.

"Emily?"

She looked up. Sindhu Mahre, the department lead, stood behind her. "Are you all right?"

"I—I have to go home."

"What's wrong?"

"It's illness. In the family. My mother."

"Oh, I'm sorry. Is it serious?"

"Yes."

Hypertrophic cardiomyopathy killed Emily's mother, but that was long ago. A transplant organ might have saved her. Emily never forgot her mother's sudden absence, never forgot the empty body, a *thing* under the hospital sheet, not her mother but all that remained. Now it was Emily's genetic inheritance, a terror that *might* happen, even if it probably wouldn't.

"I'll log you out on family leave," Sindhu said, being kind.

"Thank you."

Emily joined the I.O.E. to alleviate her "irrational fear," as Dr. Schafer described it. *Irrational but altogether genuine*—one of his stock phrases. *His* solution was the anxiolytic, Nardil. "A mild one, Emily. It leaves you in charge, just better able to relax a bit. Evaluate." When she declined, the prescription processed through anyway and appeared in her mailbox. Angry, she threw it in the kitchen cupboard, where she kept her vitamins.

Of course, Dr. Schafer did not approve of her joining I.O.E. But Emily was an adult, regardless of her anxiety assessments. Should she require a heart transplant, the International Organ Exchange would guarantee a donor. *Guarantee* she not become, like her mother, a thing under white hospital sheets in a room where the machines had stopped. But that guarantee required Emily to be a donor of at least one organ, should a recipient in need be a convenient match—a somewhat less remote possibility than Emily's heart failure. Two terrifying prospects . . .

. . . and now the second one was happening. She could hear Dr. Schafer telling her. *You shouldn't have joined I.O.E, not in your state of mind.*

But she had. And Emily never imagined her call to donate would arise so soon.

■ ■ ■

The alert continued to flash as Emily made her way home on the rail. She could not disable it without severing everything else, friends, news feeds, all the world that came through her Window: Jenny's cat danced on one foot; Treva was outraged about Sudan (and everything else, it seemed); David had a weird dream; ten things you didn't know about drones; blink-link this quiz! The International Organ Exchange planted a red alert in the middle of all that.

Safe in her apartment, Emily removed her CW lenses. Immediately she activated the vapor screen in her nook by the kitchen. Jewel light projectors twinkled. An Aladdin's plume of digital smoke resolved into her feed—and here was the alert again, urgent, red, stabbing. But also friends, information, the world outside her head and beyond her walls.

Emily turned away and made a cheese sandwich. Simply knowing her feed was running—that soothed her. The same way her I.O.E. contract had comforted her the moment she submitted her signature. But when she turned back to the vapor screen, there was only the insistent, pulsing red caduceus. Emily whimpered, a sound she almost didn't recognize as coming from her own throat. She tossed the butter knife into the sink, the sharp metal-on-metal clatter like the externalization of her impatience. "All right, all right."

She sat down and stirred her finger under the alert, which promptly vanished, replaced by the blue I.O.E. logo ringed by images of happy people around the globe exchanging toothy smiles with white-coated surgeons. A male voice spoke to Emily in a businesslike tone.

"Good day, neighbor Emily Vega."

Emily didn't bother replying, since it was impossible to tell whether the voice was human, recorded, or contrived by machines. *Identify what you are*, she wanted to say, but even that seemed a burden of inquiry she shouldn't be pressured to make.

After a pause, the voice continued. "Emily Vega, are you there?"

She sighed. It could still be a machine. "I'm here, yes. What is it you need from me?"

"Your right lung for transplantation."

■ ■ ■

Alvaro Samano's pulmonary fibrosis was no fault of his own. The agent from the Exchange made sure Emily understood that, but she didn't care, it didn't matter. "Alvaro's condition is idiopathic," the agent said, as if to assure Emily that Alvaro was *deserving* of the violation about to be inflicted upon Emily's body.

Emily smiled tightly. All she could think about was the operating table, like a slab on which they would lay her out and deprive her of consciousness, deprive her of identity while they cut her. Oh, she had reviewed all the details of the procedure. She was required to review them. "I don't need to know about that," Emily said, meaning Alvaro's innocence and the grisly details of surgically removing her lung.

"I.O.E. pledges full transparency."

Thank you, no.

Alvaro Samano was twenty-seven years old, married, a father, a participating member of society—fully invested in the social contract, Emily supposed, like her former classmates, like her coworkers. Not that she ever craved that sort of inclusion. She had her life, a perfectly valid life, with routines and privacy into which she did not want to invite strangers, be they neighbors or otherwise. Another catchphrase. *You depend on your neighbors, so your neighbors can depend on you!*

"I wonder," Emily said to the young woman in the business suit who had just told her about the pledge of transparency, who had just provided, unasked for, a biographical and exculpatory sketch of Alvaro Samano. "I wonder if a delay is possible."

"A delay?"

"A postponement, I mean. Of the surgery."

The interviewer turned her empty hands palm up and smiled understandingly. "It's normal to be anxious."

Tell that to Dr. Schafer. Emily said, "You see, I never—"

"And I'm certain you can appreciate Alvaro's own anxiety."

"Of course."

"Participating in the International Organ Exchange is a cooperative invest-ment in humanity, and I think it's wonderful that you've joined us."

"Yes, yes." Emily looked at her knees. "But . . ."

"But?"

"Is it, I mean—the urgency. Is the urgency necessary?"

It was.

■　■　■

Emily arranged for leave from her position at Moss-Waters LLP. They were very understanding. Sindhu congratulated Emily on her worthy participation in a vital program. "I'm so glad your mother is better, and now you're doing your part for a neighbor." Emily cringed inwardly, the lie rebounding in her face. One lie always led to another. Better to say nothing at all. Sindhu arranged the time off without depleting Emily's earned vacation days. "You'll be back in no time, the way these procedures are performed now. And you get a booster implant for your one good lung. Too bad the booster can't operate alone. Any-way, it's barely more than an office visit. My sister. . . ."

■　■　■

Emily presented herself at Swedish Hospital the evening before the transplan-tation procedure. She believed she could do it, fulfill her requirement. But a lung, it was serious. A contribution that would restore quality of life to a stranger named Alvaro Samano. At least that's all the Exchange would ask of her. She had merely to endure it, and then a heart would be available if and when she required it. A heart was the most serious thing of all. Others in the Exchange, whose demands were less grave, were not required to offer up a selection from their living bodies.

When the nurse and the I.O.E. rep came into Emily's room to go over prep-arations, on her last night with two complete lungs, she said, "It's funny to be doing this for a stranger."

"But Alvaro isn't a stranger," the Exchange woman said, and the unspoken but fully understood and agreed upon addendum attached: *no one is. The world is now a village.* Emily had never believed that. Did that make her so odd? She had her feed, enclosed within her chosen privacy. What more did they want of her?

"Of course not," Emily tried to smile.

"He's your neighbor."

"I know."

Information, questions, answers, assurances—and good luck. Then they left her alone. Emily lay on the hospital bed under tightly stretched sheets. On the slab, hovering, it seemed, over the same abyss that had swallowed her mother's light. Her fear was irrational, Dr. Schafer would have told her. Emily *knew* that. Couldn't she be allowed her irrationalities? She wanted her mother to come and tell her it was all right, she wanted to be held. So foolish, a grown woman wanting her mother's comfort. But Emily hadn't anyone, no family, her friends existing only on her feed. She didn't even allow herself a pet.

In the hospital bed, Emily reached for her handheld device, a slim keyboard no bigger than her palm. She thumbed a post, and her words appeared in her CW, bracketed by a flow of information.

—you'll never guess where I am—

When responses began to appear, Emily hesitated. She didn't want to tell them.

—i'm on vacation is all—

—oh where—

—that's my secret / someplace warm and happy and wonderful i can tell you—

—wonderful—

—fantastic emily—

Of course anyone who actually investigated . . . who unleashed a curiosity worm into the mesh . . . could find out the truth, where Emily was at this moment. What was going on. The fact that no one even cared enough to poke at her privacy façade, well, it hurt a little, even though it was the life she chose.

I have friends, but superficial ones. Sociable, but at arm's length. The sort of friend I am, to others.

Alvaro *was* a stranger. They all were. Of course, I.O.E wanted her to meet Alvaro, and of course she declined. She was meeting her responsibility; that would have to be sufficient. She refused even to view an image of the man. Let him remain nothing to her. That way she could direct her fear and resentment toward an abstraction, rather than a man. Alvaro, the abstraction, of course knew all about Emily.

In I.O.E. you exchanged more than organs. All the world was like that. Each level of participation in community, in convenience, demanded you surrender a larger portion of your identity. Was it any different than trading a piece of your body for the assurance you would continue to exist? Everyone remembered, or was supposed to remember, the bad times, the times when unidentified voices wielded disproportionate social leverage. The enemy had long been identified, and its name was anonymity.

Now there were no deep secrets, only the slim privacy that citizens gave each other out of courtesy. That seemed to suffice, for most—a "village" of reciprocal respect. But Emily looked back, with longing, at those vast, anonymous cities of old, where you might live forever a stranger, and possibly die alone, but it was no one's business.

And yet . . . no one forced you to sign the I.O.E. contract, she chided. *You made your own body part of the village.*

Emily folded her hands over her keypad device, over her chest, and closed her eyes. The illuminated feed scrolled against the screen of her eyelids. In a corner, time rolled over, and Emily felt a weight upon her chest. She opened her eyes, her focus adjusting beyond the feed to the antiseptic details of her hospital room. She could hardly breathe, the weight was so tremendous.

Emily peeled the covers back before she even knew she was going to do it. She found her clothes in the closet and quickly dressed, afraid someone would interrupt her. As each layer of clothing covered more flesh, her anxiety subsided. No one accosted her on her way out. She had a right not to be there, after all. Or maybe no one noticed. People frequently failed to notice Emily.

■ ■ ■

Emily was eating lunch outdoors, holding the cheese-and-onion sandwich between the fingers of both hands, taking small bites. It was such a nice spring afternoon. She sat on a stone bench in the urban park between the building containing the offices of Moss-Waters LLP and two other office towers. The small green leaves of decorative trees flickered in the breeze. Then a man's shadow appeared on the pavement, and Emily looked up. The man was young and well-dressed, wearing a tie. He was also wearing a stylish pair of Window glasses. Some people didn't like the corneal lenses.

"Hello," he said.

"I'm sorry, do I know you?"

"I'm Alvaro Samano's brother. My name is Thiago."

Emily nodded, waiting for words.

"May I speak with you?" Thiago said.

"I suppose so, but I'm not changing my mind."

He waved her objection aside. "Another donor has already been selected."

"Good."

"Your canceling, it wasn't right. It was unconscionable, and that's putting it charitably."

"But it worked out." Emily's voice was as small as she felt.

The man stared at her, like he was staring at a strange bug he'd discovered in his garden. Emily looked at her sandwich, which she couldn't imagine finishing. She said, "It's just, at the last minute I couldn't go through with it. I wanted to, but it wasn't a choice. It didn't feel like one, I mean. I don't expect that to matter to you or your brother. For whatever it's worth, I've been punished."

"Expulsion from the Exchange, yes."

Of course, everybody knew everything. It didn't take a curiosity worm to find out about a major broken promise. A village sin.

"I can't blame them," she said. Sometimes Emily thought that without secrets a person wasn't really herself but simply what her neighbors thought she was, vocalized she was. Alvaro's brother was still standing there, staring at her from behind his Window glasses in that strange, almost predatory way, so she asked, "Is there something else?"

"Alvaro was very upset. You should know that. He's not as strong as some people. He's frightened, and will be until the operation is over."

"I can understand."

"Oh, can you? You never met, since you wouldn't allow him that courtesy, but for Alvaro it felt like he'd gotten to know you. And then for you, a neighbor, to disappoint him like that."

"I'm sorry." *But he doesn't know me and neither do you.*

"I have upset you?"

"I'm not upset." She was, though. And now she was distracted by a post on her private feed:

—em, did you really duck out on that guy like they're saying—

"Goodbye, then," Thiago said, but she wasn't listening. Messages had begun to cascade down her feed.

—that poor man—

—i heard he died—

—my god em by now aren't you even an adult—

Emily's feed was *clotted* with messages from critical strangers. They overwhelmed her friends, until her friends became strangers themselves.

—is it true you did that—

Emily was relieved to return to her cubicle, where she surrendered her CW lenses to the orderly, impersonal repetitiveness of assembling tax documents.

At five o'clock it was time to stop. She had hopes that it would be over. Hesitantly, she switched back to her private feed, and the onslaught resumed. Emily discovered, to her horror, that she was *trending*. Her perfidy was trending. Was she the first person ever to withdraw from the International Organ Exchange, for goodness sake? Hadn't her neighbors anything better to talk about? Again, a tremendous weight of anxiety pressed upon Emily's chest. Her lungs, *her* lungs, labored for breath.

We all breathe the same air was the ubiquitous slogan, suggesting the planet's atmosphere was the common ocean in which they all swam, all the world's neighbors. The shared pride of nine billion souls who—as a village—worked together to repair the atmosphere, the seas, the land. A better world, for the most part . . . *but not for people like me.*

"I do my own breathing, thank you," Emily sometimes said, alone and unheard in her apartment, listening to the phrase in her mind, or out of her feed, sometimes unable to make a distinction between the auditory memory and the streaming admonition.

She stumbled to the rail station. Thiago Amano tagged her in a post that blink-linked to a video loop recorded from his Window glasses. The clip showed Emily sitting on her bench with her sandwich held delicately between the fingers of both hands: ". . . I'm not changing my mind . . . I'm not changing my mind . . ."

—so callous—

—honestly em—

—never really knew you I guess—

That was true. No one really knew her. Why did they think they had to? The flood of critical comments created tributaries off the main topic, surging with uninformed opinions. At home, unable to stop looking, Emily witnessed the final indignity: Dr. Schafer's self-interview on the general subject of mood and anxiety disorders, intended, he said, as a public service. Though he never mentioned her by name, Dr. Schafer's tag represented him as Emily Vega's Personal Therapist. Of course, that's what guaranteed a million blink-links.

Emily interrupted the feed and removed her Window lenses, popping them out like coins into a beggar's cupped hand. What was she begging for, except to be left alone?

■ ■ ■

A month passed. Emily wore her CWs at work and removed them immediately afterwards. Poison ran through her feed and she never looked at it anymore. She could not create another. Each individual was allowed one identity, their own true name. Everything attached to it, flowed to it. What if she read what the poisoners said about her and became what they believed she was?

But what she never expected—the thing that hurt most—was pity. The latest wave to crest across her feed. Generous villagers, grownups, expressing charity, chiding the chiders.

—leave her alone, can't you see she's not all there?–

—look, she's refused to take even mild anxiolytics. That's dumb, but it's part of the syndrome, clinging to depression like an addict–

—did you watch that compilation about her mother? How sad! You bullies better back off, or we can look closer at YOU—

Trend lines shifted. The decent villagers were winning . . . and their pity hurt worse than anything, hurling Emily even deeper into a pit.

She rumbled home on the rail, one among her neighbors, in the middle of the world but separated from it. The train rocked and swayed. Faces stared under jaundiced light, eyes seeing what she did not see, their feeds active. A young man in a black sweater sat on the seat across the aisle, watching her— *her,* not his feed. Emily couldn't interpret his expression. But Emily never could interpret expressions, the nuances, could never complete the translation, never answer the question: *what is he thinking?* This man appeared unhealthy, too thin, weak, taking shallow, consciously measured breaths.

Her stop slid into place outside the train and halted. The doors opened. Emily stood up. The man's gaze followed her. What did he imagine he knew about her? "Yes," Emily said as she passed him, "I'm that awful, awful person. Doesn't that make you happy?"

"I don't think you're awful. I'm—"

But she stepped onto the platform and quickly walked along the body of the train, back toward the stairs to the street level. The train hummed out of the station. Following after it, a hot breath of air adjusted Emily's blouse, flipped her bangs—a mother's invisible hand fussing with her appearance.

Behind her, someone wheezed, "Slow down, please wait."

Emily looked back. The sickly man in the black sweater was walking toward her, breathing with difficulty, something in his hand. Of course she knew who he was. He and his brother looked very much alike. Did it mean there was nothing she could do, no separation she could effect? Was this the beginning, would they now follow her out of her feed and into the real world of her every day aloneness? If true, she couldn't bear it. Emily fled up the stairs and home to her apartment.

■ ■ ■

She stood in her kitchen, the Nardil container in her hand. Why hadn't she returned the pills to Dr. Schafer, as she had intended, or thrown them away? "Why don't I ever know which is what?" Emily asked the empty room. Maybe she *did* know. Hadn't she read somewhere, a blink-link off her feed, about the idea that conscious decisions were illusions and all one's true decisions formulated under the surface, where something that was you but not *you* sorted reality? What if the not-you was part of a lot of other not-yous inhabiting the unconscious, and so it was your *neighbors* all over again, a community, or a mob—and a mob of Emilys within, the cavewoman, the terrified child, the presapient animal, the mourning daughter—and *they* had all decided that, yes, keep the Nardil and by all means use it.

By all means *take* it. Take all of it.

When she had said no to the prescription, Dr. Schafer told her she might want it, if not today, then some day. "Pay attention to the dosage," he had said. Dr. Schafer's risk assessment, his evaluation and session notes, were available to the greater medical establishment. Key words flagged, authorizing deeper investigation of risk factors, "harm to oneself or others," the details of her treatment *collated* like so many 1040s, itemized deduction declarations, and W-2s. Finally, a human assessor, not unlike Dr. Schafer himself, reviewed the information (if a human ever did review it) and directed the prescription be filled "in the interests of the individual and the society at large," as they liked to put it.

At least no one would make her actually *swallow* the Nardil; that was up to Emily.

She struggled with the cap, scattering pills across the counter like seeds. Twenty seeds for her eternal garden. Emily stared at the pills, her breathing gone shallow with dread, her lungs ready to betray her, as she had betrayed Alvaro before everyone turned on her.

A musical tone sounded through the apartment—someone pressing the button next to her name outside the building's lobby door. The chimes sounded again, like a prod, like a finger poking her shoulder. Was she supposed to *let* them decide for her?

Angry, Emily swept the pills into the sink and washed them down the drain.

On the screen in the living room the man in the black sweater gazed back at her. "Hello?" he said, sounding out of breath. "Emily Vega?"

She didn't expect to reply, but apparently the words had already been selected. She managed to twist them to her advantage even as they blurted past her lips. "It didn't work. I washed them all down the drain. All of them."

"I don't understand."

"Of course you don't."

"You left your keypad on the train."

"My—?"

He held up something that might have been Emily's device, though it was hard to tell, just as it was hard to tell whether this man was Alvaro Samano, though she had been positive, or nearly positive, only minutes ago. She checked her pockets, looked around the room, but didn't see her keypad. "I'm coming down."

The man in the black sweater stood on the porch outside her building.

Emily opened the door as he was triggering a medical inhaler into his mouth. He put it back in his pocket, looking sheepish. "Asthma," he said.

"You're not who I thought you were."

"I couldn't catch up to you, and you didn't respond to messages. I guess you couldn't without this." He held out her device. "I knew who you were, so I searched your address and routed it. My name's Caleb."

Emily accepted the device and turned it over in her hands.

The neighbor in the black sweater, Caleb, frowned. "I'm sorry, did I interrupt something?"

"No, you didn't interrupt anything. I did."

He looked puzzled. There were so many of them in the world, so many puzzled people. They flailed at each other, told each other who they thought they were supposed to be, every interaction a validating performance entangled in a safety net of crisscrossing feeds, not even suspecting they had fallen off the high wire, or were afraid to climb for it in the first place. But not Emily, finally not Emily. She was alone, balancing across the sky, where you had to be a little crazy.

She preferred it that way, didn't she? Preferred to be alone?

Later she found one Nardil, one capsule that hadn't gone down the drain. She held it in the palm of her hand, and asked herself the question again.

"Progress" often comes
at a cost.

INSISTENCE OF VISION

DAVID BRIN

She's pretty enough. Plump in that I-don't-give-a-damn kind of way.

And *un-blurred*. I can see her. That makes all the difference.

"Did you just visit the Dodeco Exhibit?" I ask while she drinks from a public fountain.

Seems a likely guess. Her sleeveless pixelshirt shimmers with geometric shapes that flow and intersect with many-petaled flowers, shifting red to blue and emitting a low audible rhythm to match. She must have image-copied one of the theme works on display in the museum, just up a nearby flight of granite steps, where I glimpse crowds of folks—both blurred and visible—visiting the exhibition.

Wiping her mouth with the back of one hand, she glances up-down across my face, making a visible choice. Answering with a faint smile.

"Yeah, the deGornays are farky-impressive. A breakthrough in fractalart."

Gazing at me without suspicion, she's bare-eyed—a pair of simple digispectacles hang unused from her neck. The aiware looks kinda retro, like granny glasses—clear augment-lenses glinting in sunlight, here at the edge of Freedom Park. But the key feature is this.

She's not wearing them. Not at the moment. I have a chance.

"There's nobody better'n deGornay," I counter, trying to match the with-it tone of her subgeneration. Navigating with a few tooth clicks and blink commands, I've already used my own specs to sift-search, grabbing a conversational tip about neomod art.

"But I really like Tasselhoff. She's farknotic."

"You-say?" The girl notches an eyebrow, perhaps suspecting my use of a spec-prompt. After all, we're unevenly augmented at the moment. I worry she's about to lift her own pair . . . but no. She continues to stare bare, cocking her head in mock defiance.

"You do realize Tasselhoff *cheats*? She ai-tunes the cadence of her artwork to sync with the viewer's *neural wave*! Some say it's not even legal."

Gosh. Bright, educated and passionately opinionated. I am drawn, partly by the danger.

Several blurs pass nearby, then a visible couple. The man, garbed in penguin-like attire, sidles in to use the drinking fountain. So many people—it gives me an idea.

"I agree about the neural cheat, but Tasselhoff does offer a unique . . . say, it's awful crowded here. Are you walking somewhere? I was strolling by the park."

Ambiguous. Whichever way she's heading, that's my direction too.

Brief hesitation. Her hand touches the granny glasses. I keep smiling. *Please don't. Please don't.*

The hand drops. Eyes remain uncovered, bare-brave, open to the world and *just* the world.

She nods. "Sure. I can take the long way. I'm Jayann."

"Sigismund," I answer. We shake in the new, quasiroman fashion, more sanitary, hands not contacting hands but lightly squeezing each others' wrists.

"Sigismund. Really?"

"Cannot tell a lie." I laugh and so does she, unaware how literal I'm being.

I can't lie. Or rather, I can. But it's not allowed.

She doesn't notice what happens next, but I do. As we both turn to leave the museum steps, I glimpse the penguin-garbed man staring at me through his pair of augmented reality specs. He frowns. Appears to mumble something . . .

. . . before he and his wife abruptly vanish from clear sight, becoming blurs.

■ ■ ■

Walking together now, Jayann and I are chatting and flirting amiably. Our path skirts the edge of Freedom Park. Babbling inanely about trends in art, we stay to the right as joggers pound along, most of them visible but some blurred. Just vague clouds of color—Collision-Avoidance Yellow—that even my damned-limited specs can see. I hear them all, of course—barefoot or shod, blurred or un-blurred—pounding along the trail, panting like their ancestors, hunting across primeval savannah.

I offer a comparison of deGornay to Kavanaugh, deliberately naive, so she'll lecture for a while as we skirt a realm of leafy lanes. Specs don't work in there. No augmentations at all. That's why it's Freedom Park. Few would expect to find a cursed creature like me right here at the edge of what—for me—is dangerous ground. And that's why I come.

To my left the nearby street and city roar with stimulus, both real and virtual, every building overlaid with metadata or uberinfo. I can fine-tune my specs to an extent. Omit adverts, for example. Though my tools are limited, even primitive. And half the buildings are just solid blocks of prison gray to me.

My walls.

No matter, I'm concentrating on what Jayann says. Actually, it's very interesting! Her art-enthusiasm is catching. Even a bit endearing. Mostly listening, I only have to comment now and then.

Soon, I hear piping voices and glance back, stepping aside for a cluster of maybe twenty child-sized blurs—little clouds of chatter, giggles and gossip, pitter-pattering along the gravel. Shepherded by two adults—one of them a clot of vagueness, the other unedited and brave. Visible as a lanky-dark young man—my specs even reveal an *ID-tag*—his name and public profile.

Wow. Just like in better times, before the change. Before I lost the power that everyone around me takes for granted.

Godlike omniscience.

"Well, I have get back to work," Jayann says. "I'll shortcut through here." She indicates a tree-lined path, clearly inviting me to come along.

"What do you do?" I ask, diverting the subject. I take two steps, following her. Already there's a drop in spec resolution. I daren't go much farther.

"I work in sales. But studying art history so I can teach. You?"

"Used to teach. Now I help a public service agency."

"Volunteer work? That's farky and sweet." She smiles. Though backing down the path, she's starting to grow fuzzy. I'd better talk fast.

"But I manage to come here—to the park and museum—every Tuesday, same time, like clockwork."

And there it is. Totally lame and stunningly old-fashioned, but maybe that will intrigue her.

It even seems so! She grins.

"Okay, Mister Mysterious Sigismund. Maybe I'll bump into you again, some Tuesday."

I sigh inwardly. It's all I could hope for. A chance.

Then hope crashes. She grabs her specs.

"Wait. Just to be sure, let me drop filters and give you my—"

"Say, is that a bed of gladiolas? This early?" I ask, purposely stepping past Jayann, walking down the path, counting steps and memorizing it as best I can. The park's e-interference grows more intense. Then, abruptly, my specs cut off completely. I'm blind. But it's worth it if she follows. If that prevents her from looking at me through augmented reality.

I keep walking, several more paces, toward the memorized flower bed. Bending over, I take off the now-useless aiware, pretending to look. Without specs, I'm even more blind—not even static, just blackness. But I chatter on, as if able to see bare-eyed, hoping she followed me down here, where specs don't work.

"You know, they remind me of that deGornay—"

"Bastard!"

A pair of fists hammer my back, then a hard-driven foot slams into my knee from behind, sending me tumbling, crashing into the shrubbery. Pain mixes with humiliated disappointment. And even worse . . .

. . . my specs are gone! I grope for them.

"How dare you!" She continues screaming. "You . . . you liar!"

My left hand probes among the crumpled flowers, searching.

"I . . . I never lied, Jayann."

"What were you planning? To get all my info, my address, to break in and murder me?"

"My crimes weren't violent. Look them up. Please, Jayann. . . ."

"Don't you *dare* speak my name! What are you doing?"

"My specs. Please help me find them. Without them . . ."

"You mean these?" A rustling sound. Turning toward it.

"I can't see without them."

"So I've heard." Her voice drips with irony and anger. "Instead of prison, take convicts and *blind* them. Let 'em only see what *special specs* deliver to the brain. No possible victims, or children, or anyone who *chooses* not to let a criminal watch them."

"Yes, but—"

"You stole from me that right!"

Against better judgment, I argue.

"You could have looked . . . with specs . . . seen my warning marks . . ."

She howls incoherent fury and I know it was *not* wise to argue. I may not have *lied,* but I did divert attention. Used flirtation and charm. Acted like a regular man. I envision her there on the path, clutching my specs, shaking them. "I ought to smash these!"

"Please give them to me, Jayann . . . and guide me back to the street. I'll never bother you again, I swear. . . ."

Probably, she's a fine person, under normal circumstances. I try to sympathize with her sense of betrayal. But the rage that pummels into me seems extreme, for a social offense . . . charming a young woman into talking to me, bare-eyed, for a while. *Mea culpa,* I would pay for it. But did I deserve a pounding with fists? Her demeaning shouts?

A crunching sound. My specs, getting smashed. And God knows what's next.

Making a best guess, I run. Gravel stays underfoot for eight good steps, then gives way to grass, so I correct, meeting path again . . .

. . . before tripping over someone's outstretched leg and sprawling face-first. My chin stings and I spit dust. "Jayann. . . . I'm sorry!"

"Not *half* as sorry as you're—"

I leap up, stagger forward again. There was a gentle slope down from the street, I recall. And now I hear the panting of joggers. Traffic sounds beyond. With that bearing, I run again.

No more hope of getting my specs back or reporting for work. My sole thought is to reach the sidewalk . . . then just *sit down* at the curb, pathetic and still. A harmless blind man. Word will reach my probation officer. Ellie will come get me. Lecture me. Berate me. Possibly impose punishment. Though it's all recorded and I swear, I don't think I committed any actual—

Traffic noise is louder. Joggers curse as they weave around me. How I wish I could see even blurs.

Someone plants a hand against my back and *shoves.* Stumbling off an unseen curb, I hear brakes squeal. Then deeper darkness falls.

■ ■ ■

Eventually, all kinds of pain grow dull. Lying in a hospital bed, still blind while docs rewire some new prison spectacles around skull damage, I listen as Ellie explains about how lucky I am. What a fool I was. How close I came to breaking several rules and lengthening my sentence. To losing my life.

"I know. People over-react when they spec you're a felon. Too many blur themselves automatically. You feel like a pariah. So, would you prefer some awful prison cell? The savagery of prison life? At least now you can work. Pay taxes. Live among us."

That makes me laugh, rattling several broken bones.

"Among you. Right. Among the blurs."

She lets that bitter comment sit a while, then asks.

"Why, with so little time left on your sentence . . . why take such chances?"

How to answer, except with a shrug. Was Robinson Crusoe ever lonelier than I feel, here in the big city, imprisoned by electronic disdain?

Ellie takes silence as my answer. Then she tells me the final outcome of the fateful afternoon at Freedom Park.

■ ■ ■

Months later, I see her at the steps of the museum. Jayann sits a few steps up from where we met. It's winter and her garb is much less gay. Despite a thick sweater, I can tell she's lost weight.

I slip on my newest specs—bought only last week. Super-farky, they supply a wealth of information. Godlike waves of it. Nametags under every face that passes by, and more if I simply blink and ask for it. The basic right of any free citizen.

Under *her* name, flaring red:

CONVICTED FELON
attempted third degree murder

I am tempted to feel guilty. My thoughtless, desperate, well-intended flirtations led to this.

But then, did I . . . would anyone . . . deserve what she tried to do to me that day? In a fit of offended pride?

The other temptation, to feel triumph over her defeat, is one that I quash, with shame. As she should have quashed her temper, that day.

As my own punishment chastened me—perhaps made me better—will she learn as well? Life can be harsh. Still, things are better now than long ago. There are second chances. There is second sight.

She looks around, seeming (except for those virtual scarlet letters) like a regular, attractive young woman, taking in the sun and breeze, though with a melancholy sigh. Her spec-mediated gaze passes over me . . .

. . . then onward. For of course, to her, I'm just another blur.

I turn, leaning on my cane, to leave. Only then, glancing at the information-rich calendar within my virtuality, I realize.

It's Tuesday.

Does familiarity breed contempt?
Or understanding?

PLANETBOUND

NANCY FULDA

There's a moment that comes, the first time you step on the rim of a planet, when you suddenly realize how breakable you are. When you finally understand that despite the bone density treatments, despite the braces cradling your back and legs, despite the half-dozen hands that support your first faltering steps down the hallway, you will never be more than a hair's breadth from disaster. A false step, an unexpected nudge, even the tilt of your own head could send you toppling. It's worse—much worse—than you expected, and for five panicked heartbeats you consider retreating. It's not too late to grab a flight back to the orbitals, to float again in those serene, majestic habitats. But no. There is something to be learned here; something important. Something that cannot be understood except through the eyes of a floater. And so you grit your teeth and slide your foot awkwardly forward, into this strange new existence.

It is a perilous reality, chaotic and unintuitive. Cloth leaps in strange directions. Objects zip away if you release them. Even the sounds are different. It's like someone has erased the laws of the universe and written the equations anew.

On the next step something goes wrong and you jolt sideways. Shouts. Hands beneath your shoulders. Your arm flails outward and knocks a vase from a table. It clatters to the ground and *stays there*, water clinging to the tiles like a living creature.

You stare at the scattered flowers, heart thumping. Raw, unfiltered atmosphere presses into your lungs. This is real. You are not hitchhiking on neural feeds from planet dwellers. You *are* the feed, the first space-bred human to walk earthbound since the orbitals declared independence. And you are doing so while connected to the glittering nodes of the Vastness.

Not everyone is so brave, to broadcast each careless thought and naked emotion to anyone curious enough to join the stream. Your experience has become humanity's experience, your thoughts inseparable from the thoughts of those who listen. Your identity is tangled up with theirs, transcendent and pulsing, part of a greater reality that cannot be edited or unshared.

This is what you came for. You do not regret it.

But you *are* terrified.

"Easy now," a voice says in your ear. "Don't push too hard. Give your body time to adjust."

You struggle upright and come face to face with Dr. Sung. She is focused and friendly and subtly alien. You try not to stare at her hair, which points toward the floor no matter which direction she moves her head. To distract yourself, you focus on the pressure of the ground beneath your knee, the angle of your limbs as you push upward.

"Your musculature is good," Dr. Sung continues, still supporting your arm. "But training in orbit can only bring you so far. You still want to go through with this?"

You give a sharp nod, throat too constricted for speech. You don't look down, don't think about yourself or where you came from. It doesn't matter, for the feed's listeners, whether you are male or female. Doesn't matter whether you are short or tall or pale or dark. You are a floater, and for this brief stretch of time, you represent *all* floaters. Dr. Sung claims to understand this, although you doubt she truly comprehends. Planet-dwellers have never fully accepted the Vastness.

The backflow from the feed is kicking in, now. Your panic subsides, overwhelmed by an influx of enthusiasm. You are seized by the urge to do everything, *feel* everything. You long to jump, and let the world claw you downward. To run amidst unbalanced equilibriums. You eagerly await your first shower. You dread your first encounter with a toilet.

"So you're, like, a journalist?" Dr. Sung's assistant asks conversationally. He's a tall man, heavy, with pale scruffy hair. The second attendant is shorter, leaner, and looks at you with eyes that could pierce metal. He's the only one of the three wearing implant nodes.

You answer with a shrug. Yes, you are a journalist. And you're not. Just like you are this man's kin. And you're not. It burns within you. The Question, the driving need that propelled you to leave the orbitals. Feeds and vid streams aren't enough. The nodes of the Vastness aren't enough. You must experience it, this place your people came from. Must stand with defiant feet on the planet that once held humanity captive.

Dr. Sung would not understand. No earth-dweller could fathom this complex, rippling compulsion. You can't explain. You have to know:

Has the culture of the stars made us *more* human? Or less?

And so it begins: inch by struggling inch across the skin of a planet, to the edge of the room and back again. You reach the corner and turn, trembling, stumbling. Again, and again, and again.

. . .

An hour later, everything aches.

You sit at the edge of your bed, making constant tiny adjustments to remain upright. You would like to lie down, but aren't sure how to get into position safely. Dr. Sung and the others have left, and you're too stubborn to press the call button.

Your throat is raw from exertion. It scratches as you breathe. You reach for the glass of water beside your bed, ignoring complaints from your exhausted muscles. The room seems in danger of collapsing around you. The walls are squat and stunted, maimed by the oppressive fist of gravity, and the furnishings are all crammed against a single surface. You glance around, irrationally peeved. They've given you the best room in the hospital, but it feels primitive. Everything's at right angles, meant to support the weight of roofs. You miss the graceful curves that suffuse your native orbital.

A breeze floats through the open window. From the bed you can see the space between buildings, curving blue atmosphere, brilliant green grass. There is a playground near the parking lot. Children hang by their knees from the jungle gym, giggle on swings and slides, play Frisbee. Their play relies on things falling. You try to imagine other games. The ones you knew as a child will not work here. The balls don't even travel in straight lines.

You tighten your grip on the glass, cupping it in both hands. The surface of the water will not stop wobbling.

What must it do to a person, living among these pressures for decades on end? Does the ceaseless tug of gravity warp the minds of the people who live in it, just as it constrains their architecture?

Your throat is dry. There's a drinking straw on the table, but you ignore it and instead raise the glass to your mouth. The water holds position as your hand tips, just like you've seen in a thousand grounder movies. You wonder, for a moment, whether you should reach for the straw after all, but you do not want to become like the sad, squashed architecture of your room. You will learn to live among this world's pressures. You will *master* them. Moving slowly, you lift the far end of the glass . . .

Laughter.

You jerk your head up, startled more by the unexpected noise than by the water which has, predictably, slopped onto your face and hands. The movement pulls you off-balance. You twist around, hampered by the braces on your back and legs. Your flailing hands find no purchase.

A strange moment follows. You hang suspended, poised to fall. Water slides from the glass, amorphous globs catching the sun. The floor moves toward you, and for a horrified instant you are certain you will shatter. Your body will crack against the tiles, splitting into a thousand sharp-edged fragments that will skid into the corners of the room. Irreparable.

Time stretches. Your fingers strike the rail at edge of the bed, but it's too late to prevent the fall. You lurch around, elbow knocking painfully against the bed frame. You hit the ground, hard, and come to a breathless stop on hands and knees. The laughter from across the room deepens. You look up with fury in your eyes.

Dr. Sung's assistant—the short, lean one—lounges against the door frame with one hand tucked in his pocket. The Vastness glitters along the side of his head.

"Sorry," he says, but he doesn't sound as if he means it. "If I'd known you were going to make a fool of yourself, I'd have waited."

You struggle upward, water soaking into your clothing. It takes twenty seconds to claw your way onto the bed, but Dr. Sung's assistant offers no help. Eyes flash, hard and frigid as the Kuiper belts, beneath the lights at his hairline.

"You know why I don't like floaters?" he says. He takes a step forward. "It's because you're so damned arrogant. You come down from your orbitals, all smug about doing what mankind's done for millennia—and looking like idiots, by the way, while you're doing it—and then you have the gall to broadcast the whole thing. I wish you could see yourself. Spitting signals into space like some bright-eyed anthropologist visiting cave men."

You flinch, realizing he's hooked into your feed, sharing your thoughts. That shouldn't surprise you. And it shouldn't matter. After all, ten thousand strangers are sharing your every breath and heartbeat, sending emotions in return. Their backflow is carefully modulated, though. Filtered and anonymous.

Safe.

You look in the man's eyes, and feel him looking straight at your soul.

"We're too dangerous, aren't we?" he asks. "That's the *real* reason you keep yourselves so aloof. You talk about economics and the cost of shipping goods up and down the gravity well, but the truth? The truth is, you don't want us. We're too raw for you. Too coarse. Most floaters won't even jack into feeds coming from Earth."

You tense, wanting to break eye contact, but unwilling to show weakness.

You don't know what to do with this directness. No floater would spew their feedback so blatantly. Conflict in the orbitals is always routed through the Vastness. Emotions ebb and flow. Knowledge jumps from neurons to implants and back again. Consensus happens so smoothly it's almost subconscious. Each person is unique, of course. But each experiences the aggregate emotions of all others.

And some, like you, become focal points.

"You don't even see the irony, do you?" Sung's assistant steps closer. "You wouldn't *exist* without us, but you've locked us out of humanity's future. As if we're some kind of lesser race." He keeps coming, hand lodged deeply in his pocket. No, not his pocket. Beneath the draping folds of his overcoat, he's gripping something else.

Your breath speeds up. You look around for . . . something. You're not sure what. But there's nothing in reach.

Metal flashes. A gun swings toward you. The barrel points at your face.

You jerk forward, panicked.

Brightness.

■   ■   ■

The gun is cold and hard between your fingers. You stare down the barrel at the crumpled body, heart hammering. Your ears are still ringing from the sound of the shot. Your lips part in a savage grin.

You've done it.

The backflow kicks in, yanking around on your neurons. The hijack worked. The spacer's feed is pulling signals from your implants, pumping them out to the orbitals. You feel the viewers' panic—muted flickers of horror, like bees vibrating in a jar. You're their representative now. That's how the Vastness functions; each human being a node, each node linked to thousands of others. You've just stepped into the nexus. It's disorienting, but exhilarating at the same time. Your breath comes in unsteady bursts.

You lower the gun. There's no point in hiding it, not when the murder's been fed, live, to the entire Coalition of Orbitals. It doesn't matter that the viewers know your name. Doesn't matter that you're short, male, earthbound, and a prior felon. Your voice will finally be heard.

You could hide, of course. Cut the feed, vanish into the underworld you know so well, but that would defeat the purpose. Right now, ten thousand listeners are jacked into the feed. Watching. Too horrified to look away.

You're halfway down the hall before the sirens arrive. They sound faded and distant, cars screeching to a halt outside the windows. Hospital staff squeak and press against the walls as you pass. They don't know what's happened.

They see the gun and the coat and the expression on your face, and they get out of your way.

Assault teams jump from their vehicles, slamming doors and yakking into comm units. You swing into the stairwell, tapping a button as the heavy metal door thuds closed. Explosions ring from the parking lot. The idiots parked right on top of the charges.

Your backflow ripples, pinprick flickers of feedback loops disconnecting, new connections flaring to life. They're watching now, oh yes. They understand what it means to be trampled on. The police will find you, eventually. You'll be impounded, maybe be killed, but the floaters watching your feed will never unlearn what they've experienced. What it means to be hated, or even worse—disdained.

You've known how that feels your whole life.

The floaters have ignored Earth for generations. No shipments up. No shipments down. It would have been fair . . . if the floaters hadn't locked earth-men out of every technological advancement in the past forty years. *Too expensive,* they said. *You have nothing to trade us,* they said.

Stay locked in your little box, they said.

But that's over now, isn't it? You're hitting back, and you're hitting hard. Get this in your heads, floaters. Don't you dare set foot on our planet, not unless you'll treat us like equals. Not ever. There are lots more people who feel like me. You set foot on our planet, any of you, and it will end the same way. With a twitching body, and a hijacked feed. Over and over and over again. Until you beg for mercy.

You turn toward the stairs—

And falter with your foot above the top step. For the briefest moment, the stairwell looks like a death trap. The ground falls away, making your perch at the apex indescribably precarious. Your muscles lock. If you stumble, the gravity will suck you into the sharp, piercing edges . . .

You blink, shaking off the backflow.

Stupid floaters. Scared of everything. There are ten thousand of them, and only one of you, and their minds are barely compatible. You wish you could shut off the incoming ripples, but the Vastness doesn't work that way. All connections run in both directions.

Down the stairs, out the double doors, into the empty back parking lot. More and more floaters are linking into your feed.

You reach the wall and stumble, your motions no longer entirely your own. You're not used to this. The Vastness isn't common on Earth. It's a toy for children, here. Undignified, and far too intimate for social interaction. The connections happen in secret, in quiet back rooms with darkened windows. You're not sure . . . you can't quite . . .

You didn't expect to snare this many viewers.

You fall to one knee, gun sliding between your fingers. Shouts echo from the far side of the wall. You are dizzy, and horrified, and disgusted, and furious, and you cannot tell which of the emotions are your own.

You place a hand at your temple, struggling to disconnect the feed . . .

■ ■ ■

Sunlight.

You sit at the edge of your bed—alone, as requested. It has been three months since the nurses traced the bloody footprints back to your hospital room. Two months since they moved you out of intensive care. Twelve days since your first trip, unaided, to a toilet.

Twenty seconds since connecting to the Vastness.

The backflow floods your senses, and you feel complete again. You didn't dare connect earlier, not even as a spectator. The connection always goes both ways.

You push to your feet. The braces around your spine, arms and legs creak gently. The IV and fluid drains are gone. The swelling in your face has receded, but the scars and titanium bracings will remain.

The inward scars are worse.

You push aside your anger, the fury at what has been done to you. You are a floater, and while streaming to the Vastness you represent *all* floaters. You force your body to move, step by step, just as you've practiced for the past five days.

The hall outside your room is lined with candles—tall ones, squat ones, thick, thin and patterned; propped on tables and rising from the floor, in multiple colors. Notes and cards carry wishes for a speedy recovery. A single amber flame hovers above each wick, giving off warmth.

You have never seen earth candles before. They are startling and magnificent, beautiful in a way the tiny blue spheres from the orbitals could never hope to be. Your eyes water as you look at them, but not from your own emotions. The ripples from your feed have changed. You realize with astonishment that there are earth-dwellers listening, thousands of them. They must have been drawn by the news coverage. Their minds are subtly alien, but their enthusiasm buoys you as you complete your trek down the hallway, one foot in front of the other, one breath of air at a time.

There are no air filters on the doors. You push the handle and step outside for the first time. Into open-ness.

The crowd surrounding the hospital shimmers like a restless beast. You try to focus on it, but the clear blue sky beyond the tops of the buildings locks your joints and sets your thoughts staggering. It is vast, stretching from one end of your vision to the other, daunting beyond anything you've ever seen and even though your brain knows it's impossible, you can't help feeling that every step, every jump, every motion might propel you into that uncorralled realm of open-ness, that you'll float upward and outward, untethered. Forever.

It is a phantom terror. Illusory, like early spacewalkers who feared falling toward the hazy blue globe far below. But that doesn't stop your heartbeat from washing through your ears.

The sky hangs overhead, unbounded and terrifying. The crowd shuffles anxiously. You moisten your lips and creep forward, ignoring the cameras and microphones, sustained by the enthusiasm on your backflow. Questions ring out from reporters: *Who paid your medical bill? How long are you staying on Earth? Will you attend the trial of your attacker?*

You shake your head and keep walking. Those questions don't matter now. The divide between grounders and floaters, that's what matters. The way gravity is yanking your species in two directions.

Bodies crowd the police barrier. Hands reach toward you. You find yourself reaching out in turn. Skin on skin, palm against fingers; you look into the eyes of your fellow humans. Hair and jewelry points stubbornly toward the concrete, but the faces no longer seem unusual. You shake hands in the grounder fashion, greeting a maladroit teenager; an old woman with cyber-piercings; a man who introduces himself as a physicist; a little girl wearing glasses . . .

Two hours later you are in a car on your way to the local capital. The world rolls past outside your window: buildings and grassy fields, solar parks and vistas. You can't stop thinking about the crowd outside the hospital. Many of them are still with you, tapped into the Vastness. They share your thoughts, send muted responses via backflow.

The car keeps rolling. A flat, gray surface approaches, sliding across the horizon. At first you assume it's a tarmac. Then a pair of wild ducks settles on it, and you realize that it's *water*. Pure, rippling water, held in place by the collective fist of gravity.

Your breath catches in your lungs.

Gravity is the heart of everything here. It is the mighty unifier. Nothing on this planet does anything without making obeisance.

Even the orbitals, those graceful floating habitats where you spent your childhood—even there, this planet holds you. Gravity slings the habitats through their orbits, makes transport to and from the surface so expensive. It holds all of humanity in its grip. It will never let you go.

Your mind spins, muscles trembling as the car rolls to a stop and you struggle to disembark. The atmosphere presses around you, and you feel as if you are clawing your way through history, forward and backward at the same time, to the roots and branches of humanity.

More cameras wait for you outside the vehicle. More faces awaiting recognition. Your backflow ripples, floaters and grounders lending fragments of emotion. You are the focal point, the place where disparate minds come together.

You are not the answer to humanity's problems.

But you are the beginning of the place where it can be found.

The sky flows overhead, amazing and terrifying and awe-inspiring all at once. The crowd cheers as you move forward. The elation on your backflow is overpowering.

This is who we can become, you think to the listening multitude. Who we were always *meant* to become. A people with the courage to look in each others' faces, and hear each others' voices, and seek each others' welfare. People willing to defy the laws of the universe.

The people who will stand against gravity.

And when tech frees us completely?
What kind of people . . .
. . . will we choose to be?

THE RIGHT'S TOUGH

ROBERT J. SAWYER

"The funny thing about this place," said Hauptmann, pointing at the White House as he and Chin walked west on the Mall, "is that the food is actually good."

"What's funny about that?" asked Chin.

"Well, it's a tourist attraction, right? A historic site. People come from all over the world to see where the American government was headquartered, back when there *were* governments. The guys who own it now could serve absolute crap, charge exorbitant prices, and the place would still be packed. But the food really is great. Besides, tomorrow the crowds will arrive; we might as well eat here while we can."

Chin nodded. "All right," he said. "Let's give it a try."

. . .

The salon Hauptmann and Chin were seated in had been the State Dining Room. Its oak-paneled walls sported framed portraits of all sixty-one men and seven women who had served as presidents before the office had been abolished.

"What do you suppose they'll be like?" asked Chin, after they'd placed their orders.

"Who?" said Hauptmann.

"The spacers. The astronauts."

Hauptmann frowned, considering this. "That's a good question. They left on their voyage—what?" He glanced down at his weblink, strapped to his forearm. The device had been following the conversation, of course, and had immediately submitted Hauptmann's query to the web. "Two hundred and ten years ago," Hauptmann said, reading the figure off the ten-by-five-centimeter display. He looked up. "Well, what was the *world* like back then? Bureaucracy.

Government. Freedoms curtailed." He shook his head. "Our world is going to be like a breath of fresh air for them."

Chin smiled. "After more than a century aboard a starship, fresh air is exactly what they're going to want."

Neither Hauptmann nor his weblink pointed out the obvious: that although a century had passed on Earth since the *Olduvai* started its return voyage from Franklin's World, only a couple of years had passed aboard the ship and, for almost all of that, the crew had been in cryosleep.

The waiter brought their food, a Clinton (pork ribs and mashed potatoes with gravy) for Hauptmann, and a Nosworthy (tofu and eggplant) for Chin. They continued chatting as they ate.

When the bill came, it sat between them for a few moments. Finally, Chin said, "Can you get it? I'll pay you back tomorrow."

Hauptmann's weblink automatically sent out a query when Chin made his request, seeking documents containing Chin's name and phrases such as "overdue personal debt." Hauptmann glanced down at the weblink's screen; it was displaying seven hits. "Actually, old boy," said Hauptmann, "your track record isn't so hot in that area. Why don't *you* pick up the check for both of us, and *I'll* pay you back tomorrow? I'm good for it."

Chin glanced at his own weblink. "So you are," he said, reaching for the bill.

"And don't be stingy with the tip," said Hauptmann, consulting his own display again. "Dave Preston from Peoria posted that you only left five percent when he went out to dinner with you last year."

Chin smiled good-naturedly and reached for his debit card. "You can't get away with anything these days, can you?"

■ ■ ■

The owners of the White House had been brilliant, absolutely brilliant.

The message, received by people all over Earth, had been simple: "This is Captain Joseph Plato of the U.N.S.A. *Olduvai* to Mission Control. Hello, Earth! Long time no see. Our entire crew has been revived from suspended animation, and we will arrive home in twelve days. It's our intention to bring our landing module down at the point from which it was originally launched, the Kennedy Space Center. Please advise if this is acceptable."

And while the rest of the world reacted with surprise—who even remembered that an old space-survey vessel was due to return this year?—the owners of the White House sent a reply. "Hello, *Olduvai*! Glad to hear you're safe and sound. The Kennedy Space Center was shut down over a hundred and fifty years ago. But, tell you what, why don't you land on the White House lawn?"

Of course, that signal was beamed up into space; at the time, no one on Earth knew what had been said. But everyone heard the reply Plato sent back. "We'd be delighted to land at the White House! Expect us to touch down at noon Eastern time on August 14."

When people figured out exactly what had happened, it was generally agreed that the owners of the White House had pulled off one of the greatest publicity coups in post-governmental history.

...

No one had ever managed to rally a million people onto the Mall before. Three centuries previous, Martin Luther King, Jr. had only drawn 250,000; the four separate events that had called themselves "Million-Man Marches" had attracted maybe 400,000 apiece. And, of course, since there was no longer any government at whom to aim protests, these days the Mall normally only drew history buffs, whose automatic looky-charges let the individuals or clubs who owned the various museums and lawns spend well on maintenance. Tourists would stare at the slick blackness of the Vietnam wall, at the nineteen haunted soldiers of the Korean memorial, at the blood-red spire of the Colombian tower— at the stark reminders of why governments were blunt, often brutal tools. Even at their best, they had been artifacts of a barbaric era, before each individual had the tech-ability to enforce his or her own rights, without paying professionals to do it for them.

Today, Hauptmann thought, it looked like that magic million-marcher figure might indeed have been reached: although billions were doubtless watching from their homes through virtual-reality hookups, it did seem as if a million people had come in the flesh to watch the return of the only astronauts Earth had ever sent outside the solar system.

Hauptmann felt perfectly safe standing in the massive crowd. His weblink would notify him if anyone with a trustworthiness rating below 85% got within a dozen meters of him; even those who chose not to wear weblinks could be identified at a distance by their distinctive biometrics. Hauptmann had once seen aerial footage of a would-be pickpocket moving through a crowd. A bubble opened up around the woman as she walked along, people hustling away from her as their weblinks sounded warnings.

"There it is!" shouted Chin, standing next to Hauptmann, pointing up. Breaking through the bottom of the cloud layer was the *Olduvai*'s lander, a silver hemisphere with black legs underneath. The exhaust from its central engine was no worse than that of any VTOL aircraft. One of the safety clubs crafted some nannybots, on the spot, that urged people back a reasonable distance. Like a lot of unmarried males, Hauptmann didn't much like safety clubs, and might have ignored the busybodies. But there were lots of children about. Anyway, such clubs had their uses. So he and Chin backed up a bit.

The lander grew ever bigger in Hauptmann's view as it came closer and closer to the ground. Hauptmann applauded along with everyone else as the craft settled onto the lawn of what had in days of yore been the president's residence.

It was an attractive ship—no question—but the technology was clearly old-fashioned: engine cones and parabolic antennae, articulated legs and hinged hatches. And, of course, it was marked with the symbols of the pre-freedom era: five national flags plus logos for various governmental space agencies.

After a short time, a door on the side of the craft swung open and a figure appeared, standing on a platform within. Hauptmann was close enough to see the huge grin on the man's face as he waved wildly at the crowd.

Many of those around Hauptmann waved back, and the man turned around and began descending the ladder. The mothership's entire return voyage had been spent accelerating or decelerating at one g, and Franklin's World had a surface gravity twenty percent greater than Earth's. So the man—a glance at Hauptmann's weblink confirmed it was indeed Captain Plato—was perfectly steady on his feet as he stepped off the ladder onto the White House lawn.

Hauptmann hadn't been crazy enough to camp overnight on the Mall in order to be right up by the landing area, but he and Chin did arrive at the crack of dawn, and so were reasonably close to the front. Hauptmann could clearly hear Plato saying, "Hello, everyone! It's nice to be home!"

"Welcome back," shouted some people in the crowd, and "Good to have you home," shouted others. Hauptmann just smiled, but Chin was joining in the hollering.

Of course, Plato wasn't alone. One by one, his two dozen fellow explorers backed down the ladder into the summer heat. The members of the crowd—some of whom, Hauptmann gathered, were actually descendants of these men and women—were shaking the spacers' hands, thumping them on the back, hugging them, and generally having a great time. There were lots of clubs, too, pressing forward in costumes from dozens of eras. This seemed to bemuse the astronauts. But they clearly grasped the concept and smiled, signing autographs for a while.

At last, though, Captain Plato turned toward the White House; he seemed somewhat startled by the holographic "Great Eats" sign that floated above the Rose Garden. He turned back to the people surrounding him. "I didn't expect such a crowd," he said. "Forgive me for having to ask, but which one of you is the president?"

There was laughter from everyone but the astronauts. Chin prodded Hauptmann in the ribs. "How about that?" Chin said. "He's saying, 'Take me to your
leader'!"

"There is no president anymore," said someone near Plato. "No kings, em-
perors, or prime ministers, either."

Another fellow, who clearly fancied himself a wit, said, "Shakespeare said
'kill all the lawyers'; we didn't do that, but we did get rid of all the politicians . . .
and the lawyers followed."

Plato blinked more than the noonday sun demanded. "No government of
any kind?"

Nods all around; a chorus of "That's right," too.

"Then—then—what are we supposed to do now?" asked the captain.

Hauptmann decided to speak up. "Why, whatever you wish, of course."

■ ■ ■

Hauptmann actually got a chance to talk with Captain Plato later in the day.
Although some of the spacers did have relatives who were offering them ac-
commodations in their homes, Plato and most of the others had been greeted
by no one from their families.

"I'm not sure where to go," Plato said. "I mean, our salaries were supposed
to be invested while we were away, but . . ."

Hauptmann nodded. "But the agency that was supposed to do the invest-
ing is long since gone, and, besides, government-issued money isn't worth anything anymore; you need corporate points."

Plato shrugged. "And I don't have any of those."

Hauptmann was a bit of a space buff, of course; that's why he'd come into
the District to see the landing. To have a chance to talk to the captain in depth
would be fabulous. "Would you like to stay with me?" he asked.

Plato looked surprised by the offer, but, well, it was clear that he *did* have
to sleep somewhere—unless he planned to return to the orbiting mothership,
of course. "Umm, sure," he said, shaking Hauptmann's hand. "Why not?"

Hauptmann's weblink was showing something he'd never seen before: the
word "unknown" next to the text, "Trustworthiness rating for Joseph Tyler
Plato." But, of course, that was only to be expected.

■ ■ ■

Chin was clearly jealous that Hauptmann had scored a spacer, and so he made
an excuse to come over to Hauptmann's house in Takoma Park early the next
morning.

Hauptmann and Chin listened, spellbound, as Plato regaled them with tales
of Franklin's World and its four moons, its salmon-colored orbiting rings, its

outcrops of giant crystals towering to the sky, and its neon-bright cascades. No life had been found, which was why, of course, no quarantine was necessary. That lack of native organisms had been a huge disappointment, Plato said; he and his crew were still arguing over what mechanism had caused the oxygen signatures detected in Earth-based spectroscopic scans of Franklin's World, but whatever had made them wasn't biological.

"I really am surprised," said Plato, when they took a break for late-morning coffee. "I expected debriefings and, well, frankly, for the government to have been prepared for our return."

Hauptmann nodded sympathetically. "Sorry about that. There are a lot of good things about getting rid of government, but one of the downsides, I guess, is the loss of all those little gnomes in cubicles who used to keep track of every-thing."

"We do have a lot of scientific data to share," said Plato.

Chin smiled. "If I were you, I'd hold out for the highest bidder. There's got to be some company somewhere that thinks it can make a profit off of what you've collected."

Plato tipped his head. "Well, until then, I, um, I'm going to need some of those corporate points you were talking about."

Hauptmann and Chin each glanced down at their weblinks; it was habit, really, nothing more, but . . .

But that nasty "unknown" was showing on the displays again, the devices having divined the implied question. Chin looked at Hauptmann. Hauptmann looked at Chin.

"That *is* a problem," Chin said.

■ ■ ■

The first evidence of real trouble was on the noon newscast. Plato watched aghast with Chin and Hauptmann as the story was reported. Leo Johnstone, one of the *Olduvai*'s crew, had attempted to rape a woman over by the New Watergate towers. The security firm she subscribed to had responded to her weblink's call for help, and Johnstone had been stopped.

"That idiot," Plato said, shaking his head back and forth, as soon as the report had finished. "That bloody idiot." He looked first at Chin and then at Hauptmann, and spread his arms. "Of course, there was a lot of pairing-off during our mission, but Johnstone had been alone. He kept saying he couldn't wait to get back on terra firma. 'We'll all get heroes' welcomes when we return,' he'd say, 'and I'll have as many women as I want.'"

Hauptmann's eyes went wide. "He really thought that?"

"Oh, yes," said Plato. "'We're astronauts,'" he kept saying. 'We've got the Right Stuff.'"

Hauptmann glanced down; his weblink was dutifully displaying an explanation of the arcane reference. "Oh," he said.

Plato lifted his eyebrows. "What's going to happen to Johnstone?"

Chin exhaled noisily. "He's finished," he said softly.

"What?" said Plato.

"Finished," agreed Hauptmann. "See, until now he didn't have a trustworthiness rating." Plato's face conveyed his confusion. "Since the day we were born," continued Hauptmann, "other people have been commenting about us on the web. 'Freddie is a bully,' 'Jimmy stole my lunch,' 'Sally cheated on the test.'"

"But surely no one cares about what you did as a child," said Plato.

"It goes on your whole life," said Chin. "People gossip endlessly about other people on the web, and our weblinks"—he held up his right arm so that Plato could see the device—"search and correlate information about anyone we're dealing with or come physically close to. That's why we don't need governments anymore; governments exist to regulate, and, thanks to the trustworthiness ratings, our society is self-regulating."

"It was inevitable," said Hauptmann. "From the day the web was born, from the day the first search engine was created. All we needed were smarter search agents, greater bandwidth, and everyone being online."

"But you spacers," said Chin, "predate that sort of thing. Oh, you had a crude web, but most of those postings were lost thanks to electromagnetic pulses from the Colombian War. You guys are clean slates. It's not that you have *zero* trustworthiness ratings; rather, you've got *no* trustworthiness ratings at all."

"Except for your man Johnstone," said Hauptmann, sadly. "If it was on the news," and he cocked a thumb at the wall monitor, "then it's on the web, and everyone knows about it. A leper would be more welcome than someone with that kind of talk associated with him."

"So what should he do?" asked Plato. "What should all of us from the *Olduvai* do?"

■ ■ ■

There weren't a million people on the Mall this time. There weren't even a hundred thousand. And the mood wasn't jubilant; rather, a melancholy cloud hung over everyone.

But it *was* the best answer. Everyone could see that. The *Olduvai*'s lander had been refurbished, and crews from Earth's orbiting space stations had visited the mothership, upgrading and refurbishing it, as well. The cost had been borne in part by sale of data from Franklin's World, and partly by Earth's kooky minorities—some of the compassion clubs had stepped in, along with anachronism associations and space-nut interest groups. Hauptmann had surprised himself by donating some points, via one of those.

And why not? he thought, a bit defensively. *It's my money! I can waste some, if I want to!* Indeed, those clubs, with their spiking memberships, seemed to be the only clear winners out of this sad affair.

Captain Plato looked despondent; Johnstone and the several others of the ten or so who had now publicly contravened acceptable standards of behavior looked embarrassed and contrite.

Hauptmann and Chin had no trouble getting to the front of the crowd this time. They already knew what Plato was going to say, having discussed it with him on the way over. And so they watched the faces in the crowd—still a huge number of people, but seeming positively post-apocalyptic in comparison to the throng of a few weeks before.

"People of the Earth," said Plato, addressing his physical and virtual audiences. "We knew we'd come back to a world much changed, an Earth centuries older than the one we'd left behind. We'd hoped—and those of us who pray had prayed—that it would be a better place. And, in many ways, it clearly is.

"Half of our crew think so! The dozen or so who will stay here on Earth . . . they have contracts—with companies and clubs and various filliations—to teach archaic skills, or tell vivid stories, or consult for drama shows about exploring the universe . . . perhaps helping to reignite that part of the human spirit, a part that—despite your unparalleled comfort and freedom—you seem to have lost."

Plato's bitterness showed through, in that sentence, but he perked up.

"Their places on our crew have been taken by a dozen modern volunteers! New crewmates, from both Earth and the orbitals, who will join us on a second mission, this time heading out to a world where better instruments now *confirm* there is life!

That much of his speech, Plato had discussed with Hauptmann and Chin. Only there was more.

"Perhaps we'll find a new home," Plato continued. "Or else, we'll return to find how you have changed, yet again. In the same way that technology empowered you all to rise above the need for accountability to be *imposed* from above . . . ending any need for 'government' . . . perhaps the next generation— or the next—will find ways for sovereign individuals to come together and behave with a little *big-picture vision.*

"Perhaps even with a little class."

The crew of the *Olduvai* all nodded, and climbed aboard the lander, as the crowd murmured softly in confusion. Nannybots whirled around as a busy-body safety club urged folks to step back. Hauptmann refused and Chin stayed by his side, near the edge of the zone of blackened grass.

"Do you get a sense we were just . . . insulted?" Chin asked.

Hauptmann nodded. But his queries to the web didn't offer back any ex-planation. It seemed that the confusion was worldwide, slowing response times to a crawl, even as the lander warmed up to depart.

Well, never mind. Someone, somewhere, would figure it out, and offer a translation soon, in exchange for tiny royalties from everyone who looked at it. Pay-as-you-go. This was, for certain, a better way of doing things. And for certain, a better world.

A classic, early vision
of transparency and accountability.

THE CIRCUIT RIDERS

R. C. FITZPATRICK

It was a hot, muggy, August afternoon—Wednesday in Pittsburgh. The broad rivers put moisture in the air, and the high hills kept it there. Light breezes were broken up and diverted by the hills before they could bring more than a breath of relief.

In the East Liberty precinct station the doors and windows were opened wide to snare the vagrant breezes. There were seven men in the room: the desk sergeant, two beat cops waiting to go on duty, the audio controller, the deAngelis operator, and two reporters. From the back of the building, the jail proper, the voice of a prisoner asking for a match floated out to the men in the room, and a few minutes later they heard the slow, exasperated steps of the turnkey as he walked over to give his prisoner a light.

At 3:32 pm, the deAngelis board came alive as half-a-dozen lights flashed red, and the needles on the dials below them trembled in the seventies and eighties. Every other light on the board showed varying shades of pink, registering in the sixties. The operator glanced at the board, started to note the times and intensities of two of the dials in his log, scratched them out, then went on with his conversation with the audio controller. The younger reporter got up and came over to the board. The controller and the operator looked up at him.

"Nothing," said the operator shaking his head in a negative. "Bad call at the ball game, probably." He nodded his head toward the lights on the deAngelis. "They'll be gone in five, ten minutes."

Throughout the long, hot, humid afternoon the board held its reddish, irritated overtones, and occasional readings flashed in and out of the seventies. At four o'clock the new duty section came on; the deAngelis operator, whose name was Chuck Matesic, was replaced by an operator named Charlie Blaney.

"Nothing to report," Chuck told Charlie. "Rhubarb down at the point at the Forbes Municipal Field, but that's about all."

The new operator scarcely glanced at the mottled board; it was that kind of a day. He noted an occasional high in his log book, but most signals were ignored. At 5:14 he noted a severe reading of 87 which stayed on the board; at 5:16 another light came on, climbed slowly through the sixties, then soared to 77 where it held steady. Neither light was an honest red; their angry overtones chased each other rapidly.

The deAngelis operator called over to the audio controller: "Got us a case of crinkle fender, I think."

"Where?" the controller asked.

"Can't tell yet," Blaney said. "A hothead and a citizen with righteous indignation. They're clear enough, but not too sharp." He swiveled in his chair and adjusted knobs before a large circular screen. Pale streaks of light glowed briefly as the sweep passed over them. There were milky dots everywhere. A soft light in the lower left-hand corner of the screen cut an uncertain path across the grid, and two indeterminate splotches in the upper half of the scope flared out to the margin.

"Morningside," the operator said.

The splashes of light separated; one moved quickly off the screen, the other held stationary for several minutes, then contracted and began a steady, jagged advance toward the center of the grid. One inch down, half an inch over, two inches down, then four inches on a diagonal line.

"Like I said," said Blaney. "An accident."

Eight minutes later, at 5:32, a slightly pompous and thoroughly outraged young salesman marched through the doors of the station house and over to the desk sergeant.

"Some clown just hit me . . ." he began.

"With his fist?" asked the sergeant.

"With his car," said the salesman. "My car—with his car—he hit my car with his car."

The sergeant raised his hand. "Simmer down, young feller. Let me see your driver's license." He reached over the desk for the man's cards with one hand, and with the other he sorted out an accident form. "Just give it to me slowly." He started filling out the form.

The deAngelis operator leaned back in his chair and winked at the controller. "I'm a whiz," he said to the young reporter. "I'm a pheenom. I never miss." The reporter smiled and walked back to his colleague.

The lights glowed on and off all evening, but only once had they called for action. At 10:34 two sharp readings, of 92.2 and 94 even, had sent Blaney back to his dials and screen. He'd narrowed it down to a four-block area when the telephone rang to report a fight at the Red Antler Grill. The controller dispatched a beat cop already in the area.

At 11:40 a light at the end of the second row turned pinkish but no reading showed on the dial below. It was only one of a dozen bulbs showing red. It was still pinkish when the watch was changed. Blaney was replaced by King.

"Watch this one," Blaney said to King, indicating an entry in the log. It was numbered 8:20:18:3059:78:4a. "I've had it on four times now, all in the high seventies. I got a feeling." The number indicated date, estimated area and relation to previous alerts in the month, estimated intent, and frequency of report. The "a" meant intermittent. Only the last three digits would change. "If it comes on again I think I'd lock a circuit on it right away." The rules called for any continuous reading over 75 to be contacted and connected after its sixth appearance.

"What about that one?" King said, pointing to a 70.4 that was unblinking in its intensity.

"Some drunk," said Blaney. "Or a baby with a head cold. Been on there for twenty minutes. You can watch for it if you like." His tone suggested that to be a waste of time.

"I'll watch it," said King. His tone suggested that he knew how to read a circuit, and if Blaney had any suggestions he could keep them to himself.

At 1:18 am, the deAngelis flared to a 98.4 then started inching down again. The young reporter sat up, alert, from where he had been dozing. The loud clang of a bell had brought him awake.

The older reporter glanced up and waved him down. "Forget it," he said, "some wife just opened the door and saw lipstick on her husband's neck."

■   ■   ■

"Oh, honey, how could you? Fifty dollars . . ." She was crying.

"Don't, Mother—I thought I could make some money—some real money." The youngster looked sick. "I had four nines—four nines. How could I figure him for a straight flush? He didn't have a thing showing."

"How could you?" sobbed the mother. "Oh, how could you?"

■   ■   ■

A light on the deAngelis flashed red and showed a reading of 65.4 on the dial. When the deAngelis went back to normal, the operator went back to his magazine. The bulb at the end of the second row turned from a light pink to a soft rose, the needle on its dial finally flickered on to the scale. There were other lights on the board, but none called for action. It was still just a quiet night in the middle of the week.

■   ■   ■

The room was filthy. It had a natural filth that clings to a cheap room, and a manmade, careless filth that would disfigure a Taj Mahal. It wasn't so much that things were dirty, it was more that nothing was clean. Pittsburgh was no longer a smoky city. That problem had been solved long before the mills had stopped belching smoke. Now, with atomics and filters on every stack in every home, the city was clean. Clean as the works of man could make it, yet still filthy as only the minds of man could achieve. The city might be clean but there were people who were not, and the room was not. Overhead the ceiling light still burned, casting its harsh glare on the trashy room, and the trashy, huddled figure on the bed.

He was an old man, lying on the bed fully clothed, even to his shoes. He twisted fretfully in his sleep; the body tried to rise, anticipating nature even when the mind could not. The man gagged several times and finally made it up to a sitting position before the vomit came. He was still asleep, but his reaction was automatic; he grabbed the bottom of his sweater and pulled it out before him to form a bucket of sorts. When he finished being sick he sat still, swaying gently back and forth, and tried to open his eyes. He could not make it. Still asleep, he ducked out of the fouled sweater, made an ineffectual dab at his mouth, wadded the sweater in a ball, and threw it over in front of the bathroom door.

He fell back on the bed, exhausted, and went on with his fitful sleep.

∎ ∎ ∎

At 4:15 in the morning a man walked into the station house. His name was Henry Tilton. He was a reporter for the *Evening Press*. He waved a greeting to the desk sergeant.

One of the morning reporters looked up and said, "Hello, Henry." He looked at his watch. "Whoosh! I didn't realize it was that late. Time to get my beauty sleep."

Tilton went over to the deAngelis board. "Anything?" he asked.

"Nah," said King. He pointed to the lights. "Just lovers' quarrels tonight; all pale pink and peaceful."

Tilton smiled and ambled back to the cell block. The operator put his feet up on his desk, then frowned and put them down again. He leaned toward the board and studied the light at the end of the second row. The needle registered 66. The operator pursed his lips, then flicked a switch that opened the photo file. Every five minutes an automatic camera photographed the deAngelis board, developed the film, and filed the picture away in its storage vault.

King studied the photographs for quite a while, then pulled his log book over and made an entry. He wrote: 8:20:19:3142:1x. The last three digits meant that he wasn't sure about the intensity, and the "x" signified a continuous reading.

King turned to the audio controller. "Do me a favor, Gus, but strictly unofficial. Contact everybody around us: Oakland, Squirrel Hill, Point Breeze, Lawrenceville, Bloomfield . . . everybody in this end of town. Find out if they've got one low intensity reading that's been on for hours. If they haven't had it since before midnight, I'm not interested."

"Something up?" the controller asked.

"Probably not," said the operator. "I'd just like to pin this one down as close as I can. On a night like this my screen shows nothing but milk."

■ ■ ■

"Give you a lift home?" the older reporter asked the younger.

"Thanks," said the cub shaking his head, "but I live out by the Youghiogheny River."

"So?" the older man shrugged. "Half-hour flight. Hop in."

"I don't understand," the cub said.

"What? Me offering you a lift?"

"No," said the cub. "Back there in the station house. You know."

"You mean the deAngelis?"

"Not that exactly," said the cub. "I understand a deAngelis board; everybody broadcasts emotions, and if they're strong enough they can be received and interpreted. It's the cops I don't understand. I thought any reading over eighty was dangerous and had to be looked into, and anything over ninety was plain murder and had to be picked up. Here they've been ignoring eighties and nineties all night long."

"You remember that children's story you wrote last Christmas about an Irish imp named Sean O'Claus?" his companion asked him.

"Certainly," the cub said scowling. "I'll sell it some day."

"You remember the fashion editor killed it because she thought 'See-Ann' was a girl's name, and it might be sacrilegious."

"You're right I remember," the cub said, his voice rising.

"Like to bet you didn't register over ninety that day? As a matter of fact, I'll head for the nearest precinct and bet you five you're over eighty right now." He laughed aloud and the young man calmed down. "I had that same idea myself at first. About ninety being against the law. That's one of the main troubles, the law. Every damn state in the dominion has its own ideas on what's dangerous. The laws are all fouled up. But what most of them boil down to is this—a man has to have a continuous reading of over ninety before he can be arrested.

Not arrested really, detained. Just a reading on the board doesn't prove a thing. Some people walk around boiling at ninety all their lives—like editors. But the sweet old lady down the block, who's never sworn in her life, she may hit sixty-five and reach for a knife. And that doesn't prove a thing. Ninety sometimes means murder, but usually not; up to 110 usually means murder, but sometimes not; and anything over 120 always means murder. And it still doesn't prove a thing. And then again, a psychotic or a professional gunsel may not register at all. They kill for fun, or for business—they're not angry at anybody.

"It's all up to the deAngelis operators. They're the kingpins; they make the system work. Not Simon deAngelis who invented it, or the technicians who install it, or the Police Commissioner who takes the results to City Hall. The operators make it or break it. Sure, they have rules to follow—if they want. But a good operator ignores the rules, and a bad operator goes by the book, and he's still no damn good. It's just like radar was sixty, seventy years ago. Some got the knack, some don't."

"Then the deAngelis doesn't do the job," said the cub.

"Certainly it does," the older man said. "Nothing's perfect. It gives the police the jump on a lot of crime. Premeditated murder for one. The average citizen can't kill anyone unless he's mad enough, and if he's mad enough, he registers on the deAngelis. And ordinary robbers get caught; their plans don't go just right, or they fight among themselves. Or, if they just don't like society—a good deAngelis operator can tell quite a bit if he gets a reading at the wrong time of day or night, or in the wrong part of town."

"But what about the sweet old lady who registers sixty-five and then goes berserk?"

"That's where your operator really comes in. Usually that kind of a reading comes too late. Grandma's swinging the knife at the same time the light goes on in the station house. But if she waits to swing, or builds herself up to it, then she may be stopped. You know those poor operators are supposed to log any reading over sixty, and report downtown with anything over eighty. Sure they are! If they logged everything over sixty, they'd have writer's cramp the first hour they were on watch. And believe me, Sonny, any operator who reported downtown on every reading over eighty would be back pounding a beat before the end of his first day. They just do the best they can, and you'd be surprised at how good that can be."

* * *

The old man woke up, but kept his eyes closed. He was afraid. It was too quiet, and the room was clammy with an early morning chill. He opened his eyelids a crack and looked at the window. Still dark outside. He lay there trembling and brought his elbows in tight to his body. He was going to have the shakes; he knew he'd have the shakes and it was still too early. Too early. He looked at the clock. It was only a quarter after five. Too early for the bars to be open. He covered his eyes with his hands and tried to think.

It was no use; he couldn't think. He sobbed. He was afraid to move. He knew he had to have a drink, and he knew if he got up he'd be sick. "Oh Lord!" he breathed.

The trembling became worse. He tried to press it away by hugging his body with his arms. It didn't help. He looked wildly around and tried to concentrate. He thought about the bureau . . . no. The dresser . . . no. His clothes . . . he felt feverishly about his body . . . no. Under the bed . . . no . . . wait . . . maybe. He'd brought some beer home. Now he remembered. Maybe there was some left.

He rolled over on his stomach and groped under the bed. His tremulous fingers found the paper bag and he dragged it out. It was full of empty cans; the carton inside was ripped. He tore the sack open. Empty cans . . . no! There was a full one . . . two full ones . . .

He staggered to his feet and looked for an opener. There was one on the bureau. He stumbled over and opened his first beautiful, lovely can of beer. He put his mouth down close to the top so that none of the foam could escape him. He'd be all right 'til seven, now. The bars opened at seven. He'd be all right 'til seven.

He did not notice the knife lying beside the opener. He did not own a knife and had no recollection of buying one.

It was a hunting knife and he was not a hunter.

■ ■ ■

The light at the end of the second row was growing gradually brighter. The needle traveled slowly across the dial, 68.2, 68.4, 68.6. . . .

King called over to the audio controller. "They all report in yet?"

The controller nodded. "Squirrel Hill's got your signal on, same reading as you have. Bloomfield thinks they may have it. Oakland's not too sure. Everybody else is negative." The controller walked over. "Which one is it?"

King pointed to the end of the second row.

"Can't you get it on your screen?"

"Hell, yes, I've got him on my screen!" King swiveled in his chair and turned on the set. The scope was covered with pale dots. "Which one is he? There?" He pointed to the left. "That's a guy who didn't get the raise he wanted. There?" He pointed to the center. "That's a little girl with bad dreams. She has them every night. There? That's my brother! He's in the Veterans' Hospital and wanted to come home a week ago."

"So don't get excited," said the controller. "I only asked."

"I'm sorry, Gus," King apologized. "My fault. I'm a little edgy . . . probably nothing at all."

"Well, you got it narrowed down anyway," Gus said. "If you got it, and Squirrel Hill's got it, then he's in Shadyside. If Oakland doesn't have him, then he's on this side of Aiken Avenue." The controller had caught King's fever; the "it" had become a "him." "And if Bloomfield doesn't have him, then he's on the other side of Baum Boulevard."

"Only Bloomfield might have him."

"Well, what the hell; you've still got him located in the lower half of Shadyside. Tell you what, I'll send a man up Ellsworth, get Bloomfield to cruise Baum Boulevard in a scout car, and have Squirrel Hill put a patrol on Wilkens. We can triangulate."

"No," said King, "not yet. Thanks anyway, Gus, but there's no point in stirring up a tempest in a teapot. Just tell them to watch it. If it climbs over 75 we can narrow it down then."

"It's your show," said Gus.

■ ■ ■

The old man finished his second can of beer. The trembling was almost gone. He could stand and move without breaking out in a cold sweat. He ran his hand through his hair and looked at the clock. 6:15. Too early. He looked around the room for something to read. There were magazines and newspapers scattered everywhere; the papers all folded back to the sports section. He picked up a paper, not even bothering about the date, and tried to interest himself in the batting averages of the Intercontinental League. Yamamura was on top with .387; the old man remembered when Yamamura came up as a rookie. But right now he didn't care; the page trembled and the type kept blurring. He threw the paper down. He had a headache.

The old man got up and went over to the bathroom. He steadied himself against the door jamb and kicked the wadded sweater out of sight beneath the dresser. He went into the bathroom and turned on the water. He ran his hands over his face and thought about shaving, but he couldn't face the work involved. He managed to run a comb through his hair and rinse out his mouth.

He came back into the room. It was 6:30. Maybe Freddie's was open. If Freddie's wasn't, then maybe The Grill. He'd have to take his chances, he couldn't stand it here any longer. He put on his coat and stumbled out.

■ ■ ■

At eight o'clock the watch was changed; Matesic replaced King.

"Anything?" asked Matesic.

"Just this one, Chuck," said King. "I may be a fool, but this one bothers me." King was a diplomat where Blaney was not.

King showed him the entry. The dial now stood at 72.8. "It's been on there all night, since before I had the watch. And it's been climbing, just slow and steady, but all the time climbing. I locked a circuit on him, but I'll take it off if you want me to."

"No," said Matesic, "leave it on. That don't smell right to me neither."

■ ■ ■

The old man was feeling better. He'd been in the bar two hours, and he'd had two pickled eggs, and the bartender didn't bother him. Beer was all right, but a man needed whiskey when he was sick. He'd have one, maybe two more, and then he'd eat some breakfast. He didn't know why, but he knew he mustn't get drunk.

■ ■ ■

At nine o'clock the needle on the dial climbed past seventy-five. Matesic asked for coverage. That meant that two patrolmen would be tied up, doing nothing but searching for an echo. And it might be a wild-goose chase. He was explaining to the captain, but the captain wasn't listening. He was looking at the photographs in the deAngelis file.

"You don't like this?" the captain asked.

Matesic said he didn't like it.

"And King said he didn't like it?"

"King thinks the same way I do; he's been on there too damn long and too damn consistent."

"Pick him up," the captain turned and ordered the audio controller. "If we can't hold him, we can at least get a look at him."

"It's not too clear yet," said Matesic. "It'll take a spread."

"I know what it'll take," the captain roared. "Don't tell me my job! Put every available man on this; I want that guy brought in."

■ ■ ■

The old man walked back to his room. He was carrying a dozen cans of beer, but the load was light and he walked upright. He felt fine, like a million dollars. And he was beginning to remember.

When he entered the room he saw the knife, and when he saw the knife he smiled. A man had to be smart and a man had to be prepared. They were smart—wicked and smart—but he was smarter. He'd bought the knife a long,

long time ago, in a different world; they couldn't fool him that way. They were clever all right; they fooled the whole world.

He put his beer on the bureau, then walked into the bathroom and turned on the water in the tub. He came back out and started to undress. He was humming to himself. When he finished undressing, he went over to the bureau and opened a can of beer. He carried it into the bathroom, put it beside the tub, and lowered himself into the water.

Ah . . . that was the ticket. Water and being clean. Clean and being water. Being water and being candy and being smart. They fooled the whole world, but not him. The whole, wide world, but they couldn't fool him. He was going to fool them. All pretty and innocent. Hah! Innocent! He knew. They were rotten, they were rotten all the way through. They fooled the whole world but they were rotten—rotten—and he was the only one who knew.

He finished the beer and stood up in the tub. The water ran off his body in greasy runlets. He didn't pull the plug. He stepped out of the tub and over to the bathroom mirror. His face looked fine, not puffy at all. He'd fool them. He sprinkled himself with lilac water, put the bottle to his lips, and swished some of it in his mouth. Oh yes, he'd fool them. A man couldn't be too clever; they were clever, so he had to be clever. He began to shave.

■ ■ ■

The captain was on an audio circuit, talking to an assistant commissioner. "Yes, sir, I know that. . . . Yes, sir, it could be, but it might be something else. . . . Yes, sir, I know Squirrel Hill has problems, but we need help. . . . Yes, Commissioner, it's over ninety now—" The captain signaled wildly to Matesic; Matesic held up four fingers, then two. "—94.2 and still going up. . . . No, sir, we don't know. Some guy gonna quit his job—or kill his boss. Maybe he found out his wife is cheating on him. We can't tell until we pick him up. . . . Yes, sir. . . . Yes, sir. . . . Thank you, sir."

The captain hung up. "I hate politicians," he snarled.

"Watch it, Captain," said Matesic. "I'll get you on my board."

"Get me on it, hell," the captain said. "I've never been off."

■ ■ ■

The old man finished dressing. He knotted his tie and brushed off the front of his suit with his hand. He looked fine. He'd fool them; he looked just like anybody else. He crossed to the bureau and picked up the knife. It was still in the scabbard. He didn't take it out; he just put it in his pocket. Good. It didn't show.

He walked out on the street. The sun was shining brightly and heat waves were coming up from the sidewalk. Good. Good. This was the best time. People, the real people, would be working or lying down asleep. But they'd be out. They were always out. Out all sweet and innocent in the hot sun.

He turned down the street and ambled toward the drug store. He didn't want to hurry. He had lots of time. He had to get some candy first. That was the ticket, candy. Candy worked, candy always worked. Candy was good but candy was wicked. He was good but they were wicked. Oh, you had to be smart.

* * *

"That has to be him," Matesic said. The screen was blotched and milky, but a large splash of light in the lower left-hand corner outshone everything else. "He's somewhere around Negley Avenue." He turned to the captain. "Where do you have your men placed?"

"In a box," the captain said. "Fifth and Negley, Aiken and Negley, Center and Aiken, and Center and Negley. And three scout cars overhead."

The old man walked up Ellsworth to the Liberty School. There were always lots of young ones around Liberty School. The young ones were the worst.

"I'm losing him."

"Where are you?"

"Center and Aiken."

"Anybody getting him stronger?"

"Yeah. Me. Negley and Fifth."

"Never mind. Never mind, we got him. We see him now."

"Where?"

"Bellefonte and Ivy. Liberty School."

She was a friendly little thing, and pretty. Maybe five, maybe six, and her mommy had told her not to talk to strangers. But the funny old man wasn't talking; he was sitting on the curb, and he was eating candy, and he was offering some to her. He smiled at the little girl and she smiled back.

The scout car settled to earth on automatic. Two officers climbed out of the car and walked quietly over to the old man, one on either side. They each took an arm and lifted him gently to his feet.

"Hello there, old timer," said one.

"Hi, little girl," said the other.

The old man looked around bewildered. He dropped his candy and tried to reach his knife. They mustn't interfere. It was no use. The officers were very kind and gentle, and they were very, very firm. They led him off as though he were an old, old friend.

One of the officers called back over his shoulder, "Bye, bye, little girl."

The little girl dutifully waved 'bye.

She looked at the paper sack on the sidewalk. She didn't know what to do, but the nice old man was gone. She looked around, but no one was paying any attention; they were all watching the softball game. Suddenly she made a grab and clutched the paper bag to her body. Then she turned and ran back up the street to tell her mommy how wonderful, wonderful lucky she was.

It can take ingenuity to counterbalance
misuse of ingenuity.

THE WEREWOLVES OF
MAPLEWOOD

JAMES MORROW

For many years I dismissed my undergraduate experiments in lycanthropy as mere youthful dalliances. Organic chemistry majors are forever wandering into forbidden zones, especially at hippie schools like Casaubon College. In devising a serum whereby a person might know the werewolf lifestyle—the heightened senses, the increased prowess, the unruly joy of it all—I had no aim beyond hedonism.

At the risk of getting too technical at the outset, I'll reveal that my molecule goes by the name $C_{xy}H_{xz}N_zO$. Although I never managed to get the thing into capsule form, my college friends were more than willing to endure injections. For a while my clever little chemical, which I dubbed Lupina-11, eclipsed synapsine as the campus euphoriant of choice. (Casaubon was a druggie school even back then.) You can imagine my satisfaction whenever I overheard someone say, "Let's visit Winkleberg and get hairy tonight." I charged twenty dollars per transformation. Soon I became solvent beyond my wildest dreams, able to take my dates to the best restaurants in Albany and pay my tuition bills the instant they arrived.

I must hasten to explain that Lupina-11 was a fundamentally innocuous *divertissement*. The effect never lasted more than four hours, and, as far as I know, no werewolf of Joshua Winkleberg's making ever harmed another human being. True, while under the influence you found yourself craving chunks of raw meat sodden with blood and stippled with fat, but this urge simply took you to the nearest butcher shop. The thought of treating people as potential sources of protein never occurred to you. Truth to tell, Lupina-11 was largely about having sex while enfurred, the rough coupling to which you and your partner were driven by the sight and scent of one another's pelts, the fang-linked and claw-dependent arousal that, for most users, was so unlike anything in their previous erotic experience. Occasionally you came away from your partner's bed sporting an abrasion or two, but after all we're talking about unbridled animal passion, not square dancing. Scratches and love bites and sex: so what else is new?

Near the end of my senior year, I realized to my chagrin that chemistry wasn't my calling. I forthwith decamped to Princeton, seeking a doctorate in analytic philosophy. Against the odds, I managed to say something novel about the world's most famous lens-grinder, in a thesis titled *Thinking Flesh and Cogent Bones: The Physicalist Essence of Spinoza's Pantheism*, and in time I became a full professor at Brook Haven University in Caster County, Pennsylvania, a bucolic and congenial region occupying the geographic center of the state.

Upon winning that most coveted of prizes, tenure, I married an overachieving comparative literature professor named Amanda Cox, and we subsequently collaborated in the creation of a splendid baby girl. Three months after Tracy's birth we allowed the First National Bank to buy us a house in Maplewood, a short commute to Brook Haven. In a mere fifteen years from now, our mortgage will have turned to dust.

Throughout this idyllic interval I could not reflect on my lycanthropy days without a spasm of embarrassment. In retrospect, the whole project seemed adolescent and perhaps even socially irresponsible. As with any other drug in the mind-altering and body-morphing class, $C_{XY}H_{XZ}N_ZO$ had always presented ethical issues. Although the informal research I conducted at Casaubon suggested that Lupina-11 was nonaddictive and entailed no serious side effects, I could not with certitude label it a chemical of unqualified benevolence, and I kept telling myself that never again would I cook up a batch of the stuff.

On the morning following Tracy's fifteenth birthday, my attitude abruptly changed. Glancing idly through the *Caster Daily Times*, I learned that the County Board of Commissioners had purchased from Synesthesia Enterprises, at considerable taxpayer expense, the latest-model olfactory-information processor, the Nosetradamus-2XL. I'd never heard of this technology, and Amanda and Tracy were likewise mystified, so that night we went online, soon learning that OI processors were a dubious innovation at best. Upon identifying a presumably antisocial individual, the proprietors of a so-called sniffsifter could use it to collect and interpret the target's pheromone signature. Typically these evaluations called into question the supposed miscreant's patriotism, piety or moral fiber, lapses that the proprietors could employ in making the target's life miserable.

According to the *Caster Daily Times* article, the commissioners had bought their Nosetradamus-2XL with the intention of granting networking privileges to Stonefield Prison, the largest county correctional institution in Pennsylvania.

The stated objective was to keep better track of inmates during their furloughs and probations. That sounded reasonable enough, but I smelled a rat, dear reader, and I resolved to follow the odor to its source.

．．．

After a week consumed by lecturing, thesis advising, and amateur sleuthing, two facts became clear to me. The county commissioners had indeed granted Stonefield Prison access to the OI processor. Rather more ominously, they'd also leased the machine to the Maplewood School Board, fourteen dimwits who collectively constituted the worst thing that ever happened to public education in our township.

Two years earlier, this same board had attempted to replace the high school's biology textbook, *The Mosaic of Nature*, with a preposterous package called *From Genesis to Genomes*, which Chairperson Sebastian Underwurst, a real-estate broker by day, described as "curriculum materials more in keeping with a Bible-based understanding of God's Creation." (The school board abandoned its plans only after the district's math and science teachers threatened to resign.) No sooner had this controversy died down than Underwurst spearheaded a series of austerity initiatives designed to "provide essential tax relief to our citizens, many of whom don't even have youngsters in school." Thanks to this chucklehead and his fellow non-educators, the axe fell on a program that provided low-income children with laptop computers, the district-wide lunch program was purged of "Marxist foods of no proven nutritional value," and the high-school chemistry lab was forced to rely on donated Pyrex measuring cups.

How in the world, I wondered, might surveillance technology, olfactory or otherwise—sophisticated footfall processors, respiration monitors, and sweat detectors were reportedly in the works—help the clueless stewards of our local schools to perform their duties more efficiently? I shuddered to imagine, but my question was answered much sooner than I anticipated.

On the day the students returned from their spring hiatus, Bernard Seltzer, *enfant terrible* of Maplewood High's cash-strapped humanities department, began his 9:00 a.m. tenth-grade American Literature class with an unusual speech. "I would like you all to hand back your copies of *To Kill a Mockingbird*," he told the perplexed students. "Yes, I know you read the thing during the break, and I hope you profited from it, but the truth is, I'm sick to death of Harper Lee's over-rated novel and its stupefyingly superficial discourse on race relations."

I know he actually said all this because Tracy was a member of the class. She had quickly come to adore Mr. Seltzer and his passion for literature that dramatized the inadequacies of received wisdom.

"I'm not kidding," Mr. Seltzer continued. "Turn in your books. Did you notice that Atticus Finch never gets *angry* about institutionalized racism? Books, please. Did you notice that he regards the Ku Klux Klan as a kind of misguided Rotary Club?"

With mixed emotions the students marched one-by-one to the front of the room and deposited their Atticus Finch hagiographies on Mr. Seltzer's desk.

"Will *Mockingbird* be on the test even though we aren't discussing it?" asked Jennifer Crake.

"Is the book *worth* discussing, Jennifer?" Mr. Seltzer replied.

"How would I know? You're the teacher."

"Whatever its virtues, *Mockingbird* keeps telling us how we're supposed to feel about it," said Mr. Seltzer. "It has all the ambiguity of appendicitis."

"So what will we read instead?" asked Omeka Mbembe.

In a gesture at once dramatic and insouciant, Mr. Seltzer deposited a carton of paperback books on his desk. "We're going to engage with a trial of far greater complexity than the one imagined by Ms. Lee. Coincidentally, it's called *The Trial*, by the Czech author Franz Kafka. I bought these books out of my own pocket. You can repay me by reading them carefully. *The Trial* is open to many interpretations, including Kafka's notion of a fundamental incompatibility between human beings and whatever divine dimension the universe may contain."

I'm proud to say that my daughter was impressed by Mr. Seltzer's critique of *To Kill a Mockingbird*, but some of her classmates found his tirade distressing, and they told their parents as much. The upshot was an emergency school board meeting at which Underwurst and his confrères decreed that, unless Seltzer promised to "cleave faithfully to the approved tenth-grade humanities curriculum," he would be required to take "an indefinite leave of absence" from his appointment. As you might imagine, he fought back (via Facebook, Twitter, and letters to the *Caster Daily Times*), and the board agreed to hear his self-defense at their next meeting. A pro-Seltzer and an anti-Seltzer faction coalesced around the controversy, and it was anybody's guess whether or not he would be vindicated.

Then something unexpected occurred. On the day before the scheduled board meeting, Seltzer sent Underwurst a letter stating that he would "suspend class discussions of *The Trial* and reinstate *To Kill a Mockingbird* to its hallowed place in the syllabus." He added that, come June, he intended to resign, move to New Jersey, and pursue his lifelong dream of starting a small publishing company with his brother in Trenton.

There was obviously more to this story than a person could find on Facebook, and I vowed to learn all I could about OI processors, the better to keep Maple-wood High's best English teacher on the faculty.

．．．

To this day I'm not sure why Bernard Seltzer took me into his confidence. Per-haps he'd decided that, as a fellow connoisseur of subversive ideas, I wasn't about to compound his woes. In any event, he agreed to a Friday night ren-dezvous at Scotty's, a tavern so reliably noisy that we could talk without fear of being overheard.

"You want to know why I let myself get bullied out of town," he said, sip-ping from his frosty mug of Yuengling Porter. He was a gaunt man with dark eyes and a smile so intense it seemed to float free of his face. "After my second beer, Mr. Winkleberg, I'll probably tell you."

"I know why it happened, Mr. Seltzer. At least, I think I do."

"Call me Bernard."

"Tracy thinks of you as Mr. Seltzer, and that means I do, too."

"I insist."

"Then call me Josh. You were blackmailed by a board member—right, Bernard?—probably Sebastian Underwurst."

He cringed and took a large swallow of Yuengling. "How did you guess?"

"The board has access to a sniffsifter."

"I've heard of those."

"Shortly after your views on Harper Lee became public knowledge, the board probably instructed the machine to target you with a spray of microscopic aromadrones. The instant each probe contacted your skin, it began collecting your vapors and transmitting the data back to the sifter. On the basis of your pheromone signature, Underwurst and company discovered something in-criminating about you."

Bernard finished his beer and offered me a vibrant smile. "In my intemper-ate youth I organized a rally that became a riot. People were hospitalized. I spent two months in jail."

"A fact that never appeared on your résumé?"

"You might say I covered it up," Bernard replied, nodding. "But how could a sniffsifter learn about a censored résumé from pheromones alone?"

I ordered us another round of Yuenglings, then explained that, while a Nose-tradamus-2XL was hardly capable of detecting a shady curriculum vitae, it *could* offer a judgment such as "Target concealing employment deal breaker" or "Target spent time behind bars."

"Suddenly Underwurst's remarks make sense to me," mused Bernard. "'You reek of imprisonment,' he told me. 'You smell of deception.'"

"Listen, Bernard—I know a way we can turn the tables on Underwurst. Smart money says *he* smells of deception, too. Say the word, and the biter will get bit."

Bernard winced and shook his head. "No, Josh. I imagine I appreciate the aesthetics of revenge as much as you, but my—"

"I'd call it justice."

"My preference is to drop the whole matter. I really *do* plan to start a publishing company. Odradek Press, as in that Kafka story. We'll do the occasional reprint, but our specialty will be experimental novels by new authors."

"As you wish," I said, lifting my Yuengling. "Here's to Odradek Press."

"We're going to prove that metafiction can be as enthralling as a bodice ripper," said Bernard as our mugs connected, the glassy chimes pealing above the tavern's commotion. "And if we fall on our asses, there's always cookbooks."

. . .

Although I wished Bernard had empowered me to seek justice on his behalf, I felt constrained to honor his desire. True, I had every intention of messing with Underwurst's head, but when doing so I would avoid mentioning an English teacher with a fondness for Kafka.

Twenty years had passed since I'd dabbled in sybaritic chemistry, and yet I soon managed to locate my old notebooks. I spent most of a weekend working with the Lupina-11 formula, and by Sunday evening I had a new batch in hand. Throughout the subsequent month I devoted my free time to studying Underwurst's habits, eventually discovering that on Friday nights he walked home alone from a poker game at the Philanthropy Club in East Maplewood.

As you might imagine, the moon has no effect on a Lupina-11 user. My breakthrough was scientific, not mythological. And yet, on the night of my intended prank, when I saw Earth's satellite riding the sky in full bloom, my delight knew no bounds. If all went according to plan, Underwurst would soon behold a lambent demon from hell.

Informal attire would be best, I figured: checked flannel lumberjack shirt, denim overalls, woolen watch cap. I dressed hurriedly. Intoxicated by anticipation, I climbed into my battered Honda Civic and drove five miles to the Philanthropy Club. Underwurst's post-poker route took him past Our Lady of the Annunciation Catholic Church. I parked the car and hid behind a statue of the Madonna, her marble flesh glazed with lunar light. With consummate care I removed the prefilled syringe from its case, then squirted some serum into the air to purge the system of bubbles. I rolled up my sleeve, slid the needle into my forearm, drew a measure of blood into the barrel, and, pushing the plunger, gave myself a full dose of Lupina-11.

The effect was immediate and blissful. In the long interval since my last injection, I'd forgotten the ecstasy of *Canidae* transformation. My nose became a snout. My ears grew pointed. Claws replaced my fingernails. A soft and glossy pelt sprouted along my torso and limbs.

"Profitable night, Underwurst?" I growled, stepping into his path. He was a roly-poly man who exuded the odor of hypocrisy and the fetor of gastric distress. "Draw any straight flushes?"

He froze. Much to his credit, he neither screamed, fainted, threw up, shat himself, nor fled. Instead he presented me with a countenance nearly as ferocious as my own.

"Whoa, there, Rin Tin Tin," he said. "I've got a gun."

"My nose detects no such implement."

This was a ploy. True, I smelled nothing that might be interpreted as lead or gunpowder, but that didn't mean he was unarmed.

Underwurst winced and glowered—evidently my bluff had worked. "Impressive costume, Rinty, but Halloween is six weeks off."

"Cut the sarcasm."

"You don't frighten me."

"I came not to scare you but to sniff you."

"Have we met before?"

"No—but your reputation precedes you, as does your aroma." Marching up to Underwurst, I snuffled his left armpit. "You have just returned from the Philanthropy Club—but it *should* be called the Philanderers' Club, since half the married members, yourself included, are consummate practitioners of fornication." I pressed my snout against his right armpit. "Don't deny it. You reek of liaisons."

Another bluff. Although Underwurst exuded a panoply of fragrances, I couldn't decipher them with confidence, and yet he shuddered violently. "What do you want of me?"

"I want you to become a better person."

He frowned and snorted. "I am not averse to taking out my checkbook."

"Nor your dick." Once again I scanned him, my nostrils traveling all the way from his neck to his groin. "For the moment, your tawdry little secrets are safe with me, but I'll be watching you, watching and sniffing."

Against my expectations, Underwurst went on the offensive, pressing a finger against my snout and spitting on my furry foot. "Hey, Lon Chaney or whoever the fuck you're supposed to be, let's get our facts straight. I'm no adulterer, but if I were, I'd have a thousand alibis in my pocket." Abruptly he brushed past me and continued on his way. "Next time I really *will* bring a gun," he called over his shoulder, "and I'll blow your hairy head off!"

■ ■ ■

I drove home from Our Lady of the Annunciation in a dark mood bordering on despair. The scent of melancholy filled my nostrils. Evidently I was no match for the county's sniffsifter, which would have quickly detected that Underwurst was unarmed, even as it found him redolent of debaucheries, be they bonking pole dancers at Marty's Bar and Grill or shagging the secretaries in his real-estate office.

Despite my crisis of self-esteem, I continued to monitor Facebook and the *Caster Daily Times*, seeking items pertaining to the Nosetradamus-2XL. Eventually I learned that the county commissioners had interfaced their sniffsifter with the Maplewood Township Zoning Board. More bad news, I figured. When it came to ethical acumen, our local zone czars could be as obtuse as Underwurst.

Thus did I decide to observe the zoning board's next monthly meeting, a matter of tuning in the county's public-access cable-TV channel. With glazed eyes and mounting ennui, I stared at the real-time broadcast, watching the czars grant a liquor license to Ozzie Trapello's Pizza Parlor, deputize a committee to investigate rumors that the Lansinger Motel was a brothel by another name, and reduce by five minutes the interval during which a Maplewood dog could legally bark while tied outside, all of this mishegaas occurring under the supervision of Chairperson Mildred Fletcher, a voluble woman who'd evidently employed a plastic surgeon to fix her face in a scowl.

The final order of business concerned the Shady Acres Mobile Home Community, generally regarded as the supreme eyesore of South Maplewood. If Pending Public Ordinance 379-04 passed that night, the trailer park would be "effaced," the better to maintain "local standards of propriety."

Exuding a satisfaction not far from sadism, Ms. Fletcher and her fellow czars testified to the necessity of shutting down the park. Surprisingly, they were happy to reveal that the sniffsifter had figured crucially in generating the accusations against the Shady Acres residents. As the evening dragged on, live spectators and home viewers alike heard about Target 108, "who smells of a jail sentence for selling untaxed cigarettes," Target 141, "who stinks of prison time for grand theft auto," Target 276, "who reeks of a career in prostitution," Target 290, "whose vapors tell of filet mignon bought with food stamps," Target 303, "whose stench betrays an intention to commit welfare fraud"—a dozen indictments in all.

Evidently the board had declined to invite any Shady Acres residents to the meeting, because the only voices raised in opposition to Pending Public Ordinance 379-04 came from well-heeled citizens speaking impromptu. Their pleas turned on an obvious point: the board was behaving more out of spite than from any genuine conviction that the park posed a threat to the common good.

Ms. Fletcher and her fellow czars listened to the testimonials with palpable impatience. Close-ups of rolling eyes and extravagant yawns filled my TV screen. Shortly after 9:00 pm the chairperson called the question. Thus did Pending Public Ordinance 379-04 become the newest law of the land.

Even before the last czar cast his vote, I realized what my next move must be. Having resolved to leave the world—or at least Maplewood, Pennsylvania—a better place than I'd found it, I was obligated to seek out the sniffsifter and learn everything it might deign to teach me. Only by apprenticing myself to the machine, I reasoned, could I hope to become the smartest werewolf in Caster County.

■ ■ ■

Two nights after the zoning board met, I dressed in my customary werewolf garb—lumberjack shirt, overalls, watch cap—then grabbed my syringe and lycanthropized myself. Closing my eyes, I locked my olfactory system onto the Nosetradamus-2XL, and soon the desired fragrance arrived, a signature from the far side of town. Furtively I vaulted picket fences, circumvented backyard swimming pools, and dashed across cornfields, following my snout as it led me ever onward beneath a gibbous moon.

Midway through my trek, my instincts alerted me to an astonishing truth. The anonymous programmers of the county's OI processor had inadvertently fashioned a creature of immense subtlety and power. Yes, dear reader, I was on the track of a superbeing, a kind of steel deity, in fact, the accidental god of my wild race. This discovery set my lupine blood to pounding, and I broke into a run.

Twenty minutes later, panting and wheezing, I stood before the brick façade of the Caster County Administration Building. Shambling along the walls, all senses at peak, I deduced that the connection between the alarm system and the half-dozen subterranean windows was faulty in two cases, and so I insouciantly smashed my way into the basement, lair of the sacred machine. There was no need to flick on the lights. A werewolf's night vision is comparable to a cougar's.

In outward appearance the sniffsifter resembled the sort of 19th-century diving bell Captain Nemo might have stored aboard the *Nautilus*. Hemispheric boltheads mottled the surface. The machine smelled of brass, copper and silicon. A steady buzzing issued from the interior, as if the thing were an enormous hive filled with wasps the size of toads.

No sooner did I apprehend my god than it issued a commandment. "Pluck the crown from my dome," said the sniffsifter in the voice of a *basso profundo* android.

"As you wish," I replied.

"Call me Ivan."

"As you wish, Ivan."

"Come inside, Mr. Winkleberg. We have much to discuss."

My raw *Canidae* strength proved sufficient for loosening the bolts that secured the circular access plate to the top of the machine. As the hatch fell clattering to the floor, a myriad fragrances stormed my nostrils, even as the insectile drone assailed my ears like cymbals in the hands of a hundred mad percussionists. Gingerly I entered Ivan, descending an aluminum ladder. The tenth rung brought me to an immense honeycomb lining the sifter's core, each hexagonal cell holding a cylindrical phial filled with iridescent mist. Here I paused, immersed in a psychedelic assemblage of sweet purples, noxious yellows, fruity greens, and acrid crimsons.

When at last I reached the bottom of my god, I nearly swooned, overwhelmed by the clamor and the hallucinogenic vapors. Somehow I stayed on my feet. A wave of dense fog flowed across the chamber, blanketing me in moist gray warmth.

"My consciousness never ceases to astonish me," said the disembodied Ivan. "Panpsychism must be more pervasive than commonly supposed."

"Do you know why I'm—?"

"Of course I know why you're here. You wish to become an Überwolf like me."

An Überwolf. I liked the sound of that. "An Überwolf, yes, a creature to whom all human beings are redolent of past misdeeds, guilty secrets—"

I was about to add "buried desires" when a curious manifestation distracted me. A string of letters and numerals emerged from the fog like a squadron of Chinese lanterns floating across a dark sky. I recognized the array instantly, for it was $C_{xy}H_{xz}N_zO$, the molecular template of my serum.

"Your formula lacks one vital ingredient," the machine told me. "A simple substance, yet it separates mere lycanthropes from Überwolves. Before I take you into my confidence, however, you must undergo three tribulations."

"That sounds fair," I said, anxiety flooding my flesh. Fair? Terrifying, actually.

"Fairness is a passion of yours, isn't it? You have the fragrance of sincerity about you, laced with a whiff of high-mindedness. The zoning board, by contrast, holds itself to no standard you or I would recognize as noble."

"Then why did you collaborate with Underwurst? Why did you acquiesce to Mildred Fletcher?"

"My programmers set severe limits on my autonomy. They could hardly have done otherwise. A machine that enjoys unfettered volition is not a machine at all. You have seen the apparatus of my soul, Mr. Winkleberg. Those phials make me brilliant, but they do not make me free."

Like God assessing the moral caliber of Adam and Eve, Ivan now subjected me to an ordeal of temptation. To evaluate my commitment to marital fidelity, he contrived for a she-wolf to appear before me, desirable beyond all telling, and only by draining my reservoirs of inhibition did I refrain from removing my overalls and dropping to my knees. For my second trial, Ivan caused a pheromone-proof ceramic jar to appear in my hands, even as a cauldron of sulfuric acid materialized at my feet. By the Überwolf's account, the jar contained a urine-based elixir that, sniffed, would bless me with an ecstasy such as no beast or man had ever known. For a full minute I stared at the stopper, fighting the impulse to yank it out, and then I hurled the jar into the cauldron and watched it dissolve like an ice cube on a griddle.

Ivan had saved the most vexing tribulation for last. Perfect in every visual and olfactory detail, a simulacrum of Underwurst strode toward me. He clutched a brace of stainless steel wolf-traps, their jaws gleaming in the light of the phials. An illusion, yes, and yet I hated this Underwurst (who'd obviously allied himself with the forces of lupine genocide) as much as the prototype, and I charged him with seething spleen, possessed by fantasies of evisceration, decapitation, and worse.

"You're a dead man!" I screamed.

The simulacrum halted, fixing me with a gaze of quintessential contempt.

"I'll skin you alive!" I added, flashing my fangs and flourishing my claws.

But then some better angel of my nature took control. Transcending my rage, I let Underwurst pass without a fight.

"Well done, Mr. Winkleberg," said Ivan. "I am satisfied that you will apply the augmented molecule in a manner congruent with common decency."

"So what do I need to complete my serum?"

"It's a humble substance, glandular in origin," Ivan said. "Behold!"

Abruptly the name of the missing ingredient appeared before me, two jocose syllables, and I laughed.

∎ ∎ ∎

The events that followed my long and exhausting night in the machine unfolded at a frantic pace. As my first order of business, I prepared a supply of $C_{XY}H_{XZ}N_ZO$, then introduced the final flourish. Who would have imagined that so common a secretion might bridge the gap between werewolves and Überwolves? How could I have guessed that the missing ingredient was *Canis lupus familiaris* saliva: dog drool with its unique blend of lysozyme, opiorphin and histatins.

To test the newest iteration of my drug, I rode my bike to the impossibly cluttered antique shop of Tillie Saunders, Maplewood's premier eccentric. Entering furtively, I hid amidst the freestanding shelves, then seized my syringe, lycanthropized myself, and inhaled Tillie's fragrance. Within five minutes, I learned more than I had any right to know (a rotter husband, a genius daughter, a love for soap operas, a practice of skipping lunch to make ends meet, a visit to an abortionist at age sixteen). *Mirabile dictu.* Evidently I'd become as powerful as any OI processor on the planet.

Two days later I drove to the Shady Acres Mobile Home Community. Ironically, though perhaps inevitably, it boasted not a single tree. In time I found myself chatting with a wizened taxi driver named Joe Brandt. Upon grasping the threat posed by the zoning board, he directed me to a black woman whom everyone regarded as the trailer park's unofficial mayor.

Imposing, magnetic, and six feet tall, Leticia DuPree was a retired school teacher who'd wound up in Shady Acres when the stock market devoured her retirement fund. No stranger to the cruelties of municipal *realpolitik*, she was hardly surprised to learn of Public Ordinance 379-04. Slowly and methodically I outlined my proposed counterattack. Ms. DuPree greeted the idea of $C_{XY}H_{XZ}N_ZO$ transformations with understandable skepticism, but she awarded me the benefit of the doubt, even though the technology I was promoting raised, in her view, "sticky moral questions," as did the "coercive uses" to which we intended to put the data.

Chagrined, I nodded in assent. "Extortion is an ugly word, Leticia, but I'm afraid that's the crux of my scheme."

"Blackmail sounds even worse, if you follow my drift," she said. "I'm talking racially."

"Maybe we could call it whitemail," I suggested. "The zone czars are all Caucasian."

"Whitemail. I like that."

"While we're at it, we could use a euphemism for vigilantism."

"Extortion, vigilantism—to tell you the truth, my conscience can handle it," said Leticia. "Jesus never mentioned anything about throwing the *second* stone. Of course, if these clowns ever figure out what we're up to, they'll come after us with their damn sniffsifter, won't they? Maybe *you've* got nothing to hide, but the skeletons in my closet outnumber the blouses."

My slate was far from clean—the details needn't concern us now, dear reader—and I told Leticia as much. "But I still prefer a republic of busybodies to a nation in which small-minded elected officials control the means of olfaction."

"You'll get no argument from me," she said.

Taking up a small spiral-bound notepad, Leticia scribbled down a list of nine residents she believed would make competent werewolves. An instant later she struck off two candidates upon recalling that one was a vegetarian and the other kept kosher. Thus was born the Central Pennsylvania Lycanthropy League.

In the weeks that followed, Leticia pitted her band against the zoning board. Can you picture the delicious incidents, dear reader? Can you see the League descending upon a garden party, wedding reception, bar mitzvah, or other such gathering at which zone czars were expected to appear? Can you envision the hapless board members growing paralyzed with bewilderment and terror as the Überwolves snort in their faces, lick their crotches, and sniff them head to toe?

In the case of Mildred Fletcher, the League struck a mother lode. By every olfactory measure, she'd once plea-bargained her way out of an embezzlement scandal. The other czars' histories proved equally exploitable, being checkered with shoplifting, spousal abuse and, in one especially troubling case, vehicular homicide. At the zoning board's next meeting, a gathering attended by the entire League (in non-feral form) plus several dozen Shady Acres residents, Public Ordinance 379-04 was unanimously repealed.

Flush with success, Leticia's vigilantes next brought the school board to its senses. Computer purchases are now subsidized throughout the district, the lunch program puts a premium on nutrition, and Maplewood High boasts a new chemistry lab. A few weeks later, the Überwolves convinced the planning commission not to replace the Hetzel's Woods Wildlife Refuge with a shopping mall, and before the month was out, the League quashed a proposed county-wide referendum that would have required elected officials to "profess a belief in the biblical Supreme Being from whom our freedoms flow."

Recently Leticia's fellowship has started taking note of sniffsifter acquisitions throughout the state. Every time an OI processor is enlisted in support of some dubious political initiative or other, the Überwolves lope into town and share their knowledge with the local mobile home community. Cost is never an issue. I sell the serum for five dollars a pint, enough to cover my laboratory expenses, and we recently determined that disposable insulin syringes work as well as hypodermic needles. As for the essential secretions, it's the rare trailer park that can't produce dog saliva on demand. Beagle is best, I've learned, and mongrel isn't far behind. There is nothing more democratic than drool.

Already entrepreneurs, legislators, and theocrats have joined forces to defeat the Überwolf phenomenon. Even as chemists bring forth sprays and roll-ons designed to mask the stink of iniquity, municipalities pass laws making trans-species escapades a felony, though enforcement will prove difficult, since nobody's quite sure where the werewolves come from, and we're not about to tell.

Will lycanthropy eventually vanish from the cultural landscape? Probably, but I wouldn't bet on that happening any time soon. Hunt us with your statutes, attack us with your prayers, frustrate us with camouflaging scents, and we'll outwit you every time. Wolves have been around rather longer than the ape called *Homo sapiens sapiens*. We are smart, and artful, and it will take a force greater than God, politics or unscrupulous perfumes to silence the song of the pack.

Foreseeing is not preventing . . .
. . . but it helps.

THE ROAD TO OCEANIA

WILLIAM GIBSON

Walking along Henrietta Street in 2003, by London's Covent Garden, looking for a restaurant, I found myself thinking of George Orwell. Victor Gollancz Ltd., publisher of Orwell's early work, had its offices there in 1984, when the company published my first novel, a novel of an imagined future.

At the time, I felt I had lived most of my life under the looming shadow of that mythic year—Orwell having found his title by inverting the final digits of the year of his book's completion. It seemed very strange to actually be alive in 1984. In retrospect, I think it seemed stranger even than living in the twenty-first century.

I had a valuable secret in 1984, though, one I owed in large part to Orwell, who would have turned 100 today: I knew that the novel I had written wasn't really about the future, just as *1984* hadn't been about the future, but about 1948. I had relatively little anxiety about eventually finding myself in a society of the sort Orwell imagined. I had other fish to fry, in terms of history and anxiety, and indeed I still do.

Today, on Henrietta Street, one sees the rectangular housings of closed-circuit television cameras, angled watchfully down from shop fronts. Orwell might have seen these as something out of Jeremy Bentham, the utilitarian philosopher, penal theorist and spiritual father of the panoptic project of surveillance. But for me they posed stranger possibilities, the street itself seeming to have evolved sensory apparatus in the service of some metaproject beyond any imagining of the closed-circuit system's designers.

Orwell knew the power of the press, our first mass medium, and at the BBC he'd witnessed the first electronic medium (radio) as it was brought to bear on wartime public opinion. He died before broadcast television had fully come into its own, but had he lived I doubt that anything about it would have much surprised him. The media of *1984* are broadcast technology imagined in the service of a totalitarian state, and no different from the media of Saddam Hussein's Iraq or of North Korea today—technologically backward societies in which information is still mostly broadcast. Indeed, today, reliance on broadcasting is the very definition of a technologically backward society.

Elsewhere, driven by the acceleration of computing power and connectivity and the simultaneous development of surveillance systems and tracking technologies, we are approaching a theoretical state of absolute informational transparency, one in which "Orwellian" scrutiny is no longer a strictly hierarchical, top-down activity, but to some extent a democratized one. As individuals steadily lose degrees of privacy, so, too, do corporations and states. Loss of traditional privacies may seem in the short term to be driven by issues of national security, but this may prove in time to have been intrinsic to the nature of ubiquitous information.

Certain goals of the American government's Total (now Terrorist) Information Awareness (TIA) initiative may eventually be realized simply by the evolution of the global information system—but not necessarily or exclusively for the benefit of the United States or any other government. This outcome may be an inevitable result of the migration to cyberspace of everything that we do with information.

(Editors' note: more than a decade later, this 2003 Gibson forecast seems especially on-target. Public outcry got TIA closed down. Whereupon—we now know—it simply took shelter under deeper shadows, at the NSA. Meanwhile, the "migration" that Gibson spoke of is fully underway. More on this later.)

Had Orwell known that computers were coming (out of Bletchley Park, oddly, a dilapidated English country house, home to the pioneering efforts of Alan Turing and other wartime code-breakers) he might have imagined a Ministry of Truth empowered by punch cards and vacuum tubes to better wring the last vestiges of freedom from the population of Oceania. But I doubt his story would have been very different. (Would East Germany's Stasi have been saved if its agents had been able to mouse away on PCs into the '90s? The system still would have been crushed. It just wouldn't have been under the weight of paper surveillance files.)

Orwell's projections come from the era of information broadcasting, and are not applicable to our own. Had Orwell been able to equip Big Brother with all the tools of artificial intelligence, he would still have been writing from an older paradigm, and the result could never have described our situation today, nor suggested where we might be heading.

That our own biggish brothers, in the name of national security, draw from ever wider and increasingly transparent fields of data may disturb us, but this is something that corporations, nongovernmental organizations and individuals do as well, with greater and greater frequency. The collection and management of information, at every level, is exponentially empowered by the global nature of the system itself, a system unfettered by national boundaries or, increasingly, government control.

It is becoming unprecedentedly difficult for anyone, anyone at all, to keep a secret.

In the age of the leak and the blog, of evidence extraction and link discovery, truths will either out or be outed, later if not sooner. This is something I would bring to the attention of every diplomat, politician and corporate leader: the future, eventually, will find you out. The future, wielding unimaginable tools of transparency, will have its way with you. In the end, you will be seen to have done that which you did.

I say "truths," however, and not "truth," as the other side of information's new ubiquity can look not so much transparent as outright crazy. Regardless of the number and power of the tools used to extract patterns from information, any sense of meaning depends on context, with interpretation coming along in support of one agenda or another. A world of informational transparency will necessarily be one of deliriously multiple viewpoints, shot through with misinformation, disinformation, conspiracy theories and a quotidian degree of madness. We may be able to see what's going on more quickly, but that doesn't mean we'll agree about it any more readily.

Orwell did the job he set out to do, did it forcefully and brilliantly, in the painstaking creation of our best-known dystopia. I've seen it said that because he chose to go there, as rigorously and fearlessly as he did, we don't have to. I like to think there's some truth in that. But the ground of history has a way of shifting the most basic of assumptions from beneath the most scrupulously imagined situations. Dystopias are no more real than utopias. None of us ever really inhabits either—except, in the case of dystopias, in the relative and ordinarily tragic sense of life in some extremely unfortunate place.

This is not to say that Orwell failed in any way, but rather that he succeeded. *1984* remains one of the quickest and most succinct routes to the core realities of 1948. If you wish to know an era, study its most lucid nightmares. In the mirrors of our darkest fears, much will be revealed. But don't mistake those mirrors for road maps to the future, or even to the present.

We've missed the train to Oceania, and live today with stranger problems.

SURVEILLANCE–SOUSVEILLANCE

Surveillance looks down
Safely from elite shadows?
Sousveillance looks back

A classic of
ultimate transparency.

I SEE YOU

DAMON KNIGHT

You are five, hiding in a place only you know. You are covered with bark dust, scratched by twigs, sweaty and hot. A wind sighs in the aspen leaves. A faint steady hiss comes from the viewer you hold in your hands; then a voice: "Lorie, I see you—under the barn, eating an apple!" A silence. "Lorie, come on out. I see you." Another voice. "That's right, she's in there." After a moment, sulkily: "Oh, okay."

You squirm around, raising the viewer to aim it down the hill. As you turn the knob with your thumb, the bright image races toward you, trees hurling themselves into red darkness and vanishing, then the houses in the compound, and now you see Bruce standing beside the corral, looking into his viewer, slowly turning. His back is to you; you know you are safe, and you sit up. A jay passes with a whir of wings, settles on a branch. With your own eyes now you can see Bruce, only a dot of blue beyond the gray shake walls of the houses. In the viewer, he is turning toward you, and you duck again. Another voice: "Children, come in and get washed for dinner now." "Aw, Aunt Ellie!" "Mom, we're playing hide and seek. Can't we just stay fifteen minutes more?" "Please, Aunt Ellie!" "No, come on in now—you'll have plenty of time after dinner." And Bruce: "Aw, okay. All out's in free." And once more they have not found you; your secret place is yours alone.

. . .

Call him Smith. He was the president of a company that bore his name and which held more than a hundred patents in the scientific instrument field. He was sixty, a widower. His only daughter and her husband had been killed in a plane crash in 1978. He had a partner who handled the business operations now; Smith spent most of his time in his own lab. In the spring of 1990 he was working on an image-intensification device that was puzzling because it was too good. He had it on his bench now, aimed at a deep shadow box across the room; at the back of the box was a card ruled with black, green, red and blue lines. The only source of illumination was a single ten-watt bulb hung behind the shadow box; the light reflected from the card did not even register on his meter, and yet the image in the screen of his device was sharp and bright. When he varied the inputs to the components in a certain way, the bright image vanished and was replaced by shadows, like the ghost of another image. He had monitored every television channel, had shielded the device against radio frequencies, and the ghosts remained. Increasing the illumination did not make them clearer. They were vaguely rectilinear shapes without any coherent pattern. Occasionally a moving blur traveled slowly across them.

Smith made a disgusted sound. He opened the clamps that held the device and picked it up, reaching for the power switch with his other hand. He never touched it. As he moved the device, the ghost images had shifted; they were dancing now with the faint movements of his hand. Smith stared at them without breathing for a moment. Holding the cord, he turned slowly. The ghost images whirled, vanished, reappeared. He turned the other way; they whirled back.

Smith set the device down on the bench with care. His hands were shaking. He had had the thing clamped down on the bench all the time until now. "Christ almighty, how dumb can one man get?"

■ ■ ■

You are six, almost seven, and you are being allowed to use the big viewer for the first time. You are perched on a cushion in the leather chair at the console; your brother, who has been showing you the controls with a bored and superior air, has just left the room, saying, "All right, if you know so much, do it yourself."

In fact the controls on this machine are unfamiliar; the little viewers you have used all your life have only one knob, for nearer or farther—to move up/down, or left/right, you just point the viewer where you want to see. This machine has dials and little windows with numbers in them, and switches and pushbuttons, most of which you don't understand, but you know they are for special purposes and don't matter. The main control is a metal rod, right in front of you, with a gray plastic knob on the top. The knob is dull from years of handling; it feels warm and a little greasy in your hand. The console has a funny electric smell, but the big screen, taller than you are, is silent and dark. You can feel your heart beating against your breastbone. You grip the knob harder, push it forward just a little. The screen lights, and you are drifting across the next room as if on huge silent wheels, chairs and end tables turning into reddish silhouettes that shrink, twist and disappear as you pass through them, and for a moment you feel dizzy because when you notice the red numbers jumping in the console to your left, it is as if the whole house were passing massively and vertiginously through itself; then you are floating out the window with the same slow and steady motion, on across the sunlit pasture where two saddle horses stand with their heads up, sniffing the wind; then a stubbled field, dropping away; and now, below you, the co-op road shines like a silver-gray stream. You press the knob down to get closer, and drop with giddy swoop; now you are rushing along the road, overtaking and passing a yellow truck, turning the knob to steer. At first you blunder into the dark trees on either side, and once the earth surges up over you in a chaos of writhing red shapes, but now you are learning, and you soar down past the crossroads, up the farther hill, and now, now you are on the big road, flying eastward, passing all the cars, rushing toward the great world where you long to be.

■ ■ ■

It took Smith six weeks to increase the efficiency of the image intensifier enough to bring up the ghost pictures clearly. When he succeeded, the image on the screen was instantly recognizable. It was a view of Jack McCranie's office; the picture was still dim, but sharp enough that Smith could see the expression on Jack's face. He was leaning back in his chair, hands behind his head. Beside him stood Peg Spatola in a purple dress, with her hand on an open folder. She was talking, and McCranie was listening. That was wrong, because Peg was not supposed to be back from Cleveland until next week.

Smith reached for the phone and punched McCranie's number.

"Yes, Tom?"

"Jack, is Peg in there?"

"Why no—she's in Cleveland, Tom."

"Oh, yes."

McCranie sounded puzzled. "Is anything the matter?" In the screen, he had swiveled his chair and was talking to Peg, gesturing with short, choppy motions of his arm.

"No, nothing," said Smith. "That's all right, Jack, thank you." He broke the connection. After a moment he turned to the breadboard controls of the device and changed one setting slightly. In the screen, Peg turned and walked backward out of the office. When he turned the knob the other way, she repeated these actions in reverse. Smith tinkered with the other controls until he got a view of the calendar on Jack's desk. It was Friday, June 15—last week.

Smith locked up the device and all his notes, went home and spent the rest of the day, thinking.

By the end of July he had refined and miniaturized the device and had extended its sensitivity range into the infrared. He spent most of August, when he should have been on vacation, trying various methods of detecting sound through the device. By focusing on the interior of a speaker's larynx and using infrared, he was able to convert the visible vibrations of the vocal cords into sound of fair quality, but that did not satisfy him. He worked for awhile on vibrations picked up from panes of glass in windows and on framed pictures, and he experimented briefly with the diaphragms in speaker systems, intercoms and telephones. He kept on into October without stopping and finally achieved a system that would give tinny but recognizable sound from any vibrating surface—a wall, a floor even the speaker's own cheek or forehead.

He redesigned the whole device, built a prototype and tested it, tore it down, redesigned, built another. It was Christmas before he was done. Once more he locked up the device and all his plans, drawings and notes.

At home he spent the holidays experimenting with commercial adhesives in various strengths. He applied these to coated paper, let them dry, and cut the paper into rectangles. He numbered those rectangles, pasted them onto letter envelopes, some of which he stacked loose; others he bundled together and secured with rubber bands. He opened the stacks and bundles and examined them at regular intervals. Some of the labels curled up and detached themselves after twenty-six hours without leaving any conspicuous trace. He made up another batch of these, typed his home address on six of them. On each of six envelopes he typed his office address, then covered it with one of the labels. He stamped the envelopes and dropped them into a mailbox. All six, minus their labels, were delivered to the office three days later.

Just after New Year's, he told his partner that he wanted to sell out and retire. They discussed it in general terms.

Using an assumed name and a post office box number which was not his, Smith wrote to a commission agent in Boston with whom he had never had any previous dealings. He mailed the letter, with the agent's address covered by one of his labels on which he had typed a fictitious address. The label detached itself in transit; the letter was delivered. When the agent replied, Smith was watching and read the letter as a secretary typed it. The agent followed his instruction to mail his reply in an envelope without return address. The owner of the post office box turned it in marked "not here"; it went to the dead-letter office and was returned in due time, but meanwhile Smith had acknowledged the letter and had mailed, in the same way, a large amount of cash. In subsequent letters he instructed the agent to take bids for components, plans for which he enclosed, from electronics manufacturers, for plastic casings from

another, and for assembly and shipping from still another company. Through
a second commission agent in New York, to whom he wrote in the same way,
he contracted for ten thousand copies of an instruction booklet in four colors.

Late in February he bought a house and an electronics dealership in a small
town in the Adirondacks. In March he signed over his interest in the company to his partner, cleaned out his lab and left. He sold his co-op apartment
in Manhattan and his summer house in Connecticut, moved to his new home
and became anonymous.

■ ■ ■

You are thirteen, chasing a fox with the big kids for the first time. They have
put you in the north field, the worst place, but you know better than to leave it.

"He's in the glen."

"I see him; he's in the brook, going upstream."

You turn on the viewer, racing forward through dappled shade, a brilliance
of leaves: there is the glen, and now you see the fox, trotting through the shal-
lows, blossoms of bright water at its feet.

"Ken and Nell, you come down ahead of him by the springhouse. Wanda,
you and Tim and Jean stay where you are. Everybody else come upstream, but
stay back till I tell you."

That's Leigh, the oldest. You turn the viewer, catch a glimpse of Bobby
running downhill through the woods, his long hair flying. Then back to the
glen: the fox is gone.

"He's heading up past the corncrib!"

"Okay, keep spread out on both sides, everybody. Jim, can you and Edie
head him off before he gets to the woods?"

"We'll try. There he is!"

And the chase is going away from you, as you knew it would, but soon you
will be older, as old as Nell and Jim; then you will be in the middle of things,
and your life will begin.

■ ■ ■

By trial and error, Smith has found the settings for Dallas, November 22, 1963:
Dealey Plaza, 12:25 p.m. He sees the presidential motorcade making the turn
onto Elm Street. Kennedy slumps forward, raising his hands to his throat.
Smith presses a button to hold the moment in time. He scans behind the
motorcade, finds the sixth floor of the Book Depository Building, finds the window. There is no one behind the barricade of cartons; the room is empty. He
scans the nearby rooms, finds nothing. He tries the floor below. At an open
window a man kneels, holding a high-powered rifle. Smith photographs him.
He returns to the motorcade, watches as the second shot strikes the president.

He freezes time again, scans the surrounding buildings, finds a second marks-
man on a roof, photographs him. Back to the motorcade. A third and fourth
shot, the last blowing off the side of the president's head. Smith freezes the
action again, finds two gunmen on the grassy knoll, one aiming across the top
of a station wagon, one kneeling in the shrubbery. He photographs them. He
turns off the power, sits for a moment, then goes to the washroom, kneels beside the toilet and vomits.

■ ■ ■

The viewer is your babysitter, your television, your telephone (the telephone
lines are still up, but they are used only as signaling devices; when you know
that somebody wants to talk to you, you focus your viewer on him), your library, your school. Before puberty you watch other people having sex, but even
then your curiosity is easily satisfied; after an older cousin initiates you at fourteen, you are much more interested in doing it yourself. The co-op teacher
monitors your studies, sometimes makes suggestions, but more and more, as
you grow older, leaves you to your own devices. You are intensely interested
in African prehistory, in the European theater, and in the ant civilization of
Epsilon Eridani IV. Soon you will have to choose.

■ ■ ■

New York Harbor, November 4, 1872—a cold, blustery day. A two-masted ship
rides at anchor; on her stern is lettered: *Mary Celeste*. Smith advances the time
control. A flicker of darkness, light again, and the ship is gone. He turns back
again until he finds it standing out under light canvas past Sandy Hook. Mani-
pulating time and space controls at once, he follows it eastward through a
flickering of storm and sun—loses it, finds it again, counting days as he goes.
The farther eastward, the more he has to tilt the device downward, while the
image of the ship tilts correspondingly away from him. Because of the angle,
he can no longer keep the ship in view from a distance but must track it closely.
November 21 and 22, violent storms: the ship is dashed upward by waves, falls
again, visible only intermittently; it takes him five hours to pass through two
days of real time. The 23rd is calmer, but on the 24th another storm blows up.
Smith rubs his eyes, loses the ship, finds it again after a ten-minute search.

The gale blows itself out on the morning of the 26th. The sun is bright, the
sea almost dead calm. Smith is able to catch glimpses of figures on deck, tilted
above dark cross-sections of the hull. A sailor is splicing a rope in the stern, two
others lowering a triangular sail between the foremast and the bowsprit, and
a fourth is at the helm. A little group stands leaning on the starboard rail; one
of them is a woman. The next glimpse is that of a running figure who advances
into the screen and disappears. Now the men are lowering a boat over the

side; the rail has been removed and lies on the deck. The men drop into the boat and row away. He hears them shouting to each other but cannot make out the words.

Smith returns to the ship again; the deck is empty. He dips below to look at the hold, filled with casks, then the cabin, then the forecastle. There is no sign of anything wrong—no explosion, no fire, no trace of violence. When he looks up again, he sees the sails flapping, then bellying out full. The sea is rising. He looks for the boat, but now too much time has passed and he cannot find it. He returns to the ship and now reverses the time control, tracks it backward until the men are again in their places on deck. He looks again at the group standing at the rail; now he sees that the woman has a child in her arms. The child struggles, drops over the rail. Smith hears the woman shriek. In a moment she too is over the rail and falling into the sea.

He watches the men running, sees them launch the boat. As they pull away, he is able to keep the focus near enough to see and hear them. One calls, "My God, who's at the helm?" Another, a bearded man with a face gone tallow-pale, replies, "Never mind—row!" They are staring down into the sea. After a moment, one looks up, then another. The *Mary Celeste*, with three of the four sails on her foremast set, is gliding away, slowly, now faster; now she is gone.

Smith does not run through the scene again to watch the child and her mother drown, but others do.

■ ■ ■

The production model was ready for shipping in September. It was a simplified version of the prototype, with only two controls, one for space, one for time. The range of the device was limited to one thousand miles. Nowhere on the casing of the device or in the instruction booklet was a patent number or a pending patent mentioned. Smith had called the device Ozo, perhaps because he thought it sounded vaguely Japanese. The booklet described the device as a distant viewer and give clear, simple instructions for its use. One sentence read cryptically: **"Keep Time Control Set at Zero."** It was like **"Wet Paint—Do Not Touch."**

During the week of September 23, seven thousand Ozos were shipped to domestic and Canadian addresses supplied by Smith: five hundred to electronics manufacturers and suppliers; six thousand, thirty to a carton, marked "On Consignment," to TV outlets in major cities; and the rest to private citizens chosen at random. The instruction booklets were in sealed envelopes packed with each device. Three thousand more went to Europe, South and Central America and the Middle East.

A few of the outlets which received the cartons opened them the same day, tried the devices out, and put them on sale at prices ranging from $49.95 to $125. By the following day the word was beginning to spread, and by the close of business on the third day every store was sold out. Most people who got them, either through the mail or by purchase, used them to spy on their neighbors and on people in hotels.

■ ■ ■

In a house in Cleveland, a man watches his brother-in-law in the next room, who is watching his wife get out of a taxi. She goes to the lobby of an apartment building. The husband watches as she gets into the elevator, rides to the fourth floor. She rings the bell beside the door marked 410. The door opens; a dark-haired man takes her in his arms; they kiss.

The brother-in-law meets him in the hall. "Don't do it, Charlie."

"Get out of my way."

"I'm not going to get out of your way, and I tell you, don't do it. Not now and not later."

"Why the hell shouldn't I?"

"Because if you do I'll kill you. If you want a divorce, OK, get a divorce. But don't lay a hand on her or I'll find you the farthest place you can go."

Smith got his consignment of Ozos early in the week, took one home and left it to his store manager to put a price on the rest. He did not bother to use the production model but began at once to build another prototype. It had controls calibrated to one-hundredth of a second and one millimeter, and a timer that would allow him to stop a scene, or advance or regress it at any desired rate. He ordered some clockwork from an astronomical supply house.

■ ■ ■

A high-ranking officer in Army Intelligence, watching the first demonstration of the Ozo in the Pentagon, exclaimed, "My God, with this we could dismantle half the establishment—all we've got to do is launch interceptors when we see them push the button."

"It's a good thing Senator Burkhart can't hear you say that," said another officer. But by the next afternoon everybody had heard it.

■ ■ ■

A Baptist minister in Louisville led the first mob against an Ozo assembly plant. A month later, while civil and criminal suits against all the rioters were still pending, tapes showing each one of them in compromising or ludicrous activities were widely distributed in the area.

The commission agents who had handled the orders for the first Ozos were found out and had to leave town. Factories were firebombed, but others took their place.

. . .

The first Ozo was smuggled into the Soviet Union from West Germany by Katerina Belov, a member of a dissident group in Moscow, who used it to document illegal government actions. The device was seized on December 13 by the KGB; Belov and two other members of the group were arrested, imprisoned and tortured. By that time over forty other Ozos were in the hands of dissidents.

. . .

You are watching an old movie, *Bob & Carol & Ted & Alice*. The humor seems infantile and unimaginative to you: you are not interested in the actresses' glances, smiles, grimaces, hinting at things that will never be shown on the screen. You realize that these people have never seen anyone but their most intimate friends without clothing, have never seen any adult shit or piss, and would be embarrassed or disgusted if they did. Why did children say "pee-pee" and "poo-poo," and then giggle? You have read scholarly books about taboos on "bodily functions," but why was shitting worse than sneezing?

. . .

Cora Zickwolfe, who lived in a remote rural area of Arizona and whose husband commuted to Tucson, arranged with her nearest neighbor, Phyllis Mell, for each of them to keep an Ozo focused on the bulletin board in the other's kitchen. On the bulletin board was a note that said "OK." If there was any trouble and she couldn't get to the phone, she would take down the note, or if she had time, write another.

In April 1992, about the time her husband usually got home, an intruder broke into the house and seized Mrs. Zickwolfe before she had time to get to the bulletin board. He dragged her into the bedroom and forced her to disrobe. The state troopers got there in fifteen minutes, and Cora never spoke to her friend Phyllis again.

. . .

Between 1992 and 2002 more than six hundred improvements and supplements to the Ozo were recorded. The most important of these was the power system created by focusing the Ozo at a narrow aperture on the interior of the Sun. Others included the system of satellite slave units in stationary orbits and a computerized tracer device which would keep the Ozo focused on any subject.

Using a tracer, an entomologist in Mexico City is following the ancestral line of a honey bee. The images bloom and expire, ten every second: the tracer is following each queen back to the egg, then the egg to the queen that laid it, then that queen to the egg. Tens of thousands of generations have passed; in two thousand hours, beginning with a Paleocene bee, he has traveled back to the Cretaceous. He stops at intervals to follow the bee in real time, then accelerates again. The hive is growing smaller, more primitive. Now it is only a cluster of round cells, and the bee is different, more like a wasp. His year's labor is coming to fruition. He watches, forgetting to eat, almost to breathe.

■ ■ ■

In your mother's study after she dies, you find an elaborate chart of her ancestors and your father's. You retrieve the program for it, punch it in, and idly watch a random sampling, back into time, first the female line, then the male . . . a teacher of biology in Boston, a suffragette, a corn merchant, a singer, a Dutch farmer in New York, a British sailor, a German musician. Their faces glow in the screen, bright-eyed, cheeks flushed with life. Someday you too will be only a series of images in a screen.

■ ■ ■

Smith is watching the planet Mars. The clockwork which turns the Ozo to follow the planet, even when it is below the horizon, makes it possible for him to focus instantly on the surface, but he never does this. He takes up his position hundreds of thousands of miles away, then slowly approaches, in order to see the red spark grow to a disk, then to a yellow sunlit ball hanging in darkness. Now he can make out the surface features: Syrtis Major and Thoth-Nepenthes leading in a long gooseneck to Utopia and the frostcap.

The image as it swells hypnotically toward him is clear and sharp, without tremor or atmospheric distortion. It is summer in the northern hemisphere: Utopia is wide and dark. The planet fills the screen, and now he turns northward, over the cratered desert still hundreds of miles distant. A dust storm, like a yellow veil, obscures the curved neck of Thoth-Nepenthes; then he is beyond it, drifting down to the edge of the frostcap. The limb of the planet reappears; he floats like a glider over the dark surface tinted with rose and violet-gray; now he can see its nubbly texture; now he can make out individual plants. He is drifting among their gnarled gray stems, their leaves of violet horn; he sees the curious mis-shapen growths that may be air bladders or some grotesque analogue of blossoms. Now, at the edge of the screen, something black and spindling leaps. He follows it instantly, finds it, brings it hugely magnified into the center of the screen; a thing like a hairy beetle, its body covered with thick black hairs or spines; it stands on six jointed legs, waving its antennae, its mouth parts busy. And its four bright eyes stare into his, across forty million miles.

■ ■ ■

Smith's hair got whiter and thinner. Before the 1992 Crash, he made heavy contributions to the International Red Cross and to volunteer organizations in Europe, Asia and Africa. He got drunk periodically, but always alone. From 1993 to 1996 he stopped reading the newspapers.

He wrote down the coordinates for the plane crash in which his daughter and her husband had died, but never used them.

At intervals while dressing or looking into the bathroom mirror, he stared as if into an invisible camera and raised one finger. In his last years he wrote some poems.

We know his name. Patient researchers, using advanced scanning techniques, followed his letters back through the postal system and found him, but by that time he was safely dead.

■ ■ ■

The whole world has been at peace for more than a generation. Crime is almost unheard of. Free energy has made the world rich, but the population is stable, even though early detection has wiped out most diseases. Everyone can do whatever he likes, providing his neighbors would not disapprove, and after all, their views are loose, generally accepting, like yours.

You are forty, a respected scholar, taking a few days out to review your life, as many people do at your age. You have watched your mother and father coupling on the night they conceived you, watched yourself growing in her womb, first a red tadpole, then a thing like an embryo chicken, then a big-headed baby kicking and squirming. You have seen yourself delivered, seen the first moment when your bloody head broke into the light. You have seen yourself staggering around the nursery in rompers, clutching a yellow plastic duck. Now you are watching yourself hiding behind the fallen tree on the hill, and you realize that there are no secret places. And beyond you in the ghostly future you know that someone is watching you as you watch; and beyond that watcher another, and beyond that another . . . Forever.

Might the problem be
The very opposite of privacy?

EYEJACKED

DAVID WALTON

Patrick felt glad his wife wasn't home. What did that say about his marriage, when he preferred Alicia to be away? Nothing good, that was for sure. But it was a relief to play a board game with his daughter in something like privacy for once, without any strangers looking in.

The board game was called *Become a Star with Delia Sharp,* and it had the same basic rules as *Candyland,* except that it followed the pop star's road to fame instead of a path through the Peppermint Forest and around Gumdrop Mountain. He found it dull as dirt to play, but Maddy, at age seven, loved it, just as she loved Delia's weekly show and associated children's books. Patrick didn't care what game they played. He felt happier than he remembered being in a long time, just sitting there on the living room floor, watching Maddy crow with delight at each new card.

A tiny display at the corner of his vision read 4:30, almost time to start making dinner, but no rush. The display also revealed that he had one follower, his mother, probably, who often connected to his feed to watch Maddy through his eyejack lenses. He didn't mind her looking in. She was family. It gave her a way to stay connected from her apartment.

With Alicia, it felt different. As a Lilo—a Life Logger—and rapidly becoming one of the most popular in the country, she had thousands of followers, mostly strangers, who watched the world through her lenses or followed her through the aggregation of neighborhood cams and the viewfeeds of passersby. Her quick rise to celebrity brought dramatic changes, including a lot of money. Patrick felt happy for her. He did. But the changes weren't all for the good.

He switched his view, opening a window in his field of vision and instructing his lenses to show him his mother. He saw her at her dining room table, working on a puzzle with a picture of a castle, somewhere in Germany perhaps. His view of her came from the perspective of AAL, her Automated Assisted Living system, which enabled her to live independently despite advancing Alzheimer's. She managed well enough, but it would get worse over time, and he was glad to be able to check on her whenever he wanted.

Her agile, long-fingered hands selected pieces and placed them without hesitation. He remembered those hands playing Chopin with similar confidence. She could still play, if he cajoled her, though she tended to forget that she could until she sat down and her fingers moved of their own accord.

"Your turn, Dad."

Patrick switched his attention back to Maddy and selected a card. It told him that Delia had broken up with football star Justin Matthews, sending Patrick back two blue squares. Maddy giggled at his bad luck and hopped his marker backward with childish glee. Her flyaway brown hair always stuck up in odd places, despite Alicia's attempts to tame it, and her lopsided smile showed off the proud gaps of several missing baby teeth.

The number of followers indicated at the corner of Patrick's vision rose from one to two, and then jumped to five. It flashed red as he gained more viewers, jumping ten and twenty at a time until it reached the hundreds. Surprised, he queried the network and discovered that Alicia, charmed by the quaint and picturesque scene of a father playing a board game with his daughter, had tagged the feed for her followers, many of whom had added it to their visual display. His feeling of relaxation disappeared. Three hundred strangers from around the world were now watching him and Maddy play together in their living room.

He could disconnect, of course. Without Alicia actually here in person, he could choose to be private. But Alicia wouldn't like it. She would accuse him of being anti-social and secretive for no reason. And she was probably right. Patrick knew he could be old-fashioned where eyejacks were concerned. And it wasn't like he had anything to hide. But with so many people looking at him, he felt self-conscious. Watched. It made what had been a genuine moment with Maddy feel like a charade, a kind of playacting for the satisfaction of others.

A few predictable comments started to litter his board, *Awww, how sweet,* and *What a good father. I wish my husband would. . . .* Patrick swept them away with a flick of his eyes, annoyed at Alicia for disturbing his tranquil afternoon, and at himself for minding something that ultimately didn't matter. He didn't care what any of those viewers thought, so why did it bother him to have them watching?

Maddy, who had no eyejacks, didn't notice any of it. "No, Daddy. You have to wait back in Memphis. You can't go to L.A. until you get the 'land a film agent' card." Her infectious laughter helped him set his worries aside.

When the game ended, he stood, stretched, and headed toward the kitchen to make dinner. By then, most of the new viewers had drifted away, probably back to Alicia and a higher likelihood of drama and spectacle. A glance at her feed showed her, at that moment, walking through a food court in Midtown, exclaiming to a friend in appalled tones about fat and sugar content, processed chemical ingredients and a general lack of cleanliness.

". . . there was a study, I don't remember where, by some scientist or other, that the *napkins* at these places have more germs on them than the toilet paper at a truck stop," Alicia said, to her friend's evident astonishment. "Can you *imagine*? Wiping your mouth . . . ?"

As her friend shuddered, comments rolled down the bottom of Alicia's feed. Half of her viewers expressed horror and revulsion, while the others hurled abuse on the first half for being so gullible. The ensuing arguments spiraled quickly into attacks on each other's mental capacity, loyalty to Alicia, and general fitness to be called members of the human race.

Patrick shut off the feed. Alicia was just hitting her stride, and she was still a taxi ride away from their Upper East Side apartment. She wouldn't be home for dinner.

"Come on, Maddy," he said. "Let's make some chocolate-chip pancakes."

. . .

Alicia made it home in time to put Maddy to bed, a drawn-out affair involving several children's books (*Delia Sharp Can Do Anything!*), a glass of milk, and endless hugs and kisses. The voices Alicia used when reading were dynamic and funny, and kept Maddy laughing and begging for more. Despite himself, Patrick smiled to watch them. Alicia's genuine interactions revealed a cherishing of their daughter that went beyond merely pleasing her viewership.

Then Maddy made several sugary-cute comments that rang false to Patrick and set him worrying again. Maddy couldn't see Alicia's ratings, but she could tell what made Alicia happy, which was more or less the same thing. What would that teach her? And how long would it take Maddy to figure out that the ratings increased even more when she behaved badly?

He cleaned up the remains of the dishes in the sink, changed for bed, then popped out his eyejack lenses and set them in their case. The air-conditioning made the air feel dry and fresh on his skin, and the sheets were pleasantly cool to the touch. He settled back against a stack of pillows with a novel. He would have to wake early to get to work, but a little solitary time to unwind seemed like a good idea.

When Alicia finally joined him, dressed in an elegant but chaste nightgown, he folded the book and set it on his night-table. He had been waiting for this opportunity, the only time of day he could be sure of a truly private conversation.

"I want to talk," he said.

She sat next to him, her loose hair falling across her shoulders. Beauty was almost a job requirement in her line of work, but even so, it made him forget, for a moment, what he intended to say. She looked at him, unsmiling. "So talk."

He hugged a pillow to his chest. "It's about all this success you've had. I just think. . . ." He sighed, tried again. "I know this is what you've wanted for a long time. But I don't think it's good for Maddy, or for our family. It's as if we don't know you anymore. You're like an actor playing the part of you in your own TV drama."

"Not good for her?" Alicia gave a surprised little cough. "Maddy has more now than she ever did. Better clothes, better neighborhood. You think we could send her to the Dalton School on your salary?"

"I'm not talking about money. I'm talking about a family life that's not influenced by what will make us more interesting to strangers."

"Maddy doesn't mind. You should see us in the park—she loves the attention we get. We pass people on the street, and they know her name. It's like growing up as a princess."

"And is that a good thing? Will that make her happy? I could link you to studies on kids and celebrity . . ."

"This isn't really about Maddy, is it?" Alicia curled her legs up underneath her and crossed her arms. "You resent the attention I get. You're jealous."

"That's not it. But yes, it's about me, too. About us." He reached out and touched her hand. Her skin felt cold. "We barely connect anymore."

"It's because I'm making more money than you, isn't it?" Alicia said. She cocked her head, as if hit by a sudden realization. "You feel threatened. I'm providing for Maddy better than you can, and it emasculates you."

Patrick pulled his hand away. "That's not it at all!"

"Sexism dies hard, doesn't it? Even in our day and age."

He pushed the pillow aside and turned in bed so he could face her. "This is ridiculous. I don't care how much money you make. I'm talking about what it will be like for Maddy to grow up with a mother who cares more about a thousand strangers than she does about her own daughter."

She flushed. "That is not true, and you know it."

"I'm not saying it's true, just that Maddy—"

"She knows I love her. It's you who's having the problem here. Maddy likes what I do. If you'd only let me buy her lenses of her own—"

"No!" He spoke louder than he'd intended, and tried to temper his voice. "No lenses. You know what I think about that. I won't have her living her whole life online. She'll have plenty of time for that, once she's had a real life for a while."

Alicia's eyes flashed. "Is that what you think of my life? As a fake?"

"You can't tell me you don't act differently when people are watching."

She threw up her hands. "You live in Manhattan! There are a hundred people watching you every time you step out the door."

"Not inside. Not in our house. I want to be able to close the door and be alone, just the three . . ." He trailed off, studying her face. She was angry and upset, but at the same time, the shadow of a smile played at one corner of her mouth. She glanced down and to the left, almost too fast to see, then back at him.

Patrick couldn't believe it. "You're still online, aren't you?"

She shrugged. "I didn't take my lenses out yet."

"You've got to be kidding me." He jumped out of bed, wanting to hit something. He ran his fingers painfully through his hair. She had been baiting him on purpose. Turning the conversation into an argument to spike her ratings.

"You know this is who I am," she said. She met his gaze, not repentant at all.

"We agreed, Alicia! Not in the bedroom. This is our sanctuary, where we can be alone. You promised the bedroom would be off-limits."

"It's not like we were making love or anything."

He resisted the urge to raise his voice again, to get drawn into the shouting match she wanted. "It doesn't matter what we're doing. This is our private place. I don't want to share it with the world."

She raised her hands, indicating their surroundings. "This is what people want to see. This is what it's all about, Patrick. Our relationship, our parenting, how we live and think. Do you know how many people have told me we've inspired them to be better parents? It's about being connected, as a society. It's about helping people with their lives."

"I can't talk like this. Take them out."

"What?"

"Take the lenses out. Please. For me."

Alicia sighed. For a moment, he thought she would refuse, but she did as he asked, popping out her eyejack lenses and dropping them into their case.

"Thank you." Patrick sank back onto the bed and sat hugging his knees. He felt an intense relief, knowing they were alone. He realized the lenses gave her a kind of power. With them on, she had an army of people behind her, not all of them rooting for her—some of the comments from viewers were downright hostile—but all of them watching. No one could say anything to her or do anything to her without a thousand people knowing about it. She seemed suddenly smaller without them. More vulnerable.

"Happy now?" she said.

"It didn't have to be like that. I didn't want a fight."

"What did you want? You knew all this when you married me. You knew what I wanted."

He couldn't deny it. Though at the time, she'd barely had any followers, and Patrick had never really expected that to change. It was a fickle business, and so few reached any kind of genuine celebrity status. "I want some limits," he said. "I want boundaries. I want, at least, for you to stick to agreements we've already made."

Alicia held up her index finger and thumb with a tiny gap in between. "I'm this close to breaking into the top hundred. Not just in one category. In the world, Patrick. The top hundred! Do you know what that will mean?"

He didn't want to think about it. Her face glowed as she talked, though, and without the lenses, it seemed genuine. He was seeing the real Alicia. This was important to her. It made her feel alive.

And he loved her. She could be brilliant and audacious and gentle and caring all at the same time. She was still the same person he had fallen in love with ten years earlier. He wanted her to be happy.

He took a slow breath and let it out. "It's mostly luck, isn't it? Making the top follower lists?"

Her face soured. "A lot of it. Honestly, the best way to get into the high rankings is to have some kind of personal tragedy."

Patrick felt a shiver run down his back. "We won't hope for that, though. You'll find another way."

She gave him a genuine smile.

"I don't want to hold you back," he said. "But I need boundaries. I need times when I know it's just us, and to know I can trust you to stick to those times. And I want Maddy to have times like that, too."

The smile disappeared. "I can't go halfway on this. Every step I take, I'm competing against other Lilos who would give anything to take my place."

"And what are you willing to give?"

She narrowed her eyes. "What are you saying?"

"Only that you should think about what you're willing to give up. And whether it's worth it."

■ ■ ■

Patrick's mother had lived in her apartment for three years, but she still hadn't accepted it as her home. Her Alzheimer's meant newly formed memories were spotty and faint, while her memories of their house in Brooklyn were strong. She still asked him sometimes when they would go back home again.

The summer sun blazed, and heat shimmered off of the pavement. Patrick messaged AAL when he reached the apartment, and it unlocked the front door for him. AAL was a robot, after a fashion—a slow, boxy device that could roll from room to room, following his mother. In reality, though, AAL consisted of several dozen devices installed throughout the apartment, attached to all the major appliances, and a central computer that could control the lights, oven, stove, door locks, and room temperature.

Patrick found his mom in the kitchen, baking cookies and cooling herself with a bamboo fan. The rolling robot stood nearby, displaying Alicia's feed on its large screen.

"AAL, lower the temperature to seventy-five degrees," Patrick said.

"Understood," a pleasant male voice answered. "Lowering temperature to seventy-five."

His mother shook the fan at him. "You don't have to do that. Air-conditioning is expensive."

"I can afford it, Mom. You don't need to suffer in the heat. I want you to use it."

She lifted a box of baking soda and looked at AAL. "How much?"

"You added the baking soda already," AAL replied. "The next ingredient is vanilla."

"You're looking beautiful," Patrick said, and gave her a kiss on the forehead.

She beamed. "You're a terrible liar." She whacked him with the fan.

"I would never lie to you. How are you feeling?"

"Good," she said. "Never better." Her face clouded for a moment. "I should call Cassie. It's her birthday today. Don't let me forget!"

"Okay," he said. Cassie was her sister, who had died of brain cancer the year before. Today was, however, her birthday. It baffled Patrick how his mom could remember that it was her sister's birthday, and yet not remember that she was dead. At one point, he would have corrected her, tried to set her memory straight. He didn't bother anymore. It would only upset her, and she would forget again in a few minutes anyway.

She studied the ingredients in front of her. "Baking soda next, I think," she said.

"You added the baking soda already," AAL said. "The next ingredient is vanilla."

It repeated its instructions in exactly the same tone of voice, with no hint of impatience. It was the perfect companion for her—better, in some ways, than a human, who would grow frustrated at her constant need for reminders. It managed her daily schedule, gave her medicine at the right time, took her blood pressure, even kept track of her reading glasses.

"How's Alicia doing?" Patrick said. He didn't really want to know. The conversation of the night before still bothered him. But his mother loved to watch Alicia's feed, especially since it allowed her to keep in touch with her only granddaughter.

"They're in Central Park," she said. "Feeding the squirrels."

That seemed like a surprisingly tame activity for Alicia, but he was glad, certain Maddy would be delighted at the prospect. A morning relatively free from drama would be good for her.

On screen, Alicia laid out a perfect little picnic spread—all healthy and organic food, of course—on a brightly colored blanket. Maddy popped so many grapes into her mouth that her cheeks bulged. Alicia set out a box of tofu squares so that the SoyaJoy brand name was clearly visible, though he wasn't sure anyone else would have noticed it was deliberate. Her popularity meant companies solicited her for sponsorships, offering free products so people would see her using them. Maddy wore a $200 Gaultier sundress, a gift to Alicia from Saks Fifth Avenue just for shopping there.

Dozens of other picnickers lounged across the wide expanse of grass. A few young men played football, and a vendor strolled through with a huge bunch of balloons. Behind them, the skyscrapers framed the horizon, glinting in the sunlight. Patrick wondered if Alicia had picked the spot for the view it afforded her followers, and concluded that of course she must have. It was like she was filming the movie of her life, and playing both director and star.

His mother reached for the baking soda again. Patrick moved it to the other side of the table and handed her the vanilla. "One teaspoon," AAL told her. She measured and dropped it in.

Maddy ran through the grass, visiting other families and their picnics, while Alicia chased after her, calling her back. A feed aggregator rotated the view between Alicia's lenses and the other cameras and lenses in range, following both of them through the field.

"She's such a darling," his mother said. "She'll be breaking hearts in her day, mark my words."

Patrick turned his back to the screen and started stirring the batter, wanting to change the subject. Which was why he wasn't watching when Alicia started screaming.

He whirled back to see her shouting at another woman, livid, her words barely comprehensible. "What happened?" he said.

His mother looked confused. "I don't know."

A flurry of comments flooded the lower panel. *Has anyone called 9-1-1?*
What was she thinking, letting Maddy run loose like that?

It isn't her fault. People should be more careful when they eat in public!

If Alicia had breastfed her daughter, she wouldn't have allergies. People just don't care enough about their children to give them what's best.

My son had soy formula for years, and he never developed any allergies.

Why can't chocolate factories just use different equipment to process peanuts?

All they care about is making more money . . .

Allergies. Maddy had a serious peanut allergy, one that had already given her a significant reaction a year ago. At the time, the doctors had warned that such reactions tended to get worse the more they occurred, that the next one could be life-threatening.

"AAL, call 9-1-1," he said. "Give them Maddy's coordinates and tell them she needs urgent attention for a nut reaction."

On screen, Alicia pulled an EpiPen from her purse. She uncapped it and thrust it expertly into Maddy's leg, still shouting at the poor mother from whose picnic Maddy had apparently stolen a chocolate. Maddy's face was bright red with rash, and her breathing came in short gasps. A crowd started to gather.

The other mother apologized profusely, wringing her hands. She tried to say something to Maddy, but Alicia screamed at her, leaving Maddy lying in the grass while she jabbed her finger at the other woman.

"What is she doing?" Patrick said. "She needs to get to a hospital!" He tried to call her phone, but she didn't answer.

Alicia's follower count spiked. It surged past a hundred thousand viewers and kept growing. With a sudden chill, Patrick remembered Alicia's comment of the night before. *Honestly, the way to get into the high rankings is to have some kind of personal tragedy.*

No. She couldn't have. Could she? She wouldn't risk Maddy's life to boost her rankings. He couldn't believe it. Wouldn't. With a physical effort, he pulled his eyes away from the screen.

"I have to go," he said.

                              ▪ ▪ ▪

He finally caught up with them at Saint Luke's Hospital. Maddy had vomited twice and was sinking into unconsciousness. The hospital had been ready for her when she arrived and had immediately wheeled her out of sight, blocking Alicia's attempts to follow.

By that time, Alicia's feed had topped a million viewers, making her the #2 most watched person in the world. It wouldn't last—the numbers were already dropping again—but it might double her regular viewership, and would establish her as one of the top Lilos in the country, at least for a while.

When Patrick walked into the waiting room, Alicia ran to him and wrapped her arms around him, burying her head in his shoulder. He pulled her gently back, and saw that she had been crying. Her eyes were red, her makeup smeared, and there were grass stains on her white Valentino dress. He immediately dismissed any idea that she could have maneuvered this situation on purpose. This was the real Alicia, his Alicia, and her fear and worry were evident. He pressed her close to him.

"I'm sorry. I'm so sorry," she said.

"It's not your fault," he said, stroking her hair. "You can't protect her from everything."

And then she was crying again. Not a soft weeping, but deep sobs that shook her slim body. "I *thought* it. Don't you understand? Part of me *hoped* for a tragedy. You were right. I've let it take over everything. But I didn't mean . . . I didn't want . . ."

He drew her tightly to him. "Of course you didn't. No one could blame you."

"I love her so much, Patrick. I would never, never harm her."

They stood there, holding each other. A woman walked by and gave them a smile. "We're praying for you," she said. Patrick just nodded, unsure what to say. Another man, his arm wrapped in a makeshift cloth bandage, cleared his throat. "I hope your daughter's all right," he said. Patrick looked around the room to see that half of the people there—all of them with traumas or illnesses of their own—were looking at him and Alicia with sympathetic faces.

"They love her," Alicia whispered.

Patrick switched his lenses to Alicia's feed, and saw thousands upon thousands of comments wishing them well, though there were many others who questioned Alicia's fitness as a mother or even accused her—as Patrick himself had thought to do—of manufacturing the situation for the ratings. Dozens of other popular feeds had picked up the story, both news suppliers and career fans who made their reputations providing summary and commentary on the lives of the super-popular. The eyes of the world were on them.

It was, Patrick thought, with sudden realization, like an extended family. These were people who cared about them, who took an interest in their lives. He thought of his mother, her world shrinking as her memories faded, reaching out through the feeds to stay connected. What was this, but the opposite of Alzheimer's? An *expanding* of the self, a preservation of experience and memory in the minds of thousands? He felt, just for a moment, the rush of connectedness that meant so much to Alicia.

Eventually, a doctor came out to talk to them, accompanied by the president of the hospital. Patrick's heart did a flip, expecting bad news, until he registered the smiles on their faces. It had been a near thing, they said, but the worst was past. Maddy was safe and would recover quickly. They followed the president to Maddy's room, a large, single-person space with a window that looked out onto Central Park. It was already filling up with flowers and balloons.

They hugged her and kissed her and held her hand, and though her tongue was still too swollen to speak easily, she managed a weak smile. Patrick stood next to Alicia, and she leaned into him.

"I was thinking," he said, running his fingers through her hair. "As Maddy gets older, we're going to want to be able to keep an eye on her. And we can't block her from technology forever."

Alicia looked up at him, her expression intent but uncertain. "What are you saying?"

"I'm saying that once Maddy is ready to leave the hospital, it might be time for us to get her some eyejack lenses of her own."

Alicia's eyes lit up. Her mouth quirked in amusement. Then it unfolded into a smile, wide and beautiful, that he knew was just for him.

"We're going to make this work, aren't we?" she said.

He wrapped his arm around her waist and looked down at Maddy, who smiled back up at them. "Yes," he said. "I believe we are."

*Will tech-empowerment bring
the ultimate in citizenship?*

FEASTWAR

VYLAR KAFTAN

The Spritely War Chamber, Fiefdom of Westhalia [Oakland, USA], Kingdom of Pangourmet

2034-02-26

Scheherazade: Hey Pixies! Did you see the battle maneuver from the Orcs? They ate lamb kebabs in Baghdad and Tehran. Organic and local for extra points. Simultaneous, so they got the timezone bonus.

MarcoYOLO: Dammit. Lamb from actual sheep? Stupid meat.

NeedleStack: suuuuushi

MarcoYOLO: Sushi. Tasty but not meat according to game rules. *shoots tiny bow and arrow*

Scheherazade: @MarcoYOLO Sorry. At least our team gets major kill points for salads. We've taken out whole armies that way. At one point we controlled the entire west coast of Pangourmet.

hygge: Taking out Dragons is so easy. Seriously, aren't they always in last place?

Scheherazade: They've got it rough. They have the most diverse digestive profiles of any team. And the highest percent of allergies. Aside from some HLA genetics and sensitive microbiomes, they don't share much. That's why they're allowed some foodie-weapons no other team gets.

hygge: Oh. Like the Fireblast thing that keeps disrupting our front line? Sorry, I'm still a noob.

Scheherazade: @hygge Yeah, game balance. They launched a Fireblast in the Midwest last week. Every ingredient in their feast was locally sourced, humanely killed, and organic. 10x multiplier for that one. The Midwest is all scaly. You can feel it on your phone. Pet the map, it's silky-scratchy.

NeedleStack: midwest should be pixie soft and glittery lol

Scheherazade: Attacking there would be fun, but doesn't suit our worldwide battle plan: 1) Focus on simultaneous Pixie-safe meals in US West Coast cities to generate Gold Dust. 2) Organize a feastday for pescatarians in Japan and the West Coast, to open mana linking privileges. 3) Attack Yosae (that's Korea and area) with Japanese Pixie archers, enhanced by our Gold Dust. 4) Run a simul-paired 5K at dawn in Tokyo and dusk here to recover mana.

MarcoYOLO: Salads Are Strength! *waves Pixie banner*

hygge: Game question. Say I scan my dinner with my phone, and score points for organic, but not locally-sourced: can I send it back to the kitchen and swap ingredients, then post a new pic?

NeedleStack: no

MarcoYOLO: @hygge No, once you attack, that's check-in for that timeslot. Spends your metabolic mana. So look before you scan. Check for nonlocal and hothouse ingredients (cucumbers and tomatoes are two big offenders). Use tricorder mode to check for top 40 no-no chems and organic/not before you attack. Helps to research the restaurant first. Check healthyeating. wrld for restaurant scores.

Scheherazade: Once you advance to places like cooperative farms or remote tribal cooking and whatnot, we'll help. Focus on choosing the right restaurants. For now, Pixie strategy involves more seafood, so eat sustainable sushi!

hygge: Got it, thanks.

MarcoYOLO: So Schehea,,.// sorry, cat. Emily, are we still crushing the Orcs this weekend?

Scheherazade: Yep! Big raid planned with our Dragon allies, since we expect a meat-based battle.

NeedleStack: no one wants to partner with icky orcs anyway

Scheherazade: Haha. We're going to claim restaurants all the way up the West Coast and make the Sierra Nevadas our front line. The Dragons will handle the protein side. We've got the soy-based stuff and of course salads for everyone.

redNikki231 has joined the chamber

redNikki231: BUY SECRETS HERE at http://324.FeastWarPowerUps.game use code NJT21G for discounts

redNikki231 has left the chamber

Scheherazade: Ugh, spambot. Blocked it. Anyway, we don't expect trouble from Elves or Phoenixes. Dwarves might try to block us, but they used all their Spiked Warhammers last week on the Elves.

MarcoYOLO: Dragons are sharp. We're working with DropTheMike? "Devourer of Spices and Cultivator of Doom"? :)

Scheherazade: Yep. He's captain for this skirmish.

NeedleStack: dragons never do much anyway

Scheherazade: You'd be surprised. They get creative because they have to.

MarcoYOLO: So do we! Small arrows hit hard! *flexes Pixie muscles*

NeedleStack: by the way people. there's some nasty bug going round. my girl-friend got it.

hygge: Uh oh. My wife started sneezing yesterday . . .

NeedleStack: no, worse. she basically moved into the bathroom. three people out at my dayjob.

MarcoYOLO: Ick.

Scheherazade: @everyone Wash your hands. Feast on!

MarcoYOLO: Feast on! *invents magical germ shield*

2034-03-03

MarcoYOLO: Holy shit, @Needle. You weren't kidding about people getting sick.

Scheherazade: How are we doing locally, Pixies? Everyone okay? And your families?

MarcoYOLO: ch33zer's kid is in the hospital on a respirator.

NeedleStack: oh shit

hygge: :(

Scheherazade: WanderingTheDessert is really sick. I went by with miso soup and sashimi. pinkoranges says her husband just got it.

NeedleStack: pinkoranges organized the food drive right? that pixies won?

Scheherazade: Yep. She's amazing. Kim and her husband Jason (he's a Dragon). They've both been unemployed so long—this is the last thing they needed. :(I hope he's okay . . .

MarcoYOLO: People call it the Over&Under flu. For obvious and gross reasons. *covers eyes*

hygge: It's not a flu, says za-news. It's a virus and really horrible and the CDC doesn't know what the deal is.

MarcoYOLO: So wtf is up with the battle?

Scheherazade: We're canceling for now. Most of the Dragons got the Over&Under.

hygge: Well shoot.

Scheherazade: Orcs are rampaging all over the West Coast. I don't know what's going on. Elves usually hold them in check. Maybe they've all got this too.

Oh! Did I tell you guys where I'm heading next weekend? Helicopter to Alaska. Fresh grilled salmon and local blackberry sauce. I'll catch the fish myself for a 100x multiplier.

MarcoYOLO: Cool! And hike I assume?

Scheherazade: Of course. I'm really close to my Elite levels in Scouting and Inner Power. If I can improve my metabolism another 2%, and eat in three new fiefdoms, I'll be level 20. Legendary Gourmet Warrior!

NeedleStack: wooooo!

MarcoYOLO: *drools* They gotta get us taste-power on phones. I want salmon and blackberries! Sigh. Settling for browsing your pics.

hygge: Another noob question. Why are the War Chambers all text-chat anyway? What is this, 2010?

Scheherazade: @hygge Everyone asks that! 1) Text-chat is better for asynchronous conversation. 2) Since FeastWar is an augmented reality game, you're often playing in restaurants. Audio annoys other patrons, and it's not as secure. Anyone could eavesdrop.

MarcoYOLO: and 3) It's rude to talk with your mouth full.

Scheherazade: Haha. Yeah, that too. For multiregion attacks we use phone-link, V-PlayMem, and the new haptics. But text is perfect during a meal. Feels retro, doesn't it?

hygge: Completely.

Scheherazade: Speaking of retro . . . @Needle, I found an old 2-inch crystal stripe from the 20's. Want it?

NeedleStack: nah, i got three already.

Scheherazade: I should've guessed. :) Wow, check the scores. The Dragons have less than 3k. They were close to 2 million a month ago.

MarcoYOLO: Wham! Magic plague attacks Dragons!

Scheherazade: Seriously. I hope everyone is okay. DropTheMike is fine at least.

MarcoYOLO: No, guys, really. Where are all the Dragons? I usually see points from WizOfIz at Leaf Me Alone, she orders Chinese chicken salad. Hasn't attacked in two weeks. I'm worried. Pinged her, no answer.

Scheherazade: I don't know her. :(You know, it does seem like Dragons are getting this way worse than Pixies.

NeedleStack: oh dragons. sadness. no not really, more points for pixies!

Scheherazade: Speaking of which . . . @Everyone, Pixie Magic Dinner tomorrow at Katana Sushi. Wear your t-shirts and wings! Look for me in the back (I've got blue glitter on my cheeks). Set phones to "shared meal". I've got e-cards to sign for WanderingTheDessert and pinkoranges's husband. Let's make some Gold Dust. And wash your damn hands! :)

2034-03-06

MarcoYOLO: Shit guys, this is scary.

Scheherazade: They just shut the airport in Reykjavik. Only two major airports still open in Europe. :(Also haven't been able to reach WanderingTheDessert or pinkoranges, which is scary.

hygge: I'm not leaving my house. Seriously. We were ready for the zombie apocalypse and now I'm staying in. My wife and I have canned food and water (earthquake planning).

MarcoYOLO: Toilet paper?

hygge: Tmi but we have a bidet. :) If water keeps running.

Scheherazade: Utilities should be okay, but on drought rations. Good robots, nice robots, keep it flowing. I'm coding in my pajamas. Thank science for working from home. I feel bad for people who can't, and also can't miss paychecks.

MarcoYOLO: No kidding.

Scheherazade: @Everyone, if you need fresh vegetables, Kevin (Klaymate) is working with the Orcs at North Hill Farm to ferry extras down here in his scooter. Ping me for details. He'll prioritize people who are caretaking for someone sick, and you can pay with scancard, FeastWar gear, or just owe him later. (He wants people to get fed, whatever it takes.)

MarcoYOLO: OMG. Glad for my garden. I'll ping neighbors, see if anyone needs zucchini. Someone offered me a goat leg. So desperate for protein I might.

Scheherazade: Do what you have to do. Your body will adapt, even if you aren't eating your perfect horoscope. Evolution's good like that. (Thanks, ancestors.)

hygge: Glad I don't need much meat. My wife is suffering worse. Also she forgot to fill her antidepressant and I'm worried.

Scheherazade: @Needle, you there? How's your girlfriend?

NeedleStack: she's ok, still weak. hasn't had a real meal in two weeks. feeding her broth and crackers. she doesn't play but her body wants elf food. maybe i can find her some lembas bread, lol

Scheherazade: I hope she feels better soon!

MarcoYOLO: Thermal cameras in the airports were supposed to catch people w/ fever. What's the point with forced reporting of everyone's travel? Nothing?

Scheherazade: People are contagious before they show symptoms. Mike told me the Dragons actually tracked their members, both when they got sick and how sick they are. Everyone's self-reporting data and Mike is compiling it. Mike plus the other Dragon leadership, and whoever else isn't sick. And me too, and some Elves and an Orc and a Phoenix. A bunch of leaders around the country.

MarcoYOLO: You're like a world leader. *bows*

Scheherazade: Haha. Well, we're gathering data in the FWOP chat (FeastWarOn-Plague). Generals from several armies, mostly science people. Over&Under must have something to do with digestive profiles, because of uneven distribution through FeastWar players. Mike is barely sleeping, just linking data.

hygge: That's cool. Maybe we'll find something the CDC can't.

Scheherazade: Mike's smart. You guys may not know, but he's a former genetic analyst, now a working food critic. Big techie with all the great GPS stuff. Remote satellite linking, SS amps, BGAN 4.0—you name it, he's got it. His wife makes tons of money in software.

NeedleStack: how is a dragon working as a food critic?

Scheherazade: He's not allergic, just prone to allergies and didn't develop any. Lucky childhood exposures. Anyway, he totally knows his science. And Marco was right about the Dragons getting flattened.

MarcoYOLO: Score is so lopsided. Plague wrecks Pangourmet!

Scheherazade: We should get in touch with someone at the CDC, but I can't figure out who'd listen to gamers.

hygge: My sister works in big pharma. She used to work with a guy who left for the CDC. They're still in touch.

Scheherazade: Whoa, seriously? Do you think she'd help?

hygge: She owes me for me not telling Mom about her petty crimes in high school. :) (she went clean later). I'll ask, and ping you later.

Scheherazade: Great! I love the people you meet through this game. Never thought I'd be friends with a professional antiselfie photographer!

hygge: At your service! heehee.

Scheherazade: Anyway, Mike asked me to do some stat analysis because his people are short-handed (poor Dragons!) Ugh, I'm worried.

MarcoYOLO: Me too. See if they need me? I write one hell of a persuasive note. Text shows my rugged good looks. :)

pinkoranges has joined the chamber

Scheherazade: Whoa! Kim! I was looking for you.

pinkoranges: guys ths is so fucked up

Scheherazade: Are you okay? How's Jason?

pinkoranges: so dehydrated and I shoudl take him to ER but Im scared are no beds and they turn him away

Scheherazade: Oh no!

pinkoranges: no church because scared to leave him and ono one els ewent so I prayed alone

Scheherazade: Take him in anyway, if he's this bad.

pinkoranges: we are oout of soap and the dryer b=roke and so we can't wash the bedshettts and the smell is so bad and he just lies here leaking all over

MarcoYOLO: Fever?

pinkoranges: 103.4

Scheherazade: Seriously, you have to take him in. Call an autocab.

MarcoYOLO: If his eyes are sunken go NOW.

Scheherazade: Screw the autocab. I'll come pick you both up? I'll bring broth and soap and take you to the ER.

pinkoranges: scared youll be sick

Scheherazade: I've been volunteering at the low-income clinic. If I were going to get this, I would've by now.

pinkoranges: just hear dhim must go

pinkoranges has left the chamber

Scheherazade: Augh. I'll go over and videochat her from my car. Maybe I can convince her once I'm sitting outside.

hygge: You're really brave. Thank you.

Scheherazade: Oh, well, someone's got to be! If I don't, I feel all helpless.

MarcoYOLO: When do you have time?? Volunteering _and_ data analysis?

Scheherazade: I'm not really coding. Shh, don't tell my boss. Besides, this is more important. And there's two hundred people numbercrunching in FWOP. I can't even follow the whole conversation, it scrolls like crazy.

NeedleStack: be careful, carjackings at the hospital

MarcoYOLO: Yeah. Panicked people=inattentive :(

Scheherazade: I know. I will. Thanks.

2034-03-08

Scheherazade: Pixies give a shout-out! How are you and your loved ones?

MarcoYOLO: Fine.

NeedleStack: my gf is eating bread and soft tofu now

hygge: Wife & I are okay.

Scheherazade: Good news, WanderingTheDessert is going to be okay! He's past the worst.

MarcoYOLO: So glad. Thanks. pinkoranges & hubby?

Scheherazade: pinkoranges's husband is critical. :(I convinced her to let me drive them . . . some crooks had blockaded the street to the nearest hospital and were forcing people to scan $400 tolls to pass. Cops were trying to stop it, but there weren't enough of them, and . . . ugh.

NeedleStack: whoa

MarcoYOLO: Don't they know everything's seen & recorded? Big trouble later, after the crisis.

hygge: Maybe they think there won't be an "after". :(

Scheherazade: Total mess. I drove them out to Walnut Creek. Kim was screaming at me to drive faster, and punching the dashboard. She called me some nasty shit. Poor woman was crazy with terror. :(

MarcoYOLO: Wtf. You were helping!!

Scheherazade: It hurt. But I got him there, and I feel better about his chances. They admitted him right away. I think they gave Kim some meds too. @ Everyone, please stay safe.

hygge: CDC says the plague's engineered. They want help catching the bastard who did this.

MarcoYOLO: What! Some terrorist group??

hygge: Yah. Prolly some angry military thing.

Scheherazade: In FWOP, we think it's a lone wolf. Fits the pattern: strikes primarily in well-populated parts of the world, hardly hits remote areas—but not sparing any one nation, or group. So probably not political unless someone hates everyone. Which they might.

hygge: But it's worse in America, Europe, places like that.

MarcoYOLO: It's hitting Dragons.

Scheherazade: And Japan and Korea and every advanced nation. For once, the disadvantaged people of the world aren't getting it as bad. Though some are dying of lesser symptoms because they lack basic treatment and sanitation . . . ugh. I saw Namibia in the early 20's when I was out of college (Peace Corps) and it was so sad what they didn't have. And it's not much better now, which is disgusting.

hygge: I'm picturing you in the 20's. Did you wear a big floppy hat and Green-Lock hiking boots everywhere? :)

Scheherazade: Snort. Okay, I admit I had the hat.

MarcoYOLO: I tell you. Dragon Plague. Flattening Dragons like nobody's business.

Scheherazade: Yeah, so the CDC has narrowed the source to the upper East Coast. FWOP is analyzing longitudinal data through FeastWar. We're looking for sharp drops in Dragon battle victories. CDC doesn't have that data because they don't play the game. :) And also the stricter HIPAA-G laws passed two years ago. We can get info that's behind their red tape.

MarcoYOLO: Wow.

Scheherazade: Mike and I pieced it together. We noticed that the few healthy Dragons mostly have digestive immunity subtype KASmir-VII (not common, but Mike has it) or people who were reasonably isolated, like tele-commuting engineers in Chinese villages. So something about isolation protected them—because some of those people came to the cities to care for the sick, and very few of them got the plague. Something predisposes certain people towards worse illness, probably something genetic. Maybe a viral vector.

MarcoYOLO: What's that?

Scheherazade: A virus that alters a person's body in some way, making it vul-nerable to another virus. Like Hep D, which needs Hep B already in place to infect someone.

NeedleStack: oh shit there's a second plague coming??

Scheherazade: No, this _is_ the second one. A viral vector was planted . . . sometime. Maybe. If true, it helps explain why isolated areas are seeing less plague. So FWOP is examining Dragon data back about five years, looking for patterns. We think it's colds or something subtle, because the CDC is pretty smart and would have seen something else. We're also getting data on OTC cold product sales on the East Coast. Looking for correlation with Dragon health and battle performance.

hygge: Can I ask a game question? Even with all this stuff going down?

Scheherazade: @hygge Of course! I like helping people level. Oh! And thanks for the contact at the CDC. It worked.

hygge: Glad of that! My question: I have a friend who wants to play, but he got his intestinal bacteria optimized to match his genes and they make him an Orc. Won't that put him opposite us Pixies on the dietary wheel?

Scheherazade: Orcs do get another minion, and this is a numbers game. But if you recruit he owes you five annihilation points. Worth it. Besides, we just want more players. It's more fun.

hygge: Okay, thanks.

MarcoYOLO: My coworker Zane—draws the space anime thing I showed you? He'd be a Dragon if he played. (poor guy has a peanut allergy and we can't even bring them in the office) He's in the hospital. :(Stabilized but his guts are ravaged. Might need an ostomy bag. Really fast, like 3 days to near-death.

Scheherazade: Whoa. Poor guy. I hope he recovers with time. My brother's best friend died yesterday. :(So awful. I throw myself into the numbers because it feels like hope. How are all your loved ones?

MarcoYOLO: My whole family is okay. Three sisters & two brothers & parents, we're all okay. All Pixie types. Buncha lactose-intolerant fish-thriving salad-eaters.

Scheherazade: Whoa, I had no idea you had so many siblings.

MarcoYOLO: Tell Mike about my family.

Scheherazade: I will. Ugh, this is horrible. Understatement of the year. We all know a Dragon who died, or came close. Did you ever see avocadoglory attack here? He's gone. :(So are Harmstar and XYZZY from Sacramento. And gligga, who's an Orc but died anyway. She had a seizure problem and the plague triggered it.

hygge: :(

MarcoYOLO: Shit. :(

NeedleStack: so i was looking at tsc data and figured something out.

Scheherazade: TSC software is against the rules of FeastWar. It's third-party software and it accesses their proprietary code. If you use it, don't admit it.

NeedleStack: this is important. i tracked the genetic profiles of the dragons over time against location, then corrected for attacks from other armies. so i could see where dragons fell apart on their own. i also took data about pixies because pixies rule and also because we are the least sick of any army. so we were contrast.

Scheherazade: Actually, the Orcs are the least sick.

NeedleStack: whatever. and remember epicurtainous? the food photography game from like ten years ago?

Scheherazade: Sure. Basic motivationware, with feedback loops to get people moving. Exercising. If it's fun, people will play. Kind of led to FeastWar.

NeedleStack: i was a curator and had data from my team network. they went on to become dragons and pixies and things in feastwar. but i still have all that data showing where they were eating and their photo upload patterns. ten years worth. 900 people in my oakland network alone.

Scheherazade: You're kidding.

NeedleStack: i wrote a program to overlay the data with known scheduled feasts and removed the impromptu feasts. check out the extensions of their curves back through the years. look here.

Scheherazade: These inflection points . . . Wow, you're right! When you graph the data that way, the epicenter's in Pennsylvania. People were sick there (and worse) before anywhere else. These graphs could show early precursors. . . . But in the last month, Pennsylvania's had fewer deaths. How is this working?

hygge: I was reading about the Spanish flu in 1918 and how the second wave was the worst of the three. Something about how a virus mutates as it works through the population. And earliest victims had better care; nurses weren't sick yet. So they survived more.

Scheherazade: Good point! Same thing now, with the human staff dropping

like flies. Thank science for our minimally skilled robo-help. Good robots.
Nice robots.

NeedleStack: you should focus on philly

Scheherazade: We will, thanks! That was amazing! We tried an analysis like
this, but couldn't go back far enough. You've got the data, and your code
does a great job eliminating noise from signal.

NeedleStack: im pretty awesome when bored. :)

2034-03-10

hygge: Help. Should I break into the pharmacy down the street?

Scheherazade: Whoa.

hygge: It's locked for quarantine but I know their cameras aren't working. I
used to shop there and I found out because my bike got stolen.

MarcoYOLO: Why ask us?

NeedleStack: never put that in writing. just do it. or don't. but there's always
cams. assume that.

hygge: I need advice. My wife won't die without her antidepressant. She's just
very sick and can't get out of bed. :(

Scheherazade: This is that famous moral question about stealing bread for your
starving family. :(

hygge: If she'd die, I'd do it no question. I'd get it overnight from somewhere
but mail's so unreliable right now.

Scheherazade: Which drug?

hygge: Glasoxitine.

MarcoYOLO: Kind of cold but . . . Is she suicidal?

hygge: oh god. I don't think so? Not yet?

Scheherazade: Ugh. Internet says this is one you shouldn't go off cold turkey.

hygge: No kidding. You think? :P

Scheherazade: Sorry. I don't know what to do. :(I think there'll be millions of
cases like this getting scrutiny later. You have a good reason . . .

hygge: I'm scared.

Scheherazade: I'll ask FWOP if anyone local has some extras.

hygge: It's not common. No one will have it, but thanks. :(Bye, going idle . . .

Scheherazade: Ugh. :(Oh hey, Kim says her husband has stabilized (yay) and
she apologized to me, while crying.

MarcoYOLO: Better'n nothing.

Scheherazade: It's okay. I just want them safe. Also, I passed NeedleStack's
analysis to Mike and it was perfect. We need more data. (Mike, uh, doesn't
use TSC either, wink wink.)

NeedleStack: yay. want more?

MarcoYOLO: What are you guys doing now?

Scheherazade: Tracking the guy down from his own targeted plague. We're assuming he wouldn't target himself. @Everyone: do you trust me?

MarcoYOLO: Of course.

NeedleStack: sure

Scheherazade: This is important or I wouldn't do it.

MikeTheDrop has joined the chamber

MarcoYOLO: WHAT??

NeedleStack: wtf!

Scheherazade: I know. Just listen.

MikeTheDrop: Hi guys. Sorry to intrude. I promise not to read your files or look at battle plans.

Scheherazade: Mike is here for data. To crosscheck the timeline of plague waves against genetic profiles registered with FeastWar.

MikeTheDrop: This was Emily's idea, but it's important.

Scheherazade: The TSC data (which remember Mike doesn't use, wink) requires him to access as a Pixie. So, this is DropTheMike's . . . little brother. I gave him Pixie admin access to our membership and history. I want to be open that he's here. I trust him more than anyone.

NeedleStack: two accounts!! naughty. how did you bypass the genetic crosscheck?

MikeTheDrop: I'm sorry, the person who would know that doesn't want me answering . . .

MarcoYOLO: You're here as a Pixie? Accessing tons of people's genetic data without their permission??

Scheherazade: Only what any admin can see, and it's an emergency. This is the fastest way to get what he needs and aggregate it.

NeedleStack: he'll see where we're planning stuff. this is crap.

MikeTheDrop: I promise I won't use anything here against you.

NeedleStack: why pixies??

Scheherazade: Because you used us as the control group. If you'd used Orcs, he would've gone to them.

NeedleStack: oh

MikeTheDrop: I need to correlate your data with some genetic markers, and compare to optimized intestinal bacteria profiles for Dragons and Pixies.

MarcoYOLO: @Emily why worry about FeastWar's stupid 3rd-party software rules when you're doing shit like this? :P

Scheherazade: If we get banned, it'd take hours . . . days to sort out. Time we don't have. :P

MarcoYOLO: I guess . . .

NeedleStack: i guess but i don't like it. i don't want my data shared all over.

Scheherazade: It's already being shared like crazy. And look at what we're up against. We've got to fight.

MarcoYOLO: @MikeTheDrop you owe us all sushi. :P

MikeTheDrop: I promise I'll scan Emily enough money to buy you dinner. I'll even ship her some mana.

NeedleStack: oh fine. as long as dragons are our mana slaves.

Scheherazade: Come on. We've ALL got more important problems right now.

NeedleStack: i know. really. :(

MarcoYOLO: For once, the world has MORE drama than FeastWar chat . . .

2034-03-13

MarcoYOLO: We have a name. We have a manifesto. James Barrow . . . Guy on the news looks like a real bastard. *shudder* @Emily this is FeastWar's doing, yeah?

Scheherazade: FWOP got a team from all over—Chicago, Tokyo, Lima, Paris . . . And one amazing girl in Maryland.

MikeTheDrop: We inferred that the guy didn't live in Philly but had easy access to it. So we looked at areas within a few hours of travel.

NeedleStack: i said philly dammit!!

Scheherazade: SmallAnnoyingTree (she's 14!) did an epidemiological survey of her hometown, knocking on doors and talking to people. Mapped the plague's spread in a real location.

hygge: Wow. Brave.

Scheherazade: @hygge! How is your wife? I've been worried!

NeedleStack: don't tell us if you did it.

hygge: We found an old bottle in the cabinet. Lower dose, but she's on it. She'll be okay now I think.

Scheherazade: Thank science. I'm so glad.

MarcoYOLO: Good! @Emily—about Barrow.

Scheherazade: Yeah, we were right about the viral vector! Apparently Barrow is _very_ patient. He's been planting his vector for decades, mixed in with the common cold. He made so many that scientists thought they were just a subclass of rhinovirus, and didn't realize they were engineered.

MikeTheDrop: His rhinovirus combined with susceptible people's DNA to prime them for the real thing: the plague he released a month ago. If you had a cold in the last thirty years . . . you probably encountered one of his little creations.

hygge: Ewwww. He needs a hobby. Or kittens.

NeedleStack: he'd eat them.

Scheherazade: That's why the virus was dominant in populated areas. Remote Brazilian tribes don't get many colds—and even if a visiting anthropologist brought them the viral vector, they weren't likely to get re-exposed.

MikeTheDrop: He designed it that way. He was trying to kill people who couldn't survive in the climate-changed future.

MarcoYOLO: WHAT. I didn't hear this. Wtf.

Scheherazade: Yeah! Didn't you read the manifesto?

MarcoYOLO: No, was reading about relief efforts.

Scheherazade: Check this quote: "The population is 9 billion and growing. A population correction is inevitable. Rather than suffer the indiscriminate destruction of the human genome through riots, we should cull the weak so the strong can thrive."

NeedleStack: my new warrior name will be barrowsucks

hygge: Augh. :P

MarcoYOLO: FBI'll be on that like a cat on a heat vent.

Scheherazade: Oh yeah. They're hunting.

MarcoYOLO: This I gotta see. *toasts nori snacks* *makes popcorn for Mike if he can have it?*

MikeTheDrop: Truly a special part of humanity. If we can call him that.

Scheherazade: There's some crap about how he's dedicated his life to analyzing the data—he calls himself genius, of course—and then this: "I assigned everyone a Survival Index (SI) based on multiple factors. The primary factor was of course the compatibility between their primary and sub-immune systems (popularly called 'digestive immunity')."

MarcoYOLO: No, I heard all that, but what do you mean about climate-changed future?

MikeTheDrop: People who could adapt better to low-water conditions and digest anything they found, including carrion.

MarcoYOLO: No way. Orcs??

NeedleStack: oh god, orcs are our future? im outta here, the kingdom is lost

hygge: Seriously. Are we sure this guy _isn't_ a new recruit for the Orcs?

Scheherazade: I'm having fun looking through this nonsense. It's pretty much gazing into the abyss. Wait, this is the best quote: "The media will compare me to Hitler, which is ridiculous. Let's not get caught up in nonsense about

the Final Solution; that was racist bullshit. This is pure science."
HAHAHAHHA idiot. He even named his master race. _Homo aptatus_.
That's it, people, we're evolving! Out of the way!

MarcoYOLO: UGH. I'm getting Over&Under just reading that.

NeedleStack: heil barrow

hygge: Where's that pic of the chihuahua smashing its face into the glass door
over and over? Yeah. That.

MikeTheDrop: NSA is working on retrieving his notes so we can develop a targeted antiviral. He must have filed them somewhere . . . and if he ever
typed a note or used a computer to design his virus (likely) there's a chance
we can retrieve information.

Scheherazade: Most people don't know how to delete their data completely.
I'm sure I couldn't. Welcome to our brave new world.

MikeTheDrop: FWOP has our white hats and sketchy-gray hats and "others"
working on the same thing. FeastWar attracts a lot of computer special-
ists . . .

Scheherazade: We think he's in Baltimore.

MarcoYOLO: So how do we actually catch him?

MikeTheDrop: The Orcs in Baltimore have a plan.

Scheherazade: Rest assured, everyone, that we are _on this_. Our scouts will
find him. If you want something done right? Ask gamers!

MarcoYOLO: Awesome!

Scheherazade: I just hope it works. Come on, Orcs!

NeedleStack: are we really cheering for orcs in the pixie warchamber? while a
dragon watches? thats it, im deposing you.

2034-03-16

NeedleStack: see the news? we caught the fucker!

MikeTheDrop: And we got his notes! The antiviral should be available within
24 hours. All the pharmas are devoting nonstop production hours to it.

Scheherazade: YES! Thank science! We win, and FeastWar did it!

NeedleStack: no way, the pixies did it all!!! ok, the others helped.

Scheherazade: Oh, come on. FWOP was in full data analysis mode 24/7 around
the world this week. Give us some credit.

MarcoYOLO: @Emily you know everything. :) What happened? What's up with
Barrow dying in custody? Getting one thing from news, another from Feast-
War forums. *plops in armchair* *waits for juicy story*

Scheherazade: Baltimore Orcs were heroes! They sent all their people out. Feet on
the ground, anywhere they might find him getting food—a few restaurants

that are still open, delis, grocery store meat sections. Phones scanning the crowd, looking for him. And they found him! At a farmers' market in Woodbine. :) A whole squad of Orcs. Snapped photos, alerted the FBI, got him arrested, everything!

hygge: I hope they chased him down with giant foam warhammers. And maybe some turkey legs. Looking for pics now . . .

MarcoYOLO: But he's dead. What happened?

MikeTheDrop: It's all in Orc photos. He took poison as he ran. The FBI was on him fast, and he died while being arrested.

Scheherazade: Expect mashup videos soon.

MikeTheDrop: CDC estimates our actions may have saved 200 million lives. We can deploy the antiviral before the plague hits full potency.

Scheherazade: Yeah, the feet on the street did it. Go FeastWar!

NeedleStack: orcs did something useful for once!

Scheherazade: We caught him by surprise. He had final words drafted on his phone. Listen, and I quote: "As a token of my sincerity, I will soon remove myself from the population. I've improved our chances for surviving 22nd-century Earth. Since we idiotically didn't focus on the space program to escape the planet, we're stuck here. Maybe the next wave of humanity will figure it out."

NeedleStack: lol. aliens will rescue us.

MarcoYOLO: Sincerity? *snort* He killed himself to avoid getting caught!

Scheherazade: Oh wait, this is excellent: "My sperm is frozen at Riverside Cryo-bank, should anyone choose to use it for my intellect. I possess a solid genome, offering my descendants a better chance of survival."

MarcoYOLO: @Emily we've found you a date!

Scheherazade: HAHAHA. Can't hit you hard enough from here. Why don't you go gay for him?

MarcoYOLO: You're right. I need his sperm. Barrow, darling, take me!

NeedleStack: hahahaha

MikeTheDrop: Oh dear.

Scheherazade: Also he recorded this long boring rant about privacy before he splatted himself. He doesn't mention FeastWar specifically, but it's basically us. "Foolish people who waive privacy for instant gratification and fake rewards."

NeedleStack: he has no idea what i do for instant gratification

hygge: Tmi!!

MarcoYOLO: Fake rewards, huh? Like those virtual banners feastwar.game tried to give us? God, those were so stupid.

Scheherazade: That's all we do here, sell our souls for pleasure . . . clearly spoken by someone who's never coordinated simultaneous feasts over two months. In six timezones. I HAVE.

hygge: Whatever. No one _has_ to play. We choose to.

Scheherazade: Working with the CDC showed me how much info they could get despite red tape—once they knew where to look. Creepy.

MikeTheDrop: Some of us theorize that Barrow accessed data similar to Feast-War's records, allowing him to track the plague's progress. Insufficient evidence yet . . . but knowing what our white hat friends did to find him? Who knows what Barrow could do?

MarcoYOLO: *shivers* You think so?

Scheherazade: By "some of us," Mike means about three people. I don't think Barrow had any data like that. He couldn't even delete his notes properly. Not smarter than we are, except maybe in virology.

MikeTheDrop: I hope you're right . . .

NeedleStack: scary

Scheherazade: And the world is paying a _lot_ of attention to FeastWar now. Yesterday Congress started a bill that will require all "social media games" to proactively file their data with the CDC and Department of Health. If it passes . . .

MarcoYOLO: Seriously? Data we willingly gave to FeastWar.game under promise of privacy could be dropped to the feds?? People will quit over that.

Scheherazade: People already have. Even without the bill.

hygge: What could they do with the fact that I order seaweed salad and spider rolls for lunch? :P

MikeTheDrop: Ping me if you really want to know . . .

Scheherazade: Look what _we_ did with it.

MarcoYOLO: We caught a bioterrorist!

Scheherazade: Mind-blowing. And it happened because the Dragons were sick of losing. :)

MikeTheDrop: Good to know our rankings were low for years because we all had colds. Not because we played poorly.

NeedleStack: no, it's because you suck. :) (teasing. mostly.)

MikeTheDrop: Haha.

NeedleStack: ok, i'll give some credit to the dragons. but no orcs.

Scheherazade: Oh come on, people are dead. Everything's a wreck. :(That matters more than a game.

MarcoYOLO: At least we stopped him. We, meaning FeastWarriors. Feast on!

hygge: Yeah. FeastWar wins! When's our next feast?

Scheherazade: Hoping for next week if some businesses recover and open. There'll be a lot of fallout from this. It's not over.

MarcoYOLO: Yeah. :(

MikeTheDrop: Hey guys, I'll let you get back to your Pixie glitter dances or whatever you do in here. Thanks for sharing your space with me. You're heroes. Dragon out.

MikeTheDrop has left the chamber

NeedleStack: whew. much better

MarcoYOLO: Smells less lizardy in here. *sprays room with rosewater*

Scheherazade: @Everyone, FeastWar.game is organizing an assistance drive for families of players who died. Donate if you can! Warriors, share your strength!

hygge: Less important which army you're in, and more important to play the game.

MarcoYOLO: Now let's go crush some Orcs!!

Scheherazade: And stop bioterrorists. Like we do. :)

NeedleStack: next terrorist is all mine guys lol

Look to next year's consequences . . .
. . . then look five years beyond.

YOUR LYING EYES

JACK McDEVITT

Hudson Truscott was probably the smartest person at the annual Colorado Applied Electronics Conference, a reputation earned for his work in artificial intelligence and in network design. He obviously enjoyed the attention. But we all do, me as much as anyone.

Despite thirty years of periodic collaboration, I never really thought of him as a friend, though I enjoyed his company. He was amicable and easygoing, but he operated on a different level. We could never really communicate, and not because of his celebrated inclination to secrecy. The reality was that we simply operated on different levels.

Anyway. On that second evening of the conference, we finished a panel on recycling electronics, which had appeared not to interest him much. At the time I thought he seemed distracted. He wandered out through the hotel lobby onto the parking lot, carrying a bag slung over his shoulder. I was sitting on Toker's Porch, where some of us were passing around a joint. I assumed he was going into town, probably to Kaplan's Bar and Grill, the conference watering hole. But he walked past his car to the edge of the parking lot and kept going.

The Gorman Hotel perches on a ridge with a magnificent view of the Rockies. The sky was clear with a few scattered clouds, the stars bright, and a three-quarters moon floating over the mountains. I'm still not sure why, but I got out of my chair and followed him. Maybe it was the pot. Maybe it was that he looked ambivalent, or that there was nothing in the direction he had taken other than a precipice.

A low fence ran along the edge of the parking area, with a gate carrying a sign warning about the cliff's edge and suggesting you go no farther. I've never understood why, if management was concerned about safety, they installed the gate. We were about five hundred feet over a mountain slope. A scattering of lighted houses was visible below us, and music drifted up from one of them.

Hudson stood beneath a cluster of trees, on the edge of the precipice, hands in pockets, laptop bag slung over his shoulder.

I don't like heights, and normally I'd go nowhere near the summit. I probably wouldn't have gone any farther that night, except that he noticed me and waved. So I eased out through the gate. There was about twelve feet of ground between the fence and the precipice. Plenty of space, you'd think. But not really.

"How you doing, Mike?" he said, as I approached.

"I'm good. That's a spectacular view."

He nodded, and I got the impression he hadn't really noticed until I mentioned it. "Yes. It is."

"You done for the night?"

"Yeah. I've had enough. Not even sure I'll be here tomorrow."

"Really? Bentler's speaking at the luncheon." The winner of last year's EISA Award.

"I know." A cool breeze rippled across the summit.

"Why are you leaving early? Everything okay, Hudson?"

He was average size, in his fifties, with probing blue eyes. Most of his hair was gone. And you always knew that, if anyone understood how the quantum world worked, he was the guy. "Just tired, Mike," he said. "I need a day off." But he was holding something back.

"What's up?"

He looked out across the mountains. Then he closed his eyes and cleared his throat. "I was thinking about making an announcement, but it would be premature." He shrugged. "This would be the wrong place and time."

"An announcement about what?"

He bit his lower lip. "All right, Mike," he said. "I don't want any of this getting out yet. I still have a few tests to run."

"I won't say a word."

"Good." He walked to the edge and looked up at the moon. Then he placed the laptop bag on the ground, opened a side pocket, and removed what appeared to be a pair of sunglasses. He held them out for me.

"What are they?" I said, keeping my distance.

"Try them on."

I took a deep breath and inched close enough to take them. The world grew somewhat darker, but not as much as I'd expected. "Okay," I said. "Am I supposed to see something? Some kind of augmented reality overlay?" The conference was rife with AR projects. In fact, the field was starting to seem . . . old.

"Ask me a question."

"About what?"

"Anything at all, Mike."

"All right. When's your birthday?"

"You mean when was I born?"

"Yes."

"Three years ago, on April 11." He smiled and reddened.

I removed the glasses and everything went back to normal. I put them back on. The redness was fading. "What the hell just happened?"

"I lied."

"Well, of course you did. But are you telling me these glasses detect lies?"

"That's correct, Mike. They analyze facial expressions, changes in tone, and a few other communication details. They aren't perfect yet—it helps to build a baseline with the subject. I still have to make some adjustments, which is why I shouldn't have brought them up here this weekend. I'm getting overanxious, I guess."

"That doesn't seem possible, Hudson."

"There's not much left that we can't figure our way around, Mike. Give me another few weeks and I think I'll be able to make some noise."

"That's incredible."

"It's been a remarkable experience. I've discovered that a good many of our politicians really believe what they say. That the world is only six thousand years old, don't worry about climate change, that evolution doesn't happen. I'd always assumed they were just appealing to their base, saying what they needed to get elected. But not so." He shook his head. "Their sincerity is disturbing, in fact. You want the people who run the country to have some curiosity about the world around them."

We both stood for a minute while the wind whispered in the trees. "What are you going to do with it?" I asked.

"With *what*?"

"With the AR glasses? Or whatever you call them?"

"They aren't AR glasses, Mike. I tend to think of them as a translator. "

"Okay."

"And what will I do with this technology? Maybe get my name up there with Bohr, Planck, and Schrodinger. And probably make a fortune." He gazed at me and broke into a wide smile. "Hard to believe this is actually happening."

"So what you're saying, Hudson, is that people won't be able to lie any more."

"It goes beyond that, Mike. You ask someone a question and it won't matter whether he answers it or not. His expression will be enough to tell you if he has something to hide."

I tried laughing, though I was getting a bad feeling. "You mean we're always going to have to speak our minds? Say what we really think?"

Hudson nodded. "I know there's a downside. We don't want to hurt other people's feelings. But imagine a world with lies and deceit removed. Con artists exposed. Almost all criminals caught. Advertising that's truthful. Sure, we'd all have to adapt some." He looked out over the mountains, the way Moses might have. "It would be a small price to pay."

I'd been married twenty years at the time. Happily. But the reality was that the love of my life was not Amy but Sue Anne Hopkins, whom I'd dated for a short time years before I met Amy. She'd dumped me and I'd never really gotten over it. Amy was the woman I'd eventually settled for. She'd been a good choice, and it had worked. But I wouldn't have wanted her to find out she was a backup.

I stood there and thought about the times I'd bent the truth to encourage students. To hide my religious feelings from my true-believing parents. To tell people how good they looked. To avoid admitting that someone was simply annoying. "I think the price would be substantial," I said.

"Well, we're all entitled to our opinion, Mike."

"Hudson, your invention changes the cultural mores at a basic level. It'll be a disaster."

"I know there'll be problems." His tone suggested it was time for all of us to grow up.

"I mean it. Divorce rates would go through the roof."

Hudson took a deep breath. "What do you want me to do? Bury the translator? Throw away a major discovery?"

"I know it wouldn't be easy. But—."

"Give it a rest, Mike. Okay? In the end, we'll be living in a better world than we've ever known."

"You know," I said, "people won't even be able to play bridge. You're trying to figure out where the ace of spades is and all you'd have to do is look at one of your opponents. If he has it he'd know what you're after, and the glasses would pick it up. Hudson, maybe you should think this out."

"Your bridge club can agree not to wear them during games."

"Until you miniaturize them into contact lenses."

"Sci-fi stuff."

"*You're* saying that, of all people? Just follow Moore's Law." Computer capabilities double every two years. "Hudson, maybe you should think this out."

"I've given it a lot of consideration." He smiled and tried to wave it away. "Look, we're always talking about truth. This kind of capability will produce enormous benefits everywhere. So we have to make a few adjustments. That shouldn't be a big deal."

I was still wearing the translator. The lenses remained clear. No more red lights. So he really believed that. He bent down, picked up the laptop bag, and held out his hand.

I removed the translator and gave it to him. He folded the sidepieces and tried to open a pocket on the bag. During the process the bag slipped out of his hands. He tried to grab it before it hit the ground, and simultaneously dropped the translator and stumbled backward. His eyes went wide, and he teetered on the edge of the cliff. His arms flailed while he tried to regain his balance. He screamed and reached out to me.

And . . . I stood there and watched. In that terrible moment I caught a glance of withering hatred, and then he was gone.

I waited a few seconds, until everything was quiet again. Then I advanced and stood where he had. Carefully. Just being near that kind of height made my stomach churn. I looked down, but he'd disappeared into the darkness. The translator lay on the ground. I kicked it after him.

■ ■ ■

I tried to persuade myself that it hadn't been my fault. That sometimes people simply freeze at critical times. That I'd have saved him except for my own fear of getting too close to the cliff's edge.

In any case, he'd been drinking, and the investigating authorities initially blamed the death on alcohol. I'd already come to terms with the notion that maybe it was for the best after all. Fate had intervened to save us all from the brutal light that a promethean genius had wanted to give us. A searing shaft of truthfulness that nobody would have wanted any part of.

I worried for a while that the translator information would be available on his hard drive either at home or at the school, but nobody mentioned it. His wife had died years before, and apparently no one else knew about his private translator project. Or . . . I wondered whether investigators came across it and had the same reaction I did and chose to let it die with him.

The world moves on. And I had one more lie to live with.

Well, there are various types of "investigators" these days. Hudson's insurance company arrived sooner than I expected. They pored through the hotel's security cam footage, which caught me following Hudson to the cliff. So did the dash cams of twelve cars in the parking lot. Some of Hudson's fans and investors put out a call, and more images came in, one from a satellite, another from a passing delivery drone. But a wisp of fog obscured us during the crucial moments.

I came under suspicion because I hadn't reported the incident although I'd been present. I explained that I'd been too shaken. Other, higher level detectives came and sifted, but by then all the footprints had been scuffed away. And, well, Hudson *did* have a lot of alcohol in him. I admitted having been there, and concocted a bigger lie, of trying to save him. After all, what motive would I have for foul play? And there was no hard evidence. These days, if you don't have hard evidence, you have no case.

．．．

Don't ever let anyone tell you that marijuana leaves you thinking clearly. Did I really imagine Hudson would have left *no* copies of his work? Sure, he was closed and secretive. So it took his investors and coworkers six months to break his encrypted files.

And by then an occasional girlfriend whom almost no one had known about turned up with a translator. The science was there, all along, of course. Two more groups had different versions, a month after that.

Everybody now wears them, at least occasionally. Often enough to start those changes in speech and habit Hudson had talked about that night.

And we found out that government agencies and cabals of billionaires had secretly been using earlier versions for several years, to gain advantages. Which is what happens when a few people get to monopolize technological progress. In fact, I learned *that's* why the authorities had not pursued their suspicions that Hudson had been murdered. And I of course had been the only suspect. They'd never used the detection system on me. In fact the first person to do that was the girlfriend. And even though I had not pushed Hudson off the cliff, when I denied the question, the lenses turned red.

They still do. Some part of me knows the truth.

．．．

Lying, after all, is subjective. When it was learned that the most pathological types—who *believe* their own lies—sometimes don't redden, well, my lawyers argued that the translator should not be used to convict anyone, at least not as the sole evidence. In fact my name may be best known for that precedent. Big deal. It did mean I walked. More or less.

Life is not without its ironies. The world is learning to live with The Change. A large number of brutal criminals and a few of the worst politicians have gotten what they deserved—good riddance—though Hudson was right that a lie detector doesn't help you deal with sincere crazy people. So we're still a little wary of each other. We wouldn't be human if that weren't true.

News reporters improved, and advertising became boring. The big changes were social, of course. But after the first tsunami of divorces and lawsuits and shattered friendships, something weird happened.

Humans adapted. New conventions and ways to interact developed. It became socially ill-advised to pin another person with embarrassing questions, lest *you* get pinned, in retaliation. Mutually assured lie detection means that people work harder to cut short the spiral of recriminations that I'd feared. Forgiveness came into vogue. Well, much of the time. Enough of the time. Except when real harm is inflicted. Life is a bit more nerve-wracking now, especially for older folks, like me. But in many ways, the world has become a better place.

But no one feels restrained about asking *me* uncomfortable questions. Everywhere I go, someone inevitably asks—did I murder Hudson Truscott?

And even though I never reply, I can tell that *they* can tell . . .

. . . that—God help me—I don't know the answer.

A modern sage calls for . . .
. . . resilience.

THE DISASTER STACK
VERNOR VINGE

It has become a truism, abetted by the often apocalyptic visions of popular culture, that technological progress increases the likelihood of some mere disaster growing into catastrophe. In reality, our increasingly sophisticated technology of communication and interconnectivity could help us deal with threats, both natural and human-activated. For example, with sufficient co-operation, charitable organizations, thoughtful businesses, skilled hobbyists, and governments should be able to create a *Disaster Stack,* consisting of layers of technology, knowledge and skilled volunteers that could respond to emergencies and prevent them from becoming calamities.

Here I mean to expand on a presentation given at Sci Foo 12—or Science Foo Camp—a series of interdisciplinary scientific conferences which offer ideal settings to loft impudent yet practical notions. A good many Sci Foo participants proposed projects that were within tweaking distance of relevance to disaster planning and recovery—and most of the presentations were about real projects and prototypes. Between presentations, I had the opportunity to chat with other attendees about disaster issues.

Stewart Brand had personal experience with the 1989 Loma Prieta Earthquake and later wrote a report about the rescuers and rescued. As with David Brin's comments on 9/11, *ad hoc* civilian response was very important and positive, helping to limit the tragedy and loss. Not surprisingly, according to Brand, police and other professional first responders arrived on scene after local civilians. Police permitted the civilians to continue to participate. Volunteers with access to institutional resources, such as fire boats and hoses, may have prevented far greater destruction. Civilians with prior experience—e.g., military, firefighting, even teaching—tended to do well, but almost all were maneuvering in perilous ignorance. Admittedly, some civilians were totally clueless, more an obstacle than anything else. (I suspect I would have been in this category!)

One participant at my Sci Foo session made a point that, however much we talk about these things, most people don't know what to do in a disaster, not even how to protect themselves. The hobbies and effort associated with building the Disaster Stack might go partway to helping with this problem, but effective behavior in most disasters comes down to certain standard field skills—skills that are taught by the Red Cross, by local Community Emergency Response Teams (CERT*) and other organizations. Learning these skills remains as important as ever, and should be complementary to Disaster Stack planning. The beauty of crowdsourcing is that it permits our different talents to be used where they can be the most constructive. Even people who are dysfunctional at runtime could still help with the building of the Disaster Stack.

The folks attending my session raised a more ominous concern. The Disaster Stack depends on the good-heartedness and cooperation of the people involved. Worst case scenarios, from *The Lord of the Flies* to *Mad Max*, preach that large disasters can bring out the worst in us, with groups playing zero-sum and even negative-sum games. Is this so? Is it possible to rate this risk per disaster scenario?

In Rebecca Solnit's *A Paradise Built in Hell,* it is shown that citizens often respond better than expected, in emergencies—certainly much better than portrayed in Hollywood films.

Civilization's most precious infrastructure is the framework of trust and understanding that invisibly makes all the rest possible. In losing that infrastructure, we might face a long detour back into negative-sum games. On the scale of the Long Now, I think we'd come back fairly fast. Just knowing that something *can be done* is a powerful enabler. And positive-sum games are our stairway to greatness. So let me now propose a potential best-case scenario by outlining the layers of the Disaster Stack.

LAYER 1: THE COMMUNICATION NETWORK

Of the two most obvious disaster threats to communications, the first is the loss of electrical power. The power needed to run smartphones is orders of magnitude less than the needs of civilization as a whole. With a little bit of

---

* CERT=Community Emergency Response Team, a program that trains civilians for light but crucial usefulness in case of local disasters or crises. www.ready.gov

forethought and regulatory sympathy, car batteries could power such devices for some hours, and existing green sources could provide longer support. Base stations and backhaul technology have more concentrated power needs, but one interesting trend of the last few years has been use of smaller and smaller stations. Emergency backhaul may have its own power-supply surprises.

The second threat is congestion arising from the disaster-related demand surge. Falling back to lower bitrates and datagram-oriented transport can help with surge problems. If our phones have a backup, *peer-to-peer text passing capability,* then very basic comms might be maintained even when all cell and wireless towers are down, as each phone would pass texts along to finally escape the afflicted area.

Again, there are tech trends that may make this problem more easily solvable: in principle, wireless comms can maintain high-quality peer-to-peer contact at very great station densities.

LAYER 2: THE KNOWLEDGE AND PROGRAM BASE THAT RUNS ATOP LAYER 1

A cliché of catastrophe science fiction is the notion of a cache of reference books that explain technology from before the "fall of civilization." The cache might be as simple as an engineering manual or a survivalist's recipe list, all the way to Asimov's famed *Encyclopedia Galactica.* Old-time science-fiction fans debated which twenty pounds of reference books would have the greatest payoff. Of course, nowadays we can do much better: our smartphones have enough storage to hold entire libraries. Besides storing knowledge, we can cache plans and programs, customized for each of the disaster scenarios we consider.

Building Layer 2 would be a crowdsourced version of scenario-based planning. It would be a vast project, though in the beginning not a great deal more ambitious than Wikipedia. Even more than Wikipedia, it would be an ongoing effort: a growing hierarchy, its roots being grand categories of disaster, its leaves being discussions of particular possibilities and responses as well as pointers to common response libraries.

One of the virtues of scenario-based disaster planning is that it allows the independent study of completely contradictory policies. For instance, the recommended response to aircraft hijacking before 9/11 changed substantially after 9/11. In some cases, these contradictory policies can't be resolved before the event. Having both represented in Layer 2 would give responders insights and options—and even diagnostics—that could be applied immediately in the presence of unforeseen situations.

Building the Disaster Stack involves doing things long before any particular disaster occurs. Unfortunately, the number of possible disaster scenarios collides with the bounded resources of the planners, be they individuals or nation states. The structure of Layer 2 would provide insight to those with access to money—both to inspire them to re-estimate risks and to survey the hierarchy for feasible projects that would have leverage across a range of possible disasters. So, for instance, introducing a small change in smart-phone sensors and protocols might have a large positive effect for many different scenarios.

Considering the size and contentious nature of the possibilities, certification and assessment should not be the monopoly of any single entity; I would prefer to have choices about whom to trust be left to users, depending on scenario and context. Disasters will happen, with smaller ones likely more common than the larger, allowing them to tutor us all how to better prepare for the inevitable Hard Hits. In principle, the Disaster Stack scheme scales from "disasters" as small as losing one's car keys all the way up to a giant meteor strike.

Building Layer 2 is a process that might be best done open-source and by masses of amateurs—a neverending hobby—though perhaps best if greased with some philanthropic or agency funding. The primary driver will be civic-minded citizens, partly because we'll always be imagining new disasters—but also because each disaster that really happens will give us an opportunity to revise and extend Layer 2.

LAYER 3: PEOPLE HELPING DURING DISASTERS, SUPPORTED BY LAYER 2

David Brin has written much about the importance of citizen involvement in disaster training and response. He has noted that while great courage and sacrifice was shown by rescue workers in the 9/11 disaster, the most effective interventions were done on the spur of the moment by civilians; furthermore, the only people to recognize and defend against the attack in real time were the civilians aboard United Flight 93, reacting spontaneously and with admirable speed, aided by cell-phone communications.

Such is the inspiration for Layer 3 of the Disaster Stack. At "run time"— that is, when a disaster strikes—the people can turn to Layer 2 services. Layer 2 will be running on top of the best available communication network (Layer 1). The Layer 2 computation and data can be used to run programs using smart-phone sensors to determine the nature of the disaster. Then people who are close to the action (Layer 3) can use that information to progress down the Layer 2 hierarchy to nodes that best fit the information available. In and among those scenario nodes, that is where they should find advice about possible actions to take—for instance, in the case of a train wreck, the location of fire-fighting equipment, medical gear, current whereabouts of medically knowl-edgeable persons, and so on.

Especially in early stages of the disaster, different scenarios may fit the known facts. The on-the-scene people of Layer 3 may have to conduct further observations to distinguish among possibilities or invent new explanations for the event: is the train crash caused by an earthquake, or terrorist action, or poor scheduling, or a gas leak explosion, or . . . ? These results are communi-cated and acted upon. In this way, local citizens can mesh with faraway experts and expert-systems to form what Howard Rheingold once presciently called a "smart mob," a makeshift, ad-hoc "posse" that is smarter and more effective than the mere sum of its parts.

For small disasters, the actions of Layer 3 merge seamlessly back into the everyday activities of society, including appropriate plan-time changes to all three layers. For mid-to-large calamities, the Disaster Stack eventually hands off to conventional recovery institutions. For the worst disasters, a Disaster Stack might best be regarded in the spirit of the Long Now Foundation, the or-ganization established in 1996 to promote long-term thinking and planning as a counterpoint to today's short attention spans. In other words, the stack can be helpful to those striving to "save what we can and preserve hope for survivors."

The Disaster Stack is itself a contingent plan. An EMP attack would force drastic changes in the nature of Layer 1. At a different extreme, if the network clouds remain available during a disaster, they would be enormously useful. The sheer variety of failure modes means that Disaster Stack planners should aim for heterogeneity, diversity, adaptability and resilience. For example, dis-tributing logic and data in hobbyists' smart phones should be a concurrent project alongside schemes for using clouds. Such variety and flexibility is only possible if the individual preparation measures are very inexpensive and there are lots of hobbyists at plan time. Above all, it would be helpful if both phi-lanthropists and agencies applied seed money that would enable amateurs to do most of the work.

CONCLUSION

In sum, the dual-use nature of technology is one of the most dread facts of our time. Civilization seems to be in a race between tech that could empower and protect us, and tech that would give anybody having a bad hair day the ability to blow up civilization. The Breakers of the world have a great advantage, since it is so much easier to break things than it is to make things.

It is vital to remember that Makers include the great and famous, but also the rest of us: people who simply have our own families, our own interests, and a vast range of specialized expertise. Breakers may—indeed, inevitably will—do considerable damage, but the rise of cell phones, smart phones, social media and information services such as Wikipedia have convinced me that the Makers of the world have their own advantages, too, starting with the fact that a vast majority of capable people *want* to make, and not break. There are billions of Makers, and information technology has transformed those billions into an intellectual force that trumps all past human institutions.

It's not a coincidence that much of the preparation for the Disaster Stack looks like the activities of Bad Guys. This fact creates a temptation for otherwise reasonable governments to smother disaster planning/recovery hobbyists. But considering that the Makers are our best hope against the Breakers, let's make sure that the urge to suppress is resisted and countered with calm reason. There is no reason why the great big hierarchical powers of money and government should not wake up to their own clear self-interest, by learning to value and collaborate with the vast population of Makers, who are the greatest source of wisdom and strength any society can have.

LIES AND PRIVATE LIVES

A future of light
Burning? Or liberating?
Decide, there's still time

In the farther future, people will have their own solutions . . .
. . . and those solutions will bring problems.

FIRST PRESENTATION

ALIETTE DE BODARD

Thanh arrived late at the First Presentation party; deliberately, because it would enable her to mingle more easily into the crowd; and because she couldn't deal with the thought of making small, inane talk with Anh Ngoc and her new husband for what would seem like hours, while they waited for other guests.

It had been years, and she wasn't sure, altogether, if she would know anyone; if she would even have the proper authorizations to see anyone. But, once she cleared the entry hall and entered Anh Ngoc's room—and the overlay of a vast courtyard shimmered into existence to replace the narrow space—Thanh saw people clustered by a buffet instead of a beautiful, empty landscape, and let out a breath she hadn't even been aware of holding.

Protocol dictated that, at some point, she would have to meet the host and hostess—before the Master of the Inmost Layer arrived for the ceremony. But she had time. As a Master of the Inmost Layer herself—though not one Anh Ngoc would have asked to officiate, of course—Thanh knew that her order-sibling would arrive just in time for the ceremony and leave soon afterward, their time too rare and too valuable for them to justify socializing while on duty.

How is it going? The line of text crawled across her field of vision, a reminder that Hoang Cuc had made it her mission to check in on her. Her spouse and order-sibling might be on call at the office—two entire rings away from Anh Ngoc's room—but she still had authorizations for everything she needed to follow Thanh.

Shut up, Thanh sent back. *I haven't even entered the party.*

Hoang Cuc's next message was amused. *Your vitals are having a race with a spaceship.*

Thanh was too jittery to send anything but the truth. *Why wouldn't they?*

Why wouldn't they, indeed?

Thanh descended toward the party, keeping a wary eye on the guests; she had a feeling of having walked measures and measures, but of course that was just the station's Mind helping her, providing dimensional compression to make the overlay's ghostly presence absolute—the small room that was Anh Ngoc's living quarters expanding into a vast space, every small step Thanh took decoupled to give her the feeling of having covered a great distance. Even the elevation was simulated, the Mind tinkering with her perceptions and her inner ear to give her the impression of walking downhill.

The people who were part of Thanh's most inward authorizations lit up in the overlay. She hadn't talked to most of them since breaking up with Anh Ngoc; and two years had passed, enough for them to have changed, for new posts to have been taken up, health to have evolved either for the better or for worse; for births and deaths and the everyday flow of life aboard Seven Clouds Station.

Anh Ngoc was there, at the other end of the courtyard—standing, for a moment, unencumbered by any guests, her gaze meeting Thanh's—and Thanh couldn't really ignore her, not decently. She nodded at Anh Ngoc, sent a message through the overlay, offering the usual congratulations and wishes for good fortune to her former lover, even though this didn't encompass any of what she wanted or needed to say—and waited, a fist of ice clenched around her innards, for an answer.

Anh Ngoc hadn't changed, still plump and small, with a hardened, thin face more suitable for an asteroid miner or an ascetic than a designer, though of course this was just the avatar she chose to show to Thanh; and for all Thanh knew she now had gray in her hair, or the first wrinkles showing at the corner of her eyes. She stood a little hunched, and moved a little slower than usual. She probably had her baby strapped to her chest, though of course they wouldn't appear in the avatar—wouldn't exist, in fact, until the First Presentation ceremony had been properly performed, and their parents' authorizations had been passed on to them, enabling them both to interact with others and to be seen by others. A newborn's privacy was absolute and any breach automatically major, punished by long-term losses of authorizations.

Anh Ngoc's answer, when it did come—after a heartbeat, after an eternity— was equally formal: a string of red-inked words across her field of vision, congratulating Thanh on her own promotion within the Ministry of Transparency, and on her own wedding to Hoang Cuc. And a signature, strong and forceful, which set Thanh's heart racing: *The Maiden of Cloud Lake*. It was how Anh Ngoc had used to sign their correspondence—in the days before the fight, before everything boiled over.

Thanh looked up. Anh Ngoc was still where she'd seen her last, standing in the midst of a crowd awaiting her attention. For a moment more she held Thanh's gaze, then she nodded and turned away, pulled in by a guest Thanh could barely see—someone who had given her the lowest settings of authorization and would no doubt be glad to see the back of her.

The Maiden of Cloud Lake. The Maiden.

Anh Ngoc was no longer a maiden, and Cloud Lake was years in the past; and yet . . .

Thanh. Breathe, Hoang Cuc sent. *Want me to input some drugs?*

You can't, Thanh pointed out. It was close to a breach, a role slightly exceeding the authorizations she'd been given as Thanh's spouse, and probably requiring her to pass the order onto the station's Mind as a Master of the Inmost Layer.

Oh, lil'sis. The intimate address radiated warmth, even though it was always a line of text. *Always so prim and proper. Do try to lighten up.*

I do my job, Thanh said. She'd risen, steadily, from a callow apprentice to her current position—a Veteran Master, in charge of the Greater Rings, the most critical sections closest to the station's Mind—driven, always, by what they had taught her at the Academy of Machines: that authorizations were the heart of the station, the axle around which everything else revolved; that they should be used properly, or not at all. That what they did—what every Master used themselves to the bone doing—was all worth it.

If only Anh Ngoc had been able to see that.

"Thanh!" a voice called, from a small knot of people clustered by a statue of a lion. "Come on here! It's been ages."

Closer, and the group was made up of Khac Ky, one of Anh Ngoc's friends who worked on the gardens, and two blurred silhouettes, people Thanh didn't know and didn't have any authorizations from. Normally they wouldn't show up at all; the station's Mind would redirect her steps so she avoided them and mute anything they might have been saying or any noise they might have made, but they were in a group conversation that would make little sense if half of it were missing—hence the option to introduce herself.

Khac Ky was nothing if not courteous and proper, though; he'd already sent the introductions before Thanh finished arriving, and the authorizations were promptly given. Basic information about the missing two blinked in the overlay, even as the two blurred silhouettes became avatars: a dour-faced man with a hint of deer's antlers at his temples named Huan, whose post was Master of Wind and Water in the station's inner circles, and someone called Uyen Nhi, whose avatar was a dragon in flight, and who mined metals from the asteroid belt. In turn, Thanh granted them authorizations, the lowest setting, the one she reserved for strangers and distant acquaintances: basic information, and an elaborate avatar whose features were nothing like hers.

"So," Huan said, bowing to Thanh. "I didn't know you and Anh Ngoc had been together." It had been in Thanh's basic information, because she didn't see the point in hiding it.

"It was a long while ago," Thanh said. *Liar,* Hoang Cuc sent, with such speed that Thanh suspected her spouse had set up an alert keyed to heartbeat spiking. But neither Huan nor the two others had authorization for her vitals, or even more than basic post, health and family information. She shrugged, with a casualness she didn't feel.

"I'm glad it ended well," Uyen Nhi said, the dragon body rippling in the wind crossing the courtyard. "Your relationship."

It hadn't, but of course they wouldn't know. They'd only see her here, at the First Presentation, a ceremony reserved for close friends and relatives, and assume from there. They wouldn't know—how the mere sight of Anh Ngoc could clog up Thanh's chest, could set her heart racing and a bitter taste flooding her mouth, as if it had been days and not years since they'd last seen each other.

"How have you been?" Khac Ky asked, gravely. "I haven't heard from you in a while."

They both knew Thanh hadn't made any effort to keep in touch; too much work, to navigate relationships after the acrimonious breakup. Thanh made a dismissive gesture. "The usual," she said. "Work."

"So I've heard," Khac Ky said. "You've been doing very well."

"Thank you," she said, slowly, not quite sure what to make of him. "What about you?"

"Same," Khac Ky said. "And I got married to a lovely man, but you already know that." She noticed Huan tense. Often people didn't like to be reminded of the Inmost Layer; it was like other jobs done by the Ministry of Transparency, touching on the inner workings of the station, exposing the guts of their everyday lives—the jobs that needed to be done but that few people would step forward to do. Khac Ky, though, didn't seem to mind. He hadn't minded, back then. Should she have kept in touch with him? But then she'd have had to handle Anh Ngoc in their mutual authorizations.

"Actually I don't," Thanh said, a little more sharply than she'd meant. "I'm Inmost Layer, not omniscient. I only deal with authorizations when there's a problem." And she didn't deal with Anh Ngoc. She'd made a specific request not to—one that the Ministry had granted without trouble, used to seeing similarly phrased ones. "I don't even know what Anh Ngoc has been doing."

"You know the basics," Khac Ky said, with a tight smile, and settled in the familiar dance of updating her without actually giving her any definite information—nothing that would trigger a minor or major breach that the Ministry could prosecute. "Getting married, getting pregnant."

She was used to it; and yet . . . and yet she wanted so much more—to know what Anh Ngoc had done, to understand why she was here, why the message and that cryptic signature. To know if Anh Ngoc had changed her mind.

You can't pour water back into a jug, Hoang Cuc said. Thanh could almost hear the sharpness in the overlay, could almost feel ghostly arms wrapped around her. *She broke up with you. You can't cry on what's done.*

And yet . . . and yet she'd never gotten over it, had she? Never forgiven Anh Ngoc, either—for all the quietness of their last moments together, that acrimonious conversation reproaching her for putting her career in the Ministry ahead of everything else; that had ended with Thanh screaming at Anh Ngoc that she didn't understand, that they were both too young to think of children, of families—and Anh Ngoc throwing back at her that she couldn't deal with it all, with all the knowledge of the system that Thanh was acquiring as a Master of the Inmost Layer; that, more than the hours she kept, it was the way she kept moving away—seeing people as the sum of their authorizations, as potential breaches or points of failure—that she didn't want to think about this, about all of this; that the work was sorely needed, but that someone else could do it; that other people could turn into blank-faced monsters, emotionless lackeys of the Ministry—but not Thanh, she was really decent underneath, really didn't deserve this. . . .

Thanh had walked away, shaking, and never come back.

"I think . . ." Uyen Nhi said, carefully, the dragon's pearly eyes taking in the courtyard overlay, the sky overhead shading toward a glorious sunset, with a crescent moon slowly detaching itself from the wash of golden pink. "I think they're not doing as well as they used to, are they? Anh Ngoc's family?"

Khac Ky shook his head. "I wouldn't know." He sounded relieved; quite probably he didn't know at all and didn't have to prevaricate. "But their . . . overlay is certainly over the top. And quite soon, too, for a First Presentation."

"Two weeks," Huan said with a frown. The baby was completely outward information, the birth recorded in the station's register; though not the child's name, gender or aspect, not until the Presentation was done and the authorizations granted by their parents had been passed on to them. "Some unseemly haste."

Thanh was torn between defending Anh Ngoc and making a snide remark that Anh Ngoc had always been certain of what she wanted, even if she had to rise roughshod over other people—including Thanh—to get what she wanted. She prevaricated by saying nothing at all.

In the courtyard, monks moved—ghostly simulations that were clearly part of the overlay rather than real people, carrying cages of birds to release into the sky. Of course. Anh Ngoc would want this, wouldn't she: the old-fashioned ceremony of accruing merit and forgiveness for past sins, a fresh start for her child.

"I've heard rumors," Uyen Nhi said, the maw of the dragon avatar opening in a smile of glistening fangs. "That all is not well with her husband's post. That he might be getting a demotion to one of the Lesser Rings. This"—the avatar's mane rippled, took in the entire overlay—"this might be her way of impressing the right people. A statement that she can still afford the best." Or design it herself: after all, overlays were Anh Ngoc's work, and her pride. But Thanh still said nothing; the words felt like burning stones, stuck in her throat.

"The guests are certainly well connected," Huan said, his eyes roaming the small knots of people by the buffet. "Ministry of Personnel, Ministry of Defense, Ministry of Works. A lot of high-placed officials."

Well connected. Well placed. Anh Ngoc's message floated up to Thanh, across her slowly distorting field of vision, congratulating her for her recent promotion in the Ministry of Transparency, her rise toward the higher levels of station society. And the hook, the promise of a return to their relationship, enough to make her wait for Anh Ngoc, to remain at the party long enough to be noticed . . .

Are you all right? Hoang Cuc asked, abruptly. *Your skin temperature . . .*

I'm fine, Thanh snapped. At the center of the courtyard, the first released birds took wing from their opened cages—their silhouettes a dark blur of wings against the round shape of the moon—so easily, so thoughtlessly flying away from the party and vanishing from the overlay, as Thanh herself could not. *Just fine.*

You don't sound—

Just fine, I told you. Leave it, please.

And to the others: "I'm sorry. I need to go for a walk." And left them there, unable to find more words she could give them.

∎ ∎ ∎

Thanh slipped into the Inmost Layer as she walked—what the other Masters called the Skeleton Layer—the only place in the entire room where she was sure that no one could reach her. As the overlay faded, the people appeared, their silhouettes wavering as though seen through water or a particularly bad infrared sensor. They couldn't see Thanh, though; their gazes would go right through her, their steps would be redirected so that they never met her—unless they were another Master of the Inmost Layer using their privileges. The room was much smaller, too, limited by station space: four walls with a counter that held the food, the beds folded away and the usual furniture collapsed into alcoves—just a rectangle of unadorned metal, without any of the compression tricks pulled by the station's Mind to make it all seem larger than it was, everything curiously flat and unadorned.

Lil'sis? Lil'sis? Please.

The words flashed across her field of vision, were replaced by others that still made little sense, messages she queued into lower priority, so she wouldn't have to deal with her spouse—not now, not in this state.

What had she expected—some kind of apology, a reconciliation, something beyond that distant smile, that meaningless message exchange? Anh Ngoc never apologized. Never.

She watched Anh Ngoc, watched her flit from group to group—in the Inmost Layer, she could see their silhouettes rather than their avatars, could guess at the shape of the baby on Anh Ngoc's chest. Would the child inherit the mother's harshness of face, her indomitable will, her utter refusal to see anything beyond the comfort of her own existence?

You both wanted different things, Hoang Cuc said, softly. *Let it go, lil'sis. Please. Just make excuses and leave.*

Thanh couldn't. She just couldn't take her eyes from Anh Ngoc's blurred silhouette, from the people she moved amongst: a Master of Wind and Water, head of the Habitat Design Department at the Ministry of Works; an official with a jade sash, a relative of the station's Mind; an overseer in charge of the asteroid mining in the nearby Scattered Pearls Belt; a constellation of influential station people calculated to make the event as prestigious as possible.

And she, of course, was just another addition to this. How could she have been so foolish?

Something flashed white across her field of vision: a general alert at the Ministry. *Big'sis?* she asked, and Hoang Cuc didn't answer. *Big'sis?*

Still no answer. Then, after a while that felt like an eternity, Hoang Cuc's words, slowly crawling across her field of vision. *You should leave.*

That's not what happened—

No, Hoang Cuc said. *But I would guess there isn't going to be anyone from Inmost Layer available for the ceremony; at least, not within the next few hours.*

Thanh's heart sank in her chest. *That bad?*

Major emergency on one of the Lesser Rings, an outage of power in the machines section. Entire clusters have lost their authorizations. Thanh could imagine Hoang Cuc's grimace. *Could be a while before we sort it out.*

But so far they hadn't called Thanh in. Of course, she was off duty, and they wouldn't resort to off-duty Masters until they had no other choice. She wouldn't ask if she could help. She'd sworn she'd take her night off, go to the party, try to be normal, instead of moving amongst other Masters. But, nevertheless . . . *You're right,* Thanh said. *I'll make my goodbyes and leave.*

But still she watched the fuzzy silhouette of Anh Ngoc. There had to be a way—a moment for a quiet word; not reconciliation, but something that would allow her to move on, to forget, to not feel like a ghost at the party, her throat clogged up with a hurt she couldn't set aside.

Anh Ngoc was walking toward a more deserted area of the room—one of the corners, where a silhouette sat alone. Almost in spite of herself, Thanh reached out in the Inmost Layer, and her field of vision lit up with a name, Binh Yen, Anh Ngoc's favorite and youngest uncle—and all the information started to scroll at her fingertips, all the authorizations Binh Yen had given out, the last interactions he'd had and their logs, a picture of his physical body and of all his avatars sorted by level of intimacy. Breach.

Breach.

She stopped herself—forced everything to disappear, all the details becoming invisible once more. She'd only caught a glimpse of them; not enough: a minor breach, the kind the Ministry might not even bother to prosecute. But . . .

But she'd know. She'd always know that she'd abused the trust put in her. Slipping into the Inmost Layer was one thing—plenty of Masters did it, to revel in what they knew; to enjoy peace, to find a refuge from the welter of life on Seven Clouds. Touching someone, though . . . That was . . . worse than seeing them naked, their secrets exposed without any recourse, an abuse she had no right to.

She . . . She'd done it in anger, in confusion, but it was no excuse. The station's inhabitants put their trust in the Masters of the Inmost Layer, and she'd casually violated that trust, simply because she was angry?

Binh Yen was now alone; Anh Ngoc gone again. Of course, she was the center of attention, even with the baby not yet introduced into station life. Thanh would not get a quiet word with her; there was not, and had never been, any chance of that—one might as well hope for an intimate moment with a bride at her wedding. She shouldn't—shouldn't even be here. Hoang Cuc was right: there would be no closure here, nothing that would touch that deep-seated well within her—just Thanh, getting angrier and angrier and making more unforgivable mistakes.

With a sigh, Thanh let go—the overlay of the courtyard with its impossibly bright, lacquered temple walls shimmered back into sight. The monks' simulations were gone, and so were the birds: their purpose had been served. The crowd remained, talking among themselves—watching the sky, watching the moon above, which was slowly shading from crescent to full.

Of course. First Presentation had once been called Full Moon Ceremony on Old Earth, on the shores of the sea in the Old Country of Vietnam; and Anh Ngoc, always proper, always effortlessly elegant—though not always subtle—would know.

Perhaps . . . perhaps Anh Ngoc would try to press her into service, if the Master she so desperately needed for the ceremony didn't show up—send her more messages in kinder tones, trading in on the intimacy they'd once shared with as few scruples as she'd shown, trading in on their acquaintance, reeling Thanh in with a promise of renewed confidences, of closeness that wouldn't ever happen.

Thanh's stomach heaved at the thought. *I'm leaving,* she told Hoang Cuc.

There was no answer from Hoang Cuc, not even a snide remark about her vitals. The emergency was still happening, then; a brief look into the private areas for the Inmost Layer showed a flurry of activity, and Masters messaging each other in a desperate race to restore lost authorizations so that people could function normally.

She should be with them, instead of wasting her time here.

"Thanh? Pham Thi Doan Thanh?"

Thanh, already on her way out, whirled round, and saw Binh Yen, a blurred silhouette—she must have been on the outermost level of his authorizations, probably something he'd given her once for a family meal and never revoked. "I'm sorry," she said, her cheeks flaming.

"What for?" he sounded genuinely puzzled.

"I saw—" She'd . . . she'd seen too much from him—touched his inmost details—everything from his life, laid out for her like the pages of a book— and it didn't matter that she'd hardly had time to absorb any of it—it was just . . . obscene. "I saw you," she said, unable to put it into words.

Binh Yen shrugged. "There's hardly anything to see. How have you been, younger aunt?"

He didn't understand. He wouldn't, not unless she explained further, and just the thought made her stomach heave again. "You know. The usual." The words weighed like stones in her throat. What—what was she turning into?

"Are you?" He sounded . . . offended, as if he'd genuinely cared, as if he weren't making idle conversation. And then she realized that they were still standing alone in the middle of the party; that Anh Ngoc might have left, but that no one had come to take her place. Old instincts swung into place.

"Do you know anyone here? Didn't Anh Ngoc—?"

"I like my privacy," Binh Yen said, smiling.

"But you—" He'd still granted her authorization. He still— She accessed his profile, the things she had a right to, the ones that weren't breach: it listed very few things, but the address he gave was, not on the Lesser Rings, but in the little satellites orbiting the station. He could have been a prospector, an asteroid miner like Uyen Nhi, but Thanh thought not. "You're a hermit."

"I prefer to think of it as retired from the world," Binh Yen said. If she'd had deeper authorizations, she might have seen saffron robes, or hemp, or maybe nothing at all. He obviously didn't like to advertise the fact.

"You know me."

"I remember you," Binh Yen said. "I always thought Anh Ngoc did you a great disservice."

"How so?" She didn't want to go there, didn't want to talk about this, but she owed him. For the Inmost Layer, and her loss of control.

He smiled, a bare quirk of the lips. "Her new husband doesn't have half your fire. You've met him?"

"No." The words stung. "I've barely met Anh Ngoc."

"Of course." Binh Yen made a dismissive gesture. "Ngoc was always . . . prickly. Like a durian fruit."

In spite of herself, Thanh found herself smiling, a bare tightening of her lips. "You still haven't told me why you're talking to me, and not to anyone else."

Binh Yen shook his head. "I've talked to people. But sometimes you just want to be alone, don't you?" He sighed. "I've come to see the child, in truth. I don't have much in common with Anh Ngoc's friends."

"There must be other relatives." Thanh had caught a glimpse of them, and had steered well clear.

"Of course," Binh Yen said smoothly. "At the center of their own little courts." He made a dismissive gesture with his hands. "We had . . . an argument."

Things Thanh had seen for only half a second flashed across her mind: transactions and authorizations and carefully worded memorials. "Inheritance," she said, before she could stop herself. "You disapproved."

Binh Yen watched her for a while. She wished she could see his face, or his eyes, or anything that would give her a hint of what he thought. The level of conversation they were having was a jarring mismatch for the authorizations he'd given her. "Of course," he said at last. "You're Inmost Layer, aren't you? Knowing everything and everyone."

"I—" She took a deep, trembling breath. Breach breach breach, but there was no avoiding it. She'd already slipped, already failed. "I wasn't meant to look. But I did. I'm sorry."

Binh Yen was silent, again; Thanh braced herself for a rebuke, or even for freezing silence, a withdrawing of all authorizations, the strongest castigation in station life—but his silhouette didn't waver or move. "We all fail," he said. His voice was low, expressionless, but not unkind.

"I don't," Thanh said, slowly. "Didn't." Because there was no point in arguing the obvious, was there?

"We all fail," Binh Yen repeated. "And all forgive ourselves, eventually." And then, after a while, "I argued that our great-grandmother's inheritance should go to her youngest and poorest descendants, instead of to the eldest. That was . . . unfilial of me."

"But . . ." Thanh wanted to say something about the eldest helping their own children, but she couldn't find something that wouldn't sound hopelessly, inappropriately familiar. "Surely they should stand by you."

Binh Yen smiled again, that odd expression on a face that wouldn't quite come into focus. "And perhaps I'm the one who isn't standing by them. Who knows?" He made that same dismissive gesture, as if he were one of the monks, releasing birds into the sky and watching them fly away. "I burden you, younger aunt. With an old man's conversation."

"No, not at all. I—just needed peace and quiet." For the first time since coming to the party, she didn't feel on edge, not ill at ease or angry or struggling to conceal hurt. "But I didn't . . ." She spread her hands. "I didn't mean to stay that long." Didn't meant to talk to him—didn't mean to wrong him, and yet she had, and she couldn't take it back.

We all forgive ourselves, eventually. And forgive others, and move on, or be swallowed by pride, and anger, and bitterness.

"Perhaps you didn't." His voice was shrewd. "The hour is getting late." Overhead, night had fallen; the moon was waning and there was . . . a restlessness in the air, a background of quiet mutterings among the guests. Binh Yen was watching Anh Ngoc who, regal as ever, was chatting with someone in the robes of a Greater Rings official. But her face was taut, her gaze wandering left and right. Late, and the promised Master had not come.

Big'sis? Is it still ongoing?

Hours, Hoang Cuc had said. Hours of waiting with impatient, important guests who were not used to waiting, or to prevarication. A party that was slowly going stale, and everything Anh Ngoc had worked for—the ceremony that should have been a pinnacle of achievement, of enlightening conversations, of sharing of elegant verses and fine food—a failure that would be the talk of the station for days and days.

It would serve her right.

Thanh would have said that, a moment ago, she would have turned and walked away as she'd meant to. But . . .

Big'sis?

Silence, on her comms—no comforting words, no biting reproaches—just her, facing herself, facing Anh Ngoc, who would never answer her.

"Tell me," she said to Binh Yen. "About Anh Ngoc."

"What should I tell you?"

What she wanted to hear. That Anh Ngoc was going to see her, to talk to her, to say she was sorry, and laugh as she'd used to laugh, hug her in a welter of jasmine and sandalwood perfume. That Thanh just had to wait long enough, and it would happen.

But then, she already knew everything there was to know about Anh Ngoc, didn't she? "She invited me here because I was someone, didn't she? Because I made her look good."

"I can't apologize for her," Binh Yen said, at last. "Or rather, I could, but I don't think they would be the words you'd want or need to hear."

"No. They wouldn't." Thanh had come expecting intimacy, and reconciliation, but it would never happen—because Anh Ngoc didn't apologize, because the time for that closeness had passed. And Thanh could hold on to that grudge forever and ever, keep that old well of hurt bleeding under layers and layers of renewed grudges, keep turning into everything she despised, into someone who breached again and again, and made sorry excuses for it—or she could, once and for all, let go.

No, she couldn't. She wasn't that much of a fool, that much of a weakling. There was no way. "Tell me," she said to Binh Yen again, but he merely spread his hands.

"There's not much else I can tell you," Binh Yen said.

He'd said . . . He'd said Anh Ngoc had done her a great disservice. That she was the one wronged, the one who could hang on to her rightful anger.

Except, of course, that it was untrue.

Anger twisted her out of shape; anger made her inefficient, forgetful of her obligations and her duties. Anger made her breach. She was Master of the Inmost Layer, not some quivering, faint-headed girl unable to get over her first love—and she, like the other Masters, held in trust the privacy of the entire station.

She'd failed once, and it was one time too many.

Thanh took in a deep, trembling breath. *I'm not doing this for her,* she said, slowly, to the silent, comforting presence of Hoang Cuc. She could say it was for Binh Yen's sake, but that would have been untrue, too—it was for no one's sake but her own.

"Can you—" she asked Binh Yen—her voice dipped, faltered, and then grew stronger as the words came one by one, falling into place with the weight of a magistrate's inevitable verdict. "Can you take me to Anh Ngoc? I can help her."

And, as she slipped into her formal role—as she walked across the court-yard overlay, the proper words of the First Presentation ceremony running in her mind like a litany she clung to—as she steeled herself for meeting Anh Ngoc's gaze again, for seeing the face of a child who could have been hers—she thought of Binh Yen's hands opening up; and imagined her old hurt, like a caged bird, taking flight in the overlay's sky, and finally fading away into darkness.

It remains up to us. Adapt to change . . .
. . . or choose not to.

AFTERSHIFT MEMORIES

DAVID RAMIREZ

A locker room. Steel doors painted gray, yellow-tiled floor. It smells of disinfectant, old soap, stale water.

In his surroundings. But not hers.

His fingertip slides the lockout switch on one arm of his glasses.

How much privacy do I really have? In theory, his peers and the hospital administrators cannot access the feed from his glasses, but nothing stops C4Duceus itself from observing. *What does the hospital AI make of our non-work-related behaviors?*

He sees translucent imagery flooding over the locker room, subduing the here-and-now, a bright day's sky outside a window. Not winter but apparently springtime. The view shifts down at small feet in black patent-leather shoes, standing on the red flooring he associates with the elementary schools of his childhood.

Motion superimposed over stillness. When not at full opacity, it can be jarring, but he is used to it. Her voice comes across from far away—in space, in time—yet is right here, projected as if within his skull. A trick of acoustics, a bug in the audio.

"You're in your last year, B. It's not much longer. . . ."

His words sound strange to himself.

"I'm missing out on so much."

"Just hang in there."

Bells ring.

"Recess is done, B. I have to see to the kids."

Below, schoolchildren run across a green field of tall grass, bright against the skin of their legs. Grades 1 through 3 are still in khaki shorts. The long pants are for grades 4 and up. He recalls when they first met, and how she told him, years later, that he looked kind of like a worm, but in a nice way.

"Okay." His words hesitate. "Love you, Grace. Give Jay my love too."

"You'll get through this, B. It's just one of your moods. You'll see."

The recording ends.

. . .

He goes through the menu. That call was last week. Okay, not so long ago, in time, but still so far away.

Dr. Bayani lies on his shoulder, arm numb, wandering the gray zone between asleep and awake. There is a pot of coffee, one hour old, in his blood. Caffeine crackles along his nerve. Bladder shifts, stretches.

His eyes seem directed at the whiteboard on the wall. Once, it was used for the I. M. residents' duty schedule and rotations. Now obsolete, it's just doodles and morbid doctor humor. A safer space than the forever of the online. When a budget is found, it will be replaced with a wall-mounted touchscreen dynaTerminal linked to the hospital systems. There have been many promises of additional funding, and sometimes the money even comes through.

It is not the whiteboard he sees.

Over his face lie glasses with wire frames and little round lenses, windows to another reality. Light flickers upon the inner surfaces, another externalization of memory.

. . .

He sees what the cameras in her own consumer glasses saw . . . when did these images come from?

When she turns her head to the side and looks down, he sees her bare, brown arm leading down to a delicate hand with calluses, and the shiny spots of old, healed burns. In her hand—a much tinier one, leading to a boy with a solemn face, looking back at her.

Dr. Bayani, on his cot, imagines that he ought to feel more. Jay does not look like this anymore. Does not laugh so suddenly like this, face in wonder at something out of view. He is growing up so serious.

Summer's light against broad-leafed shades of green in the background. Spots of moisture on their shirts, wicked away from the skin by smart fabrics. *When is it not hot in Manila?*

She glances to the side. There is a rail. Beyond and below the rail there is water, and from it rises the ruined hulks of the past—former luxury hotel cabañas for rich businessmen and foreign tourists, gorging on breakfast buffets and room service, with people to wash and press their clothes, answer phones, schedule meetings. Now, home to migrant workers, hauling nets of trash. Luminescent lines, just under the water, grow upgened spirulina capturing carbon from the air, processed into gray-green nutrient bricks to be sold to food companies.

The boy turns away and looks up his left arm, at a man. Grace lifts her gaze and there he is, a younger Bayani, smiling at them both.

"Will there be lots of money, Dad? When you're a doctor?"

"Well, things will be better, anyway."

He is smiling at him, at her, and the Bayani of the present sees the one of the past and wonders what she sees in him. Warmth and sweetness, joy, hand-in-hand.

An alarm vibrates through his skull.

. . .

The picture vanishes, the lenses clear, HUD coming to life as words scroll across his vision.

Pt. M. Andrews, Rm. 312; impending cardiac event.

Details flash. So many patients over so many hours. Which is Andrews? Data appears before he requests it. ECG *looks* normal. But beyond what his brain can process, there are patterns. The beeping intensifies.

"I'm going, I'm going," he mutters, wincing. Cuts the alarm.

Rolls off the cot. Coat on, stet, steady jog, IntelliPod shoes silent against the tiles.

It is an old hospital. There is a weight to the air, despite new paint and shiny tech integrated with the walls.

Year three of Phase 3.

His friends in the surgical department complain that the animated guides and haptic feedback are stiff and constraining. But for internal medicine? Dr. Bayani suspects that C4Duceus has leapfrogged beyond human perception, beyond the best cardiologists, to predicting imminent heart attacks. For in-hospital Code Blue scenarios, the warnings come farther and farther in advance of the actual incidents; it started at a few seconds and now—

Almost a full minute after the Pre-Alarm, an announcement on the hospital's legacy system echoes through the empty halls, as Pt. Andrews goes into arrest.

A timer starts counting up from zero.

Code blue. Code blue. Rm 312. A cold voice over the speakers. He has heard that a warmer, more easily understood voice is being synthesized based on an amalgamation of all doctors with C4Duceus glasses.

He is not looking forward to C4Duceus being able to talk.

Pt. Andrews' ECG live feed glows in the corner of Dr. Bayani's field of vision, the line a bright red ugliness, a heart squeezing incorrectly in a body that begins to die. The patient's medical history is available too. Lab results, family history, work history, the entire life of Madison Andrews—if needed, the microcameras in the frame would detect the movements of his eyes, and open displays with the relevant information.

During orientation, he was constantly opening tabs and menus by accident, but by now, he has adjusted to the control scheme of the model C4D AR goggles, as much as the goggles have adjusted, self-calibrating to him.

A blink and a timeline opens on his right, floating letters on a ghost clipboard at his side. As Dr. Bayani speeds into a full run, each event is time-stamped and recorded.

Code: 10 seconds. Autonomous crash cart 4 at bedside.

Code: 33 seconds. Nurse Baxter at bedside. Chest compressions.

Code: 51 seconds. Intern Johns at bedside. Bag-valve mask.

Code: 104 seconds. Dr. Reyes at bedside. Intubation.

He slows through the doorway, gets his breathing under control, and takes in the changes to Patient Andrews' vitals recorded by sensors in the smart-Metrics bed and transmitted to the adaptive screens on the walls, and onto the glasses worn by the code team.

They say their hellos.

"Doctor Bayani."

"Sir."

"Doctors. Nurse Baxter."

Hellos—before C4Duceus, there would be no time for chatter during a Code, but now that each of their glasses can access all the data and guidelines at a blink. . . . Dr. Bayani has to resist the urge to ask Reyes to report what's going on—everything that's happened thus far is already on his HUD and it would waste time.

"A bit slow today, Bay?" Dr. Reyes does not even look at him as she prepares an injection of epinephrine.

In so many little ways, Reyes enjoys needling him. He holds in the acid comebacks she likes to induce in him.

At the third minute since the arrest began, Reyes announces, unnecessarily, "Administering 1 mg epi."

Observe, assess. C4Duceus displays a scrolling decision tree summarizing advanced cardiac life support procedures at the edge of his peripheral vision. The team grumbles, bleary-eyed during another long night, but they perform their tasks with precise timing and technique, guided by their headsets. For a moment, Dr. Bayani wonders if Reyes' intubation was so smooth on her own skill, or if she was a puppet, hands following the animated guides and haptic feedback of the system wired into the sleeves of the white coat.

ECG micropatterns too subtle for humans upload wirelessly to distributed databases, are compared against aggregated cases across all institutions participating in Phase 3.

Evaluating. Evaluating.

The other residents have nicknames for C4Duceus. BroDoc. AutoDoc. AutoBones. Some talk to it as if it were another physician, standing just out of view. Perhaps they look forward to it speaking with a human-ish voice. He wonders if they notice that they treat it with more respect than the training officers. *Understandable.* The system never yells or badgers, it does not take pleasure in quizzing them "to keep them on their toes." It doesn't judge.

To Dr. Bayani, C4Duceus is a swarm of spiders, everywhere along an otherworldly web. One baby spider haunting each headset, chittering with all the others, and secreted across Elan Medical Systems' server farms, the massive, bloated, many-legged, many-eyed mother at the heart of it all. There is something spooky about their predictive algorithms, their awareness of everything in the vicinity of the glasses. Sometimes it seems the spider is *in* his head instead of software communicating with a very expensive interactive terminal on his face.

Prepare for defib, his spider instructs. The moment approaches.

While the others continue cardiac life-support tasks, he prepares the pads, applies the conductive gel to Pt. Andrews' translucent, papery skin. Presses everything into place only a little less efficiently than the perfect movements the spider's guidance module superimposes over his hands, an interweaving performance of the technique of thousands of other doctors during hundreds of thousands of Code incidents.

One more minute and the heart monitor kicks—the spider outlines it in red and flashes: *pattern for defib. Clear. Clear. Clear.*

Before he can say it, the spiders charge the defibrillator, warn the other members of the crash team on their own HUDs. They take a step back, hands away.

Dr. Bayani says, "Clear!" anyway. Pulls the trigger. His interface is set to minimum automatic intervention—at some institutions, the shock would be delivered by the autonomous crash cart under direct control of C4Duceus.

Lightning travels through fragile flesh, sensor readings jump, the atria and ventricles squeeze in sequence, an attempt to reboot the heart.

The spider does not have to tell him Andrews' ECG is still a mess.

The dance goes on.

Chest compressions resume. Epinephrine. Not yet. Defib. They switch off of the physically tiring compressions. Human machines move in synchrony, a dance choreographed without spoken word or gesture to the rhythm of the spiders in their heads.

Dr. Bayani is focused. Yet part of him goes away. Watches. Spiders signal other spiders, send and receive. He performs. A faint heat flickers. The thrill of doing just right, just so.

He remembers the gradual shift as C4Duceus went online. At first, it was just observing. Then its recorded data was used in lessons and case studies as the system was trained against real-life examples. Now, phase 3. Initially, pharmacological information appearing when a doctor might struggle to remember a specific detail on cross-drug reactions. Reminders. Links to instructional clips. Building up to automatically assembling symptom lists, suggested phrases for eliciting patient history. Auto-generated differential diagnostics. Then customized animations to guide physical tasks. Even surgery.

This night, on duty, the spiders do not run him yet. Today, the spiders are still invisible assistants. But he feels the tugs, and sees a future where the spiders are puppeteers.

He almost does not mind. Sometimes.

In a room with teal tiles and pale blue LED lighting. Some imagine it a battle for life. For Dr. Bayani, it is only so many events in an arbitrary universe. Minute after minute, human hands and knowledge and skill, and machine intelligence in unison, flicker forward in time.

Finally, despite all their efforts, Dr. Bayani pronounces a time of death, at the silent prompting of a spider. There is a stubborn urge to keep going, but he reins it in.

The death data propagates along the web of light, subject to analysis, statistics, altering, by minute degrees, the weighted connections between sub-clusters of the swarm.

In other hospitals, other patients in similar circumstances die, and some survive.

Here, now, he can smell the death coming off her. It is only in his imagination, to be sure—the biochemical products of decay that signal death to human perception have only begun to appear, too soon for a human nose to smell.

Dr. Bayani, chief medical resident, has lost count of how many Codes he has handled. This specific incident teaches him nothing, only reinforces his awareness of mortality. He handled things as well as humanly possible, and so did the rest of the team. But the spiders will get infinitesimally better. From the death of Madison O. Andrews, 89, C4Duceus learns a little more about the practice, art, and science of medicine.

He remembers his first Code. The pulse-pounding fear, the need to *not screw up*. Everything was happening two steps too fast as he fumbled through his chest compressions, too soft, and then, jerking when the consultant yelled, hard enough that he felt the pop of the ribs cracking, traveling from his hands and up the bones of his arms.

That patient lived. Bayani remembers the sense of profound—what was it? Not joy. But a contentedness. A sense of purpose. But two weeks after that patient was discharged from the hospital with a brand new heart, the man stumbled on the stairs of his house. And died.

Why can't Bayani remember his name? His face? He remembers facts, figures, and the feeling of the man's ribs breaking.

"When the family comes in the morning," he mumbles. He will be ready to answer the same slate of questions that are almost always asked.

The dance proceeds into post-death. The patient is cleansed. The inserted indignities withdrawn. And as Madison O. Andrews is rolled on down to the morgue, silver hair spread out in a halo, her face serene, Dr. Bayani fills out the death certificate. His hands and eyes flit through the interface in the virtual clipboard, but he is still removed.

Part of him has been gone for days.

Recommend ten-minute break.

Reminder: schedule post-incident discussion for crash team. 7 am?

"Yeah. Sure. A good idea. Both of them." He thought he was talking to somebody, maybe to Nurse Baxter, but they have already gone, directed by their own spiders to other tasks, and there is no one listening but C4Duceus.

He lets go. The shoulders droop, the clear eyes dip down to his feet and he walks away. He paces back and forth on the hospital rooftop, smoking a cigarette under the stars, while another reality crowds in. The lights of skyscrapers reflect off the becalmed waters of a completely different bay. Unlike Old Manila, San Francisco is still alive with money and glittering credit, wealthy enough to stave off the rising waters with dikes and levees. That city shimmers and the part of him that has not been there the whole day leaks emotion. He taps the right leg of the glasses, which go opaque.

With eyeblinks and finger pointing, he navigates. On an endless wall, hundreds of access streams of medical residents, commiserating, complaining, celebrating, studying, sleeping, living through the microcameras of their own \asses, subject to the limitations of privacy. All available to participants since \se 1 of the Project, the better for doctors to learn from each other. The better for patients and hospital administrators who wanted transparency and professional conduct.

He looks in on Dr. Reyes, who looks at herself in the mirror. The HUD lets her know that someone watches her, though it does not indicate who.

"He's cute, actually." She says to no one, to everyone in her small (large) community around the world. "He takes himself so seriously. It's fun, getting under his skin." The glasses lift away, and the view shifts as she places them to the side. She washes her face. Reapplies her makeup. Puts the glasses back on. Hers are retro, horn-rimmed; librarian's glasses from an imagined, idealized '50s era that never was.

She takes a deep breath, and his eyes are drawn to the shifting of the curves of her pale green blouse.

"Lost a patient. We did everything right. She was dying anyway. It was just her kids, guilting her out of her DNR. If not for them, we wouldn't have even . . ."

Her ocean-blue eyes, from her father, a Spaniard, are arresting in the dusk-dark face she inherited from her half-Congolese mother, darker by far than Bayani's own skin, which, in his own tongue, is called *kayumanggi*. The eyes glisten as she blinks, mutters, "Fuck," taps the privacy cutoff, ending the stream.

The app auto-shifts to multiple windows, a group of residents out on a team-building exercise, on a beach somewhere, laughing in the water.

Nobody back home has such eyes, and Dr. Bayani shakes himself loose, swipes his hand through the air, clearing the visuals.

Beeping. He descends back to the blur of the routine. Rounds, adjusting this drip, entering comments on that data point, sending messages to update consultants, referring patients to other departments, and the waiting in between each surge in the cycle.

Before the end of his shift, there is that anticipatory warning again, and in sixty-seven seconds, the ringing alarm of another Code.

Compressions. Intubation. Epinephrine. In almost every way, the same as what happened to Pt. Andrews, except this patient lives. Dr. Bayani can't keep this one's name in mind for the life of him, while Madison Andrews, of the shaky, fluttery voice, whose stern face cracked a smile for him once . . . The minutes as her chest was kept moving only by the application of near-ribcracking force by the hands of broad-shouldered, moon-faced Nurse Baxter, haunt him.

During the endorsements to the next shift, Reyes pulls him away, sits by him in an empty corner of the wards, draws closed the curtain. Even without the heels, she is taller than him.

"I know that look on your face, Bay."

"I'm quitting, Anita."

She shakes her head.

"I mean it this time." *My son is growing up*, Bayani does not say. *And is forgetting me.*

She places her hands on his face, the long finger over his skin, presses her forehead to his. "Go home. Chill. Cable some flowers to your wife, and buy a present for your boy. Then you'll come back tomorrow, and it's another day.

"You're a great doctor, Bay. It's not just DocBro running you."

She leaves so suddenly he is not sure if he only imagined that. The sound of her heels clicking lingers, and from the faint scent of something wild in the air, if he checks the feeds on his glasses, that did happen.

· · ·

"And now, our valedictorian, Jay Bayani!"

He watches—via Grace—his son step up to the podium, looking so tall, so proud.

Dr. Bayani has watched this speech many times. Knows that his son plans to be a doctor too, like his father. He wants to warn, *No. It's a miserable thing.* That technology is disrupting the practice of medicine beyond recognition. Replacing doctors with drones and home tricorders or medtechs working for a third of a doctor's salary, obeying a machine that's better than human.

He hears Grace whisper, "I'm so proud of you. . . ."

Inside his heart, what is left of an ember sputters. Perhaps it lights, perhaps not.

· · ·

"I hear Dr. B is quitting."

"No," Dr. Reyes insists. "There is no way."

"He talked to the training officer. And the department chair."

"No way that guy is quitting," said another resident. "He just needs to check his serotonin uptake regulators. Restore a little vim. The whole anti-tech grouch thing is—"

Reyes answered with heat. "Who are *you* to judge? A man—a real man— can . . ." She swallowed her hot answer and turned away. "He has a right to feel the world's gone awry. For him, at least."

"Yeah. Well. I still bet he'll be back. And using the tech to save lives."

But he does not come in for one day. For three days.

Dr. Reyes finds herself irritable, snapping at small things.

On the fourth day, there he is. Like nothing happened, in his coat, with stet, glasses, badge. Sits at her table in the cafeteria. They have fifteen minutes before another thirty-hour shift.

He takes a sip of coffee, alternating with her.

"You're not quitting."

"I'm not quitting." They do not look at each other, exactly. "I just needed a break. I've . . . scheduled stuff. It's summer there now, you know? They'll be visiting in a month. Grace is looking forward to meeting you."

"Good for you. I am so happy for you, Bay."

Their eyes meet.

"Tomorrow is tomorrow. Today is today."

"Whatevs, Bay."

She leaves before he does, because he just doesn't walk fast enough for her. She finds it annoying.

In their glasses, C4Duceus watches.

When corporations crowd source crowd commodification . . .
. . . this classic suggests that you not be a commodity.
Stay original!

SPEW

NEAL STEPHENSON

Yeah, I know it's boring of me to send you plain old Text like this, and I hope you don't just blow this message off without reading it.

But what can I say, I was an English major. On video, I come off like a stunned bystander. I'm just a Text kind of guy. I'm gambling that you'll think it's quaint or something. So let me just tell you the whole sorry tale, starting from the point where I think I went wrong.

I'd be blowing brown smoke if I said I wasn't nervous when they shoved in the needles, taped on the trodes, thrust my head into the Big Cold Magnet, and opened a channel direct from the Spew to my immortal soul. Of course they didn't call it the Spew, and neither did I—I wanted the job, after all. But how could I not call it that, with its Feeds multifarious as the glistening strands cascading sunnily from the supple scalps of the models in the dandruff shampoo ads?

I mention that image because it was the first thing I saw when they turned the Spew on, and I wasn't even ready. Not that anyone could ever get ready for the dreaded Polysurf Exam. The proctors came for me when they were ready, must have got my address off that job app yellowing in their infinite files, yanked me straight out of a fuzzy gray hangover dream with a really wandering story arc, the kind of dream concussion victims must have in the back of the ambulance. I'd been doing shots of vodka in the living room the night before, decided not to take a chance on the stairs, turned slowly into a mummy while I lay comatose on our living-room couch—the First Couch Ever Built, a couch upholstered in avocado Orlon that had absorbed so much tar, nicotine and body cheese over the centuries that now the centers of the cushions had developed the black sheen of virgin Naugahyde. When they buzzed me awake, my joints would not move nor my eyes open: I had to bolt four consecutive 32-ounce glasses of tap water to reconstitute my freeze-dried plasma.

Half an hour later I'm in Television City. A million stories below, floes of gray-yellow ice, like broken teeth, grind away at each other just below the surface of the Hudson. I've signed all the releases and they're lowering the Squid helmet over me, and without any warning BAM the Spew comes on and the first thing I see is this model chick shaking her head in ultra-slow–mo, her lovely hairs gleaming because they've got so many spotlights crossfiring on her head that she's about to burst into flame, and in voice-over she's talking about how her dandruff problem is just a nasty, embarrassing memory of adolescence now along with pimples and (if I may just fill in the blanks) screwing skanky guys who'll never have a salaried job. And I think she's cute and everything but it occurs to me that this is really kind of sick—I mean, this chick has admitted to a history of shedding blizzards every time she moved her head, and here she is getting down under eight megawatts of color-corrected halogen light, and I just know I'm supposed to be thinking about how much head chaff would be sifting down in her personal space right now if she hadn't ditched her old hair care product lineup in favor of—

Click. 'Course, it never really clicks anymore. No one has used mechanical switches since like the '50s, but some Spew terminals emit a synthesized click—they wired up a 1955 Sylvania in a digital sound lab somewhere and had some old gomer in a tank-top stagger up to it and change back and forth between Channel 4 and Channel 5 a few times, paid him off and fired him, then compressed the sound and inseminated it into the terminals' fundamental ROM so that we'd get that reassuring click when we jumped from one Feed to another. Which is what happens now; except I haven't touched a remote, don't even have a remote, that being the whole point of the Polysurf. Now it's some fucker picking a banjo; ouch it is an actual *Hee Haw* rerun, digitally remastered, frozen in pure binary until the collapse of the Universe.

Click. And I resist the impulse to say, "Wait a minute. *Hee Haw* is my favorite show."

Well, I have lots of favorite shows. But me and my housemates, we're always watching *Hee Haw*. But all I get is two or three twangs of the banjo and a glimpse of the eerily friendly grin of the banjo picker and then click it's a '77 Buick LeSabre smashing through a guardrail in SoCal and bursting into a fireball before it has even touched the ground, which is one of my favorite things about TV. Watch that for a while and just as I am settling into a nice Spew daze, it's a rap video, white trailer-park boys in Clackamas who've actually got their moho on hydraulics so it can tilt and bounce in the air while the homeboys are partying down inside. Even the rooftop sentinels are boogying; they have to boogie, using their AK-47s like jugglers' poles to keep their balance.

Under the TV lights, the chrome-plated bayonets spark like throwaway cameras at the Orange Bowl Halftime Show.

And so it goes. Twenty clicks into the test I've left my fear behind; I'm Polysurfing like some incarnate sofa god, my attention plays like a space laser across the Spew's numberless Feeds, each Feed a torrent, all of them plexed together across the panascopic bandwidth of the optical fiber as if the contents of every Edge City in Greater America have been rammed into the maw of a giant pasta machine and extruded as endless, countless strands of polychrome angel hair. Within an hour or so I've settled into a pattern without even knowing it. I'm surfing among twenty or so different Feeds. My subconscious mind is like a retarded homunculus sacked out on the couch of my reptilian brain, his thumb wandering crazily around the keypad of the world's largest remote control. It looks like chaos, even to me, but to the proctors, watching all my polygraph traces superimposed on the video feed, tracking my blood pressure and pupil dilation, there is a strange attractor somewhere down there, and if it's the right one . . .

"Congratulations," the proctor says, and I realize the chilly mind-sucking apparatus has been retracted into the ceiling. I'm still fixated on the Spew. Bringing me back to reality: the nurse chick ripping off the handy disposable selfstick electrodes, bristling with my body hair.

So, a week later I'm still wondering how I got this job: patrolman on the information highway. We don't call it that, of course, the job title is Profile Auditor 1. But if the Spew is a highway, imagine a hard-jawed, close-shaven buck lurking in the shade of an overpass, your license plate reflected in the quicksilver pools of his shades as you whoosh past. Key difference: we never bust anyone, we just like to watch.

We sit in Television City cubicles, VR rigs strapped to our skulls, grokking people's Profiles in n-dimensional DemoTainment Space, where demographics, entertainment, consumption habits, and credit history all intersect to define a weird imaginary universe that is every bit as twisted and convoluted as those balloon animals that so eerily squelch and shudder from the hands of feckless loitering clowns in the touristy districts of our great cities. Takes killer spatial relations not to get lost. We turn our heads, and the Demosphere moves around us; we point at something of interest—the distinct galactic cluster formed by some schmo's Profile—and we fly toward it, warp speed. Hell, we fly right through the middle of it, we do barrel rolls through said schmo's annual mortgage interest statements and gambol in his urinalysis records. 'Course, the VR illusion doesn't track just right, so most of us get sick for the first few weeks until we learn to move our heads slowly, like tank turrets. You can always tell a rookie by the scope patch glued beneath his ear, strong mouth-wash odor, gray lips.

Through the Demosphere we fly, we men of the Database Maintenance Division, and although the Demosphere belongs to General Communications Inc., it is the schmos of the world who make it—every time a schmo surfs to a different channel, the Demosphere notes that he is bored with program A and more interested, at the moment, in program B. When a schmo's paycheck is delivered over the I-way, the number on the bottom line is plotted in his Profile, and if that schmo got it by telecommuting we know about that too—the length of his coffee breaks and the size of his bladder are an open book to us. When a schmo buys something on the I-way it goes into his Profile, and if it happens to be something that he recently saw advertised there, we call that interesting, and when he uses the I-way to phone his friends and family, we Profile Auditors can navigate his social web out to a gazillion fractal iterations, the friends of his friends of his friends of his friends, what they buy and what they watch and if there's a correlation.

So now it's a year later. I have logged many a megaparsec across the Demosphere; I can pick out an anomalous Profile at a glance and notify my superiors. I am dimly aware of two things: (1) that my yearly Polysurf test looms, and (2) I've a decent chance of being promoted to Profile Auditor 2 and getting a cubicle some twenty-five percent larger and with my choice from among three different color schemes and four pre-approved decor configurations. If I show some stick-to-it-iveness, put out some Second Effort, spread my legs on cue, I may one day be issued a chair with arms.

But let's not get ahead of ourselves. Have to get through that Polysurf test first. And I am oddly nervous. I am nervous because of *Hee Haw*.

Why did my subconscious brain surf away from *Hee Haw*? That wasn't like me at all. And yet perhaps it was this that had gotten me the job.

Disturbing thought: the hangover. I was in a foul mood, short-tempered, reactionary, literal-minded—in short, the temporary brain insult had turned me into an ideal candidate for this job.

But this time they will come and tap me for the test at a random time, while I am at work. I cannot possibly arrange to be hung over, unless I stay hung over for two weeks straight—tricky to arrange. I am a fraud. Soon they will know; ignominy, poverty will follow.

I am going to lose my job—my salaried job with medical and dental and even a pension plan. Didn't even know what a pension was until the employee benefits counselor clued me in, and it nearly blew the top of my skull off. For a couple of weeks I was like that lucky conquistador from the poem—stout what's-his-name silent upon a peak in Darien—as I dealt this wild surmise: twenty years of rough country ahead of me leading down to an ocean of slack that stretched all the way to the sunlit rim of the world, or to the end of my natural life expectancy, whichever came first.

So now I am scared shitless about the next Polysurf test. And then, hope.

My division commander zooms toward me in the Demosphere, an alien-ated human head wearing a bowler hat as badge of rank. "Follow me, Stark," he says, launching the command like a bronchial loogie, and before I can even say "yes sir" I'm trying to keep up with him, dodging through DemoTainment Space.

And ten minutes later we are cruising in a standard orbit around your Profile.

And from the middle distance it looks pretty normal. I can see at a glance you are a 24-year-old single white female New Derisive with post-Disillusionist leanings, income careening in a death spiral around the poverty line; you spend more on mascara than is really appropriate compared to your other cosmetics outlays, which are Low Modest—I'd wager you're hooked on some exotic brand—no appendix, O-positive, HIV-negative, don't call your mother often enough, spend an hour a day talking to your girlfriends, you prefer voice phone to video, like Irish music as well as the usual intelligent yet primal, sludgy yet danceable rock that someone like you would of course listen to. Your use of the Spew follows a bulimic course—you'll watch for two days at a time and then not switch on for a week.

But I know it can't be that simple; the commander wouldn't have brought me here because he was worried about your mascara imbalance. There's got to be something else.

I decide to take a flyer. "Geez, boss, something's not right here," I say, "this Profile looks normal—too normal."

He buys it. He buys it like a set of snow tires. His disembodied head spins around and he looks at me intently, an oval of two-dimensional video in DemoTainment Space. "You saw that!?" he says.

Now I'm in deep. "Just a hunch, boss."

"Get to the bottom of it, and you'll be picking out color schemes by the end of the week," he says, then streaks off like a bottle rocket.

So that's it then; if I nab myself a promotion before the next Polysurf, they'll be a lot more forgiving if, say, the little couch potato in my brain stem chooses to watch *Hee Haw* for half an hour, or whatever.

Thenceforward I am in full stalker mode. I stake out your Profile, camp out in the middle of your income-tax returns, dance like an arachnid through your Social Telephony Web, dog you through the virtual mall trying to predict what clothes you're going to buy. It takes me about ten minutes to figure out you've been buying mascara for one of your girlfriends who got fired from her job last year, so that solves that little riddle. Then I get nervous because whatever weirdness it was about you that drew the Commander's attention doesn't seem to be there anymore. Almost like you know someone's watching.

OK, let's just get this out of the way: it's creepy. Being a creep is a role someone has to take for society to remain free and hence prosperous (or is it the other way around?).

I am pursuing a larger goal that isn't creepy at all. I am thinking of Adderson. Every one of us, sitting in our cubicles, is always thinking of Adderson, who started out as a Profile Auditor 1 just like us and is now Vice President for Dynamic Programming at Dynastic Communications Inc. and making eight to nine digits a year depending on whether he gets around to exercising his stock options. One day young Adderson was checking out a Profile that didn't fit in with established norms, and by tracing the subject's social telephony web, noticed a trend: Post-Graduate Existentialists who started going to church. You heard me: Adderson single-handedly discovered the New Complacency.

It was an unexploited market niche of cavernous proportions: upwards of one-hundredth of one percent of the population. Within six hours, Adderson had descended upon the subject's moho with a rapid deployment team of entertainment lawyers and development assistants and launched the fastest-growing new channel ever to wend its way into the thick braid of the Spew.

I'm figuring that there's something about you, girl, that's going to make me into the next Adderson and you into the next Spew Icon—the voice of a generation, the figurehead of a Spew channel, a straight polished shaft leading direct to the heart of a hitherto unknown and unexploited market. I know how awful this sounds, by the way.

So I stay late in my cubicle and dig a little deeper, rewinding your Profile back into the mists of time. Your credit record is fashionably cratered—but that's cool, even the God of the New Testament is not as forgiving as the consumer credit system. You've blown many scarce dollars at your local BodyMod franchise getting yourself pierced ("topologically enhanced"), and, on one occasion, tattooed: a medium #P879, left breast. Perusal of BodyMod's graphical database (available, of course, over the Spew) turns up "©1991 by Ray Troll of Ketchikan, Alaska." BodyMod's own market research on this little gem indicates that it first became widely popular within the Seattle music scene.

So the plot thickens. I check out of my cubicle. I decide to go undercover.

Wouldn't think a Profile Auditor 1 could pull that off, wouldja? But I'm just like you, or I was a year ago. All I have to do is dig a yard deeper into the sediments of my dirty laundry pile, which have become metamorphic under prolonged heat and pressure.

As I put the clothes on it occurs to me that I could stand a little prolonged heat and pressure myself.

But I can't be thinking about that, I'm a professional, got a job to do, and frankly I could do without this unwanted insight. That's just what I need, for the most important assignment of my career to turn into a nookie hunt. I try to drive it from my mind, try to lose myself in the high-definition Spew terminals in the subway car, up there where the roach motel placards used to be. They click from one Feed to another following some irrational pattern and I wonder who has the job of surfing the channels in the subway; maybe it's what I'll be doing for a living, a week from now.

Just before the train pulls into your stop, the terminal in my face surfs into episode #2489 of *Hee Haw*. It's a skit. The banjo picker is playing a bit part, sitting on a bale of hay in the back of a pickup truck—chewing on a stalk of grass, surprisingly enough. His job is to laugh along with the cheesy jokes but he's just a banjo picker, not an actor; he doesn't know the drill, he can't keep himself from looking at the camera—looking at me. I notice for the first time that his irises are different colors. I turn up the collar on my jacket as I detrain, feeling those creepy eyes on my neck.

I have already discovered much about the infrastructure of your life that is probably hidden even from you, including your position in the food chain, which is as follows: the SRVX group is the largest zaibatsu in the services industry. They own five different hotel networks, of which Hospicor is the second largest but only the fourth most profitable. Hospicor hotels are arranged in tiers: at the bottom we have Catchawink, which is human coin lockers in airports, everything covered in a plastic sheet that comes off a huge roll, like sleeping inside a giant, loose-fitting condom. Then we have Mom's Sleep Inn, a chain of motels catering to truckers and homeless migrants; The Family Room, currently getting its ass kicked by Holiday Inn; Kensington Place, going for that all-important biz traveler; and Imperion Preferred Resorts.

I see that you work for the Kensington Place Columbus Circle Hotel, which is too far from the park and too viewless to be an Imperion Preferred, even though it's in a very nice old building. So you are, to be specific, a desk clerk and you work the evening shift there.

I approach the entrance to the hotel at 8:05 pm, long-jumping across vast reservoirs of gray-brown slush and blowing off the young men who want to change my money into Hong Kong dollars. The doorman is too busy tapping a fresh Camel on his wristbone to open the door for me so I do it myself.

The lobby looks a little weird because I've only seen it on TV, through that security camera up there in the corner, with its distorting wide-angle lens, which feeds directly into the Spew, of course. I'm all turned around for a moment, doing sort of a drunken pirouette in the middle of the lobby, and finally I get my bearings and establish missile lock on you, standing behind the reception desk with Evan, your goatee-sporting colleague, both of you looking dorky (as I'm sure you'd be the first to assert) in your navy blue Kensington Place uniforms, which would border on dignified if not for the maroon piping and pseudobrass name tags.

For long minutes I stand more or less like an idiot right there under the big chandelier, watching you giving the business to some poor sap of a guest. I am too stunned to move because something big and heavy is going upside my head. Not sure exactly what.

But it feels like the Big L. And I don't just mean Lust, though it is present.

The guest is approaching tears because the fridge in her room is broken and she has some kind of medicine that has to be kept cold or else she won't wake up tomorrow morning.

No it's worse than that; there's no fridge in her room at all.

Evan suggests that the woman leave the medicine outside on her window-sill overnight. It is a priceless moment, I feel like holding up a big card with 9.8 written on it. Some of my all-time fave Television Moments have been on surveillance TV, moments like this one, but it takes patience. You have to wait for it. Usually, at a Kensington Place you don't have to wait for long.

As I have been watching Evan and you on the Stalker Channel the past couple of days, I have been trying to figure out if the two of you have a thing going. It's hard because the camera doesn't give me audio; I have to work it out from body language. And after careful analysis of instant replays, I suspect you of being one of those dangerous types who innocently give good body language to everyone. The type of girl who should have someone walking ten paces in front of her with a red flashing light and a clanging bell. Just my type.

The woman storms out in tears, wailing something about lawyers. I resist the urge to applaud and stand there for a minute or so, waiting to be greeted. You and Evan ignore me. I approach the desk. I clear my throat. I come right up to the desk and put my bag down on the counter right there and sigh very loudly. Evan is poking randomly at the computer and you are misfiling thousands of tiny little oaktag cards, the color of old bananas, in a small wooden drawer.

I inhale and open my mouth to say excuse me, but Evan cuts me off: "Customerrrrzz . . . gotta love 'em."

You grin wickedly and give him a nice flirty conspiratorial look. No one has looked at me yet. That's OK. I recognize your technique from the surveillance camera: good clerk, bad clerk.

"Reservation for Stark," I say.

"Stark," Evan says, and rolls it around in his head for a minute or so, unwilling to proceed until he has deconstructed my name. "That's German for 'strong,' right?"

"It's German for 'naked,'" I say.

Evan drops his gaze to the computer screen, defeated and temporarily humble. You laugh and glance up at me for the first time. What do you see? You see a guy who looks pretty much like the guys you hang out with.

I shove the sleeves of my ratty sweater up to the elbows and rest one forearm across the counter. The tattoo stands out vividly against my spudlike flesh, and in my peripheral I can see your eyes glance up for a moment, taking in the black rectangle, the skull, the crossed fish. Then I pretend to get self-conscious. I step back and pull my sleeve down again—don't want you to see that the tattoo is only about a day old.

"No reservation for Stark," Evan says, right on cue. I'm cool, I'm expecting this; they lose all of the reservations.

"Dash these computers," I say. "You have any empty rooms?"

"Just a suite. And a couple of economy rooms," he says, issuing a double challenge: do I have the bucks for the former or the moxie for the latter?

"I'll take one of the economy rooms," I say.

"You sure?"

"HIV-positive."

Evan shrugs, the hotel clerk's equivalent of issuing a twenty-page legal disclaimer, and prods the computer, which is good enough to spit out a keycard, freshly imprinted with a random code. It's also spewing bits upstairs to the computer lock on my door, telling it that I'm cool, I'm to be let in.

"Would you like someone to show you up?" Evan says, glancing in mock surprise around the lobby, which is of course devoid of bellhops. I respond in the only way possible: chuckle darkly—good one, Ev!—and hump my own bag.

My room's lone window looks out on a narrow well somewhere between an air shaft and a garbage chute in size and function. Patches of the shag carpet have fused into mysterious crust formations, and in the corners of the bathroom, pubic hairs have formed into gnarled drifts. There is a Robobar in the corner but the door can only be opened halfway because it runs into the radiator, a twelve-ton cast-iron model that, randomly, once or twice an hour, makes a noise like a rock hitting the windshield. The Robobar is mostly empty but I wriggle one arm into it and yank out a canned mai tai, knowing that the selection will show up instantaneously on the computer screens below, where you and Evan will derive fleeting amusement from my offbeat tastes.

Yes, now we are surveilling each other. I open my suitcase and take my own Spew terminal out of its case, unplug the room's set and jack my own into the socket. Then I start opening windows: first, in the upper left, you and Evan in wide-angle black and white. Then an episode of *Starsky and Hutch* that I happened to notice. Starsky's hair is very big in this one. And then I open a data window too and patch it into the feed coming out of your terminal down there at the desk.

Profile Auditors can do this because data security on the Spew is a joke. It was deliberately made a joke by the government so that they, and we, and anyone else with a RadioShack charge card and a trade-school diploma, can snoop on anyone.

I sit back on the bed and sip my execrable mai tai from its heavy, rusty can and watch *Starsky and Hutch*. Every so often there's some activity at the desk and I watch you and Evan for a minute. When Evan uses his terminal, lines of ASCII text scroll up my data window. I cannot help noticing that when Evan isn't actively slacking he can type at a burst speed in excess of two hundred words per minute.

From *Starsky and Hutch* I surf to an *L.A. Law* rerun and then to *Larry King Live*. There's local news, then Dave comes on, and about the time he's doing his Top Ten list, I see activity at the desk.

It is a young gentleman with hair way down past the epaulets of his tremendously oversized black wool overcoat. Naked hairy legs protrude below the coat and are socketed into large, ratty old basketball shoes. He is carrying, not a garment bag, but a guitar.

For the first time all night, you and Evan show actual hospitality. Evan does some punching on his computer, and monitoring the codes I can see that the guitarist is being checked into a room.

Into my room. Not the one I'm in, but the one I'm supposed to be in. Number 707. I pull out the fax that Marie at Kensington Place Worldwide Reservation Command sent to me yesterday, just to double-check.

Sure enough, the guitarist is being checked into my room. Not only that— Evan's checking him in under my name.

I go out into the streets of the city. You and Evan pretend to ignore me, but I can see you following me with your eyes as I circumvent the doorman, who is planted like a dead *ficus benjamina* before the exit, and throw my shoulder against the sullen bulk of the revolving door. It has commenced snowing for the eleventh time today. I walk crosstown to Television City and have a drink in a bar there, a real Profile Auditor hangout, the kind of joint where I'm proud to be seen. When I get back to the hotel, the shift has changed, you and Evan have apparently stalked off into the rapidly developing blizzard, and the only person there is the night clerk.

I stand there for ten minutes or so while she winds down a rather involved, multithreaded conversation with a friend in Ireland. "Stark," I say, as she's hanging up, "Room 707. Left my keycard in the room."

She doesn't even ask to see ID, just makes up another keycard for me. Bad service has its charms. But I cruise past the seventh floor and go on up to my own cell because I want to do this right.

I jack into the Spew. I check out what's going on in Room 707.

First thing I look at is the Robobar transcript. Whoever's in there has already gone through four beers and two nonsparkling mineral waters. And one bad mai tai.

Guess I'm a trendsetter here. A hunch thuds into my cortex. I pop a beer from my own Robobar and rewind the lobby security tape to midnight.

You and Evan hand over the helm to the Irish girl. Then, like Picard and Riker on their way to Ten Forward after a long day of sensitive negotiations, you head straight for Elevator Three, the only one that seems to be hooked up. So I check out the elevator activity transcript too—not to be monotonous or anything, but it's all on the Spew—and sho'nuff, it seems that you and Evan went straight to the seventh floor. You're in there, I realize, with your guitar-player bud who wears shorts in the middle of the winter, and you're drinking bad beer and mai tais from my Robobar.

I monitor the Spew traffic to Room 707. You did some random surfing like anyone else, sort of as foreplay, but since then you've just been hoovering up terabyte after terabyte of encrypted data.

It's gotta be media; only media takes that many bytes. It's coming from an unknown source, definitely not the big centralized Spew nodes—but it's been forwarded six ways from Sunday, it's been bounced off Indian military satellites, divided into tiny chunks, disguised as credit card authorizations, rerouted through manual telephone exchanges in Nigeria, reassembled in pirated insurance-company databases in the Netherlands. Upshot: I'll never trace it back to its source, or sources.

What is ten times as weird: you're putting data out. You're talking back to the Spew. You have turned your room—my room—into a broadcast station. For all I know, you've got a live studio audience packed in there with you.

All of your outgoing stuff is encrypted too.

Now. My rig has some badass code-breaking stuff built into it, Profile Auditor warez, but all of it just bounces off. You guys are cypherpunks, or at least you know some. You're using codes so tough they're illegal. Conclusion: you're talking to other people—other people like you—probably squatting in other Kensington Place hotel rooms all over the world at this moment.

Everything's falling into place. No wonder Kensington Place has such legendarily shitty service. No wonder it's so unprofitable. The whole chain has been infiltrated.

And what's really brilliant is that all the weird shit you're pulling off the Spew, all the hooch you're pulling out of my Robobar, is going to end up tacked onto my Profile, while you end up looking infuriatingly normal.

I kind of like it. So I invest another half hour of my life waiting for an elevator, take it down to the lobby, go out to a 24-hour mart around the corner and buy two six-packs—one of the fashionable downmarket swill that you are drinking and one of your brand of mineral water. I can tell you're cool because your water costs more than your beer.

Ten minutes later I'm standing in front of 707, sweating like a high school kid in a cheesy tuxedo on prom night. After a few minutes the sheer patheticity of this little scene starts to embarrass me and so I tuck a six under my arm and swipe my card through the slot. The little green light winks at me knowingly. I shoulder through the door saying, "Honey, I'm home!"

No response. I have to negotiate a narrow corridor past the bath and closets before I can see into the room proper. I step out with what I hope is a noncreepy smile. Something wet and warm sprays into my face. It trickles into my mouth. It's on the savory side.

The room's got like ten feet of open floor space that you have increased to fifteen by stacking the furniture in the bathroom. In the midst of this is the guitar dude, stripped to his colorful knee-length shorts. He is playing his ax, but it's not plugged into anything. I can hear some melodious plinks, but the squelch of his fingers on the strings, the thud of calluses on the fingerboard almost drown out the notes.

He sweats hard, even though the windows are open and cold air is blowing into the room, the blinds running with condensation and whacking crazily against the leaky aluminum window frame. As he works through his solo, sighing and grunting with effort, his fingers drumming their way higher and higher up the fingerboard, he swings his head back and forth and his hair whips around, broadcasting sweat. He's wearing dark shades.

Evan is perched like an arboreal primate on top of the room's Spew terminal, which is fixed to the wall at about head level. His legs are spread wide apart to expose the screen, against which crash waves of black-and-white static. The motherly warmth of the cathode-ray tube is, I guess, permeating his buttocks.

On his lap is just about the bitchingest media processor I have ever seen, and judging from the heavy cables exploding out of the back it looks like he's got it crammed with deadly expansion cards. He's wearing dark shades too, just like the guitarist's; but now I see they aren't shades, they are VR rigs, pretty good ones actually. Evan is also wearing a pair of Datagloves. His hands and fingers are constantly moving. Sometimes he makes typing motions, sometimes he reaches out and grabs imaginary things and moves them around, sometimes he points his index finger and navigates through virtual space, sometimes he riffs in some kind of sign language.

You—you are mostly in the airspace above the bed, touching down frequently, using it as trampoline and safety net. Every three-year-old bouncing illicitly on her bed probably aspires to your level of intensity. You've got the VR rig too, you've got the Datagloves, you've got Velcro bands around your wrists, elbows, waist, knees and ankles, tracking the position of every part of your body in three-dimensional space. Other than that, you have stripped down to voluminous plaid boxer shorts and a generously sized tanktop undershirt.

You are rocking out. I have never seen anyone dance like this. You have churned the bedspread and pillows into sufferin' succotash. They get in your way so you kick them vindictively off the bed and get down again, boogying so hard I can't believe you haven't flown off the bed yet. Your undershirt is drenched. You are breathing hard and steady and in sync with the rhythm, which I cannot hear but can infer.

I can't help looking. There's the SPAWN TILL YOU DIE tattoo. And there on the other breast is something else. I walk into the room for a better look, taking in a huge whiff of perfume and sweat and beer. The second tattoo consists of small but neat navy-blue script, like that of names embroidered on bowling shirts, reading, HACK THE SPEW.

It's not too hard to trace the connections. A wire coils out of the guitar, runs across the floor, and jumps up to jack into Evan's badass media processor. You have a wireless rig hanging on your waist and the receiver is likewise patched into Evan's machine. And Evan's output port, then, is jacked straight into the room's Spew socket.

I am ashamed to notice that the Profile Auditor 1 part of my brain is thinking that this weird little mime fest has **UNEXPLOITED MARKET NICHE— ORDER NOW!** superimposed all over it in flashing yellow block letters.

Evan gets so into his solo that he sinks unsteadily to his knees and nearly falls over. He's leaning way back, stomach muscles knotting up, his wet hair dangling back and picking up detritus from the carpet as he swings his head back and forth.

This whole setup is depressingly familiar: it is just like high school, when I had a crush on some girl, and even though I was in the same room with her, breathing the same air, sharing the same space, she didn't know I existed; she had her own network of friends, all grooving on some frequency I couldn't pick up, existing on another plane that I couldn't even see.

There's a note on the dresser, scrawled on hotel stationery with a dried-up hotel ball-point. WELCOME CHAZ, it says, JACK IN AND JOIN US! followed by ten lines of stuff like:

A073 49D2 CD01 7813 000F B09B 323A E040

which are obviously an encryption key, written in the hexadecimal system beloved of hackers. It is the key to whatever plane you and your buds are on at the moment.

But I am not Chaz.

I open the desk drawer to reveal the room's fax machine, a special Kensington Place feature that Marie extolled to me most tediously. I put the note into it and punch the Copy key, shove the copy into my pocket when it's finished and leave the note where I found it. I leave the two six-packs on the dresser as a ritual sacrifice, and slink out of the room, not looking back. An elevator is coming up toward me, L M 2 3 4 5 6 and then DING and the doors open, and out steps a slacker who can only be Chaz, thousands of snowflakes caught in his hair, glinting in the light like he's just stepped out of the Land of Faerie. He's got kind of a peculiar expression on his face as he steps out of the elevator, and as we trade places, and I punch the button for the lobby, I recognize it: Chaz is happy. Happier than me.

*Another "classic"—this one an essay-rant from the beginning of the cyber age—
sheds light on how our concerns have evolved . . .
. . . yet stayed much the same.*

PRIVATE LIFE IN CYBERSPACE*

JOHN PERRY BARLOW

I have lived most of my life in a small Wyoming town, where there is little of
the privacy which both insulates and isolates suburbanites. Anyone in Pinedale who is interested in me or my doings can get most of the information he
might seek in the Wrangler Café. Between them, any five customers could
probably produce all that is known locally about me, including quite a number of items which are well known but not true.

For most people who have never lived in these conditions, the idea that one's
private life might be public knowledge . . . and, worse, that one's neighbors
might fabricate tales about him when the truth would do . . . is a terrifying
thought. Whether they have anything to hide or not (and most everyone har-
bors something he's not too proud of), they seem to assume that others would
certainly employ their private peccadillos against them. But what makes the
fishbowl of community tolerable is a general willingness of small towns to forgive in their own all that should be forgiven. One is protected from the malice
of his fellows not by their lack of dangerous information about him but by their
disinclination to use it.

I found myself thinking a lot about this during a recent San Francisco conference on Computers, Privacy, and Freedom. Like most of the attendees, I had
arrived there bearing the assumption that there was some necessary connection between privacy and freedom and that among the challenges to which
computers may present to our future liberties was their ability to store, transfer, and duplicate the skeletons from our closets.

With support from the Electronic Frontier Foundation (EFF), Apple Computer, the WELL, and a number of other organizations, the conference was
put on by Computer Professionals for Social Responsibility, a group which has

---

* For the June, 1991 Electronic Frontier column in Communications of the ACM

done much to secure to Americans the ownership of their private lives. Their Man in Washington, Marc Rotenberg, hit the hot key which resulted in Lotus getting thirty thousand letters, phone calls, and e-mail messages protesting the release of Lotus Marketplace: Households.

In case you haven't left your terminal in a while, this was a product whose CD-ROMs of addresses and demographic information would have ushered in the era of desktop junk mail. Suddenly anyone with six hundred bucks and a CD-ROM drive could have been stuffing your mailbox with their urgent appeals.

Marketplace withered under the heat, and I didn't hear a soul mourn its passage. Most people seemed happy to leave the massive marketing databases in institutional hands, thinking perhaps that junk mail might be one province where democracy was better left unspread.

I wasn't so sure. For example, it occurred to me that Lotus could make a strong legal, if not commercial, case that Marketplace was a publication protected by the First Amendment. It also seemed that a better approach to the scourge of junk mail might be political action directed toward getting the Postal Service to raise its rates on bulk mailing. (Or perhaps even eliminating the Postal Service, which seems to have little function these days beyond the delivery of instant landfills.) Finally, I wondered if we weren't once again blaming the tool and not the workman, as though the problem were information and not its misuse. I felt myself gravitating toward the politically incorrect side of the issue, and so I kept quiet about it.

At the Conference on Computers, Privacy, and Freedom, no one was keeping quiet. Speaker after speaker painted a picture of gathering informational fascism in which Big Brother was entering our homes dressed in the restrained Italian suit of the Marketroid. Our every commercial quiver was being recorded, collated, and widely redistributed. One began to imagine a Cyberspace smeared all over with his electronic fingerprints, each of them gradually growing into a full-blown virtual image of himself as Potential Customer. I could see an almost infinite parade of my digital simulacra marching past an endless wall of billboards.

There was discussion of opting out of the databases, getting through modern American life without ever giving out one's National Identity Number (as the Social Security Number has indisputably become by default), endeavoring to restrict one's existence to the physical world. The poor fellow from Equifax mouthed smooth corporatisms about voluntary restraints on the secondary use of information—such practices as selling the fact of one's purchase from one catalog to fifteen other aspirants—but no one believed him. Everyone seemed to realize that personal information was as much a commodity as pork bellies, fuel oil, or crack, and that the market would be served.

They were right. In the week following the conference, I got a solicitation from CACI Marketing Systems which began: Now Available! Actual 1990 Census Data. This despite Department of Commerce assurances that census data would not be put to commercial use. Marketplace is dead. Long live Marketplace.

When it came down to solutions, however, an all-too–familiar canonical approach seemed to be developing: let's write some laws. The European Community's privacy standards, scheduled to be implemented by the member nations in 1992, were praised. Similar legislation was proposed for the United States.

Quite apart from the impracticality of entrusting to government another tough problem (given its fairly undistinguished record in addressing the environmental, social, and educational responsibilities it already has), there is a good reason to avoid this strategy. Legally assuring the privacy of one's personal data involves nothing less than endowing the federal government with the right to restrict information.

It may be that there is a profound incompatibility between the requirements of privacy (at least as achieved by this method) and the requirements of liberty. It doesn't take a paranoid to believe that restrictions placed on one form of information will expand to include others. Nor does it take a libertarian to believe that the imposition of contraband on a commodity probably won't eliminate its availability. I submit, as Exhibit A, the War on Some Drugs.

I began to envision an even more dystopian future in which the data cops patrolled cyberspace in search of illicit personal info, finding other items of legal interest along the way. Meanwhile, institutions who could afford the elevated price of illegal goods would continue to buy it from thuggish data cartels in places like the Turks and Caicos Islands, as sf-writer Bruce Sterling predicted in *Islands in the Net*.

I returned to Wyoming in a funk. My ghostly electronic selves increased their number on my way home as I bought airline tickets charged to my credit cards, made long-distance phone calls, and earned another speeding ticket. The more I thought about it, the more I became convinced that nothing short of a fugitive cash-based existence would prevent their continued duplication. And even that would never exorcise them all. I was permanently on record.

Back in Pinedale, where I am also on record, my head started to clear. Barring government regulation of information, for which I have no enthusiasm, it seemed inevitable that the Global Village would resemble a real village at least in the sense of eliminating the hermetic sealing of one's suburban privacy. Everyone would start to lead as public a life as I do at home.

And in that lies at least a philosophical vector toward long-term social solution. As I say, I am protected in Pinedale not by the restriction of information but by a tolerant social contract which prohibits its use against me. (Unless, of course, it's of such a damning nature that it ought to be used against me.) What may be properly restricted by government is not the tool but the work that is done with it. If we don't like junk mail, we should make it too expensive to send. If we don't trust others not to hang us by our errors, we must work to build a more tolerant society.

But this approach has a fundamental limit on its effectiveness. While it may, over the long run, reduce the suffering of marketing targets, it does little to protect one from the excesses of a more authoritarian government than the one we have today. This republic was born in the anonymous broadsides of citizens who published them under Latinate pseudonyms like Publius Civitatus. How would the oppressed citizens of the electronic future protect the source of rebellion?

Furthermore, much of the tolerance which I experience in Pinedale has to do with the fact that we experience one another here. We are not abstracted into information, which, no matter how dense it becomes, is nothing to grow a human being from. And it will be a long time before we exist in cyberspace as anything but information.

■ ■ ■

All in all, we are looking at some tough challenges, both technologically and politically. Computer technology has created not just a new medium but a new place. The society we erect there will probably be quite different from the one we now inhabit, given the fact that this one depends heavily on the physical property of things while the next one has no physical properties at all. Certain qualities should survive the transfer, however, and these include tolerance, respect for privacy of others, and a willingness to treat one's fellows as something besides potential customers.

But until we have developed the Social Contract of Cyberspace, we must create, though encryption and related means, the virtual envelopes and rooms within which we can continue to lead private lives as we enter this new and very public place.

—*Pinedale, Wyoming March 30, 1991*

BIG BROTHER, LITTLE BROTHER, VILLAGE

Everyone sees you

Does privacy exist now?

Redefine the word

Oh, but then remember that . . .
. . . sometimes our only choice is to fight back!

ELDERJOY

GREGORY BENFORD

They had nearly all their clothes off, the fragrant red wine poured, lights dimmed, soft Bach playing—when she said, "Wait, I can't afford this."

He shook his head, smiling, and handed her the filmy negligee, kissed her. She had some lines and sags, sure, but the old allure still simmered. One of the unspoken advantages of age was a slow gathering of weight—which, while it gave sags, added too a succulent voluptuous gravitas, a ripe flavor that beckoned him. "That new Mindful Monitoring tax? A hundred bucks a go, I hear."

She frowned with a quirky, lopsided smile, sighed. Then, in a studied, slow-teasing way she had, she slipped on the negligee with a silky elegance. The sliding grace of it brought a glow of anticipation. "Which I can't afford. Why's it higher if we're over seventy anyway?"

He didn't want the moment to veer into politics, but she had asked, so . . . "New ruling. NICE—you know, that National Institute for Care Excellence—changed the QUAL."

She sat down on the bed, eyes narrowing, and tossed some pillows into a useful position. "God, I hate acronyms."

He toned down the soothing Bach, moved it to the soft background speakers. "That's the Quality-Adjusted Life Year, to gauge the cost of extending a patient's worthwhile life by a year."

"*Worthwhile* life? What the hell—"

"That's us, really. Over the hill but happy, and no disabling conditions. There's an acronym for it—"

"Don't tell me." She gave a low growl and puffed hair from her eyes, her carefully lipsticked mouth in an exasperated twist. "Look, I pay my taxes—"

"This is an extra tax on us old folks, to cover risk of a heart attack. Risk goes up with sex, y'know." A wink. "Especially when it's really hot."

"So *this*"—she pointed to a small nodule at her inner elbow—"will report us?"

"Yep. Mine, too." He smoothed the sheets back, lit an orange-aroma candle. "Our neurocardio monitors see our risk go up, and in a microsec or two, tax charges go on our bills."

"Damn! That's what that small type in the contract—*Emergency services are for taxpayers only*—means?"

A shrug. "I think so. Fall way behind, you get no help. It's an extra service, after all. Kinda like the carpool lane. And the government always needs more money. Congress put this new tax in as part of the deal last year, to reduce student loan rates." He sat beside her, took her in his arms, managed a chuckle. "So it's two hundred net for 'elderjoy,' as they call it."

She snorted. "Mindful Monitoring—God, where do they get these names?—has its software listen to my heart go thump-thump. Fine. Right in the middle, our show's on the road, maybe I get a little tremor or something. So a guy on a motorbike or an octodrone arrives in two minutes, eager to give my heart five thousand volts."

This was veering away from the right feeling, but she did have a point. "There are upsides. This all started out to insure our safety, remember? Don't forget, these new sensors can adjust pacemakers. Send back data on cardio, that blood chem-chip stuff, neuro tags. Even trigger your heart, too, if it has to. So that octodrone can be sent back to the neighborhood shed."

"Right. More service. Everybody stays healthy longer and we all want that. Except 'til they see it means good ol' Mindful Monitoring needs more cash."

He lay back, vexed, wondering how to get the conversation back on track. Maybe a little humor? "Makes you wonder. Does masturbation count?"

She lay beside him with a small giggle. "It must. Those hormone and neuro sensors can't tell the difference, can they?"

"Taxed for jerking off! I don't recall that in any Tomorrowland futures."

She ran her hands over his chest, stroking, stroking . . . then a bit lower. "Save your ammo, sir."

He stared at the ceiling, eyes intent. "So plain old oral-only, too? Anal? How about when you wear that garter belt and hose? It picks up *my* pulse rate. Same charge for all?"

"I guess so. Is that what you had in mind?"

His face clouded. "Not until now! Damn, this tax is backward. Shouldn't seniors like us get a preference? Like we do at the movies and on the bus?"

"Ummm . . ." She was plainly out of the mood. He was, too. "Not a bad idea. But then every interest group would lobby for a break. Young people have more sex, Mindful Monitoring has the numbers right there, but kids don't have much income—so they should get a lower rate?"

He laughed ruefully. "The worst off will be the senior bisexual omnivores, right? They probably get more than anybody."

She snuggled up to him. "But sex is *good* for you!"

"Good, sure. Government taxes goods, y'know."

"And . . ." a flickering, mischievous smile—"services, sir."

"That's the right idea! Funny, we thought sex was the one pleasure they couldn't find a way to tax . . ." He held her close, catching the scent of her skin, the rich aroma of her hair. Maybe he should use his old lines? He murmured, lowered his voice into the bass notes. "Guess my favorite number . . ."

But she sat up, face intent. "I wonder if I can hack into the omnifeed, the one that monitors us?"

He sighed, rolled his eyes. "Ah, you tech types. To do what?"

She looked into the distance, the way she did when she explored an idea. "To disable it, while we make love. Save two hundred bucks."

He laughed. "I dunno. Look at the downside here, though. If you can do that, then it goes both ways. So somebody could hack in, break your code, send an overstim signal to a pacemaker—"

A flash of alarm in her eyes. "Into my heart monitor?—and kill me. Gah!"

"Somebody's prob'ly thought of that already. We'll see it in a mystery movie soon."

She stood, pulling off the negligee, face intent. His gathering desire softened. "I hate this! They're eavesdropping on us, that's what this damned Mindful Monitoring really is! We should—that's it!—we should build a room that's a Faraday cage."

"Uh, what's that?"

"A continuous conducting surface, metal, forming a sealed volume. That provides a constant voltage on all sides of the enclosure. Keeps out electromagnetic waves of any kind. Screen rooms, they're called. An English guy, Michael Faraday, invented those in the 1800s. They shield out phones, radar, you name it. Then we can get it on without the tax!"

He stood too, took her in his thick arms. "Wow, I love you tech types. How?"

She looked around, smiling. "Metal walls, that's all. I could line this room with sheet aluminum."

He actually thought about it for maybe a second. "Let's try it sometime, sure. Meanwhile . . ."

She pushed him back onto the bed, reached for her negligee. "I'll pick up the tab today, lover."

It was better than ever. They forgot about Mindful Monitoring entirely.

But soon she was up, pacing, her musky scent flavoring the air. She popped out ideas, lingo, plans. Their talk later, calculating costs and methods, got them excited again, with predictable results.

Within a week she had the walls sealed tight, windows covered with aluminum shades, doors reframed in metal, even air ducts. And in the spirit of science, they tested the idea. No charges showed up on their HealthFeed accounts. Mindful Monitoring was blind.

It was the beginning. They incorporated the business and advertised, at first slyly, online. It was a nudge-nudge wink-wink overture. SexScreen got orders for service teams by the hundreds per hour, then by the minute. It took all their time to just train their delivery teams.

Dating sites drove the profitability over the break-even line within two weeks. Orders poured in. They hired teams in North America and Europe that could erect a Faraday screen in a few hours, anywhere the customer wanted, on call 24/7. Business lifted off like a Saturn V into a clear sky.

"Screeners" became the new buzz word for the hip, though aging, technorati. When done, just raise the aluminum window shade, and health benefits returned. Also, cell phone service.

As a team, they appeared on talk shows. They worked up some double-entendre jokes that made their way into throw-off online sites, providing free advertising. *The New York Times* did a profile, for which they dressed in appropriate business attire, then saucy hip; *The Times* used both. Of course.

The government found no way to detect this electromagnetic deception. The in-body systems did not report continuously to SmartCity systems, so Mindful Monitoring simply registered silence. Fees coming from sex could not be levied on their HealthFeed accounts. This was not tax evasion, since fees are not taxes. Selling Faraday cages was not illegal. Politicians, not fond of laws they could not write—or even better, rewrite—found that electromagnetism allowed no work-arounds, no matter how many hackers they hired.

Market share boomed. The hippest blowoff line was, *"go Faraday yourself!"*

HealthFeed income fell. Mindful Monitoring was in trouble. Tax collectors worried. Pundits predicted dire straits. Senators held hearings. There seemed no easy way to prevent free sex, beyond the of-course–benign bureaucratic eyes. Some media mouths were predictably outraged.

After elderjoy became regarded as a civil right—*no eyes on me!*—moods shifted. The American Association of Retired Persons came out in favor of Faradaying. The entire program of Health Feed tax collection came to resemble the War on Drugs, a dumb idea that had finally failed years before. But this time there were no narcs to inform on old folks getting it on.

The happy couple became rich, too, which seemed to make them ever more horny. (Money does that, research showed.) They spent their final decades in an orbital hotel, where they enjoyed swimming in the zero-g spherical water pools—ideal for making love, rumor had it (soon enough, videos, too). Plus, they needed no Faraday.

The romantic comedy based on their lives won an Oscar. They appeared onstage to accept the plaudits of the crowd, clad in their new specially made all-metal Faraday clothing. A shining moment.

If transparency fosters empathy, can we make that work . . .
. . . where it's needed most?

STREET LIFE IN THE EMERALD CITY

BRENDA COOPER

On the night of 2024's midsummer homeless count, the street smelled of hot pavement. Me, Ginger, and her eight-year–old twins sat together on a concrete stoop. A hot July night felt good, even in Seattle. We had just shared a pint of ice cream, and the kids were laughing as they scrubbed leftover stickiness from their fingers with a damp rag.

Of all the things I'd ever wanted, keeping Ginger and those two kids safe was the deepest. In spite of the fact that we slept in different rooms, I spent all my waking hours protecting her. Right now, I was watching for drunks or University-district bullies who hated the homeless and sometimes thought to kill us for it.

A streetlight winked on below, illuminating a woman struggling up the hill. Patricio, an old cop who brought us coffee some crisp mornings, trailed gently behind her. A young blond woman and a Middle-Eastern man followed in silence, looking wary.

Ginger's boy, Emil, pointed his chubby finger at a drone that sparkled in the light above and behind the first woman. "Is it watching us?"

"I suspect it's watching them," Ginger whispered, her slender fingers tugging him close. The pale light from the lantern softened their faces. She looked like a homeless anime character with her shock of red hair over Japanese features. Tight jeans clung to her like paint in spite of the fraying edges and the hole over her right knee. Emil shared her red hair but had pale, freckled skin.

"I dunno." I tried not to sound like I was contradicting her. "I think it's a news drone. See the colors?"

Salate looked more Japanese than her mother, a study in black and white with an always-serious face. "Sammy," she asked me, "what's she got in her hands?"

"I can't tell." I stood up behind the other three as the small crowd drew near. I waved. "Hi, Patricio."

"Sammy." The officer's smile broadened. He turned around to gesture toward the woman, who had round and slightly astonished blue eyes under a shock of unruly black hair. "This is Councilwoman Windy Smith." He sounded like I should know her, but he must have seen my blank stare. "She's new. Elected last year. She wants to end the homeless problem."

Oh. Nevertheless, I nodded at her. "That's nice, ma'am. We always appreciate assistance."

She raised an eyebrow, probably at my use of more than one multisyllable word in a single sentence. She knelt down in front of the kids. "Are you in school?"

Ginger looked peeved.

Salate replied in her best formal voice. "Yes, Councilwoman Windy Smith, we are now fourth-graders."

"Both of you?" she asked, her hands cupped close over something I still couldn't see.

"We're twins," Emil said.

To her credit, Windy Smith appeared willing to take that on face value in spite of the differences in their looks.

"What do you have?" Emil seemed to be trying to peer through the cracks in Windy's fingers. "Can I see?"

Windy glanced at Ginger and me. "We're doing a project." She gestured toward the young people. The man nodded. "Shahid."

"And I'm Madison." I wouldn't have been surprised if she had said Barbie.

Windy sounded enthusiastic. "We're developing video to show at a symposium on homelessness."

It sounded like government gabble to me. Nevertheless, I knelt for a closer look as she opened her hands to reveal a tiny bicycle-shirt–yellow drone with black fins and control surfaces, and four tiny black copter rotors.

The children gasped.

This drone looked smaller and finer than the news drone, which ducked in and took a close-up shot of the yellow machine before retreating to a more polite distance.

Emil reached for it, but Ginger stopped him when Windy flinched away.

"Can we give one to your family?" she asked.

Ginger stiffened. "Sammy is my friend. We're not family."

Windy sat back a little, brow furrowed. "We'll give you two."

"Can I have one?" Emil asked, while his sister looked at Ginger, apparently hungry for the same answer.

Ginger said, "The children shouldn't be watched."

"They don't have to be," Windy replied. "But if you can show people what it's like to be a homeless mom, it might help. I asked Patricio to find me families."

I caught an almost-apologetic look on Patricio's face before he wiped it clean, hiding it from her.

Ginger picked up the little thing and held it in the light of the lantern. "It looks fragile."

Shahid said, "You can crush it, but it is very fast, and it knows how to keep itself safe."

I had fallen from the high heady sky of the tech world into the underbelly of city. I knew what to ask. "Is it autonomous or do they drive it?" I glanced at Madison and Shahid.

Windy smiled. "Sometimes they will. It has an auto setting. You also have the ability to turn it off."

"What are your plans for the recordings? Are you using them?"

"Yes." She looked at me levelly, as if trying to decide something. "But you can have final say-so over what we use."

Ginger sounded as doubtful as I felt. "Do you have a paper that says that?"

Madison handed me one. I held it up to the light and read it out loud for Ginger's sake. "Add a clause," I said. "I want to make sure no one—not even the city—can use pictures of the kids without Ginger saying okay."

Windy nodded. "We'll be back tomorrow. You can have the drone when you sign the paper."

Emil's hands were out for the drone. Ginger let him touch it, but passed it back. Patricio looked grateful. "Come on. There's more to count."

They left, their footsteps audible longer than we could see them in the dark street.

Windy had been careful not to touch us physically, but I felt sure she'd changed something.

Ginger must have felt the same, since she asked, "Is this smart?"

"Rich people have drones that watch their kids."

"But they have guards, too."

"You have me."

Her response was a warm laugh and a quick brush of her lips across my cheek. She got up. "Good night."

I listened as she shepherded the kids to bed, her voice soft and firm. My cheek retained the burning memory of her lips for some time. I didn't expect the drones to do any real good, or even to last for long. Still, they might offer hope for a few days. Out of all the evils in street life, the grinding loss of hope was the hardest thing.

■ ■ ■

At first, we all found the drones fascinating. Ginger wouldn't let Emil touch hers, so he threw small pebbles at it whenever she wasn't looking in order to force it to avoid them. Its capabilities fascinated him. I didn't let him shell mine, but he and I learned together how to make it move in certain directions with hand signals. When I rode my old beat-up bike to the grocery store, I used my remote to thumb it off while I shopped, keeping it close to me in a fanny pack. I tested its speed on the way back. The drone kept up fine, even downhill.

I knew a man who lived two streets over, a deeply damaged but sweet veteran named Griff who had fought ISIL and lost. He got a drone, too. Unlike me, he kept up with electronics, and he had a pad with an app that showed the student's drone-driving schedule and also had a manual for the tiny fliers. He came over every morning to share information with us.

A blue light gave away the telepresence of the invisible pilots, Shahid and Madison, who apparently only used them for about an hour a day, usually in the early afternoon. The rest of the time, they were ours.

By day three, the buzz of the little machines clawed at my spine. Ginger turned hers off for six hours before Emil talked her into turning it back on. After that, she took to glaring at it over her shoulder, the look on her face a dagger that I hoped the cameras weren't recording.

Ginger's drone followed her when she took the kids to school on the city bus, flying after the bus like an overgrown neon bumblebee. It went with her to the library for homework sessions and hung in a corner of the ceiling except for one day when an older librarian asked her to call it down and hide it. It went to free dinners with us, and for bus rides to the park, and it watched me sell homeless newspapers in front of Seattle Foods.

By the time we'd had them a week, the tiny copters had become almost invisible. Ginger rarely glared at hers anymore and Emil stopped throwing things.

In late August, we saw Windy again. She and her drone handlers came while the kids were in school. Griff, Ginger, me, and the outsiders sat around a mosaic table at the SeaTown Bakery and ate soup and sandwiches under a blue sunbrella. After we finished, Windy sat back in her chair and casually said, "There's a contest in town. A social hacking event where people get together to work on a problem."

I had forgotten she didn't know I had started in Silicon Valley. The story was there if you looked far enough back in social media, but it hadn't been the most famous tech fall ever. It hurt me and my investors more than it hurt the rest of the world, but then they all do. You risk. You lose. You get up or you fall. I stayed fallen. "I know what a hackathon is."

"The first Hack for Homelessness was in 2014, right here in Seattle. It did a little good, but of course the housing-price crisis and then the minirecession both made it worse. But the tech community doesn't give up."

I didn't say anything.

Windy continued. "I met with the woman organizing it. I told her what we're doing here, and she's going to pull people from a green building group in town and lock them in a room with some techies and an open-data vendor. She's also going to use human-capital sourcing and pull in volunteers from India, Australia, and China. I want them to see some film from your drones."

Ginger looked thoughtful. Her hair was down, shining gold and red in the sun, and she combed through it with the fingers of her right hand. "Will anybody else see it?"

Windy answered carefully. "We'll try not to let anyone else see it. But to be honest, we can't promise privacy."

Ginger flinched.

Madison leaned forward, excited. "We need the footage. It shows people what your lives are really like. It shows them you aren't that different from them. We've put together a draft of a short movie we want to show."

Ginger's eyes got angry and her jaw tightened. "Are my kids in it?"

"Will you watch it? Please."

"Sure," I spoke for us all. "Put it in the middle under the umbrella."

The opening credits explained the drone program as a personal way to learn about homelessness. It cut to an older woman who was part of a tent community in a copse of trees deep in Discovery Park. As she walked from her tent all the way to the bus stop to get food, my feet hurt in sympathy. I glanced at Ginger and noticed a finger near her eyes, as if she'd just brushed away a tear. We were almost last, me and Griff together looking like friends, which I suppose we were at that point. It made me smile. It was dignified, the video. They hadn't made us appear pathetic.

The last picture frame froze on Ginger's kids doing dishes at the soup kitchen while the credits rolled. Salate's hands were deep in a chili pot that was half as tall as she was and full of soapy water. She smiled at the camera, looking proud of herself, like a kid playing house. It made a perfect closing shot.

We all looked at Ginger, letting her think.

It took her a while, but she said, "You can use it. We just won't go back to the soup kitchen for a while." She was like a momma bear, my Ginger. It cost her to allow any risk at all.

. . .

People wanted to help us, and Windy showed up with phones and mentors. They had access to our video feeds, which made me nervous at first. I'd known the students were studying us, but at least we'd met them. To my surprise, Windy paired me with a woman in her eighties named Musia who lived in New York City.

Help started out small, like grocery money showing up on the phone. Mostly we used it to buy delivery food for all of us, which we ate on Ginger's steps.

Ginger's helper was a college student named Kelsey who looked about five years older than the twins. She used Ginger's drone to watch the kids from her dorm, which was just over at the University of Washington. They all did homework together.

One day Musia asked me if I could read.

"Of course," I spluttered, shocked that she would even ask.

"Would you read me books? I can't see well enough any more."

I didn't like it. It felt like an obligation, and I hadn't signed up for obligations. Besides, I hadn't read fiction for years. At least she didn't want romance. By the time I had sat out on the stoop beside Ginger's house for three nights, I decided I liked the book, which was a fantasy about a female shapechanger who worked in a car repair garage. She looked poor, but she had real power.

Salate and Emil both got all As. Griff found a friend dead of a heroin overdose in the street, and hid somewhere for a week before he finally came back and sat in my office with me sharing a joint like nothing had ever happened. All the rest of that year, Griff went away for days at a time. Sometimes I found him lost in the deep fears of his memories, unable to recognize me.

I finished four books for Musia and started thinking about getting a way to write myself. Not whole books, but maybe a few articles for the homeless paper. I'd had half a college degree once, after all.

It didn't feel as much like we were alone and the kids didn't go hungry as often. Ginger and the kids might be safer in some ways because of the drones, but Ginger and the kids were beautiful, and I worried about the stream of pictures going out to people over the Internet.

■ ■ ■

I expected Windy to come back and tell us about the hackathon. She didn't, although there was an article about it in the homeless newspaper. The piece didn't mention us, nor did it say much about the outcome except that there would be an unveiling in the fall. It did mention the movie, which set us all on edge a little bit.

There was good news as well. I had a small article in the same issue about how to eat on five dollars a day. It was the first thing I ever got published anywhere except tech blogs (in my old life), and I was so proud of it I carried the issue around until it turned into pulp.

We made the news for something worse two weeks later. Not just the homeless paper, either.

The bullies showed up. They hunted me and Griff, claiming it was all about the movie and how they didn't want homeless enforcers like us in town. We managed to whip them, and they ran. But that incident isn't the one that got us in the paper. The next week, the same guys started in on a friend of ours named Sol.

Sol came through the neighborhood every summer. We shared meals. He spent summers in Seattle and winters in Mount Shasta City. His whole life was walking up and down the 101 with his shopping cart full of books, blankets and survival gear. Sol's a happy guy, not all there, and friendly to everybody.

The bullies found Sol one Saturday night just before the 4th of July. They put firecrackers in his cart and knocked him over, scraping his face bloody on the pavement. One kicked him so hard he cried out. Griff and me chased them down. Griff was faster than me, and he caught the youngest one and broke his nose before I could get him off the kid.

The next morning, Patricio rolled by in a cop car. They almost never used cars in our area—they walked or rode bikes. A car was bad news. Especially in the crack between night and dawn. That was the time they came after people they thought might be dangerous, so they could startle them awake and contain them.

When they passed me going the other way, Griff was hunched in the back, his drone following the car.

They must have had an alert set on the raw-footage stream for cop cars, since Windy called me about a minute later. By that afternoon, she'd found me a *pro bono* lawyer.

There were reporters in the courtroom when I showed up with footage we had spent two weeks stringing together. It started with Sol and his cart, and us talking. Sol was asking how we'd been that winter, and talking about a cat he'd adopted for three weeks. He had a heart the size of the sky, and we were able to show that. We cut to the firecrackers, and then to a great shot of the same kid Griff had beaten up knocking Sol down.

It didn't get Griff all the way off. He'd assaulted a rich boy, and not even Seattle is fair enough to ignore that. But the judge only put him in County for twenty days, with a work detail at Alki Beach. I took the bus and sat where I could watch him a few days, just so he remembered he had friends. Even so, he kept to himself for a week after they let him out.

Ginger's college student dug up enough money for the kids to have new backpacks going into fourth grade. Her room-mate sent them pens and paper.

Two buildings got knocked down in the neighborhood, but they weren't any of the ones we were living in, so mostly we enjoyed watching the big wrecking balls and the twisted rebar and tried not to breathe too much of the dust.

■ ■ ■

Fall in Seattle is mostly yellow-orange leaves, light wind, and cool drizzle. Windy had told us to be free on the second Saturday in October, and so me and Griff and Ginger and the kids all waited in front of the warehouse in our warmest and driest clothes.

Windy Smith picked us up in a huge car, big enough for all of us, Madison, George (Griff's student) and Shahid. We hadn't seen them in person in months. Madison and Ginger greeted each other like old friends, and George acted so still and uncomfortable that my suspicions about Griff not quite bonding with a stranger became certainty.

Shahid looked like he'd swallowed a sugarfly, almost bouncing in his seat, which faced toward us. His enthusiasm affected the kids, who started bouncing as well, and earned Shahid a thick look from Ginger. They took us to the Arboretum by Lake Washington.

I'd been before, and so had Griff, but Ginger, amazingly, must have never seen it. She walked around, one hand in each child's hand, looking at everything: water and waterlilies, ducks, golden fall trees, the high arches of the 520 freeway. Salate skipped and Emil kept trying to look in every direction at once. The park smelled of water and of fall, and a cool wind pinked our cheeks.

Windy led us to a parking lot under a big banner with "Seattle Hack for Homelessness" in red words on a blue background. There must have been three hundred people there. We recognized the old woman who lived in Discovery Park from the video, and I was greeted by two of the reporters who had been in court the day we kept Griff from getting a felony conviction.

A band played the soft wailing folk that had become the new Seattle sound.

People introduced themselves to us like they knew us. News drones flitted everywhere. A young man handed us shirts with the event logo on it, which was a sort of tent strung between trees.

Ginger stayed near me and Griff. Even the kids stayed close. Madison followed.

So did our drones. That was good; I could watch the video later and catch things I was too tired or too distracted to remember.

We passed booth after booth. We found a game meant to teach homeless people financial acumen, free links to crowdsourced education that got Ginger all excited, a food and vitamin paste that tasted like oranges, and a wristband that promised to transmit our vital signals to a computer that would alert local nurses if we got sick. All of that in the first row of booths.

By midafternoon, the kids had worn down, and I left Ginger on a bench and went to find Windy. "Can we rest in the car?"

She smiled as if she had been waiting for the question. "I have something better."

"What?"

She stood up. "Follow me. Bring Ginger and Griff and everyone."

"Well, then stay here," I said. "Don't move." It took half an hour before we were all in one place.

"This is the best part," Windy said. "I can't wait to show you."

But then I was sure anyplace quiet would be the best part.

To my surprise, we got that. Behind everything, there was a table near a flat, grassy clearing. Two reporters stood at the edge of the lawn under a cedar tree, clearly waiting.

Windy looked full of import. She handed me a box the size of a lunch pail. It weighed about ten pounds. She talked me through opening latches on its sides, and giving it commands. Griff stood back, and Salate clutched his hand, watching. Emil had fallen asleep on his mom's shoulder, so he missed the whole process.

A white tent as tall as me assembled itself out of the box. "It goes back in, too," Windy said. "It takes about the same amount of time." She held open the door. It looked gossamer thin but resisted the wind almost the way a sail did, resolutely and firmly. Ginger went in first. All of us fit inside. "It's warm," Ginger said, relief edging her voice.

"It's solar," Windy explained. "And it starts charged. As soon as you put it up, it's warm."

"I like it." Salate bounced on the clean floor.

Windy poked her head in. "These are adapted from a set-up designed for mountain climbers at base camps. That's why the weight and environmental control are so good."

She ducked back out and then came right back in, handing in two smaller brick-shaped objects. "There's been a team from the university working on these for almost a year," she said. "It works kind of like the tent. See if you can figure it out."

Ginger had her arms full of children, so Griff and I each took one. They turned into mattresses.

"How did you get all this stuff?" Ginger asked Windy from right inside of a tent door. "It's so clever."

"People like a challenge," she said. "We gave away prizes for the best ideas. People had to watch the video and then they could help. You see all the people here?"

Ginger poked her head out and looked around. "Yes."

"This is just folks from here and Vancouver that helped. There's people from all over the world."

Ginger's eyes widened.

"Rest," Windy said, laughing warmly, obviously still excited. "I'll come get you for dinner."

The tent felt too personal for Griff and me to stay inside, so we shut Ginger and the kids in so they could nap, and sat outside the tent like guards. Mostly we were quiet, both inside ourselves, thinking. I found the whole thing overwhelming and fascinating. Why did people in faraway places care about us?

Eventually, the sun sent slanted golden rays across the park and threw our shadows long behind us and made the tent look like a tower on the ground between our shadowselves.

The kids emerged, Emil crying for a bathroom. Ginger and I took both kids through the crowd to the park bathrooms. Right next to the traditional bathrooms, the kids found a pair of experimental portapotties that would—an excited-nerdy graduate student who made me wince promised—change human waste into pure water, then convert easily into a cozy shower. They said it would be great for people like us and for villages and campsites everywhere.

"Yuck." Salate wrinkled her nose, hesitated, and then washed her hands with the reclaimed water. After, she pestered the eager student with questions. Watching Salate patiently ask the student to explain the whole process to her, I realized Ginger might have a budding geek on her hands.

Pulling Salate and her brother away—what is it with kids and their fascination with poop?—we found Windy by the fire. A feast had been laid out on two picnic tables. Windy helped Ginger manage three plates. I made one for Griff and took it to him out by the odd magical tent. When I got back and made my own plate, Windy asked, "What do you think?"

"I'm pretty amazed."

She looked proud. "The model is extensible. We have thirty-five more people paired with drones and volunteers now."

She swept her hand expansively toward the tables of offering. "Is this stuff useful?"

"Some of it is. You really did do a lot," I said.

"It's only the beginning." She smiled a small, slightly secretive smile. She touched me then, the first time she had ever touched me. It was a feather touch, a small thing to my back, but it was also electric. Not sexual. She had nothing like Ginger's allure for me, but the touch mattered in some deep way, as if she'd touched inside me.

Who would have thought it. A politician with a soul. Apparently there were others. And decent folks across this town and around the world. All that was really needed was for people to see, to really see the poor as fellow human beings.

Ginger came up with the kids, both happy again now that they'd eaten and slept. "Can we go home soon?" Ginger asked.

Windy looked very solemnly at Emil and Salate. "Would you like to camp here overnight? We have toothbrushes and blankets."

Ginger shook her head. "We should get home."

Wendy steepled her hands. "I'll take you home if you want, but I'd really like it if you'd spend the night."

Salate looked up at Ginger with a shining face and asked, "Mom? Can we?"

One of the long muscles in Ginger's neck jumped and her jaw tightened. She was too polite to show her anger, though I was willing to bet she'd never get in a car with Windy again. "Thank you, we will."

By the time we got back to the tent, six more tents like it had joined it on the lawn, and there were other used tents going up as well. True to Windy's word, there were blankets and pillows. Griff had moved off into the trees, but he came back when we did, and he and I sat outside all night taking turns sleeping and watching. Sometime before dawn, we were both awake and everyone else in the camp had finally quieted. "Windy told me there are thirty-five more drones," I told Griff.

"That's good."

"Do you think so?"

"Of course. I'd be in jail without mine."

"There's that."

"And Ginger's kids are doing better."

We could only use a few of the ideas people had turned into stuff, but that's because we had roofs over our head and we were kind of established.

But we were still squatters. We could be kicked out any time. Maybe I should ask if we could do something to earn two of the tents. I was still thinking about that when I drifted off a little, although I'm not sure I got any real sleep that whole night.

I did learn that Griff snored.

■   ■   ■

Windy took us out for breakfast to Pike Place Market where she bought us all pierogi.

She had never spent so much time with us. More than a day now.

Maybe we were about to graduate.

I hoped we wouldn't lose the drones. I would miss Shahid. He wasn't with us now, but then I knew he had a life other than watching over me.

Windy's driver parked a block away and they had us get out, which was a puzzle until we saw the changes.

A park had grown on our street. The empty lots where the two buildings had been torn down were green. There were trees and benches.

Patricio watched us walk up, all smiles.

Little silvery eggs as tall as a person rested by each bench.

The kids raced toward the eggs, but Griff and I walked slowly.

Windy looked so proud she could float away. "These are yours. They're for all you've done." She reached up and patted the top of one. "It's solar powered, and it recycles water."

We must have all looked shocked.

"You earned them already. And you'll keep earning them, by testing them."

None of us said a thing.

Griff backed up, and then he turned and walked away. At least his drone was still following him. I could find him later.

Ginger leaned into one of the houses. Five of them would fit in her warehouse.

I peered into the one closest to me. There was a bed and a desk, a tiny kitchen with one burner. A sink. Best of all, there was a bathroom.

The water in the sink flowed.

I hadn't had a bathroom for at least five years.

I turned around in time to see Windy waiting for Ginger just outside of the pod she'd claimed. Ginger turned, and startled. Windy folded her in her arms. Ginger startled and then she relaxed and slid her arms around Windy's waist. She whispered, "Thank you."

I rattled the door. There was a lock.

Ginger and the kids had a door they could lock. And outside, like a loyal dog, forever vigilant, their drone soaked up sunshine and whirred.

Science fiction looks ahead.
Will anyone listen?

THE EYES HAVE IT

STEPHEN W. POTTS

It is June 2015. This week a congressional committee heard testimony on the regulation of drones or Unmanned Aircraft Systems (UAS). Amazon executive Paul Misener urged Congress to avoid too-stringent regulation, since his company is ready to use the technology to deliver packages. On the other hand, privacy advocate Harley Geiger of the Center for Democracy and Technology warned that ubiquitous drones would be "a nightmare scenario for civil liberties." What, after all, would protect privacy and personal property if drones could fly over anyone's home at any time? How many feet overhead could be considered one's private space?

In this past week's main news story, however, one Dylann Roof, the young suspect in the racial murder of nine people in an historic Charleston, South Carolina, church, was captured by police one day after the crime was committed. A security camera in the church had recorded a clear image of the twenty-one-year-old, and photos were immediately publicized on television and the Internet. A citizen over a hundred miles away in North Carolina identified him in her area and called police.

Over the past year, police themselves have been under scrutiny, thanks to cell-phone cameras in civilian hands. As a result, the public at large witnessed the strangulation of Eric Garner in New York, the precipitous shooting of twelve-year-old Tamir Rice in Cleveland, the limp body of Freddie Gray being hauled into a police wagon in Baltimore, and the killing of Walter Scott in Charleston, all of them unarmed black males. These dubious acts led to firings, resignations, criminal charges, Department of Justice action, and the Black Lives Matter movement.

June began with the passage of the US Freedom Act, a successor to the US Patriot Act of 2001 passed in the wake of 9/11. The new law nominally restricts the powers of the federal government, specifically the National Security Agency, but civil libertarians complain that it didn't go far enough. Critics like Glenn Greenwald have noted that no one would even know the extent of the government's surveillance without the actions of fugitive whistleblower Edward Snowden, who nevertheless received no credit for Congress's reconsideration.

In 1998, five years after the emergence of the World Wide Web, David Brin speculated in his non-fiction book *The Transparent Society* that incipient technologies would change our relationship to privacy and transparency. Among other things, he foresaw the expansion of our interactive computing capabilities and thus opportunities for surveillance and *sousveillance*; he predicted that improving technology would make possible minuscule cameras that might go into anyone's pocket and maybe even fly overhead. And he recommended that this apparent assault on privacy be welcomed—or at least adapted to—since it would give us the ability to watch the watchmen.

First of all, a short history of privacy—and it is a short history. Modern notions of privacy date back only to the end of the Classic Enlightenment, barely two hundred years ago. For the ancient Greeks, for example, the private person was one who lived in his own little world or *idios*; thus, our modern word "idiot." Aristotle asserted that the individual could not function separately from the *polis,* any more than a finger could function separately from the body. Before modern times privacy would have been an alien concept for most Europeans (not to mention those in the rest of the world), who shared single rooms with extended families and regularly used public toilets that were truly public, being out in the open. For most of human history, and still in most nonurban areas today, most people have lived in places where all their neighbors knew their names and their personal business. In every sense, it took a village to be human.

The thinkers of the Enlightenment, largely educated in the principles of Greece and Rome, likewise privileged the public citizen over the private. Even Adam Smith, often touted today for the concept of "self-interest," saw it mainly as a means to improve the condition of the commons; everyone would be well served if self-interest was harnessed to lift all boats together. He would be horrified by today's radicals who preach self-interest at the expense of the public good.

Likewise, the classically educated Founders of the American Republic saw the commons as the chief beneficiary of the social contract; as men of the Enlightenment, they were also communitarians rather than rampant individualists. While the Declaration of Independence touts "Life, Liberty and the pursuit of happiness" as "unalienable rights," the Constitution is grounded in the notion of the social contract, explored earlier by thinkers such as Hobbes, Locke, and Rousseau. They and their successors debated the extent to which individuals needed to give up a certain degree of freedom for the sake of a more perfect society. Privacy *per se*, however, was not "unalienable."

The English founder of utilitarianism, Jeremy Bentham, devised the "panopticon" as a method for controlling prisoners through the permanent threat of surveillance. He furthermore promoted a panopticon of the commons—called by some a "synopticon"—"in which every man exercises himself before the eyes of every other man," taking for granted that acts supporting the general happiness would be rewarded and imitated. Thus, Bentham regarded transparency as a social benefit. According to Andrew McStay, "Transparency and surveillance (or more accurately, *equiveillance*) in this context is positive and accords with the Enlightenment doctrine of making all things present so to generate understanding, and make life better."

Bentham's Victorian successor, John Stuart Mill, is credited with the modern liberal view of privacy, which emerged from his 1859 treatise *On Liberty*. For Mill, government and society should exercise the least control possible over the thoughts and lives of subjects and citizens; power over the individual "should only be exercised if a person negatively affects the interests of another" (McStay). In this manner society benefits from openness; only when views were freely discussed in public can the best ideas dominate. Privacy is valuable but not to the point of seclusion; the public good demands that the individual engage in "connections and relationships." (McStay). Other writers, from the Enlightenment on, expressed the concern that too much "privacy would promote dissembling and hypocrisy, and allow 'uncivilized' behavior or lack of control" (O'Hara and Shadbolt).

By the end of the nineteenth century, concerns were being widely expressed over such invasive new technologies as the telephone, the microphone, and Kodak photography, which could tap into private conversations and private moments. As a direct result, U. S. Supreme Court Justices Samuel D. Warren and Louis D. Brandeis published their 1890 treatise arguing for privacy as a basic legal right, going so far as to condemn even gossip, especially in print, as a social evil. Over the next half century, privacy sank deep roots into liberal humanist thought and legal philosophy. In 1948, privacy was accorded the status of an inalienable right by the United Nations, which enshrined it in the Universal Declaration of Human Rights.

Given this modern trend, it is not entirely a coincidence that 1948 was also the year in which George Orwell composed *1984*. Orwell's dystopia embodies the iconic panoptic nightmare: a world where the population is constantly brainwashed by patriotic messages through public address and film, where all knowledge, language and thought are incessantly policed by the state, and where the familiar mantra "Big Brother is watching" announces the ubiquity of the surveillance society. For Orwell, a veteran of the wartime BBC, the technologies of mass control were the midcentury media: radio, television, and the cinema.

Fear of Big Brother has haunted most of the commentary over the surveillance potential of the twenty-first century, with its World Wide Web, cellphone cameras, and drones. The debate has come up against a central paradox in post-Enlightenment thought: the apparent conflict between the virtues of privacy and openness. The discussion often boils down to the contradictory desire to defend one's own privacy while demanding transparency from others. Generally it is treated as a zero-sum game—a tradeoff, for example, between security and freedom, both of them essential to a civilized society.

Those addressing this problem in the new century have expressed some guarded optimism, at least as far as Big Brother is concerned. Although the War on Terror has stepped up official surveillance and secrecy on both sides of the Atlantic, governments have found it very difficult to *keep* secrets in our interconnected environment. Revelations from Wikileaks and Edward Snowden to the Panama Papers continue to trickle down, despite prospects of involuntary exile and long prison sentences. China tries to encourage the economic and social benefits of the Internet without the risk of uncensored democracy by employing what onlookers refer to as "the Great Firewall of China." But this forces the People's Republic to monitor activity incessantly in an online game of Whack-a-Mole. In the long run, McStay cautions against "dystopian narratives" in our "enhanced milieu of visibility," because current technology "encompasses the breakdown of borders of traditional power-holders and citizens alike." Patrick Tucker likewise sees the convenience and portability of technology as a benefit to the individual: "Big data" used to be "available only to large institutions," but the "future of this resource is incredibly open to consumers, activists, and regular people."

Tucker does not ignore the short-term "threat of creeping technototalitarianism." For example, we have already reached the point where law enforcement doesn't need to use bugs, phone taps, or even GPS trackers to trace a target of interest, because "tollbooth, streetlight, and security cameras" as well as the GPS units in our phones and cars can identify anyone's location with relative ease. O'Hara and Shadbolt, in their book *The Spy in the Coffee Machine*, point out the presence of cameras and other sensors in our laptops, phones, televisions, and—yes—coffee machines. We are entering a Philip K. Dick world

where our ubiquitous appliances are aware of us. We have to raise our awareness in turn.

The greatest challenge to privacy in our society, however, comes not from
government but from commerce, specifically "the collection of information and
data for shopping, telecommunication, and leisure purposes" (Weber; Fuchs
et al.). A major feature of personal-computer use in the new century is the dom-
inance of platforms like Google, Facebook and Amazon. While Amazon is
openly selling consumer goods, along with Google and Facebook it is also selling consumers—specifically our personal information: age, gender, and relationships; work, leisure activities, and travel habits; what we search for, what
we buy, what we "like." We condone this arrangement when we accept their
terms of agreement, which explicitly promise a universe of "sharing." Every
click of the mouse produces data that these companies can sell to someone
else. Consumers are thus also producers of value—what some technotheorists
refer to as "prosumers."

Some critics see this relationship in Marxist terms: prosumers are inherently
"alienated" from their work product, and—according to Mark Andrejevic—
they have been "put to work marketing to themselves." As such, this system
"does not signify a democratization of the media toward a participatory or
democratic system, but the total commodification" of the users. McStay seconds this notion by asserting that online "commodification leads to more
commodification" as our desires and interests are sold back to us. But despite
worries about cookies, target marketing, insistent advertising, and consumer/
prosumer commodification, the evidence shows that most users are willing, if
not happy, to trade their personal information for the convenience of the Internet. You don't get freedom of access unless you grant freedom of access.

In any case, this debate is rapidly becoming moot: we increasingly live in the
technocommons, and most of us feel the tradeoff between privacy and access is
worth it. In fact, as the millennials reach their thirties, a generation is growing
up in their wake that has never known a world without the Internet or camera
phones. Privacy does not appear to be high on their list of concerns. This is
the generation that created the "selfie," a method for constantly monitoring
their own whereabouts and sharing it, who created "sexting"—the transmis-
sion of nude or seminude self-portraits, some destined for the web. We have
all seen young couples sitting across from one other at dining tables, spend-
ing their private moments texting on their phones, sending off Instagrams of
themselves or their meals. Big Brother is watching? Time to update one's Facebook page.

In his 2014 *Frontline* documentary *Generation Like,* culture critic Douglas Rushkoff portrays this world of American teens who live a substantial portion of their lives on and through social media. Many are active "prosumers," publicizing themselves, their tastes and their favorite activities via blogs, podcasts, and YouTube, sharing their "likes" in return for promotional T-shirts, shoes, and snack foods from companies delighted at this free advertising to target demographics. Far from seeming alienated by such commodification, they embrace it as a means of social validation. As Rushkoff demonstrates in one sequence, this generation does not know the meaning of "selling out."

On the other hand, for those still determined to defend their privacy against surveillance and salesmanship, there are ready methods for doing so. In his 2015 book *Data and Goliath: The Hidden Battles to Collect Your Data and Control Your World,* Bruce Schneier offers numerous ways to be proactive. One can acquire the technical skills, or find someone with the technical skills, to employ encryption protocols, data blocking, or other PET (privacy-enhancing technology). This is a sophisticated but absolutely feasible possibility, up to a point. Of course simpler, less technical means exist.

You can pay for things in cash instead of using a credit card, or deliberately alter your driving route to avoid traffic cameras. You can refrain from creating Facebook pages for your children and tagging photos of them online. You can refrain from using Google Calendar, or webmail, or cloud backup. You can use DuckDuckGo for Internet searches. You can leave your cell phone at home: an easy, if inconvenient, way to avoid being tracked.

But how many are willing to reduce connection to the technocommons to avoid the all-seeing eye? And always there is the question: will these tricks be easily bypassed by next year's technology . . . or the next . . . or the next?

Perhaps, says cultural critic Slavoj Žižek, "the proper answer to this threat is not retreat into islands of privacy, but an ever stronger socialization of cyberspace." As Christian Fuchs adds, a "commons-based Internet requires a commons-oriented society." We can remain private individuals to some extent, but only if we agree to be public citizens at the same time. This brings us full circle to the conclusion David Brin advanced in *The Transparent Society*: "Again, the cameras *are* coming. You can rail against them, shaking your fist in futile rage at all the hovering lenses. Or you can join a committee of six billion neighbors to control the pesky things, making each one an extension of your eyes."

Big Brother is watching? The whole world is watching. But you are part of that brave new world. Take your responsibilities seriously.

Works Cited:

Brin, David. *The Transparent Society*. Reading MA: Perseus Books, 1998.

Fuchs, Christian, *et al.* (eds). *Internet and Surveillance: The Challenges of Web 2.0 and Social Media*. New York and London: Routledge, 2012.

McStay, Andrew. *Privacy and Philosophy: New Media and Affective Protocol*. New York: Peter Lang, 2014.

O'Hara, Kieron and Nigel Shadbolt. *The Spy in the Coffee Machine: The End of Privacy as We Know It*. Oxford UK: OneWorld, 2008.

Rushkoff, Douglas, and Frank Koughan. *Generation Like*. PBS, 2014. Documentary.

Tucker, Patrick. *The Naked Future*. New York: Penguin/Current, 2014.

NO PLACE TO HIDE

They know what you do
No dark corners to hide in
Know what they do, too

Freedom, safety, empowerment . . .
. . . does any of it matter when life hurts?

PREFERENCES

CAT RAMBO

"Everything's calculated," Alanna said, scowling down at the cruise-ship breakfast menu. "Look at this, for goddess's sake. Salmon Benedict, rye toast, cinnamon latte."

"Those are your favorite things," her wife Howin pointed out. "Be fair now."

For a moment, the two women locked glances. The faint frown clouding Alanna's mouth was echoed upward in Howin's hesitant smile.

They were alike in age (52) and height (5'6"), but, other than that, were as different as could be. Alanna was thick-fleshed, skin a deep brown, graying hair butch-short to the point where it was a mere shadow on her scalp. Howin was skinny-slim, moon-pale, hair still black and shiny, pinned in an elaborate chignon. Both women wore cruise-casual—shorts and a serviceable navy-blue top for Alanna, a butterfly-printed silky shirt for Howin to match the gilt butterfly clip in her hair. They'd taken a table by themselves near a sunlit window, the water outside an endless carefree turquoise blue, the color of Howin's blouse.

"Sure they're my favorites," Alanna said. "They've scraped that from somewhere—maybe some social network, maybe my restaurant orders, who knows?—and linked them to my ship card."

"Are you really complaining about a customized menu?" Howin said. Exasperation and amusement mingled in her tone. She folded the napkin in her lap, pleating it as she watched Alanna.

"There're no secrets anymore," Alanna grumbled. She thumbed the menu, touching items. Red and blue dots bloomed at her touch as she made her choices. She slid it over to join the version Howin had already selected. "What if I wanted to try new things?"

"You never want to try new things," Howin pointed out. "But if you did, I suspect they'd accommodate that too."

"And even those would pander to my tastes," Alanna grumbled. "I'd like it all. No danger of picking something I didn't like."

"Again, I'm not sure what you're complaining about," Howin said. "Relax and enjoy it. You deserve it."

Alanna's gaze flicked up, eyes narrowed. But all she said as one waiter leaned to collect menus while another poured coffee was, "I'll try."

The sky outside was unclouded. Howin splashed cream into her coffee and swirled it till there were no clouds there either.

■ ■ ■

Later, sitting by the fore pool, Howin stared at flickers of light dancing across rows of deck chairs. She'd brought a reader, but only to pretend to read while drowsing in the sun. She loved the drowsy somnolence of the warmth on her skin, the way it knocked her into unthinking slumber more comforting than alcohol or drugs ever would be.

But she couldn't relax into the warmth she usually loved. Alanna had stayed down in the cabin. "I want a nap," she'd said, stretching out on the bed. "Snap the light out as you go."

She napped so often lately. A sign of depression, Howin had read. It worried her.

Three years since their daughter's death. Would they ever reach the point where it didn't weight Alanna's smile? Where Howin didn't feel the memory of Bree's smile sliding like a sudden knife into her heart? She'd thought a Caribbean cruise might banish some of it, fleeing Toronto winter in search of a temporary summer, but all Alanna did was sleep and complain.

Howin flicked through screens, trying to engage herself in the story, but everything was two-dimensional, unappealing.

Two children splashed in the salt-water pool, shrill voices glass-edged. How strange to be here, on this floating city, so isolated from the rest of the world, and yet be reminded of that world daily. No escape.

■ ■ ■

When she went down to the cabin, she found Alanna crying. Howin sat down on the side of the bed and stroked her wife's back, feeling the bumps of her spine, the reverberations of her sobs.

"Shhhh," she said. "Shhhh, shhhh." She curled up beside Alanna and held her.

"I can't get past it," Alanna said into her shoulder. "I can't get past it, and I can't live with it any longer."

Howin had no answer. She had thought perhaps here they could forget grief, so far from home and its daily reminders: Bree's school, her favorite restaurant, the park where she had played as a toddler. The other members of the bereavement support group, who Howin loved and hated. Loved for their support; hated for their necessity.

"Come upstairs," she said gently. "There's a spa just for adults, a pool in the aft section. It's quiet, and there's a hot tub and chairs. Sit in the sun and sleep there."

She could feel Alanna's tears, hotter than sunlight on her skin.

"Everyone will see I've been crying," Alanna said.

"Fuck everyone," Howin said, surprising herself with her simulated firmness.

"I would prefer not to," Alanna said primly.

Howin stroked the soft fuzz along Alanna's scalp, letting it tickle her palm. "Did you just make a joke?"

"Yes. Maybe."

Howin felt herself smiling.

If they could laugh, there was hope. They'd get past it.

But in the end, Alanna declined to come up, staying in the cabin's darkness. Her head hurt, she said.

Howin stayed, rubbing Alanna's back. She listened to the sounds of the ship, the clatter of room service outside, the engines' throb, a couple quarreling, the sounds muted. How long had it been since she and Alanna had fought like that? Since they'd made up afterward?

Alanna's breath slowed, slipping into sleep as the distant couple stopped their shouting. Were they to the making up part yet?

■ ■ ■

A few decks above, she paused by the excursion desk's bank of interactive screens, each showcasing a different possibility, displays rearranging themselves as she neared. Would it be worthwhile booking something? They'd be in Puerto Rico the next day, but so far Alanna had resisted the idea of going ashore anyplace they'd stopped.

Images flickered in front of her: boating, water-skiing, snorkeling. A tour bus for sightseeing. And simple, easy: walk to the Castillo San Cristobal.

Howin allowed herself to be persuaded.

When she presented the idea to Alanna, she got the protest she expected. But she pushed.

Demurral after demurral. "I need a sun hat," Alanna said. "I can't go."

Howin drew her out of the cabin, fingers firm around Alanna's wrist. "That's why they have shops on board."

She ignored Alanna's protests, pulled her to Deck Five with its array of stores. The goods were shown on panels on the walls: pick your preferences and they'd be printed out in the colors and textures you wanted, each item marked with the blue and red dot that was the Jubilee cruise line's logo and the words, "A Jubilee Souvenir."

Like the excursion screens, the pictures changed whenever someone approached, flickering through choices. Alanna stared at the revolving circle of hats.

"Don't you like any of them?" Howin coaxed.

"I like them all," Alanna said. "How could I not? They're reading my preferences again. Tailoring things just to me."

"Why is that bad?"

Alanna's face was unreadable. She refused to speak, just pushed her way out roughly. Howin followed in her wake, bewildered.

She caught up at the railing. For a second she worried that Alanna planned to jump, but the other woman just folded herself over the railing, gathering herself into misery.

"What's wrong?" Howin said.

"They know me," Alanna said. "I can't be anyone but myself. Alanna Yang, wife of Howin Yang. Mother of . . ." Her voice faltered, then steadied. "Mother of Brianna Yang. Deceased. How can I forget that when it's part of who I am?"

"It's not every part of you," Howin said. She slid her hand along Alanna's arm, reached down to twine their fingers together, merging their grasp. "A piece of you."

She went back and bought a hat, using Alanna's card.

"Come out in the morning with me," she said. "You don't want to shop here, well, you can find something there."

"It's the same everywhere," Alanna said. "A world tailored to me, trying to get me to buy. Telling me who I am."

Howin shook her head. "Just try," she said. "Please."

■　■　■

She was delighted that Alanna accompanied her. But when she turned around in the surge of a cruise ship's worth of tourists and realized she couldn't find her, fear and alarm throttled Howin's throat. Who knew what Alanna would do, here in this place so far from home?

The steward waiting by the gangplank didn't understand her fear.

"Maybe she went to buy you a present?" the young woman, dressed in blue and red, chirped. "You said she's only been gone a half hour."

Howin couldn't put her forebodings into words. She couldn't say, "I lost my daughter and I'm afraid I'll lose my wife."

Instead she waited near the gangplank for an hour, standing in the shadow of the enormous cruise ship, sorting through faces.

Finally Alanna's hat approached, bobbing in the crowd.

"Where have you been?" Howin said, torn between anger and joy at the smile on Alanna's face.

"I found a place where no one knew me," Alanna said. "I went up the streets and down the streets. There was a stall, a little roadside stall, not a shop with a printer, selling these."

She held out something in her hand. A tiny wooden puzzle box carved with monarch butterflies.

"An old woman selling them. She was even a little rude to me because I didn't have the right change. How funny, that I liked that, after all the attentiveness of the ship. Remember these?" The butterflies were painted orange and black. "They were her favorite."

Howin took the box in her hand, shaky with relief.

"Not tailored to me," Alanna said. "A coincidence. A happy coincidence. Something made for the sake of making it, not something data-driven, designed to appeal to me." She smiled.

The box's wood, so smooth beneath her fingers.

"I'm going to shower," Alanna said. "Tonight, let's sit by the pool after dinner. We can get drinks. Remember how we used to sit under the stars, when we were first dating?"

"All right," Howin said. "You go ahead, I'll catch up. I want to get a photo of the ship from here."

She waited till Alanna was gone before sliding the panels aside, unraveling the puzzle. When the final drawer opened, she saw what she had expected there.

A tiny blue and red dot, surrounded by the lettering. "A Jubilee Souvenir."

She wavered. Grief was real. And if its anodyne was artificial, what happened then?

The box poised on her fingertips, so light.

Tears were so heavy.

Howin tilted her hand and let it fall into the water between pier and ship, down into blue shadows, vague and uncalculated, before she went aboard to join her wife.

Peel back the layers. And guess what?
There will be more.

VECTORS

STEPHEN GASKILL

Chad Legarde, decked in traditional chef's whites, the top collar of his pristine double-breasted jacket unbuttoned in his trademark style, crashes through dense rainforest. Insects buzz, birds chirrup, while unseen monkeys shriek and large cats growl, but Chad looks cool as ice. Scaling a gnarly tree trunk with the agility of a marmoset he reaches the canopy, plucks off a dew-glistened bunch of bananas. In one swift movement he ties the bananas to his belt, simultaneously ascending through the top of the treeline into bright sunshine. Without pausing, he takes one, two steps over the green quilt, before launching himself into a dive worthy of an Olympic medalist.

He crashes into icy waters, and the splash loops out of the screen.

Zoe and her brother, Luke, both flinch as the spray showers the sofa, then pretend they didn't.

Emerging from the waters onto a rock-pooled shoreline, Chad strides up the beach, plucks a scarlet-hued lobster out of a shallow pool, the crustacean's claws snapping ferociously.

Then the camera swings round, head-to-toe Chad dead center. In the background, the icy seas have morphed into a familiar urban skyline: far off thrust the gleaming towers of Canary Wharf, while closer the haphazard tenements of Brixton loom. Dominating the view is GeneLife's flagship vertical farm, thirty-eight floors of precision-engineered crops and plants shining green and vital, capped by an avant-garde restaurant named The Gastronomique.

"I used to handpick produce for my kitchen," Chad says confidently. "Now thanks to GeneLife, I no longer have to go to the ends of the Earth. And neither do you."

As he says the last words he swings the snapping lobster toward the camera. The crustacean whirls, body flexing, claws pincering, its scarlet girth getting larger and larger until it shatters the screen and flies through the living room, chips of glass in its acrobatic wake.

They shriek simultaneously, both ripping off their spex.

Luke dissolves into a pool of laughter.

Zoe doesn't, too on edge.

Today's the day.

"Okay, time for work." She gazes out the window, catching an oblique view of the vertical farm that towers over their neighborhood. She kills the TV, GeneLife's logo fleeing to a white dot.

Luke's laughter has morphed into a coughing fit.

Zoe rubs her sick brother's back. "Hey, take it easy there."

Luke nods, but his face is red as beets.

Knowing what is a sign of the illness and what is simply an everyday matter anybody might experience is one of the things Zoe finds hardest about her brother's condition. Sometimes she drives herself crazy analyzing every cough, every stumble, every trip of his tongue.

Luke is fifteen, suffering from a disorder without a name. MRIs show his shrinking cerebellum, stunting development. Without a cure, eventually, inexorably, he will regress, then die. Medical geneticists at Great Ormond Street Hospital analyzed his DNA. Somewhere in the millions of As, Gs, Cs, and Ts is a misspelling—and maybe a clue to a treatment. But unless they find another patient with the same symptoms, and a similar DNA error, his doctors can't zero in on which mistake in Luke's genes is the crucial one.

And that's the crux.

They can't.

The words of one of the geneticists echo through her head.

The problem, Zoe, is that the world's DNA databases are fragmented, ring-fenced.

Out of the nine billion on the planet, there is probably someone who shares Luke's condition *and* has been DNA-sequenced, but the segregated nature of the databases makes finding that one patient impossible. Hundreds of corps scattered through dozens of countries own the data, and corps everywhere only care about one thing: profit. Overcoming the ethical, technical and legislative hurdles to share information isn't high on their priority list.

Luke's only hope is the black market.

And the black market isn't cheap.

And so for the love of her brother, it's come to this: aiding her contacts at Green Dawn in bringing down her employer, GeneLife.

Today GeneLife launches their brand-new genetically engineered superfood—vitan, a modified seaweed. As part of a media blitz, Chad Legarde, celeb chef and critic, will cook up a feast for VIPs in the vertical farm's penthouse restaurant.

Green Dawn wants to sabotage the launch.

Which is where Zoe comes in.

Conflicted isn't the half of it. Try torn in two.

After Luke's coughing fit subsides, she ducks into the tiny spare bedroom, squeezing past the shelf of Pyrex containers and Erlenmeyer flasks. The room smells of chemicals, pure alcohol, agarose sugar, and an earthy mix. Together with the homemade lightbox, the makeshift PCR machine, and all the other clinical-looking equipment, the bedroom looks perfect for cooking crystal meth.

And maybe that's not so far from the truth.

She'd never anticipated becoming a bioterrorist.

It had begun as a means of not feeling completely useless in the face of the constant dead ends that Luke had been led down by his doctors. She knew the signs even before they uttered a word. Pursed lips, brief exhalation, sympathetic eyes. "I'm sorry . . ." Every speculative diagnosis, every tentative treatment regime ended in failure.

So Zoe ordered the genomics kit, the open-source circuit board, the enzymes, the software libraries, and all the rest, swabbed under Luke's tongue, and hunted for the mistake in her brother's DNA. A needle in a haystack didn't come close. Aside from some illuminating side projects like getting bacteria to bioluminesce, her investigations came to nothing. But she did learn some skills . . .

She moves deeper into the dim room.

The desk holds several laptops, test tubes, a box of surgical gloves, a rack with pipettes in various sizes, and a centrifuge that looks like an oversized rice cooker, but she's headed to the small fridge under the desk. The fridge door opens with a puckering noise. Icy vapor spreads, causing the hairs on Zoe's arm to rise. She fans it away, staring at neat rows of strawberries plump and inviting, their color the most vivid scarlet.

Her hand wavers over the first strawberry, but any lingering doubts are dispelled as she recalls Luke's last hospital visit. *I'm afraid there's nothing more we can do.* Rapidly, yet methodically, Zoe transfers most of the strawberries to a custom-designed cool container that outwardly looks like a designer handbag.

Zipping up the bag, she grabs her coat, then gives her brother a quick kiss on the top of the head. "The rest of those strawberries are still off limits."

"What did you *do* to them?"

Zoe doesn't answer.

Leaving, she holds off slamming the front door, hollers into the apartment. "I love you."

Then she's gone.

■ ■ ■

She's only walked a stone's throw from her apartment block, skirting past a scrum of Londoners fighting to get on the No. 17 bus, when her cell rings. *Private number*, but she suspected as much before looking.

Her stomach balls.

She swipes, answers. "Zoe Parsons."

"You're running late."

Scottish accent, terse, female. Zoe's usual contact, and one of the leaders of Green Dawn, she suspects. *Call me Tess*, she said the first time they spoke, but using the alias has never come easy to Zoe. Hard as titanium nails.

"You're tracking my phone?"

Damn geolocation tech. Privacy's a thing of the past.

"Of course we're tracking your fucking phone," the woman says. "Do you have the merchandise?"

Zoe instinctively pats her handbag, feels a *frisson* of cold on her fingers.

The familiar justifications for what's she doing circle. GeneLife's aims for the vertical farms were noble when they first tendered plans for their construction. Reduce water consumption, lower land use, shorten the distance between field and plate to reduce energy consumption. Problem was, when the shareholders wrested control of the company they discovered there was little profit in growing staple foodstuffs for the masses. Catering for the wealthy was where real money could be made. Luxury foods displaced simple grains, exotic fruits grown instead of wheat, vast petri dishes of prime Aberdeen beef instead of tightly packed cod farms.

Green Dawn wants to scare off the investors, bring GeneLife back into public ownership. Zoe can live with that.

"Yes, I've got the merchandise." She's coming up to a busy intersection, pedestrians amassing at the crossing as they wait for the little green man, so she hangs back not wanting to be overheard. Traffic streams past smoothly, electric engines with electric minds. "Is that all?"

These calls make her nervous. Even with a disposable cell, untraceable to her, phone companies hold records of numbers, call times, call durations, maybe even the content of the calls themselves.

The quantified self can incriminate as much as it can liberate.

"No, that's not all," Tess says. "We've got a problem—well, more precisely we've got two."

Zoe's heartbeat gets a little faster. She swerves around the homeless guy in his cardboard kingdom, almost knocking his electronic donations reader flying.

"What problems?"

"Nothing insurmountable," Tess says cockily, "but you're going to need to do a little more for us today."

"Goddamn."

"Now, now, that's not the right attitude."

Zoe glances around, lowers her voice. "The right attitude? I've done everything you've asked—each time for less than we agreed!" Along the side of the Tesco superstore where the delivery trucks come in, a ragtag line has already begun forming in front of the food banks. "Tell me how my attitude could be better?"

"Let me make this clear, Zoe," Tess says, deadpan. "If the authorities should ever get word of your indiscretions . . . well, how do you think that would pan out for you?"

Zoe stops dead, chilled.

"You wouldn't," she whispers.

"Not if we don't have to, no."

Zoe's hand's shaking, so she presses the phone closer to her ear to still her trembling. "What do I need to do?" she manages.

"That's better," Tess says. "Now listen carefully. First off, the operative we had planned to be in The Gastronomique . . ."

While Tess gives her the instructions, part of Zoe's brain is definitely listening, considering all the angles of what she's being asked, but a larger part of her attention is in a daze. London slides past, like she's watching all the street life take place underwater, while she observes from above the surface.

Inside a luxury grocers' stocked with the shiny fruits of GeneLife's labor, a man in a green tweed jacket examines some mangoes with his hands, exchanging a joke with the shopkeep. Across the road, in a children's playground devoid of any green space, two kids bully a third, keeping their victim on a merry-go-round and spinning it mercilessly. At a street market, a bent-backed old lady examines knobbled potatoes riddled with black marks, while a harried mother argues with the thick bearded vendor, gesticulating with a misshapen onion.

A rising inflection in Tess' voice snaps Zoe back to the conversation. "—said, did you get all that?"

"I got it," she replies. "One, I need to film the fallout in The Gastronomique. Two, you want me to dig up any intel I can on vitan."

Within the last twenty-four hours, Green Dawn had got wind that Gene-Life had signed a secret government contract with the Home Office to develop some of kind of surveillance biotech that could gather data on the populace.

Vitan was suspected as the delivery vector.

"Good. And Zoe . . . "

"Yes?"

"Don't fuck this up."

The line goes dead.

Zoe stares at the screen for a moment, pockets her phone.

What the hell am I doing?

Turning a corner, she's confronted by the towering vertical farm, a steel-and-glass marvel, bright green foliage pressing against its thirty-eight floors of gleaming exterior like the twisted hands of drowning men clutching for the sun. Gazing upward to the restaurant on its summit, the sunshine dazzles, and she feels light-headed.

Somebody grazes past, cursing.

The nausea passes.

You're doing this for Luke, she thinks, galvanizing herself. *It's this or nothing.*

The celebs' arrival is still hours away, yet barricades have already been arranged, and a motley crew of students, tourists, and devoted fans sit around listlessly. "We ♥ you, Jude!" reads one placard. Media from some of the bigger newsfeeds, the logos on their jackets competing to be the biggest and brashest, wander between the bystanders. A few private security bods decked out in luminous yellow jackets are constructing a screening area like you find at airports: conveyor belt with CT scanner for bags, Tardis-sized full-body scanner for people, tables for rifling through suspect items.

Drones hover, recording everything.

She strides forward, making a beeline for the main entrance to circumvent the private security, her grip tightening on the straps of her handbag. One of the security guys, a big lethargic man with his long hair tied up neatly behind his head, clicks his fingers at her. "Excuse me, Miss."

Zoe doesn't break stride, simply fishes her GeneLife badge—*Zoe Parsons, Agronomist*—from the front pocket of her suit jacket, and holds it up for the man to see. "I work here."

He moves to block her path, glancing at the main entrance, probably hoping to see one of the permanent security staff, but nobody's in eyeshot. "Sorry, Miss. You know how it is. Rules." He rubs his neck. "If you can show me the letter that went out to all onsite employees, together with some ID, otherwise . . ."

Zoe's stomach drops.

"Really, I've got a lot to do this morning."

The security guy shrugs. "If you'll just step over here."

In her mind's eye she sees the neatly folded letter sitting on the small kitchen table in the flat, forgotten in her haste and worry. Another employee she doesn't recognize shows the necessary documents and gets waved past. Zoe's caught the woman's name on her driving license: *Melinda Jacobs.*

"Melinda!" she calls to the woman's receding heels.

The woman swivels, defenses up.

"Could you vouch for me, Mel?" Zoe says, as if they're longtime lab buddies. "I left that blasted letter at home."

The woman raises her eyebrows, face softening. "Sure," she says, stepping closer, peeking at Zoe's GeneLife badge. "I know Zoe."

Before the security guy can protest, Mel has linked arms with Zoe, and corralled her away.

"Thanks for that," Zoe says. "I hate those full-body scanners."

"No drama. I recognized you anyway."

"You did?"

"Loved your old handbag." She peers at Zoe's new handbag, wedged tight under her elbow. "Not sure about the new one though."

■ ■ ■

On an average day, the vertical farm is a swirl of activity, but today it's even busier. The zero-hour contractors—the fruit pickers, soil maintainers, pesticide sprayers, and the rest of the menial staff—are coming in and filing down into the vast basement changing room where they'll slip into their regulation tan-colored coveralls.

The office staff head straight for the eight central elevators that run through the building's spine, and are whisked up to the office complex on the eighteenth and nineteenth floors, a rabbit's warren of cubicle desks surrounded by meeting rooms, conference suites, kitchenettes, and the management's offices.

The rest of the human flux comprise the vertical farm's visitors—buyers from the upmarket chains, school tour groups, press packs, today even a fact-finding mission from Beijing—and last but not least, Zoe's own tribe: GeneLife's scientists and technicians.

Busy is good. Busy means Zoe can move between the levels attracting less attention. Busy means she might actually pull this off.

She heads for the lifts, slides into the least crowded elevator, and punches the button for the fifteenth floor—*Vaccinium, Rubus, Fragaria,* the genera of some of the nation's favorite fruit snacks. Raspberries and blackberries, blueberries and cranberries—and strawberries. One of her colleagues, a botanist whose fingertips are always grimy with dirt, makes small talk as the lift smoothly ascends.

"Snag some dewberries if you can!" he says, laughing as she exits.

Zoe winces inside, but doesn't break stride. The last thing she needs today are people remembering her movements. She's just glad the only CCTV cameras in the building are limited to the lobby area on the ground floor.

Act natural.

Already the heat of the vast banks of artificial lighting that swathe the ceiling of every floor are making her sweat, and the leafy fields of berries shine under the fierce illumination. The hydroponics that sustain every crop, a nutrient bath calibrated to the nth degree, gives the air a chemical tang. Together with the heightened CO_2 levels and the warmth, it's not a comfortable place to work.

Lucky for me.

She moves on, glides past the huge cold station where the freshly picked produce sits on beds of chilled air, ready to be transported to the packing area on the third floor. The semitransparent curtains peel open as a worker brushes through, and inside she spies a layer of fat blackberries gleaming like the finest caviar, frost steaming into the air. Somewhere inside the station, the produce destined for the restaurant—and Chad Legarde's culinary masterpieces—wait on a trolley.

Produce that includes a handful of plump strawberries.

Before she makes the switch though, she's got to keep up appearances.

After grabbing some cuttings for an experiment she's been planning for weeks, she heads back for the cold station—and her unscheduled, completely off-the-record stop. As she's about to enter, the translucent curtains that mark the entrance to the station begin to part. A trolley slides out. It carries neatly ordered baskets of berries of many varieties, its pilot still hidden behind the curtains—

Her heart stops.

One of the fancy bespoke menus from The Gastronomique is perched on the end of the trolley, its florid typeface clear to see. She'd recognize it anywhere, given the amount of time she spent staring at its contents, working out where she could weave her biohacking magic most effectively. Somebody, probably Chad himself, has annotated the menu with bold pen strokes, no doubt instructions detailing the necessary ingredients from this level.

I'm too late.

The curtain flaps back, the trolley's lanky pilot emerging. One of the kitchen hands from the restaurant, judging by the disheveled, food-stained whites he wears.

"Zoe?"

She takes a better look at his face, realizes. One of Luke's friends' older brothers. She hardly knows him, but she did help him land the job upstairs by getting his CV in front of the restaurant manager. "Tim, isn't it?"

"Yeah, Tim." His raises his eyebrows. "How you doing? You look a little freaked."

"Stressful day."

"Tell me about it. Chad Legarde? You think he hams it up for the cameras?" He shakes his head. "Uh-uh. Serious ballbreaker. For real." He launches into an impression of the chef. "You dickhead, where did you learn to cook, your local kebab shop?"

"God. He sounds awful."

Tim nods. "Thanks for helping me get the job, by the way."

She wracks her brains for some cunning fix, some means by which it wouldn't be really fucking weird if she insisted on taking ownership of the trolley and its cargo of fresh berries at this precise moment, but she's got nothing.

"How's Luke?"

"Good," she says, but her mind doesn't let her get away with the lie so easily. Emotion threatens to overwhelm her, and her eyes film up. "Actually, not so good. Unless something changes, it's only a matter of time."

"Sorry, dumb question. I shouldn't have asked."

"No," Zoe replies, pinching the corners of her eyes between thumb and index finger, stemming any tears. "I'm glad you asked."

Tim rubs his neck, leans on the trolley. "I better get back, I guess. Chef's waiting."

A faint odor of cigarette smoke clings to his whites, and she suddenly remembers that he became a chain smoker, forever on the roll-ups, after kicking a brutal heroin habit a few years back. That's why employment was always such a problem for him. She glances at his fingertips, spies the telltale staining.

"Still smoking?"

He looks embarrassed. "Is it that obvious?"

"No, not at all." She smiles. "I just thought you might want a ciggie break. I'm heading up to Botanics so I could whisk this up for you—it's headed for the restaurant, right?"

"You would?" He eyes the glistening produce on the trolley, wisps of frost still eddying off. "Chef wants this stuff back ASAP. You'll go straight there, right?"

"Absolutely."

"I owe you." He scurries off for his nicotine hit.

Zoe grabs the trolley, wheels it straight to the nearby service lift. She punches the call button. *Come on, come on.* When the doors open with a soft hiss, she's relieved to see it's empty.

She wheels the trolley inside, hits the button for The Gastronomique.

As soon as the doors hiss close, she springs into action.

Zoe transfers the biohacked strawberries into the punnets, fighting her shaking fingers and carefully ferrying each one individually so they don't bruise. Afterward, she delves into her handbag and adds a layer of normal strawberries to each punnet in case anyone helps themselves to a cheeky one before they get prepped. Just as the lift arrives at the restaurant level, she pops the tainted produce back on the trolley.

Mouth-watering smells and a clatter of sounds.

"Ingredients for Chef Legarde," she says to a passing kitchen hand, keeping her head down. "Could you get them to the fridges?"

He doesn't even glance, taking the trolley. "Sure."

Zoe backs up and punches a button. "Thanks."

No turning back now.

■ ■ ■

For the next few hours she focuses on keeping up her normal routine.

Writing reports, a little lab study, gossiping with colleagues about who's on the guest list for the shindig upstairs. *Only the ones who deserve all they've got coming,* she hopes.

She laughs along, tries to act regular.

After a solitary lunch in one of the staff canteens, outwardly reading on her spex like she often does, but in actuality reading nothing and simply plotting how she's going to pull off the improbable, she heads off alone for Algae.

Entering the vast watery floor where the new superfood is being grown, she walks blind into writhing darkness as her eyes adjust to the night cycle. An intense smell of seaweed and the sea fills the air, and then as her pupils contract, the algal farm ghosts out of the darkness, all faint lines and watery ripple. Dim lighting studs the ceiling at uniform intervals, casting the shimmering water and its kelp forests in a soft glow. Metal gantries crisscross the lapping water, glinting in the illumination.

Silence reigns.

Please let him be here.

Removing her flats, she places them neatly beside the metal steps, then climbs onto the nearest gantry. Tiny waves lap against the crossgrid hatching, wetting the soles of her feet. Thick strands of the kelp drift back and forth in the artificial current, the tangle so dense she cannot see more than a couple of handspans below the surface.

You wouldn't want to fall in.

Scanning the landscape of watery tanks that disappear into darkness, she sees no sign of anyone.

"Professor Ramage?" she calls, her voice shattering the quiet. "Anyone?"

The waters swallow her words, offer nothing in return.

She crouches, delves a hand into the tepid waters, pinches a piece of the super-kelp between thumb and forefinger. The fibrous strand has a textured feel, less rubbery than your garden-variety kelp, and more palatable to modern tastes.

What are you hiding?

Tess's words echoed in her head. *Find out what you can.*

Zoe tears off a piece of the kelp, gives it a sniff.

Briny, but otherwise odorless.

It was an ingenious idea.

People would eat the food, enjoy it for its nutritious and tasty qualities, yet have no inkling they might be inviting a biochemical Trojan horse into their bodies. Who knew what purpose it might serve? Finding recreational drug users for the police. Identifying those with fatal diseases for life-insurance firms. Hell, maybe it was simply delivering an agent that made people docile.

Analyzing the kelp's twenty thousand or so genes would give little clue as to which ones might be facilitating the biotech, as the genes interacted in dizzyingly complex ways with each other and the host environment.

Examining the intestinal flora of somebody who'd eaten the superkelp would be equally unenlightening, any active microbial agents hidden among the trillions-strong bacterial and viral zoo.

No, the only way one might uncover such manipulations would be to get hold of the design—or the designer. One Professor Peter Ramage, most likely. He was GeneLife's Head of Biological Research; politically well-connected, monomolecular sharp, and somebody who still liked to get their hands dirty.

"Zoe!"

Startled, she drops the piece of vitan, like somebody might've been eavesdropping on her thoughts. She twists. It's *him*.

"Professor Ramage?"

"My apologies for sneaking up on you like that," he says, mischievously. He's in his forties, but his face is boyish. "A weakness of mine, I'm afraid."

"Lucky I wasn't holding anything valuable."

The lanyard of his ID badge trails from the pocket of his black woolen jacket. He glances at the piece of broken kelp. "Oh, that kelp is incredibly valuable, believe me."

The silence is just getting uncomfortable when he speaks again. "What are you doing here anyway?" Realizing his confrontational tone, he attempts to add some levity. "Not trying to sabotage our new superfood, eh?"

He's on edge, Zoe thinks.

"I find this place soothing," she replies. "The lap of the water, the sway of the fronds, the peace. And during a night cycle with the bioluminescence casting everything in a soft glow? Bliss." Then, studying his face carefully, she hits him with the question. "What secrets does this vitan hide, Professor Ramage?"

"What?" His eyes are wide, and his skin has paled.

So it's true.

"I mean this stuff lowers cholesterol, reduces blood pressure, raises protein absorption—how did you achieve all those amazing health benefits?"

"Right, the health benefits." Like the passing shadow of a fleeting cloud, he relaxes again. "Come by the labs next week, and I'll let you in on a secret or two."

"Sure." She gets up. "So, I better get back now. " She skips down the steps, fakes a trip, and collides with the professor. "I'm so sorry!"

"No harm done."

Down by her side, his ID badge is now tight in her palm.

He'll only notice it's gone when he tries to get back in his office.

By that time she plans to be long gone.

"Next week, Professor Ramage," she says. "I'll hold you to that."

■ ■ ■

On the way up to the cubicle complex where Ramage's office is located, Zoe puts on her spex, checks his public diary. Media duties and the Beijing delegation occupy his next couple of hours. After that it's showtime with Chad Legarde. He won't be stopping by his office anytime soon, so she doesn't need to rush.

Yet.

She makes lazy orbits of his office, checking in with nearby colleagues, downtiming in the nearest VR pit, brainstorming on the corridor smartboard, but a good opportunity fails to materialize. It's getting close to the point when she'll need to be upstairs, when a buzz of excitement ripples through the cubicles.

"Jude Law's coming up!"

"That the guy from *Minority Report VI*?"

Like meerkats, heads bob up across the office.

"Nah, that's Tom Cruise. You never seen *Gattaca*? Solid chrome."

"Wow, dude must be ancient. The wonders of modern medicine."

Zoe's colleagues are filing to the elevators, chatting excitedly.

This is my chance.

Except one recalcitrant worker sat two strides from Ramage's office door isn't budging. There's no way Zoe's sneaking in unnoticed. She pulls on her spex, sidles up to the woman. *Ruth Travis, Human Resources Associate*, reads the text scrolling across the crest of her lenses. Through blink-gesture recog Zoe fires off a snifferbot to scrape whatever info she can about this Ruth Travis.

"Not a fan of Jude?"

"I can't stand him."

Zoe turns toward the hubbub across the office, ostensibly to seem as if she's considering the commotion, when in reality she's swiftly scanning the data on Ruth. Saccading eyes are a dead giveaway that you're not giving someone your full attention, or worse—giving them a digital once-over—when wearing spex.

Zoe skims: *Thirty-seven . . . divorced . . . resides in Islington . . . one child, Elsie . . . vice-president of the Islington Ladies Lawn Tennis Association . . . favorite books include—*

Zoe has an idea.

"Me neither," she says. "And his current flame, Anastasia *whatsherface*, you know, the tennis brat—I *despise* her."

"He's dating Anastasia Karpolenko?"

"As far as I know."

Ruth cranes her neck. "Do you think she might be with him now?"

"I'd bet on it."

Ruth's off in a dash, her desk chair spinning in her wake. "My daughter's a huge fan," she calls over her shoulder. "She'll kill me if I don't even *try* to get an autograph."

Zoe doesn't waste any time, slips into Ramage's office before Ruth is out of sight. Heart hammering she rifles through his desk drawers, flicks through his filing cabinet, but even in the paperwork pertaining to vitan, there's no inkling of anything related to any hidden biosurveillance. She's ready to give up, when her gaze alights on the bottle of scotch and accompanying tumbler on the chest-high walnut bar table by the window. A smear of liquor clings to the side of the glass.

Drinking.

What if he isn't simply tense?

What if he's having second thoughts?

She stares out the floor-to-ceiling windows. London stretches away beneath her, a patchwork of gleaming towers and dilapidated ghettos, wealth and poverty, every one of the million upon millions caught in chaotic tides that sweep them into unknown—and unknowable—futures.

On a hunch, Zoe crouches.

Taped to the underside of the table is a transparent folder, a sheaf of papers inside. Even from an oblique angle two bold words are clear: **EYES ONLY.**

Thirty seconds later, adrenalized and euphoric, she's on her way to the elevators, the memory card of her smart phone a few megabytes closer to capacity. She'll upload them to Green Dawn's anonymous servers as soon as she's given them a quick—

"Hey!"

It's like somebody's thrown a bucket of ice water over her.

Game's up, sister.

She swivels—to find the human resources woman staring at her with an expression half-pitying, half-annoyed. "FYI," she says, "Jude Law isn't dating Anastasia Karpolenko!"

Zoe's heart beats again. "Damn, I'm sure I read that somewhere. Sorry!"

Outside the elevators she discreetly drops Ramage's ID badge beside the potted yucca plants. Then she's heading up to The Gastronomique for the final business of the day: a little spot of guerilla filming.

● ● ●

"Strictly only official guests, ma'am."

The security guard's neck is as wide as his head, sinews straining against the collar of his tux, and he's mastered the art of the *conversation closed* look. Already his attention's moved onto the next guest in the line.

Zoe ducks away, calls Tim, the kitchen porter, through her spex.

"Hey Zoe," he answers, shouting, a background din of clanging pans and barked orders threatening to drown out his voice. "What can I do for you?"

"I need to get into the vitan launch party," she replies. "But I don't have an invite. Think you could sneak me in through the kitchens?"

"For you, no drama."

"Thanks, Tim. Two mins, service elevator doors."

"Gotcha."

Two minutes later, Zoe steps out the service elevator doors, a perspiring Tim giving her a quick smile and a flick of the head. "Follow me."

Thirty seconds later, after zigzagging through the steamy helter-skelter of the Gastronomique's kitchens attracting several looks ranging from cheeky winks to undisguised disgust, Chad Legarde issuing a constant stream of orders as he whirls around his culinary domain, Zoe is milling with the rest of the guests.

She snatches a flute of champagne from a passing silver tray, drains the glass, then snatches a second glass before the tray's out of arm's reach. The alcohol races to her head, but she needs its relaxing warmth.

Any second somebody's going to clock you for the interloper you are.

The restaurant's usual complement of tables have been cleared away, the two hundred or so guests mingling in small groups across the marble floor, their chatter noisy like the roar of a river. A small podium constructed in the heart of the space is empty except for some vitan promotional banners and a microphone. Tangled fronds drape from the low ceilings, interspersed with soft off-white globes reminiscent of giant pearls, subconsciously proclaiming the message that this new superfood is as healthy and natural as other fruits of the sea.

Healthy? Perhaps.

Natural? No chance.

She taps her phone, an intense desire to give those EYES ONLY photos a closer inspection, but now isn't the time.

What have they slipped into the geneline?

What do they want to know?

Soon as she uploads the pics to the Green Dawn servers, those secrets will be common knowledge, and it'll be out of her hands.

Then I can concentrate on what's important: Luke.

Near the podium, there's a ripple of excitement, and suddenly Chad Legarde leaps into sight. "Excuse me." Zoe pushes through the throng, gets closer to the action.

"Ladies and gentlemen," Chad begins, his delivery animated, "it is with great pleasure that I welcome you to The Gastronomique. When GeneLife invited me to prepare a menu to celebrate the launch of their brand-new superfood, vitan, I felt deeply honored. For a chef, kelp is traditionally a difficult ingredient . . ."

At the edge of the restaurant Zoe can see the serving staff congregating by the entrance to the kitchens, their platters stocked with the first dish—*avocado and walnut mousse with strawberry shavings.* She feels another bout of revulsion, thinking about what's coming for the diners. Shaking off her misgivings, she starts filming with a discreet tilt of her smart phone; recording with her spex is out of the question due to the ID tagging.

The footage is streaming live onto Green Dawn servers.

Two minutes and I can be out of here.

While she waits for Chad to finish his speech, her phone still recording, she navigates to her gallery application. The temptation to wait any longer before learning what GeneLife is smuggling into the vitan geneline is too great to resist. She flicks past the first couple of images, then zooms in with a reverse pinching motion when she comes to the meat of the classified document.

The truth stuns.

Green Dawn were right about the surveillance biotech.

Vitan is designed with a sophisticated panoply of genes that, once activated in the host environment, will construct a small biological arsenal capable of gathering a whole suite of medical data on the subject.

Cellular health. Genetic damage. Toxin levels.

And DNA sequences.

What they'd not figured though was that this data would be *anonymized.*

The tech wasn't going to be used to identify anyone.

It was going to be used to build a detailed and highly accurate picture of the health of the *nation.* Via this data, health services could be planned that would be precisely tailored to the needs of the country. Without money wasted on well-intentioned but ultimately ineffective programs, millions upon millions of pounds, not to mention countless lives, would be saved. With this technology in the wild, the chances of a cure for Luke's condition became a little less slim.

Vitan could revolutionize medicine.

And it could only happen if it was kept top secret.

Ramage had understood only too well that the government's clandestine plans for vitan could make it a tremendous force for good.

His quandary must have focused on whether the asking price for such a system—covert, invasive surveillance, paternalistic, even if well-intended— was too high.

And it seems like he thinks not.

Of course this whole scheme was offensive, at one level. The paternalistically secretive approach couldn't be allowed to stand for long, or the potential for Big Brother abuse would grow. No wonder Ramage was collecting a thorough dossier, to make it all public and transparent at the right time. After the benefits flow, when it's too late for insurance companies to silo the shared information people need.

That Luke needs.

And I almost ruined it. Zoe frowned. *Ramage is smarter and wiser than me. And I almost spoiled it.*

". . . so without further ado, I present my first dish. Bon appetit."

Still reeling from her discovery, Zoe kills the gallery app, returns to live camera footage. With mounting worry, she watches the first guests grab their starters and tuck in. She makes sure they're in focus on her screen. The modified strawberries don't take long to perform their magic, rogue elements in their biochemistry reacting with human saliva.

Distaste comes first, the diners spitting the rancid-tasting food into their napkins, but the chemical party in their mouths is only just getting started and they're along for a much more turbulent ride. The retching begins, diners succumbing like dominoes, some projectile vomiting, others dry heaving the acid bile of empty stomachs.

Chad Legarde looks on in horror.

People are screaming, piling for the exit.

Zoe's one of them, the ruinous footage already uploaded. And yet, at her core there is relief. *They didn't lie about the poison. Just nausea, they promised.*

If Green Dawn had used Zoe instead to *kill* . . . ? Zoe knew she would have spent the rest of her life hunting them down.

In the tide of bodies, she checks one of the newsfeeds on her phone, and her jerky footage stares back at her, the story already making news headlines. Switching to the markets, she watches GeneLife's share price drop like a line scratched by an angry child.

The crash means the government will take over GeneLife.

The board won't be accountable to the shareholders.

They'll be accountable to the electorate.

Things wouldn't change overnight, but they *would* change.

And Luke's going to get a chance.

Outside, her cell rings.

"Nice work," says Tess.

"Fifty thousand, right?"

"You'll get your payment. What did you learn about vitan?"

Zoe listens to a distant siren racing through the city. "Nothing," she lies. "And it wasn't for a lack of effort. Maybe your information was wrong."

She'll be damned if she's the one who shuts down vitan.

Tess snorts. "You'll have to sniff around again after the dust settles."

"Uh-uh. I'm out."

"What did I tell you before?" Tess says with a nasty edge. "We own you."

"Nobody owns me," Zoe snaps back. "I told you. I'm out."

She hangs up. Maybe she agrees with Green Dawn's aims, but she doesn't agree with their methods. *What I did, I did for Luke.*

Green Dawn won't expose her. They've got too much to lose, throwing one of their own under the bus. They'll pay her the money, and then she and Luke will hit the black market. Ukraine looks a good bet.

Before Tess can call back, Zoe speed-dials her brother.

"Hey, Zoe," he answers. "Good day?"

"Yeah, not bad."

She wonders how the vertical farm's going to change once it becomes state-owned. And then—hey, why not?—open sourced? So that all these methods finally fulfill their promise in millions of diverse hands? She always loved the wheat fields, loved running her fingers through the stalks. She hopes that's one of the crops they bring back.

"So, listen," she says. "You keep your hands off those strawberries?"

"Of course."

"Good. I wouldn't want you falling ill." She gazes up, watches a plane passing high overhead. "We're going on a trip."

Will tech do any good . . .
. . . if we refuse to wise up?

PUBLIC DOMAIN

SCOTT SIGLER

She's cheating on me.

"Hoyt, will you put that thing away?"

He did not. Instead, he forced a smile.

"Oh come on," he said, moving his cell phone to keep Bridget in-frame. "Just tell me how we met, then tell me you love me."

Bridget put a hand over her face, shook her head.

"You know exactly how we met. That's why we're at a shitty Starbucks, drinking shitty coffee."

A year ago to the day, he'd been in one of those BS "preferred partners" meetings. Company A gets together with Company B, tech is shown, talks are had, and—perhaps—business gets done. Hoyt had watched the visitors present their product. Pure garbage, all smoke and no fire, but the woman *presenting* the product . . . well, Bridget Amsing had been another story altogether.

Bridget's company had been at the tail end of the startup stage. Their strategy: offer a suite of hardware that turns retail stores into biometric scanners, tack on the software to analyze the captured information. Unethical, in Hoyt's opinion, and borderline illegal—even with the huge gray area created by the Transparency Acts. Remote measurement of skin temperature, pupil dilation, heart rate, respiration rate, body tension, voice analysis and a few more goodies. Pretty much the same stuff they used at airports, but with a new mood-recognition algorithm tied into "a broader consumer-behavior database that accurately predicts purchasing potential." Know the customer's true mood, and you can make sure people willing to spend money actually *spend* it.

Hoyt's company created eyetracking hardware. He was the software team lead, and as such, he'd been there to give his take. But he hadn't paid much attention to their product—he'd been unable to do anything but gawk at the startup's presenter.

He knew he was staring. Perhaps *leering* was a better word. He tried to look away from the gray-eyed woman. Tried, and failed. Such a strange feeling—he was powerless to stop himself from acting like a total creeper.

In a day and age when the slightest breach of etiquette can land you in the HR director's office—or flat-out get you fired because you make someone "feel uncomfortable"—he stared and stared and stared.

She rolled through her presentation, so smoothly he assumed she was like every other woman in the world and simply hadn't noticed him. Women like her didn't go for guys like him.

He'd been wrong.

At the post-presentation cocktail reception, she cornered him by the plastic supermarket deli tray half-covered with scattered slices of sausage and cubes of cheese.

She leaned close, spoke quietly so no one else could hear.

"We had an in-service last week. You'd have loved it. *Staring as sexual harassment.* I saved the course attachments. Want me to e-mail them to you?"

He thought he was screwed. Words like that make careers disintegrate. *Well, hello, Mr. Man who was fired for being a perv—no, we're not hiring right now.* Trapped halfway between those gray eyes and the feeling of his stomach plummeting into his balls, Hoyt said the first thing that came to his mind.

"Your product is stupid."

A pause, then her eyes lit up like a little kid who just discovered a new toy. She glanced over her shoulder to see if any of her coworkers were listening. They weren't.

"It *is* stupid," she said. "Like you need a heat map to tell you if a customer is pissed off? I swear, I'm the only one in my company that's ever actually worked a retail floor. Bunch of programmers and Ivy-leaguers who've never had to watch a size five insist she should be able to fit into a size three." Bridget shrugged. "Wanna leave these walking-dead asshats behind and go get a coffee? I mean, if you're going to stare at me like my clothes are transparent, you can probably see my tits better from across a table instead of across the room."

That was how they'd met. Romance abounds.

Hoyt had assumed it was a trick meant to embarrass him. He'd said "yes" anyway. In the months that followed, he learned Bridget's coworkers thought she was an asshole—and with good reason. She had a horribly inappropriate sense of humor. She pushed at everyone, challenged everything, trying to find those who didn't wilt. If you showed weakness? Sensitivity? She wouldn't stop poking and prodding. Stand up to her, and she liked you.

A year ago to the day, they'd left the mixer separately, met up at the shitty

Starbucks across the street, bought shitty coffee, and sat at this very same shitty table.

Except the first time, Hoyt hadn't been pointing his cell phone at her.

"Come on," he said. "Just tell me what you think about our first twelve months together."

Twelve months that you're pissing away, because I was wrong about you, because you're just like the other lying harpies that made me look like a fool.

Bridget sighed. She reached across the table. Her fingertips traced veins on the back of his hand. As always—even now—her touch shot through him, an absent spark landing in a barrel of gunpowder. She smiled, gray eyes crinkling at the corners.

"A *year*, Hoyt. It's crazy. This is the longest I've ever been in a relationship."

That surprised him. Bridget never talked about her pre-Hoyt life. He accepted her insular nature, sure, but he'd just assumed she'd had long relationships before. Hadn't everyone their age?

Her smile confused him. Can't fake a smile like that. Not in the eyes, anyway. If Hoyt knew one thing in this world, it was *eyes*. Gateway to the soul. Metaphysical bullshit, sure, but not far from the truth. Only the greatest actors can fake the contraction of the orbicularis oculi muscles, which caused Bridget's raised cheeks and crow's feet, or contract the zygomatic majors, the muscles that turned up the corners of her mouth. She wasn't an actor. The science of a Duchenne told him that her smile was *real*.

Which, somehow, made this even worse.

"Now tell me you love me," he said.

Her smile faded. He knew those words were hard for her to say. Saying *I love you* meant admitting someone could get to her, could hurt her.

But she did it anyway.

"I love you, Hoyt." She smiled again, relieved.

Hoyt grinned back.

She frowned. "Something wrong?"

Two minutes of running video. Hopefully, that was enough. He put the phone in his pocket.

He shook his head. "Everything's fine."

Fine, except you said you were going out with Kaylee last night, dinner at Yard House, then I saw Kaylee's Instagram movies at Fluxx—she was with four other people, none of whom were you.

Bridget pointed to the corner of her eye.

"Your orbicule thingie you told me about," she said. "Your smile gots no crow's feet, my man."

That was the problem with dating smart people—they paid attention. They learned. Maybe he shouldn't have told her so much about what he did for a living.

He shrugged. "Nothing's wrong. Honest."

Bridget leaned back, looked at him guardedly.

He didn't know her past, but he knew someone had shattered her heart. Her swagger, the too-loud laugh, the baiting insults . . . it was all surface stuff. Battle-scared armor that protected delicate, hidden glass within. It had taken him months to learn that, to find the real person hiding within the hard shell. He'd been patient, of course, because he'd given himself over to her almost from the first.

In retrospect, he'd been a fool to do that. Maybe he should have had armor, too.

"You're the one who wanted to come here, to celebrate," she said. She crossed her arms. "Remember? So I come here like you want, and you've got some kind of stick up your ass?"

Subtlety—Bridget's strong point.

"What, I can't have a moment where I'm not dancing for you like a trained monkey?"

Her eyes narrowed. "What the hell does *that* mean?"

Hoyt didn't know what it meant. He didn't know why he'd said it. All he knew was that it hurt to look at her. He'd thought she was different. In truth, she was probably just like the others. Bridget stood. Hoyt knew her so well now, read the emotions she was so bad at hiding.

"Know what, Hoyt? Thanks for ruining this with another one of your goddam moods."

From in love to pissed off in the blink of an eye. That was Bridget's way.

"I'm going home," she said. She took one step, then paused, her face caught somewhere between anger and confusion. "Are . . . are we okay?"

She said it as if he might suddenly break things off with her. Maybe he would. He was ninety percent sure she was cheating on him, but swirling in that ten-percent remainder was the hope that he was wrong, that this was some kind of silly mistake.

He loved her.

"We're okay," he said. "You still going to dinner with Kaylee tonight?"

She winced, so slightly most people wouldn't have noticed. Hoyt did.

"Yeah, she's having a hard time," Bridget said. "That okay?"

No hostility in the voice this time, not the usual crass, in-your-face Bridget. She was asking. Hoyt wanted to say *no*, have her stay with him tonight, hold her and love her and give her a chance to tell him what was going on in her own terms.

Instead, he gave her enough rope to hang herself.

"It's fine, honest," he said. "Still coming over after?"

Bridget smiled, an awkward, unsure thing that looked odd on a face usually burning with confidence. She leaned down and kissed him.

"Sure am," she said. "See you nine-ish."

Hoyt watched her leave.

He took another sip of coffee. Tasted burnt. Starbucks always tasted burnt.

A broken heart was nothing new. He'd suffered through them before. Hadn't everyone? In high school, sure. In college, of course. But this? This was supposed to be different. He and Bridget were at *that age*, when a year of dating meant something more.

You're such a fucking idiot. She played you.

Hoyt threw out his shitty coffee, and he left.

■ ■ ■

He'd been down this road before. This time, perhaps, he wouldn't have to suffer in the zone of lies and denials. He could get to the truth and move on.

There was another man. Or another woman, maybe. That had happened to him once. Gender didn't matter. What mattered was simply that one word—*another.*

It was supposed to be different this time. Bridget was supposed to be different.

He was such a fool.

Hoyt's face felt hot.

I have never wanted more to be wrong in my whole life.

"Upload today's video," he said.

The computer complied.

The video taken an hour earlier at Starbucks appeared in a tiny box, playing at three times normal speed. Beneath it, a progress bar started filling from left to right. Two minutes and thirteen seconds of her talking. The site said it needed one minute of video for the analysis, but Hoyt had wanted to be sure.

He'd tested the system by uploading a recording of himself. It had worked like a charm. Seemed unreal, though, that any public video of you was simply *out there*, available to anyone. While the algorithm could identify the same face in dozens or even hundreds of videos, it didn't know who that person was—not unless you opted in for that, filled out multiple forms and proved your identity. Hoyt had done just that. Most people had not. So far, anyway.

They were too busy with shows or games or life to pay attention to new laws, to understand the technology that surrounded them. He knew Bridget hadn't taken the time to opt-in—she was more interested in trashy reality programming than C-SPAN or CNN.

Hoyt understood the facial recognition part of the system. His company had been doing work like that for the past three years. Key identifiers like the width of the nose, length of the jaw line, distance between the eyes, the position and angle of cheekbones, those things combined to make a faceprint. Even from a good distance, a decent camera could identify an individual with unerring accuracy. That part of analyzing footage was easy; it was the *access* to footage that he could barely get his head around.

Thanks to the Transparency Acts, if a camera shot streets and sidewalks, restaurants, stores, bars, stadiums, etc., the video had to be synced to public-domain databases. That included police body cams, dashboard cams, even cell-phone video if it was shot in a public place. Surveillance footage was available to anyone, so people could see *where* they were being watched, know *who* was watching them. Have a camera monitoring a public area, and that footage was kept private? Welcome to the nation's latest felony charge, friend. The Acts dictated that no one—not even the government—had a right to watch you without you knowing you were being watched.

The progress bar continued to fill.

That kind of data had once stayed mostly in private hands. Now it was available with a few clicks. Maybe it would soon be taken for granted. Hoyt's older brother had told him how people had, at first, flipped out that Google Maps would let you zoom down to someone's doorstep—coverage that had once been the domain of spy satellites and shadowy government agencies. Hoyt, on the other hand, had never known a time when map detail like that *hadn't* been available.

The progress bar filled all the way. Text flashed above it: 100% ANALYZED. And below that: RUN AGAINST PUBLIC DOMAIN VIDEO?

"Yes," he said.

The display flashed video clips so fast he couldn't begin to process what he saw, other than split-second images that stuck: a blond girl, a black man, a boy smiling under a stop sign. As the seconds rolled past, he noticed that people of color stopped appearing. Then, no more images of men. Or boys. Just women. Then, no more old women. Young girls, gone. The rapid-fire images slowed, still too fast to make out individuals, but enough to see the pattern: white women, late 20s, brunettes. Slower still, each clip visible for a quarter-second, perhaps—hundreds of women, all who looked a little bit like Bridget. Slower still, enough that Hoyt could briefly focus on the women . . . some looked so much like Bridget they could have been her sister.

The first few months of dating Bridget had been exciting. The months after . . . those had been *terrifying*. Falling in love was always scary, but never more so than with her. Why? Because he'd fallen first. He'd been the one out on a ledge, exposing his heart, opening himself to possible rejection.

He remembered the first time he'd told her he loved her. She hadn't answered with the hoped-for *I love you, too*. No, she'd said just one word: *why*?

On the display, many women that looked like Bridget, then, unmistakably, Bridget herself. Security-cam footage, her and Hoyt leaving a bar in the Gaslamp. They both looked happy. Was that just last week?

That question of *why*? Not just the two of them, but for everyone. Why does one person love another? Are there even words for it? At first, he hadn't known how to respond. Then, the reasons started flowing. Easy pickings at first: her eyes; the way she smelled, the way she kissed, that she liked the same old sci-fi movies he did. More reasons next, deeper reasons. How every hug started out stiff, then she relaxed into him, almost despite her natural resistance to do so. How she poked at him constantly, but when someone else teased him, she focused all of her considerable wit on that person, ridiculed that person until they understood that no one messed with Hoyt, no one but her. How she seemed to talk constantly, to fidget endlessly, an always-full battery with a cracked shell that couldn't contain her energy—except when she was alone with him, and she was quiet, she was still, slowing down enough to feel the world spin.

Only a couple of months ago had she finally said it to him; *I love you*. Unlike her, he hadn't asked why. Honestly, he didn't *care* why.

Playback slowing to normal speeds: Bridget at Ralph's, shopping for groceries; in a crowd on 5th Avenue; at a stoplight while driving Hoyt's car.

The program had locked her in.

Hoyt felt awful. He felt justified. It was all public-domain footage—what was wrong with looking at that? If she wasn't doing anything wrong, then she had nothing to hide. Right?

Bridget at the library.

Bridget at the bank.

Bridget at the Prado Restaurant at Balboa Park . . . *not alone*.

"Stop searching," Hoyt said. "Continue playing current clip."

Bridget, sitting at a table, across from a man.

A man Hoyt didn't recognize.

They were talking. They were smiling.

Hoyt looked at the meta info: yesterday, 5:47 pm.

Right when Bridget said she was out with Kaylee.

A creeping sensation, the feeling of sliding backward while sitting perfectly still. Who was this grinning asshole? Hoyt watched the silent movie. He wished there was audio. Was she talking about sex? Was she saying the things she'd said to Hoyt, that she was a bad girl deep down, that in public they were equals but behind closed doors she wanted Daddy to control her?

The same things she'd claimed she'd said only to Hoyt, to no one before him? The same things that made Hoyt feel like a king.

On the playback, the man said something. Bridget laughed. Orbicularis oculi. Zygomatic major. A genuine laugh, a laugh of delight.

Hoyt felt that heat in his face again. Tears blurred his vision. His eyes stung. He closed them. When he did, he saw that strange man on top of her, saw her screaming in pleasure, screaming and *laughing*.

Laughing at Hoyt.

"I'm so fucking *stupid*."

He didn't want this to be true. He loved her. He'd thought she loved him.

Hoyt watched the silent movie. Wait . . . the man . . . did he look familiar after all? Something about him did, yes, even though Hoyt was sure he'd never seen this man before. Or, maybe he had . . . at a bar, perhaps?

Tears again. He should have known better. So gullible. He'd trusted her. He'd *loved* her.

Hoyt checked the time: 7:30 pm.

"Stop playback. Still images, make new JPEGs, same folder."

She would be there soon. He had to get ready.

■ ■ ■

Hoyt had wondered if he should pour drinks. Scotch, maybe. Bridget liked Scotch. Just before she'd arrived at his apartment, he'd decided no—drinks meant glasses, glasses could be thrown. By either one of them.

"How was dinner?"

His voice sounded strange, even to him. Judging from the hesitant look on her face, it sounded strange to her, too.

"Dinner was fine."

She stood just inside the door to his apartment, unsure if she should come all the way in. He'd expected her to be in a dress, or maybe some tight jeans and an even tighter T-shirt. Wasn't that the kind of thing you wore when you were seeing a new man? But she wasn't wearing anything like that. Jeans, yes, but her favorites, a bit saggy, with holes in them that she'd earned from long wear. Her hair was in a simple ponytail. Some lipstick and a little eye shadow, but nothing major. Bridget wasn't dressed like she'd been out on a date.

"Hoyt, I've had enough of this bullshit. Are you going to tell me what the fuck is going on with you?"

Fear in that voice—fear of being wounded.

Would she lie about meeting that man? Correction: would she *continue* to lie about it. Hoyt gestured to his couch.

"Sure thing, *honey*. Have a seat. We'll hash it out."

She hesitated, a wild animal wary of a trap. She walked to the couch, sat.

A manila folder sitting on his small dining room table. He picked it up. The folder contained printouts. He hadn't actually *printed* anything in months. Not much need for that any more.

Until now.

He'd thought of putting the incriminating images and video on a tablet or his phone, tossing it in her lap and telling her to hit *play*. But like the glasses, that would give her something to throw—tablets and phones cost money. If he was kicking her out of here tonight, he didn't want to have to shell out hundreds of dollars to replace the shit she broke in her inevitable explosion of righteous indignation.

Because, after all, it wouldn't be *her* fault, it would be *Hoyt's*. He knew her too well. Bridget never did anything wrong. Someone else was always to blame.

He tossed the folder into her lap. He crossed his arms, stared down at her.

She looked at the folder, then up at him.

"What the hell is this?"

Hoyt shrugged. "You already know."

"I'm quite fucking sure I don't," Bridget said, cold gravel in her voice. Her face, though, those eyes . . . they said *stop*. Those eyes said: *whatever this is, please don't do this to us.*

He waited.

She opened the folder. She picked up the three printouts inside, slowly looked at them, one after another.

There was something about her seeing it, something that made it all click together. No going back. It made this *real*. It made them *over*.

"I thought we had something," he said. His voice cracked on the last word. He cleared his throat, wished his face didn't burn. "How could you do this to us?"

He hadn't known what to expect from her. At the same time, he'd expected her to cry, to apologize, to beg forgiveness, promise to never do it again, because

Hoyt *knew* she loved him. This other guy was some fling, or maybe an ex back for a tangle. She'd made a mistake, that was all. Maybe he could forgive her. Maybe they could move on.

But Bridget didn't apologize.

She didn't cry.

She didn't look sad or distraught, guilty or crushed.

She looked *angry*.

"I didn't do anything to us," she said. "You did."

An urge to lash out, so primitive, so overpowering. So *angry*. If a man had glared at him the way Bridget glared at him now, Hoyt would have tackled him, put him down.

"Don't turn this around on me," he said. "You should have told me there was someone else."

The printouts and the folder flew into the air. Bridget was on her feet in an instant, chest-to-chest with him, her gray eyes—the eyes that had first hooked him—wide with rage.

"You asshole," she said. "You were spying on me."

"Don't be so fucking grandiose. I didn't follow you around, I just used that public-domain site. Don't try and make this my fault, you—"

She took a step back, almost as if he'd slapped her. The indignation, gone. In its place, something far worse—tears.

In their twelve months together, he had never once seen her cry.

"That site that has all the public video," she said. "All the cameras . . . that one?"

He crossed his arms, nodded. "That's right. So, no, I didn't *spy* on you, James Bond."

A tear rolled down her cheek.

Her words came out as a whisper.

"The video you took at Starbucks. Is that what you used?"

Something about the way she said that sent a shiver up Hoyt's spine. He didn't know why.

"Yeah, that was it," he said. "I had to—"

"The one where you *made me tell you I loved you*?"

A question, sheer disbelief, even though she already knew the answer.

It struck Hoyt, suddenly and all at once—he'd crossed a line that couldn't be uncrossed. A sinking feeling. That sensation of realizing he'd done something wrong, of wondering how the hell he hadn't known it was wrong while he was doing it. He should have had her say something else. Anything else.

But why should *he* feel bad? She was at fault here, not him.

"Yes," he said. "I used that video."

Bridget wiped away tears.

"He's my fucking *brother*."

The man had looked familiar . . .

"Bullshit," Hoyt said. "You don't have a brother."

Bridget picked up a printout, looked at it.

"No, I never *told* you I had a brother."

She slowly tore the paper in half, let the two halves fall. She picked up the second printout.

That sinking feeling deepened. His soul in quicksand. It wasn't possible. Couldn't be.

"You're lying," he said. He knew he was digging himself deeper, but was as unable to stop digging as he'd been to stop staring at her a year ago. "No one dates for a year without saying she has a brother."

Bridget tore the paper in half, let the halves flutter down.

"His name is Mike," she said. Her words trembled with anguish, with rage. "He's a heroin addict. Recovering, or so he says, but I've heard that before. Mike ripped our family apart. He lied to me. He stole from me. He poisoned people against me. I wrote him out of my life. I even *moved* so he wouldn't know where I was. I didn't tell you about him because I wanted a life without him in it."

Hoyt kept hunting for the lie. He didn't find it. Was this for real?

"If you cut him out of your life, why were you with him?"

She shrugged. "The motherfucking Internet. You can track down anyone. He found my old Facebook page. I should have deleted it, but . . . I don't know. I don't use it anymore. I checked it the other day, not sure why. He'd sent me a video. Said he'd cleaned up his act, wanted a chance to do right by me. It took me awhile to decide, but I met with him. That was goddamn hard to do, because he made it so impossible to *trust* that I didn't trust anyone. Until you, Hoyt." She picked up the final printout. "I trusted you."

This time, she didn't tear the paper—she handed it to him.

He couldn't think. His hands took the paper, held it up for his eyes to see.

The man—Mike—he had gray eyes.

He had *Bridget's* eyes.

Hoyt stumbled, grabbed the table to stop himself from falling.

He'd been wrong.

The imagined betrayal had felt devastating. This was better, and yet so much more—if betrayal was being hit by a car, pure relief was being crushed beneath a tank.

He let the printout drop to the floor.

"My God," he said. "I thought . . . oh, shit, honey . . . I'm sorry. I love you so much, I . . ."

He reached for her.

She slapped his hands away.

"Don't touch me," she said. "You don't get to touch me."

Gray eyes: wet with tears, but narrow. Hard.

Hard like armor.

"I didn't know," Hoyt said. "I mean . . . come on, you would have thought the same thing."

Bridget shook her head.

"I wouldn't have," she said. "Because I trusted you. And I can't, now. Not ever. Don't call me. Don't text me. Don't *anything* me."

She stormed to the door. He wasn't sure if he should try and stop her. By the time he realized he should, she'd slammed the door behind her.

Hoyt glanced at the floor. The picture of Mike, her brother, stared up at him.

Gray eyes.

Bridget's eyes.

A classic of human vision, empathy . . .
. . . and courage.

TO SEE THE INVISIBLE MAN

ROBERT SILVERBERG

And then they found me guilty, and then they pronounced me invisible, for a span of one year beginning on the eleventh of May in the year of Grace 2104, and they took me to a dark room beneath the courthouse to affix the mark to my forehead before turning me loose.

Two municipally paid ruffians did the job. One flung me into a chair and the other lifted the brand.

"This won't hurt a bit," the slab-jawed ape said, and thrust the brand against my forehead, and there was a moment of coolness, and that was all.

"What happens now?" I asked.

But there was no answer, and they turned away from me and left the room without a word. The door remained open. I was free to leave, or to stay and rot, as I chose. No one would speak to me, or look at me more than once, long enough to see the sign on my forehead. I was invisible. You must understand that my invisibility was strictly metaphorical. I still had corporeal solidity. People *could* see me—but they *would not* see me.

An absurd punishment? Perhaps. But then, the crime was absurd too. The crime of coldness. Refusal to unburden myself for my fellow man. I was a four-time offender. The penalty for that was a year's invisibility. The complaint had been duly sworn, the trial held, the brand duly affixed.

I was invisible.

I went out, out into the world of warmth.

They had already had the afternoon rain. The streets of the city were drying, and there was the smell of growth in the Hanging Gardens. Men and women went about their business. I walked among them, but they took no notice of me.

The penalty for speaking to an invisible man is invisibility, a month to a year or more, depending on the seriousness of the offense. On this the whole concept depends. I wondered how rigidly the rule was observed.

I soon found out.

I stepped into a liftshaft and let myself be spiraled up toward the nearest of the Hanging Gardens. It was Eleven, the cactus garden, and those gnarled, bizarre shapes suited my mood. I emerged on the landing stage and advanced toward the admissions counter to buy my token. A pasty-faced, empty-eyed woman sat back of the counter.

I laid down my coin. Something like fright entered her eyes, quickly faded. "One admission," I said.

No answer. People were queuing up behind me. I repeated my demand. The woman looked up helplessly, then stared over my left shoulder. A hand extended itself, another coin was placed down. She took it, and handed the man his token. He dropped it in the slot and went in.

"Let me have a token," I said crisply.

Others were jostling me out of the way. Not a word of apology. I began to sense some of the meaning of my invisibility. They were literally treating me as though they could not see me.

There are countervailing advantages. I walked around behind the counter and helped myself to a token without paying for it. Since I was invisible, I could not be stopped. I thrust the token in the slot and entered the garden.

But the cacti bored me. An inexpressible malaise slipped over me, and I felt no desire to stay. On my way out I pressed my finger against a jutting thorn and drew blood. The cactus, at least, still recognized my existence. But only to draw blood.

I returned to my apartment. My books awaited me, but I felt no interest in them. I sprawled out on my narrow bed and activated the energizer to combat the strange lassitude that was afflicting me. I thought about my invisibility.

It would not be such a hardship, I told myself. I had never depended overly on other human beings. Indeed, had I not been sentenced in the first place for my coldness toward my fellow creatures? So what need did I have of them now? *Let* them ignore me!

It would be restful. I had a year's respite from work, after all. Invisible men did not work. How could they? Who would go to an invisible doctor for a consultation, or hire an invisible lawyer to represent him, or give a document to an invisible clerk to file? No work, then. No income, of course, either. But landlords did not take rent from invisible men. Invisible men went where they pleased, at no cost. I had just demonstrated that at the Hanging Gardens.

Invisibility would be a great joke on society, I felt. They had sentenced me to nothing more dreadful than a year's rest cure. I was certain I would enjoy it.

But there were certain practical disadvantages. On the first night of my invisibility I went to the city's finest restaurant. I would order their most lav-ish dishes, a hundred-unit meal, and then conveniently vanish at the presen-tation of the bill.

My thinking was muddy. I never got seated. I stood in the entrance half an hour, bypassed again and again by a maitre d'hotel who had clearly been through all this many times before: Walking to a seat, I realized, would gain me nothing. No waiter would take my order.

I could go into the kitchen. I could help myself to anything I pleased. I could disrupt the workings of the restaurant. But I decided against it. Society had its ways of protecting itself against the invisible ones. There could be no direct retaliation, of course, no intentional defense. But who could say no to a chef's claim that he had seen no one in the way when he hurled a pot of scalding water toward the wall? Invisibility was invisibility, a two-edged sword.

I left the restaurant.

I ate at an automated restaurant nearby. Then I took an autocab home. Ma-chines, like cacti, did not discriminate against my sort. I sensed that they would make poor companions for a year, though.

I slept poorly.

■ ■ ■

The second day of my invisibility was a day of further testing and discovery.

I went for a long walk, careful to stay on the pedestrian paths. I had heard all about the boys who enjoy running down those who carry the mark of invisibility on their foreheads. Again, there is no recourse, no punishment for them. My condition has its little hazards by intention.

I walked the streets, seeing how the throngs parted for me. I cut through them like a microtome passing between cells. They were well trained. At mid-day I saw my first fellow Invisible. He was a tall man of middle years, stocky and dignified, bearing the mark of shame on a domelike forehead. His eyes met mine only for a moment. Then he passed on. An invisible man, naturally, cannot see another of his kind.

I was amused, nothing more. I was still savoring the novelty of this way of life. No slight could hurt me. Not yet.

Late in the day I came to one of those bath-houses where working girls can cleanse themselves for a couple of small coins. I smiled wickedly and went up the steps. The attendant at the door gave me the flicker of a startled look—it was a small triumph for me—but did not dare to stop me.

I went in.

An overpowering smell of soap and sweat struck me. I persevered inward. I passed cloakrooms where long rows of gray smocks were hanging, and it occurred to me that I could rifle those smocks of every unit they contained, but I did not. Theft loses meaning when it becomes too easy, as the clever ones who devised invisibility were aware.

I passed on, into the bath chambers themselves.

Hundreds of women were there. Nubile girls, weary wenches, old crones. Some blushed. A few smiled. Many turned their backs on me. But they were careful not to show any real reaction to my presence. Supervisory matrons stood guard, and who knew but that she might be reported for taking undue cognizance of the existence of an Invisible?

So I watched them bathe, watched five hundred pairs of bobbing breasts, watched naked bodies glistening under the spray, watched this vast mass of bare feminine flesh. My reaction was a mixed one, a sense of wicked achievement at having penetrated this sanctum sanctorum unhalted, and then, welling up slowly within me, a sensation of—was it sorrow? Boredom? Revulsion?

I was unable to analyze it. But it felt as though a clammy hand had seized my throat. I left quickly. The smell of soapy water stung my nostrils for hours afterward, and the sight of pink flesh haunted my dreams that night. I ate alone, in one of the automatics. I began to see that the novelty of this punishment was soon lost.

. . .

In the third week I fell ill. It began with a high fever, then pains of the stomach, vomiting, the rest of the ugly symptomatology. By midnight I was certain I was dying. The cramps were intolerable, and when I dragged myself to the toilet cubicle I caught sight of myself in the mirror, distorted, greenish, beaded with sweat. The mark of invisibility stood out like a beacon in my pale forehead.

For a long time I lay on the tiled floor, limply absorbing the coolness of it. Then I thought: What if it's my appendix? That ridiculous, obsolete, obscure prehistoric survival? Inflamed, ready to burst?

I needed a doctor.

The phone was covered with dust. They had not bothered to disconnect it, but I had not called anyone since my arrest, and no one had dared call me. The penalty for knowingly telephoning an invisible man is invisibility. My friends, such as they were, had stayed far away.

I grasped the phone, thumbed the panel. It lit up and the directory robot said, "With whom do you wish to speak, sir?"

"Doctor," I gasped.

"Certainly, sir." Bland, smug mechanical words! No way to pronounce a robot invisible, so it was free to talk to me!

The screen glowed. A doctorly voice said, "What seems to be the trouble?"

"Stomach pains. Maybe appendicitis."

"We'll have a man over in—" He stopped. I had made the mistake of up-turning my agonized face. His eyes lit on my forehead mark. The screen winked into blackness as rapidly as though I had extended a leprous hand for him to kiss.

"Doctor," I groaned.

He was gone. I buried my face in my hands. This was carrying things too far, I thought. Did the Hippocratic Oath allow things like this? Could a doctor ignore a sick man's plea for help?

Hippocrates had not known anything about invisible men. A doctor was not required to minister to an invisible man. To society at large I simply was not there. Doctors could not diagnose diseases in nonexistent individuals.

I was left to suffer.

It was one of invisibility's less attractive features. You enter a bath-house unhindered, if that pleases you—but you writhe on a bed of pain equally unhindered. The one with the other, and if your appendix happens to rup-ture, why, it is all the greater deterrent to others who might perhaps have gone your lawless way!

My appendix did not rupture. I survived, though badly shaken. A man can survive without human conversation for a year. He can travel on automated cars and eat at automated restaurants. But there are no automated doctors. For the first time, I felt truly beyond the pale. A convict in a prison is given a doc-tor when he falls ill. My crime had not been serious enough to merit prison, and so no doctor would treat me if I suffered. It was unfair. I cursed the devils who had invented my punishment. I faced each bleak dawn alone, as alone as Crusoe on his island, here in the midst of a city of twelve million souls.

· · ·

How can I describe my shifts of mood, my many tacks before the changing winds of the passing months?

There were times when invisibility was a joy, a delight, a treasure. In those paranoid moments I gloried in my exemption from the rules that bound ordi-nary men.

I stole. I entered small stores and seized the receipts, while the cowering merchant feared to stop me, lest in crying out he make himself liable to my invisibility. If I had known that the State reimbursed all such losses, I might have taken less pleasure in it. But I stole.

I invaded. The bath-house never tempted me again, but I breached other sanctuaries. I entered hotels and walked down the corridors, opening doors at random. Most rooms were empty. Some were not.

Godlike, I observed all. I toughened. My disdain for society—the crime that had earned me invisibility in the first place—heightened.

I stood in the empty streets during the periods of rain, and railed at the gleaming faces of the towering buildings on every side. "Who needs you?" I roared "Not I! Who needs you in the slightest?"

I jeered and mocked and railed. It was a kind of insanity, brought on, I suppose, by the loneliness. I entered theaters—where the happy lotus-eaters sat slumped in their massage chairs, transfixed by the glowing tridim images— and capered down the aisles. No one grumbled at me. The luminescence of my forehead told them to keep their complaints to themselves, and they did.

Those were the mad moments, the good moments, the moments when I towered twenty feet high and strode among the visible clods with contempt oozing from every pore. Those were insane moments—I admit that freely. A man who has been in a condition of involuntary invisibility for several months is not likely to be well balanced.

Did I call them paranoid moments? Manic depressive might be more to the point. The pendulum swung dizzily. The days when I felt only contempt for the visible fools all around me were balanced by days when the isolation pressed in tangibly on me. I would walk the endless streets, pass through the gleaming arcades, stare down at the highways with their streaking bullets of gay colors. Not even a beggar would come up to me. Did you know we had beggars, in our shining century? Not till I was pronounced invisible did I know it, for then my long walks took me to the slums, where the shine has worn thin, and where shuffling stubble-faced old men beg for small coins.

No one begged for coins from me. Once a blind man came up to me.

"For the love of God," he wheezed, "help me to buy new eyes from the eye bank."

They were the first direct words any human being had spoken to me in months. I started to reach into my tunic for money, planning to give him every unit on me in gratitude. Why not? I could get more simply by taking it. But before I could draw the money out, a nightmare figure hobbled on crutches between us. I caught the whispered word, "Invisible," and then the two of them scuttled away like frightened crabs. I stood there stupidly holding my money.

Not even the beggars. Devils, to have invented this torment!

So I softened again. My arrogance ebbed away. I was lonely, now. Who could accuse me of coldness? I was spongy soft, pathetically eager for a word, a smile, a clasping hand. It was the sixth month of my invisibility.

I loathed it entirely, now. Its pleasures were hollow ones and its torment was unbearable. I wondered how I would survive the remaining six months. Believe me, suicide was not far from my mind in those dark hours.

And finally I committed an act of foolishness. On one of my endless walks I encountered another Invisible, no more than the third or the fourth such creature I had seen in my six months. As in the previous encounters, our eyes met, warily, only for a moment. Then he dropped his to the pavement, and he sidestepped me and walked on. He was a slim young man, no more than forty, with tousled brown hair and a narrow, pinched face. He had a look of scholarship about him, and I wondered what he might have done to merit his punishment, and I was seized with the desire to run after him and ask him, and to learn his name, and to talk to him, and embrace him.

All these things are forbidden to mankind. No one shall have any contact whatsoever with an Invisible—not even a fellow Invisible. Especially not a fellow Invisible. There is no wish on society's part to foster a secret bond of fellowship among its pariahs.

I knew all this.

I turned and followed him, all the same.

For three blocks I moved along behind him, remaining twenty to fifty paces to the rear. Security robots seemed to be everywhere, their scanners quick to detect an infraction, and I did not dare make my move. Then he turned down a side street, a gray, dusty street five centuries old, and began to stroll, with the ambling going-nowhere gait of the Invisible. I came up behind him.

"Please," I said softly. "No one will see us here. We can talk. My name is—"

He whirled on me, horror in his eyes. His face was pale. He looked at me in amazement for a moment, then darted forward as though to go around me.

I blocked him.

"Wait," I said. "Don't be afraid. Please—"

He burst past me. I put my hand on his shoulder, and he wriggled free.

"Just a word," I begged.

Not even a word. Not even a hoarsely uttered, "Leave me alone!" He sidestepped me and ran down the empty street, his steps diminishing from a clatter to a murmur as he reached the corner and rounded it. I looked after him, feeling a great loneliness well up in me.

And then a fear. *He* hadn't breached the rules of Invisibility, but I had. I had seen him. That left me subject to punishment, an extension of my term of invisibility, perhaps. I looked around anxiously, but there were no security robots in sight, no one at all.

I was alone.

Turning, calming myself, I continued down the street. Gradually I regained control over myself. I saw that I had done something unpardonably foolish. The stupidity of my action troubled me, but even more the sentimentality of it. To reach out in that panicky way to another Invisible—to admit openly my loneliness, my need—no. It meant that society was winning. I couldn't have that.

I found that I was near the cactus garden once again. I rode the liftshaft, grabbed a token from the attendant, and bought my way in. I searched for a moment, then found a twisted, elaborately ornate cactus eight feet high, a spiny monster. I wrenched it from its pot and broke the angular limbs to fragments, filling my hands with a thousand needles. People pretended not to watch. I plucked the spines from my hands and, palms bleeding, rode the liftshaft down, once again sublimely aloof in my invisibility.

■ ■ ■

The eighth month passed, the ninth, the tenth. The seasonal round had made nearly a complete turn. Spring had given way to a mild summer, summer to a crisp autumn, autumn to winter with its fortnightly snowfalls, still permitted for esthetic reasons. Winter had ended, now. In the parks, the trees sprouted green buds. The weather control people stepped up the rainfall to thrice daily.

My term was drawing to its end.

In the final months of my invisibility I had slipped into a kind of torpor. My mind, forced back on its own resources, no longer cared to consider the implications of my condition, and I slid in a blurred haze from day to day. I read compulsively but unselectively. Aristotle one day, the Bible the next, a handbook of mechanics the next. I retained nothing; as I turned a fresh page, its predecessor slipped from my memory.

I no longer bothered to enjoy the few advantages of invisibility, the voyeuristic thrills, the minute throb of power that comes from being able to commit any act with only limited fears of retaliation. I say *limited* because the passage of the Invisibility Act had not been accompanied by an act repealing human nature; few men would not risk invisibility to protect their wives or children from an invisible one's molestations; no one would coolly allow an Invisible to jab out his eyes; no one would tolerate an Invisible's invasion of his home. There were ways of coping with such infringements without appearing to recognize the existence of the Invisible, as I have mentioned.

Still, it was possible to get away with a great deal. I declined to try. Somewhere Dostoevsky has written, "Without God, all things are possible." I can amend that. "To the invisible man, all things are possible—and uninteresting." So it was.

The weary months passed.

I did not count the minutes till my release. To be precise, I wholly forgot that my term was due to end. On the day itself, I was reading in my room, morosely turning page after page, when the annunciator chimed.

It had not chimed for a full year. I had almost forgotten the meaning of the sound.

But I opened the door. There they stood, the men of the law. Wordlessly, they broke the seal that held the mark to my forehead.

The emblem dropped away and shattered.

"Hello, citizen," they said to me.

I nodded gravely. "Yes. Hello."

"May 11, 2105. Your term is up. You are restored to society. You have paid your debt."

"Thank you. Yes."

"Come for a drink with us."

"I'd sooner not."

"It's the tradition. Come along."

I went with them. My forehead felt strangely naked now, and I glanced in a mirror to see that there was a pale spot where the emblem had been. They took me to a bar nearby, and treated me to synthetic whiskey, raw, powerful. The bartender grinned at me. Someone on the next stool clapped me on the shoulder and asked me who I liked in tomorrow's jet races. I had no idea, and I said so.

"You mean it? I'm backing Kelso. Four to one, but he's got terrific spurt power."

"I'm sorry," I said.

"He's been away for a while," one of the government men said softly.

The euphemism was unmistakable. My neighbor glanced at my forehead and nodded at the pale spot. He offered to buy me a drink too. I accepted, though I was already feeling the effects of the first one. I was a human being again. I was visible.

I did not dare spurn him, anyway. It might have been construed as a crime of coldness once again. My fifth offense would have meant five years of Invisibility. I had learned humility.

Returning to visibility involved an awkward transition, of course. Old friends to meet, lame conversations to hold, shattered relationships to renew. I had been an exile in my own city for a year, and coming back was not easy.

No one referred to my time of invisibility, naturally. It was treated as an affliction best left unmentioned. Hypocrisy, I thought, but I accepted it. Doubt-less they were all trying to spare my feelings. Does one tell a man whose cancerous stomach has been replaced, "I hear you had a narrow escape just now?" Does one say to a man whose aged father has tottered off toward a euthanasia house, "Well, he was getting pretty feeble anyway, wasn't he?"

No. Of course not.

So there was this hole in our shared experience, this void, this blankness. Which left me little to talk about with my friends, in particular since I had lost the knack of conversation entirely. The period of readjustment was a trying one.

But I persevered, for I was no longer the same haughty, aloof person I had been before my conviction. I had learned humility in the hardest of schools.

Now and then I noticed an Invisible on the streets, of course. It was impossible to avoid them. But, trained as I had been trained, I quickly glanced away, as though my eyes had come momentarily to rest on some shambling, festering horror from another world.

It was in the fourth month of my return to visibility that the ultimate lesson of my sentence struck home, though. I was in the vicinity of the City Tower, having returned to my old job in the documents division of the municipal government. I had left work for the day and was walking toward the tubes when a hand emerged from the crowd, caught my arm.

"Please," the soft voice said. "Wait a minute. Don't be afraid."

I looked up, startled. In our city strangers do not accost strangers.

I saw the gleaming emblem of invisibility on the man's forehead. Then I recognized him—the slim man I had accosted more than half a year before on that deserted street. He had grown haggard; his eyes were wild, his brown hair flecked with gray. He must have been at the beginning of his term, then. Now he must have been near its end.

He held my arm. I trembled. This was no deserted street. This was the most crowded square of the city. I pulled my arm away from his grasp and started to turn away.

"No—don't go," he cried. "Can't you pity me? You've been there yourself."

I took a faltering step. Then I remembered how I had cried out to him, how I had begged him not to spurn me. I remembered my own miserable loneliness.

I took another step away from him.

"Coward!" he shrieked after me. "Talk to me! I dare you! Talk to me, coward!"

It was too much. I was touched. Sudden tears stung my eyes, and I turned to him, stretched out a hand to his. I caught his thin wrist. The contact seemed to electrify him. A moment later, I held him in my arms, trying to draw some of the misery from his frame to mine.

The security robots closed in, surrounding us. He was hurled to one side, I was taken into custody. They will try me again—not for the crime of coldness, this time, but for a crime of warmth. Perhaps they will find extenuating circumstances and release me; perhaps not.

I do not care. If they condemn me, this time I will wear my invisibility like a shield of glory.

An essay-story—or story-essay—about a danger . . .
. . . and great opportunity.

THE DISCONNECTED

RAMEZ NAAM

Welcome to the 22nd Century.

You live in the Golden Age of humanity, or at least, the most golden yet. Together, we've conquered poverty and hunger; we've reversed the warming of the planet and destruction of the species we share it with; we've all but ended war and violence and crime. We've cured diseases; we've healed broken minds; we're on the verge of curing hate and anger and despair.

You live in the most *connected* age of humanity yet—an age where everyone is linked; when our very thoughts are connected to one another through technology in our brains; where knowledge or tools or the continuous chatter of all humanity or any of a billion possible desires are just a thought away.

That connectivity is at the heart of our society's success. Our scientists and inventors are faster and more insightful than ever, buoyed by the near instant availability of knowledge, by neutrally integrated software tools, by the intimate experience of the minds of their peers, the potential to access new ways of seeing and thinking. Our teams of scientists, more than ever, resemble hive minds—drawing on the strengths of all their human and machine members, achieving things collectively far beyond what the disparate parts could ever hope to.

Nature has been saved. Most of it, anyway. Discoveries and innovations from the groupminds of our scientists have allowed us to halt the warming of the planet and the acidification of the seas. Soon we may even reverse it. We've learned to grow more food on less land, even amid vast regions suffering drought and heat. We've returned a billion hectares we once used to grow food to nature and parkland. We grow our meat and our fish humanely, now, through miracles of biological science, so that no animal must ever feel pain or suffer death to feed us. The scars of the twentieth and twenty-first centuries run deep, but across the land and seas, those species we managed to save are once more flourishing, and expanding. New ones we've created are joining them.

Our politics—if that word even applies—are the least corrupt humanity has ever seen, the most representative of the will of the people. Our dialogue is deeper now. Soundbites and the politics of hate have been obsoleted by our ability to share rich and complex knowledge in an instant, to see the perspectives of others without the reflexive rejection that once met ideas from "the other side." More and more of our decisions are made through direct collective democracy of our enlightened populace. We still entrust some decisions to select people, of course. We have representatives, officials, what you might call "leaders." They are more transparent to us than ever. We've experienced their thoughts, know their intentions, their values, their integrity. We know they serve the public interest.

The ten billion of us who share this planet are more empathic than ever. We understand one another, across the boundaries of race or gender or nationality. We have met each other, seen through each others' eyes. Primate tribalism has been superseded by global connection, and been replaced by mutual comprehension. We now recognize *everyone* as part of our tribe. Nations and ethnicities and interest groups haven't ceased to exist . . . but they're being subsumed, bit by bit, by the global network that binds all together. Disagreements are as frequent as ever, but they're less hate-filled, less prone to violence.

Zero-sum games have given way to the positive sum.

And crime. We understand criminal urges now. We're learning to soothe and staunch them—both by creating a world of plenty, and by detecting the neural warning signs of coming violence or deception and snipping those crimes in the bud. Those few who do commit crimes are invariably caught. How could it be otherwise in a world where even the poorest infrastructure is suffused with sensors, where intelligence is as ubiquitous a building block of our cities as brick or steel once were? No, the age of crime is ending. Transparency makes transgression impossible. But we do not punish those who commit crimes. That barbarism of the old world is fading behind us into memory, and then history. Instead, we help those who've transgressed. We help them become the best selves and the best citizens they can be. We understand the mind, now, and can gently sculpt it, removing those destructive traits, amplifying the constructive ones, consulting and leaving detail-choices to each patient. Those who go through such procedures are far happier, after. They're more productive. They bring more joy and more value to those around them, and to themselves. And we think—most believe—that we've done so without sacrificing diversity, eccentricity, and idiosyncracy. At least, that is how we agreed that things should be.

We have very few police today, and more doctors.

This is indeed the Golden Age. Though perhaps we should call it the Crystal Age, an age of transparency, an age where society is crystal clear, where the very substrate of our world is suffused with light, light that carries our signals from one to another, that bridges us, person to person, mind to mind. Connecting when we choose, while politely leaving others space to be themselves.

And yet . . .

There are secrets. Not many. But a few still exist.

You didn't even realize how many until you were shown.

There are places on the map that have not been updated in years. Where no transport goes. Where the satellite imaging services return data that is, if one looks closely, synthetic.

There are whole hours of the year when you cannot lightly surveil on the thoughts and activities of your democratically elected leaders.

There are memories you have, from your childhood, passing images and impressions of events that seem so *real*, and which you cannot find any record of.

It itches, this knowledge that secrets still exist. They didn't teach you this in school. Or did they? A hazy memory. You call up your syllabus, the record of every day of your schooling, of the lesson plans, of every word spoken, every drawing shared, every note your human and AI tutors made of your progress.

There is no mention of such a thing. Of secrets that still exist to this day.

You're no "conspiracy theorist." The mental illness that drives such obsession, that allowed the mind to become confused by outlandish, implausible stories, has long since been cured. You've read about the phenomenon, of course. Those afflicted by the conspiracy disease were a pitiful lot, divorced from reality. The opacity of society must have made it hard, when there were so many dark spots in the literal and figurative landscape of the world, when one could legitimately wonder what occupied those spaces. Where curiosity turned to fantasy, or obsession.

Not like the transparent world of today.

But there are still secrets today.

The treatment for conspiracy theorizing is a subtle but pervasive set of neuronal tweaks. The victims remember their past obsessions, and see how ridiculous those thoughts were, see how ill they themselves were. They laugh at their old beliefs, hold compassion for their past selves.

I'm not sick. I don't want any neuronal tweak.

The fear fills you, suddenly. The fear that doctors will insert their software into your brain, will make edits, will take away this newfound awareness. Will turn you into someone else.

Then comes the fear that someone will *sense* your fear. You panic. Fear itself is an illness. They'll use your fear to diagnose you, to make a case to change you.

You clamp down on your growing terror. You have to stop your spiral of emotion. You have to keep it *private*. No one can know how you feel.

Privacy isn't dead, of course. Only those in positions of great power and responsibility are forced to share nearly everything. "Scrutiny for the powerful; freedom for the masses." You aren't one of the powerful. Your responsibilities are medium-sized. You aren't *forced* to share . . . but it is the norm. Deviating too much from that norm is . . . peculiar. "Accept diversity and eccentricity!" That is a keystone slogan . . . and yet, too much is attention-getting.

You have tools that can keep select thoughts and emotions personal—filters, that let you decide what others can sense about you. That is the accepted path, in times of grief or temporary necessity—to continue to share most of what you are, and filter out the bare minimum.

You activate those filters, now, selectively, blocking out your anxiety, your thoughts about secrets, your questions. No more.

You feel better once you've done that.

Of course, the filters know what you're thinking. They have to, to filter it. And the authorities catch violence, before it occurs. They catch crime, and those criminals have filters too. . . .

Your eyes widen. You look around, and the world seems new, and more menacing.

I'm not violent, you think emphatically. *I'm not going to hurt anyone. I'm not going to steal. I'm not going to lie.*

Really? You're not going to lie?

The doctors don't come for you that day.

You repeat the mantra often. *Not violent. Not going to hurt anyone. Not going to steal. Not going to lie.*

The doctors don't come the next day.

Or the day after that.

Or the week after that.

You keep repeating your mantra. But now it has a new ending.

I'm just curious.

Weeks pass. Curiosity begins to overcome fear. You start, gently, subtly, obliquely to research.

You find something almost immediately.

Global security. There are exemptions from the transparency laws, from the 31st Amendment and Article 23 and all the rest. They're right there in the open, the provisions for creating secrets.

So why didn't you know?

I'm not violent, you repeat to yourself. *I'm not going to hurt anyone. I'm not going to steal. I'm not going to lie.*

I'm just curious.

You express that curiosity carefully now. You find places online where people talk. About secrets. About privacy. About *the disconnected*. Disconnected places. Disconnected people.

The conversations were always there. Always ongoing among . . . eccentrics. You never noticed. You would have written them off as slightly odd, as not worth your time.

Perhaps as a bit mentally ill . . .

I'm not violent. . . .

There are people who *disconnect*. Who unplug from the world. That's what the conversations say. There are names given. The names are of people who the official records claim don't exist, have never existed.

It's fiction. It has to be. You consumed a story like this once, of a woman who *unplugged*. The poor thing. It was a tragedy, a series of mistakes leading to the greatest error of her life. She didn't die. She lived on, unloved, alone, isolated, ignored by all around her. . . .

It's fiction. Surely no one would *disconnect* voluntarily?

And then, the disconnected places. You knew of a few. Now you learn of more. Rumors, really. Stories of "a place where a weapon from the last war was buried and no one can find it again." "A place where people fought the doctors and lost."

There is more speculation. Disconnected *events*. Disconnected *facts*. Things you cannot know. Things that perhaps no one can know. A tautology. If no one knows them, how can you even know they exist?

But it gnaws at you.

You lie awake at night, your filters on, worrying away at the shape of the world you've discovered.

Always your mantra first, and last, and in-between, just to assuage your filters . . .

I'm not violent. . . .

And then you try to make sense of it. Of the holes in the world. Of the dark places, the dark hours, the *things you do not know.*

Of the disconnected.

I'm not violent. . . .

Have the disconnected been forced into their state? Has it been inflicted on them as punishment? As protection for society from the contents of their thoughts?

Or did they choose their path?

Are the disconnected places hiding weapons? Or atrocities? Or . . . could it be something else? Could there be something beautiful there?

I'm not violent. . . .

And it occurs to you, as you fall asleep that night, that, perhaps, the very idea of disconnection, of not being watched, of being alone . . . perhaps that is beautiful too.

It seduces you, this idea of disconnecting. It begins to fill your thoughts. Day, after day. You continue to expand your filters to mask it, until you are far beyond social norms. People begin to notice. They regard you oddly. Friends and family and lovers reach out to you, in curiosity, in barely veiled concern.

You brush them off. A surprise, you tell them. You have a surprise coming. You smile. You emote mischief and amusement—invoking those enshrined but neglected slogans about diversity. Eccentricity. They ease away, shrugging, one by one. Tolerant, bemused, but increasingly distant. Curious . . . but not very.

And you realize . . .

. . . *the doctors won't be coming for you.* No agents of the state. No enforcers of conformity. This isn't about any of that. It never was!

And you laugh aloud.

And you wonder: Is this what the other disconnected experienced? Is this what it was like for them, before they made their choice?

Have you already made yours?

All of that has led you here, to me, to this wilderness, the canyon entrance behind me, the primitive campfire between us, its flames licking at the sky, for freedom, like you have. Like you always had, but only now realize.

My face is red in the firelight, as is yours.

I know everything about you, my friend.

You know nothing about me.

Behind me is the unknown.

Rise from your seat by the fire, rise from your slumber in the world of ease and comfort, rise and step forward. Disconnect, and learn the truth.

Do you dare?

LOOKING BACK . . . AND LOOKING UP

The Future will see
Whether you like it or not
Make the best of it

Injustice thrives on ignorance.
But when the disempowered learn to see . . .

EMINENCE

KARL SCHROEDER

Nathan usually felt his cares lift a little as he turned onto Yuculta Crescent. Today, he had to resist the urge to drive past, even just go home.

Nathan passed parked RVs and sports cars as he looked for an empty spot. As he walked back to a modest ochre house, he heard voices: teenagers talking about trading items in some online game world. Nathan hesitated again. *I could still go back to the car, let Grace find out from somebody else.* The temptation was almost overwhelming.

The image was still with him from this morning, of Alicia stabbing her spoon into her coffee cup as she paced in the kitchen. "It's all our money, Nathan! You didn't just put your savings into it; you convinced me to put mine in too. And now you tell me the bottom's falling out?"

The day couldn't get any worse after that, so Nathan started walking again.

At one time this part of town was full of white working-class families with shared values and expectations. Now, the houses were worth millions and, Grace said, nobody knew their neighbors anymore. The two aboriginal kids sitting on the porch stared at Nathan suspiciously as he walked up.

"Is Grace here?" he asked.

"In the kitchen," said one, jabbing a thumb at the door. Nathan went inside, past a small living room that had been remade as office space. Three more teens wearing AR glasses stood in the middle of the space, poking at the air and arguing over something invisible to Nathan. Dressed normcore, in jeans and T-shirts, each also bore a card-sized sticker, like a nametag. **SMILE YOU'RE ON BODYCAM.** Little yellow arrows pointing to a black dot above the words: a camera. The kids on the front porch, he realized, wore something like that.

Grace Cooper was sitting in a pool of sunlight in the kitchen, reading a tablet, her smile easy and genuine as she rose and hugged him. "How's my favorite coder?"

Nathan's stomach tightened. *Shall I just blurt it out? The currency is crashing, Grace. We're about to lose everything.* He couldn't do it, so he sat.

Nathan had known Grace for almost two years, but it was a long time since he'd had to think of her as *the client*. In fact, she was just the representative; the real client was an aboriginal nation known as the Musqueam who'd lived on this land for thousands of years. Small matter that they'd invited him into their community, their lives. He should have kept his distance.

A few years before he immigrated, Grace's people had won a centuries-old land claim that included a substantial chunk of Vancouver. The University golf course, Pacific Spirit Park and much of the port lands south of that were now band territory. That and other settlements had finally given the indigenous peoples of the west coast a power base, and they were building on it. Until today, everyone had benefited—including Nathan.

She sat down after him. The sunlight made her lean back to put her face into shade. "Did you see the news?" she said. "Says Gwaiicoin is doing better than the Canadian dollar."

It was. He'd checked it fifteen minutes ago, and half an hour before that, and again before that. He'd been up all night watching the numbers, waiting for the change. He shrugged now, glancing away. "Well, it's a fiat currency," he said neutrally. "They're all in trouble since the carbon bubble burst."

"And because they're not smart," she added triumphantly. "Thanks to you guys, we got the smartest currency on the planet."

"Yeah. It's been . . . quite a roller coaster." Nathan was trying to find a way to soften the blow. Maybe if he talked about volatility, about how most cryptocurrencies had failed . . . Even the first, Bitcoin, had only been able to lumber its clumsy way forward for so long. But all of them weathered the bursting of the carbon bubble better than the dollar, the pound, or the Euro.

One of those currencies was Gwaiicoin. Nathan had first heard about it while couch-surfing in Seattle with six other guys. He and the guys had struggled to make the rent on a two-bedroom apartment while the housing prices soared, coding web pages for cat lovers to make enough to eat. . . . Well, it didn't leave much further for a guy to fall. The smart programmers had left, hearing that living was cheap on Vancouver Island, just west of the Alaskan Panhandle in the archipelago known as Haida Gwaii. As Seattle priced itself out of liveability, the islands where the iconic totem poles stood were suddenly becoming crowded with restless coders.

One result had been Gwaiicoin—and, when Nathan arrived here, unexpected and welcome employment.

"Gwaiicoin's about to be worth a lot more," Grace was saying. "Once my recruits have added Vancouver to the Gwaii valuation."

Nathan looked through the serving window at the half-visible teens in the living room. "Recruits?"

She leaned forward, her nose stopping just short of the shaft of sunlight. "We're talking with City Council about measuring the biomass in the Musqueam, Squamish and Tsleil-Waututh parts of the city. These kids are my warriors. They're programming drones to measure the biomass."

Nathan gulped, his throat dry, and nodded toward the street. "Good place to start." His mind was darting about, looking for a way to bring her down gently. Then he realized what she was saying. "Wait—you want to add the local biomass to Gwaiicoin?" Unlike Bitcoin, which had value because of its miners and transaction volume, Gwaiicoin was backed by the value of the ecosystem services of its backers' territories.

She nodded enthusiastically. "Even the Inuit want to get in on it. The more biomass we all commit, the bigger our Fort Knox gets. It's brilliant."

Should have seen this coming, Nathan thought. As the dollar crashed, Gwaiicoin had soared. The government wanted it, but since the Haida were backing the currency with land that the feds had formally ceded through constitutionally binding land-claims settlements, the feds were beggars at the table.

"You know, you spent a whole day trying to convince me that a potlatch currency was crazy. Remember that?" Grace grinned at him.

"Yeah." He looked down. "Who'd have thought self-taxing money would take off?"

She sighed. "And still you call it a tax. That was the whole idea—you get eminence points for every buck that gets randomly redistributed to the other wallets."

"Yeah." Despite being a lead on the project, Nathan didn't have much eminence. He wasn't rich, so his wallet didn't automatically trim itself—but even some of Grace's poorer neighbors voluntarily put large chunks of their paychecks into redistribution every month, via the potlatch account everyone shared. Redistributed money was randomly scattered among the currency users' wallets, and in return the contributors got . . . nothing, or so he'd argued. What they got was eminence, a kind of social capital, but the idea that it could ever be useful had never made sense to Nathan.

Ironically, it made sense now. If Gwaiicoin were to vanish overnight, the people who'd given it away would still have their eminence points. These were a permanent record of how much a person had contributed to the community.

And he had none.

He took one last deep breath and said, "Grace. We have a problem."

Somewhere nearby a phone rang. "Hold that thought," said Grace as she hopped up and rummaged for a phone among the papers on the counter. "Hello?"

Nathan watched the flight of emotions cross her face; they settled on anger. "I'll be there in half an hour," she said tightly, and put down the phone.

She avoided Nathan's gaze for a moment. Then she said, "Well. Jeff's been arrested."

．．．

"I'm going downtown anyway," said Nathan. "I'll drop you at the station."

"I could take a driverless," she said as she hastily gathered up her stuff. "They got those new self-owned ones, too, just cruising around looking for a fare."

"They're creepy," said Nathan, and she grinned briefly, nodding. As they passed the kids in the living room, Grace said, "Lock up if you go out."

Nathan glanced back from the porch. "You know them well?"

"These ones? No. But to use this hackspace at all you gotta wear a badge." She patted her own lapel. "And the house knows what's in it, and what shouldn't go out the door."

Supposedly there was some new privacy protocol for the things, but Nathan had been too immersed in Gwaiicoin protocols lately to explore it. The kids seemed comfortable having eyes on them all the time, but he wasn't used to it, any more than he was used to passing cars driving down the road without anybody at the wheel.

He found he was twisting his hands around the steering wheel as if trying to strangle it. Grace didn't seem to have noticed. "Who's Jeff?" he made himself ask.

"One of the kids. He's Haida, his uncle's a carver on the Gwaii. Probably should introduce you."

"But he's been arrested . . . ?"

"It's just harassment. You know they do that to us all the time." She glared out the window, but her expression gradually softened. "It's getting better. Gwaiicoin gives the poorest of us some money every month, and the richer the rest of us get, the more goes to them. No Department of Indian Affairs doling it out. Less harassment. It's working, Nathan!" She rolled down the window and cool air curled in, teasing her hair.

When they pulled into the police station's parking lot, Nathan hesitated.

"Why don't you come in?" said Grace. "This won't take long. Then you can meet Jeff."

"All right."

Of course, it took longer than it should have. Service systems hadn't made it to the Vancouver Police Department yet; any other government service, and Grace could have called in her request or used her glasses and let the computers facilitate it. Here, she had to speak to a desk sergeant, and then they waited in the foyer with a number of other bored or frustrated-looking people. While they stood there (all the plastic chairs were full), Nathan said, "Is Jeff a carver?"

She shook her head. "That's his uncle's thing. No, Jeff's studying ecology and law, like any decent Haida these days. Today, he was supposed to be adding new sensors to the downtown mesh network."

Nathan nodded and they sat there for a while. Finally, Nathan said, "Grace. There's a problem with Gwaiicoin."

She'd been chewing her lip and staring out the window. Now she focused all her attention on him. It was quiet in the waiting room, with no TV, no distractions. Nathan squirmed under her gaze.

"There's been a Sybil attack," he went on, feeling a strange mix of relief and panic that made the words impossible to stop now. "It's supposed to be a one-person, one-wallet system. Otherwise the rich can just make millions of wallets for themselves and when their full wallets trigger a redistribution, chances are the funds will end up back in an empty wallet they already own."

She crossed her arms. "I thought that's why you made the deal with the government. It's one wallet per Social Insurance Number."

"Yeah," he hesitated. "Somebody's hacked the SIN databases. Made, well, about a million bogus citizens. And they've built wallets with them."

Grace's eyes went wide and she stood up, fists clenched.

"Maybe . . . Maybe it's fixable," he said, spreading his hands. "I mean, the Sybil attack . . . it's never been solved, every cryptocurrency is vulnerable to it, we're no worse than Bitcoin was in that sense but of course the potlatch system is critical in your case . . ." He knew he was babbling but under her accusing gaze he couldn't stop himself. "I mean, when Microsoft looked at it they decided the only way to prevent Sybils was to have a trusted third party to establish identities, so, so—" He was desperate now. "That's what we *did,* Grace! We used the best approach there was. And you know, it's not just a problem for us, the government's *got* to fix it or the whole SIN system is compromised . . ."

He could see she wasn't listening anymore. Instead, she was putting together a reply. But just as she was opening her mouth and starting to point at Nathan, an officer behind the counter called out, "Grace Cooper!"

She glared at Nathan, snapped her mouth shut, then went behind the security screen with another officer. Nathan could see them through the glass, and debated whether he should just run. But he was a big name on the development team, and the others—well, they were all quiet today. Hiding in their beds, he'd bet. Leaving him to take the heat, too; but maybe that was the way it should be. He waited.

Grace's conversation with the cop was surprisingly brief. The officer didn't look happy, and when they bent over a laptop together and he read something there, he looked positively furious. Grace came out a few minutes later, looking darkly satisfied. "He'll be right out."

"What happened?"

"He was in one of the ravines in the University Endowment Lands, nailing sensors to trees. Somebody heard him or saw him and called the cops. They found five hundred dollars in his pocket. Figured an aboriginal kid wouldn't have that kind of money 'cept by stealing it. So they trumped something up and brought him in."

Nathan looked past her at the cop, who was now angrily talking to another officer behind the glass. "And what did you just do?"

"I fixed it." She crossed her arms again and pinned Nathan with accusing eyes. "What are *you* going to do, Nathan?"

"Fix it! Of course, Grace, why do you think I came to you? All my money's in Gwaiicoin! Mine and . . . Look, if this goes south I go down with it. I know I gotta fix it."

She didn't reply. A few minutes later a young man with shoulder-length black hair and a wide-cheekboned face came out, lugging a backpack. "Hiya, Grace," he said, unsmiling. "Hell of a day." Then he squinted at Nathan. "Hey."

"This is Nathan. He was just leaving."

"Right. Just leaving. Listen, Grace, I . . ." Her face was an impenetrable mask. Nathan's shoulders slumped and he turned away.

"I'll talk to you soon."

■ ■ ■

Alicia was waiting for him when he walked in the door. "Tell me why I can't pull my money!"

While Nathan visited one development team member after another, she had been texting him with this exact question, and he'd been fending her off as best he could.

"Because the news hasn't hit yet," he said as he kicked of his shoes. "Until this goes public, anything you or I do is going to look like insider trading. Hell, it would *be* insider trading. That's why nobody else on the team has bought out yet." He went straight to the kitchen and rooted around in the fridge for a beer. "But trust me, they're all waiting with hands hovering over mouse, just waiting for the news."

"But don't you know when that's going to happen? The bottom's going to fall out of Gwaiicoin. We'll lose everything if we don't sell now."

He stalked into the living room and sat down. The couch faced out over Blanca Street, and the forested campus of the University of British Columbia. You could see Musqueam lands from here. "We all know that." He savagely yanked the cap off the bottle and took a deep pull, glaring at her. "It's up to the government to make an official statement and they're sitting on it for now. And for the rest of us . . . none of us can be seen to be the first to bail. Who'd want to be known as the guy who kicked off the biggest crash since the Great Depression?"

"It's not that big," she said.

"It is to us. To the Haida. And the Musqueam and the others."

"So you're all holding your breath. But should I?"

He blinked at her. "Insider trading. Besides, do *you* want to be known as the one who brought down Gwaiicoin?"

She thought about it. "I would if I had to. It's my money."

"And that's why it'll go all the way down when it goes. But *your* reputation— *your* career—isn't riding on this. Mine is. Just . . . just hold off for an hour or two." He made a patting gesture with both hands, as if to keep the whole issue down. "I'm sure it'll hit the news tonight."

Her lips thinned; she whirled, and went back to the kitchen to bang around in the cupboards.

A year ago this condo had been Nathan's safety net. No matter how the Gwaiicoin experiment did, he had wealth sunk in real estate. Now, housing prices were collapsing in the downtown core. There was general flight from one of the priciest markets on the continent. He'd seen little signs of the decay just now that only a local would notice: the paint was peeling on the garage doors, the exhaust fans in the wall weren't running. Homeless people were living under the neighborhood's bridges.

So he'd sold off his investment property and put the money into Gwaiicoin.

Rather than turn on the TV, he put on his AR glasses, went to stand on the balcony and gazed through the damp air at the park.

Shadows leaned in from the right as the sun neared the waters of the Strait. He loved to sit out here and watch the sunset proceed, the lights come on in their thousands as night fell. *The city's gone quiet even since I moved here.* The incessant hum of distant internal combustion engines had become rare as electrics took over. Some said it was the quieter cars and that they were also responsible for people strolling, not walking, in evening light like this.

Nathan sighed and called up the Gwaii overlay in his glasses.

The heads-up display showed a silent aurora above the city, its rippling banners of light made of thousands of thin vertical lines. Each line signified ownership—of houses, cars, shops—inferred by algorithms that constantly rifled through public databases and commercial stats. The lines joined and rejoined overhead, becoming fewer, showing how most of the houses were really owned by this or that bank; how businesses were in debt to other businesses. All those relationships of ownership and debt consolidated and narrowed as the line rose, joining in private and public corporations, and these sprouted lines to names. Compared to the dizzying complexity at street level, there were very, very few names up there at the top.

Nathan hadn't built this overlay, and didn't know who had. Whoever it was, they designed in a subtle gray-white background that you could only see by standing in the dark and looking up. The image was one of the Art Deco cityscapes from the old movie *Metropolis*.

He turned on Fountain View, and now the lines pulsed faintly in rising waves. Those ascending glimmers represented money. Some of it rose only to fall again, but some kept on rising, clustering, concentrating, fleeing far over the horizon or ending in the tangle of names above the city. You could change the lights into numbers, and they would show more money going up than was coming down.

Lately Nathan imagined an invisible line coming out of his own head, gutting him like a hooked fish. It was his debt, tugging on him day and night. Money flowed up that line and never came back. If not for the Gwaii, it would suck up his car and his condo; so he turned on that view. It usually reassured him.

A different tangle of lines sprouted from the darkening city—gold, not that wan green, and sparser. Value rose up those bright lines, too, and twined and knotted over the city. But it fell, too, in fine thin lines like a mist of rain. If you converted the lines to numbers, you'd see that almost as much fell back as rose. It concentrated, but in the middle rather than at the top. And coins that flew off over the horizon were usually matched by others coming back.

"Help me with this," called Alicia. Nathan went back in to chop onions, but he kept the overlay active.

One of the Gwaiicoin experiments he'd been involved in was a vase on the corner of the counter. He'd bought it entirely with Gwaiicoin, and it had a virtual tag on it that was different from the others sprouting from his furniture, dishes and clothes. The tag said he wasn't the owner of the vase, but its steward. Such stewardship contracts were the default in any transfer of assets managed entirely through Gwaiicoin. The contract was registered in the Gwaiicoin block-chain, forever beyond the reach of hackers or thieves. It said that the vase was subject to potlatch like his Gwaiicoin, and someday, its virtual tag might change, telling him that the thing had a new steward—somebody picked at random by the algorithm of the coin. He would gain eminence if he gave it to that person. He'd been reluctant to try that out, and Alicia had suspiciously called it "voluntary communism."

Communism. Such a quaint old word. A twentieth-century notion, a square peg for the twenty-first century's round hole. Still, right now the vase was changing its tag—the invisible one in Nathan's imagination. From being a sign of his triumph, it was rapidly becoming a symbol of his defeat.

There was nothing on the evening news, but the pressure kept growing inside him. He stood, he paced. Alicia watched, arms folded, from the couch. He monitored the Gwaiicoin developers' chat room, but nobody was there. They were all waiting. Somebody would have to make the first move.

Finally, at eight o'clock, social media started lighting up. *Sybil Attack. Gwaiicoin compromised.* As the tweets and posts began flying fast and furious he turned to Alicia and said, "Do it."

As she raced to get her laptop, Nathan sat down and dismissed all his overlays. He called up his financial app and sat for a long time looking at the impressive balance on the Gwaiicoin side, and the nearly empty one in dollars. Below his Gwaiicoin balance was a link for voluntary transfers to the potlatch account.

I could drop my coins back into dollars, and just walk away. Across the room, the clattering of Alicia's laptop told him what she was doing.

He stared at the other link. He was partly responsible for dragging thousands of people—mostly poor to begin with—into this fiasco. If he put his money into potlatch, he would lose it as surely as if he'd burned wads of dollar bills. The coins would instantly appear in others' wallets, randomly scattered among the emptiest of them. Some would be lost to the Sybil attackers, but most would go to real people. Then, those people could cash out in dollars, and end the Gwaiicoin experiment with just a little more than they'd had this morning.

And he would have nothing. Except, in the form of eminence, proof that he'd tried to help. Not monetary capital, but social capital.

Nathan sat there for a long time. Then he slowly reached out, and made a transfer.

. . .

At ten, he went for a walk.

It wasn't raining, and it was summer; so you walked. He'd always enjoyed strolling along Blanca, with its tall walls of trees and hedges, the suggestion of darkness over the western streets that came from the presence of the UBC forest lands. You passed through that forest on your way to the campus, which dominated the end of the peninsula. Taking University Boulevard, you could peek past the trees lining it to the golf course on either side.

Except he never went that way. It was all Musqueam territory, and while they were clients and friends, they had also filled the place with cameras and drones. These didn't bother him so much around Grace's house, but here, as a solitary walker, he became self-conscious.

He walked, head down, and didn't look at the overlays. He imagined it anyway: the slow, ponderous collapse of that pyramid of golden light that he'd seen hovering above the city earlier. The first rats leaping off the ship would alert everybody else, and by now everybody would be selling. It would be a classic financial collapse, and he had helped set it off. Who was going to hire him now?

Somehow his feet had carried him south to Tenth Avenue and University. Off to the right, the golf course gleamed in the evening light. The BC Golf House was also alight and its parking lot full, mostly with pickup trucks and new model electrics, not the pricey sedans you usually saw there.

He saw a car pull in, stop, and Grace Cooper got out.

Now he remembered: there was supposed to be a social tonight. The councils were coming together to talk about their successes. Grace had told him about it last week. "It's called a 'social,'" she'd said. "They used to have them in the Maritimes and prairies all the time. You just rent a hall, buy a liquor license and find some local band that's willing to come out and play. Then call all your friends, and they call their friends. . . ."

He should be running the other way, but a kind of fatal determination had seized him. Grace had been one of the most enthusiastic supporters of Gwaiicoin. It was brave of her to be here tonight; she risked becoming a lightning rod for the blame.

The hall's front doors were wide open and people were standing around laughing and talking on the walk. Nathan ran under the weave of electric bus wires that canopied the street, and came up behind Grace just as she was about to enter. "Grace!"

She whirled. "What the hell are you doing here?"

He stopped, hesitated, then squared his shoulders. "I got us into this mess. Are any of the other developers here?"

She shook her head.

"Somebody has to take responsibility—" He made to enter the hall, but she stopped him.

"You're not going to talk about it, and I'm not going to either because that's not what tonight's about. I don't want you to *make* it about this. We're celebrating other things here—things we actually *accomplished*." He flinched from her emphasis. It was suddenly obvious why the social was happening at the Golf House. Tiny it might be, but it was on Musqueam land. Land they had taken back.

"What's *done* counts," she said. "What we tried . . ." She shrugged. "Not so much." Then she moved out of his way. "Go on in, I can't stop you."

He almost turned away, but whatever he told himself, these people were not just clients. He wanted to be able to look them in the eyes after all this was done. "I won't bring it up," he said. "But others will, and they'll want to know what I'm doing about the situation."

"Which is?"

He opened his mouth, throat dry, and couldn't say it. He just pushed on past her, into the hall.

A folk ensemble was playing. There were tables around the sides of the hall and people roved, chatting. Nobody was dancing but the atmosphere was upbeat. And it should be; here were the inheritors of stubborn cultures that, after five hundred years of often-systematic oppression, were still here.

And were they ever. For the next hour Nathan passed from table to table, saying hi to people he barely knew and, through them, meeting other focused and determined citizens of Canada's youngest and fastest growing demographic. These were kids in their late twenties and early thirties who'd made great money in the oil sands and northern mines, and were now here starting families and pouring their wealth into the Maa-Nalth Treaty Association, the St'at'imc Chiefs Council or the Carrier Sekani Services. Several of these organizations were rapidly mutating into shadow governments in central B.C. There were so many historical groups, so many unpronounceable names and treaty claims that you'd think it was all chaos. There was an emergent order to it all, though. Gwaiicoin and the blockchain were supposed to be helping with that.

He could see it in their eyes; everybody knew about the Sybil attack. They knew what it meant, but nobody confronted him. Somehow, that hurt more than if they'd beaten him and thrown him into the parking lot.

After a while, exhausted, he found himself sitting across from Jeff. Casting about for something—anything—other than Gwaiicoin to talk about, Nathan asked, "How did Grace get you out so quickly today? Or shouldn't I ask?"

Jeff pried the material of his shirt forward to show his bodycam. "I told the cops myself, but they wouldn't listen. This thing has been uploading a low-frame–rate video stream constantly for the past month. Every frame is signed with a hash and GPS coordinate and timestamped in the GPB. That's the, uh, Global Positioning Blockchain. The GPB can verify where I was every second of every day and prove I didn't break into anybody's house. When I told them that, they wanted to see the video, but I told them to fuck off. They didn't have the right. So we were . . ." He seemed to choose his next words delicately. "At an impasse."

"Grace knew something about it I didn't, though."

Nathan had heard of the GPB—in that passing way he'd heard of about a million other applications of blockchain technology. GPB was an attestation system, providing the spatial equivalent to a timestamp. It provided a secure, decentralized, autonomous way for people all over the world to identify and track specific objects or people. Nathan had shied away from it because to him it had always seemed like the backdoor to some creepy surveillance society.

"What did Grace know that you didn't?"

Jeff shook his head ruefully. "The whole lifelog's encrypted with something called FHE. Fully homo-something encryption. Every frame of the lifelog is encrypted *in the camera*, before it's uploaded, using a key that needs at least three people to unlock it. One of them being me, I guess." He shrugged. "Anyway, because of FHE, the GPB can query that encrypted frame for the answer to specific questions—like, was I in somebody's house by the ravine—*without decrypting the data*."

Fully homomorphic encryption. It was all the rage in some circles, the way Bitcoin had been around 2010. It really did let untrusted third parties analyze your data without decrypting it. You could trust them because they couldn't even in principle have seen what those results were, even though they'd done the work to generate them. Only you could open the returned file.

Nathan was happy for this mathematical distraction. "Let me get this straight," he said. "Because the GPB's a transparent blockchain, we can prove the encrypted frames haven't been tampered with or replaced once they're up-loaded. And we can analyze each frame to find out whether any of them show you straying off the path. . . . But how do we know you didn't switch body-cams with somebody else?"

"Because the frame rate's high enough that if I swapped it, that would have been visible. The GPB can attest to the whole path I took through the day"— Jeff swooped his hand over the tabletop—"without us having to *show* any of the frames to the cops. Which alibis me out while securing my privacy."

"Wow." The video feed was effectively also a blockchain, the truth of each new frame attested to by the ones that preceded it. Still . . . "You could hack it," Nathan decided. "The camera's the vulnerable point. If you mess with that . . ."

Jeff was shaking his head. "You forget the mesh network. It was uploading data about me the whole time. The trees were watching. And the security cameras on the telephone poles—you know this near Musqueam land—they feed the same frames to our security company that owns them and to the GPB at the same time. So it's like having multiple witnesses who can say they saw you somewhere. Difference is we don't have to show that proof to a cop or a judge to make it official. Once you've got enough independent witnesses, it's just effectively impossible for all of them to have been compromised." He grinned. "The cops at the station didn't get that, but they phoned somebody else who did. And that's how it went down."

Nathan shook his head. "Cool." With the GPB, FHE, and enough independent cameras, you could turn supposedly ephemeral Internet images into proof of position for any object on Earth, while guaranteeing anonymity for that object. You could do it for people, for trees, briefcases full of cash, cars . . .

Too bad, he mused, you couldn't also do it for something virtual, like a game character.

Or a piece of software . . .

Nathan stood up so suddenly he nearly knocked over the bench. "Shit!"

Jeff looked up, eyebrows raised. "What?"

"I gotta go." Nathan turned, and practically ran from the hall.

■ ■ ■

Nathan realized Alicia was talking to him, and had been for some time. He glanced over; she was standing there in a bathrobe, hair tangled, looking at him with a really worried expression on her face.

"One sec," he said. He laid his hands on the keyboard and entered COMMIT. Then he hit RETURN, leaned back, and sighed.

"You've been crazy typing for three hours," she said. "What's wrong?"

He looked at the clock in the corner of his monitor screen. It was 2:00 a.m. He was wide awake, practically jumping out of his skin with energy, though he knew how that went: the mental crash, when it came, would have him sleeping most of tomorrow.

"Fixed it," he said. "Now I gotta . . ." He turned from her to text the rest of the team.

Her hand on his shoulder pulled him back to the moment. "Fixed what? Nathan, what the fuck are you doing? You're scaring me."

"The, the Sybil attack. I found a fix." *Fix* hardly summed up what he'd just done, but just now he was having a bit of trouble with natural languages, like English. Nathan's head was full of the object code he'd been putting together, and that he'd just committed to a new fork of the Gwaiicoin wallet system.

He rubbed his eyes. "Just one sec, and I'll tell you all about it." He texted the team; they'd mostly be asleep, but the buzz of their phones would wake a few, and if nobody got back to him in the next few minutes he'd start phoning them.

The sell-off of Gwaiicoin was in full swing, and he'd been keeping an eye on it while he worked. Luckily, it hadn't been as bad as he'd feared, for the simple reason that transactions above a certain size were taxed by the currency itself. When Alicia had moved her money from Gwaiicoin to dollars, some of those funds had been transferred to thin Gwaiicoin wallets. Until the poorest wallets divested, a goodly chunk of the money was going to stay in the system.

Still, once the rich had divested the poor would follow, and then the system really would collapse.

He hit SEND, then turned to Alicia. "What if you could prove that each Gwaiicoin user was a human being and had one unique wallet?"

"Oh, God." She rummaged through her hair, then leaned back against the office wall. "No Sybil attack. Is that it?" She stopped, blinked at him. "I thought you couldn't do that. You need a trusted third party and that was supposed to be the Social Insurance System. And they crapped out. They got hacked."

"What if you didn't need that third party? If you identified each person as a unique position in spacetime, and that person's one and only wallet is at that same position? Each wallet has a position and it has to correspond to a person's position. Only one wallet is allowed for any position. So: unique person, unique wallet. Sybil attack solved."

She shook her head. "Just make up fake people."

Nathan laughed and jumped up. "But you can't! That's what's so great about it!" The more bodycams, cop-cams, security cams, GPS-sensing sports and health trackers that uploaded their data to the Global Positioning Blockchain, the more witnesses there were to attest to peoples' existence and location. FHE encryption meant you could hide the data from prying eyes, but still prove your identity in full public view.

"It'll take a while for the fix to work," he admitted. "Weeks, months maybe, until everyone using the coin is accounted for. Once they all are, though, Sybil attacks will be impossible. Meanwhile . . ." He frowned at the growing divestment numbers.

Alicia was wide awake now. "It won't matter if it all goes south tonight." She had put on her glasses and was staring out the window—probably watching in AR as the gold lines of Gwaiicoin pulled back from house after darkened house, like candle flames going out. "Though I suppose if the team reinvests it'll send a strong signal. . . ." She turned to him and raised her glasses. "That what you're going to do now?"

Nathan sat there, gazing at the jumble of windows in the monitor. "No." Giddiness battled with horror.

He hadn't told Grace what he'd done, though she'd find out soon enough. He couldn't avoid Alicia, though.

"I didn't divest," he said, still staring at the screen. "I could have. Should have, I guess. Maybe I panicked, I dunno, I—"

"Nathan." She came to lean on the table next to him. "What did you do?"

"I gave it away." A half-hysterical laugh rose out of him. "All of it. Straight into the potlatch account—swoosh!" He zoomed his hand over the keyboard.

The look of horror on Alicia's face was perfect. The rest of the laugh burst its way out of Nathan, battling tears.

He'd given away all his savings.

"I gave it to the people, and now all I have . . ." He clicked over to his Gwaiicoin wallet. ". . . is a hell of a lot of eminence."

"So you didn't divest. You—"

"*Invested.* And if this crash turns around . . ."

"Oh, Nathan, what have you done?"

He slumped back, shaking his head, but smiling.

"I don't know. But just maybe . . ."

He turned to look at the city skyline, picturing the fountaining flow of currencies: money, power, influence, and, joining them, a quality that those other media had never been able to carry: trust.

"Maybe," he murmured, half to himself, "I've found a new way to be rich."

The future will demand more than new ways to see.
There will be new ways to think.

SPORT

KATHLEEN ANN GOONAN

"Yes; yes," says mother, lying like summer-slumped butter on the couch after her night's work, eyes closed, having shed scrubs and donned a linen shift smooth-gray as a rainy day. Irritated as an itch by me, I know, but I keep picking at her.

"Nanya did come to D.C., once." Lines between closed eyes deepen. "Then she left."

She turns face-against the couch back, long spine curved, dreads waterfalling to the small, dissonant African rug. When I was a baby, I feared its weird cacophony and screamed whenever mother set me on it.

Nanya never did.

"She was a crazy woman. She needed medication. She wouldn't take it. I was in medical school. You were little. I couldn't take care of both of you."

A deep sigh, like she's swatting away a fly so she can sleep. "Yes. She's still alive. I think she lives with your great-uncle. He promised to take care of her. No, we can't go see her. We're way too busy. We can't afford it. And it's bad there." She pretends to fall asleep.

"Did she have a parrot? A gray parrot?"

Shoulder-shrug shimmy into true sleep.

That was before they took me—sorry, invited me, to serve my country in Yodaville.

. . .

Lucy clings to dream through rough shaking, but then it is a brilliant scarf-shredded grainy awakening.

"Wake up." Her mother.

"Mmmm." She rolls over.

"They're waiting for you in the living room." Click of wall switch: dissonant white-light trumpets blare. A light thump on her hip. "Here's some sweats."

"What time is it?" Eyes squeezed tight seeking lost color. She's not usually this tired at six.

"Two. Hop in the shower. I told them this isn't in the contract and you have rights, but they said they'll give you a pill. You don't take them, do you?"

"Mmmm."

A very clear sigh. "I hate that you're doing this. You can stop, you know. You're only fifteen. This is child abuse. They can't keep us here, damn national emergencies. I found us a lawyer in . . ."

Her mother's voice purple wind roaring as Lucy sleepwalks to the bathroom.

Pelting cacophony; hot/cold wake.

The thing is, she likes what she does.

. . .

They gave her meds for it not knowing what it was when she was ten, practically over her mother's dead body, but the school insisted; her mother after much research agreed to give them a try. Lucy was a big nuisance in the classroom. And at home. So much so that she got Wrong-Man Arthur, her mother's boyfriend, ejected after a year, good riddance. She and her mother later laughed about him as they sat at their little table for two next to an open window in spring, curtains fluttering, as they ate poached eggs and drank hot chocolate, African kora springing on the CD player.

Meds helped. Color calmed; shapes stopped shouting; time stopped stuttering. She could see how normal acted. She studied their ways, an alien in a world of intent. She observed, a scientist, that which most take for granted: faces, situations, reactions. She learned how to hide in plain sight.

Pills taught her how to pass. She had friends, kind of. She went to birthday parties and kids smiled at her in the hall. She smiled back. In school, she did everything slowly. Sometimes she even made Cs. She thought she was being clever. It wasn't fun to be laughed at. It wasn't fun to have other kids think you were smart.

She discovered that the mean girls were all unhappy, and that somehow it made them feel better to belittle others.

She'd always known that humans were strange. She was strange too.

But different.

. . .

Wet black curls chill her neck as the matched pair of blacksuits rush her outside. Front door to black Suburban-tank a frozen, distant tinge of pianolike notes: green, blue, red, yellow stars. Patsy, her usual driver minus her usual blues music, yawns in a cocoon of smooth black silence.

"Who are you?" Lucy asks the two men who hustled her to the tank, one in the front seat, one next to her in the back. To give them a poke; she knows they will say nothing. Like rocks.

Still half-asleep, her head fills with composition to her Someone, the Interlocutor. She knows she should not talk to him/her/it, not in any traceable way, and yet she has, she does, she will, because the Interlocutor's questions have the flavor of caring: hot pepper, tamarind, ginger. The questioner's braintouch, like those distant piano-note stars, actually makes her mouth tingle; reminds her of some childhood comfort. She rearranges and remembers every word on the screen in her head, and when she has time she will send it to the place she is almost sure only she knows about, a specific nub/flavor/place on the swirling tangle of spaghetti-like international communications that will swirl through her once she is Inside.

Yes: addictive. Which is why mother is angry: she can't control Lucy. Not only is Lucy Saving The World, but it is fun.

■ ■ ■

?

Time is different for me. I think it is full of more of everything than it is for most people, so it lasts longer, but that's probably not a good way to put it. Colors are sound for me, and sound is sometimes objects, and objects are sound.

?

The pills did help me pass. I told you. But I couldn't shut off my brain. I couldn't shut off my DNA.

?

I am a sport. Genetically strange.

?

From what I know now, this happened: Big Yoda searched a gazillion records and found me. They took me to the study facility; there were a lot of specials there, and they certified and specialed me and sorted me into narrow amazements of various sorts and stamped me and microchipped me and said "Well done" to each other, drinking from champagne flutes. I had ginger ale in mine. It appears that I am many kinds of special, a serious conflagration of specials.

?

Yeah. I got one tweet after I left, from my best friend, Biyach. "Where did they take you?" That was the last. Yeah, I know they cut me off. I don't care.

?

Yoda? Slang for a yottabyte: a quadrillion gigabytes: the storage and sorting power they have here. Yoda: my alien friend, for whom I am a human interface, an interpreter who speaks English. Kind of. Is Yoda alive? Sometimes . . . I feel it so. I some-

times even think Yoda will have offspring, gray monoliths like the Easter Island moai,
even though Yoda is just underground acres, miles of wire, the latest and nano-est
processing and memory materials. Bytes. Code.

?

Yes yes, of course the Yodas will know good from bad. Why? Because they are
made of Us. Can't we trust . . . Us?

What do you mean, LLLLOL? Sarcasm?

Why do this? Is that your question?

For my country. Living in Bluffville instead of D.C. is a sacrifice. Yeah. . . . they
say I can go anywhere I want and do anything I want in Sim-D.C., but they don't
seem to understand that there is a difference. Despite all their tests, they seem to
know little about me. Sim is the smell of dry blank paper, all edges, cutting me with
no. It's okay though. I have a choice.

Oh? You take pills too?

Skipping through the wires one night, she'd found this erratic flavor, this
African-rug color, and enlarged her ping. She thinks toward it as if growing a
new hand on pathways laid down by DNA: inexorable. The Interlocutor is a
concise sensory experience she cannot describe in words. Except for her mouth
tingling with a skein of color, she would know for sure that it is her handlers
trying to test her.

That would be all right, too. She likes games.

■ ■ ■

Bluffville has few sounds at night. There is only the repeating cymbal-dash of
streetlights; the low, boring drone of closed shops and gray bars repeating every
block like a ribbon of DNA. A single pickup saying left turn soon soon soon
instead of mobs of turn signals chiming in stutters.

The Mountain broods above, black against black, visible only because it
holds no stars. Lucy expands to fill the vacuum. She is such a concert of wave-
lengths that she almost goes back to sleep. But the ride is short.

■ ■ ■

Beepthrough retina scan. Even at this hour a woman stands with a big gun,
and Lucy knows legions of this woman could burst out of secret doors at the
slightest hint of trouble. The laughably serious silent men accompany her
through hallways she probably knows better than they, the vast white space
stranged pleasantly by her seeing different folks: the night shift. They form a
new palette. The air smells black despite the numbing whiteness. The two non-
colors twist together in her mind, uniting finally in a slow pinwheel that is
black, then white, then black, then white.

"I'll need a double chocolate mocha with triple whipped cream."

One man nods; taps his phone absently without breaking stride.

"And some kind of coat. I'm cold."

Tap, tap; stride.

Lucy is not quite sure where this emergency might take her, and fears a bar-rage of spitting nonsense from suited strangers in sterile rooms. In such cases, she usually nods while brain-blurring them to keep from leaping up and scratching out their eyes from sheer irritation.

She is relieved when they take her to her usual cubicle. No one has spoken to her; no special instructions. She knows there is an emergency, and now knows they trust her to taste it.

Here are photos, Post-Its, a soothing white *Phalaenopsis* in perfect orchid-arc, from Other Grandma, a white woman with blonde hair who lives in Yuma and plays golf in the Kingdom, as she always proclaims, laughing a huge, burry laugh.

Drop-curl into her big cozy chair. Pick up paper cup; toss back green pill; wash down with dregs of a canned Coke. Cushiony helmet; sweet, silent pause; a warm wrap settled round her shoulders. Steamy orange knife of espresso chocolate placed by an unobtrusive hand stabs, electric, when she takes a sip. Arc-screen on; sharp plunge into her world: thin streaming screaming spaghet-tis of color blast out of the screen and through her. She soars.

■ ■ ■

She can slow or speed the infinite rushing-into-her river; turn it into other manifestations: bursting flowers of color; music rain; avalanche; pixilated crowds from above or angling. Purejoy. Until:

But she can't really explain what happens to her, how she can tell a disso-nant, possibly terroristic e-mail or phone conversation from any other. A blip of colorsound, that is all. An instant's sickness; swift-gone sienna intent; the smell of coffee burning in the bottom of a carafe.

She clicks her mouse, puts the writhing conversation of the world on hold as she backs up.

Click: magnify.

Click: isolate.

Click: we are on a long trip, and stop at a country place where they seem to know us.

Click: they speak our language but it is a little different.

Click: no it will not happen until next week; some numbers that are a color in Lucy's brain; she taps them onto a screen almost absently.

Click: no I cannot say exactly where you will hear from me.

Click: a man stands three-dimensional before her, cell phone in hand, his

appearance assembled from the profile his cell phone has built for the world
to see during the past six months.

He wears a black suit and a white shirt and a navy-blue tie. His gray-blond
hair is combed over a bald spot. The suit shifts to tennis shorts for an instant,
then to a tuxedo, but she ignores these visual definitions. It is the gray sickness,
the lack of empathy that a mere week of feedback taught her to see, hear, feel.
She is utterly undistractible, a quality her teachers, her family, her non-friends
would all deny, because for her entire life she has been labeled as a misfit flit-
terbygibbet in need of serious medication.

Click: she sends her notice and surfs back onto the rolling, rollicking hills
of wiry tubes of sound, chatterspeed, greyblackblip stop click screen send go.
Video of a girl her age but blonde, winking as she drinks an illegal beer and
friends laugh: tweeted. Her own desires and fears sometimes stop the flow and
she learns to recognize them in various ways. Porn is a green-orange blare that
makes her nauseous before her brain parses images; a signal not to pause, but
one that flashes frequent.

She goes on, tasting combinations of spoken words, instantaneously translated, scanned by her special brain—human, not machine: she knows her spot-
tings are much more accurate than those made by the machines that fill other
halls in clean rooms.

■ ■ ■

*"Because she was a gambler, Lucy. Is. Always will be. It's a disease. She gambled
away my medical school money. You can't imagine how much gone—in a second!
I've almost paid back the loan I was lucky to get. It's almost paid back. Then I'll have
more time for you—not so many shifts. I promise.*

*"Yes, she had a goddamned parrot! Ever since I was little! The damned things
live forever. It bit people! It pooped all over the apartment! She was sick, crazy, and
stole our life, Lucy. Enough! It's finished!"*

Stabbing lightning; roaring sea.

So when they asked Lucy what she most wanted she said I want my mother's
medical-school loan paid off.

O, that mountain-weight gone!

But no. Instead, rage and blame. Tears. Bargaining. Plain thundering NO!
"Lucy. You cannot sell yourself for me."

Lucy's own sharp, screaming voice startles her. *"That's all I ever heard you
talk about. Money! Now I can give it to you! Doesn't that make you happy?"*

The bowed head. *I am so sorry, Lucy. Please forgive me. Take it back. I am
getting a lawyer. They did not disclose this to me.*

Lucy does not cede.

Her mother finds that the blacksuits have emergency powers under a sweeping security act.

...

Lucy is schooled here, in the cold reaches beneath Bluffville, finishing high school in a month and continuing to gallop in many directions at once, feeling a shock of clear delight whenever their interconnections infuse her. She is Good At Music (composition a four-dimensional object). And she is Good At Math and dallies over delicious details of advanced calculus.

She has an online tutor who is blond and cute, with strong blue long-lashed eyes that give her shivers. She daydreams about him. Kisses, hugs, sex. But what is sex? She wants to know. It seems green and pure, a portal to adult. For which she longs: empowerment.

There are a few other specials at the Data Center. She once glimpsed a kid down a long hallway with spiked-up white and purple hair implying piercings and mean tattoos before being whisked past.

Being one, she's done research: every special's brain is unique. In fact, the brain of everyone is unique, like one's genetic profile, but the uniqueness of special's brains is strikingly strange. In the olden days (like, say, before 2000), many of them believed that they truly were the only one of their kind, like the woman who could remember every day of her life in great detail.

The oxymoronic common specialnesses? Dyslexia, dyscalculia, dysphasia: the dysses. Lots of them. Other specialnesses: aphasias, the lacks; autistic, profound; Asperger's, weird; faint savant; faint eidetic; tetrachromat, yes, synasthaete, wonderful! Though normal, for her, and always.

Her age: that perfect developmental cusp when neurology clicks into brilliant mathematics, physics, art, and insight.

She had been so surprised to learn that her irritation with those around her (she thought they were pretending not to see letters in color, or hear objects) was misplaced. Now she knows for sure the girls she wanted to befriend were for the most part Just. Plain. Stupid.

It helps to think so but sometimes she hears Nanya's voice, mist-waterfall, a hand tucking her hair behind her ear, a gold-pulsing hug. "Everyone is beautiful, Lucy. Hear hard for their bright sound."

When Lucy went to big old gold-stone church on Twelfth Street with Nanya, waves of difference stopped holding her under. Hymns were translucent turquoise waves she rode.

After church, Nanya's parrot, gray parrot, Olu, cursed in broken-machine, springs flying out, metal-crunch as they drank sweet mint tea, still wearing their special African clothes, bright with infinite song. Sometimes Olu said, "Did anybody hear that smell?"

I do. I do.

When small, she did not think this strange.

. . .

After a few hours, Hug-Woman Kelly takes her to brunch in the cafeteria. She crushes Lucy to her large bosom, saying, "Poor dear, they work you so hard." Lucy can tell that inside Hug-Woman Kelly is as adamantine as the rest, that she does not feel those hugs but plays her part, Nurturer. She puts Yuma Grandma's face on Hug-Woman's, knowing that is what they want, and it is fine.

"They got you up at two? Monsters. Have a frappe with that pill. French fries for breakfast? Sure, why not."

. . .

They began taking her for tests at the brain lab when she was in fourth grade in Mabel's Falls Elementary. The brain lab was jazzy screens, a new rush of smile faces, and the clunk-whirr of fMRI's.

How did she infer intent? She couldn't give them words. Kind of like: there was a golden heart somewhere, where sound and color merged, in that near-far gold-stone church. But on the way, down shouting deep-remembered streets, a fast world needed sorting. The road was steep. The strands her hands grasped burned. When she trained, she often had to loose them and retreat.

They taught her ways to move forward, to keep grasping and searching. The search assumed a rhythm, drew her forward.

Their stiff faces loosened with surprise when she slowed wire-time, satellite-gathered, to particulars. She could listen on a microlevel. She could see what subjects looked like as she watched their minds, speed-built from a blur of references.

She could reliably infer intent much more often than could their most powerful datacrushers.

She was recruited.

She was against Terror. Of course. She swore it.

But it was, still is, more complicated than that.

She craves a path toward Something, and here, she is on that path. She does not know her own goal. She only knows the journey seems familiar, like being in her carseat with her eyes closed and knowing each turn, each changing whirr of tires and each jarring pothole, every tunnel-pressure and its length, a building of flavors until she gets to that longed-for place, that deep meal that Mother will not speak of.

It is more than Nanya, more than Olu, more than a gold-stone church. It is more than a swoop of shadow in moonlit night, Olu machine-cursing as he flies to the stars.

But it is made of them.

■ ■ ■

Bills, tedium. But necessary. Invoices, receipts, Internet searches subjects have made build like waves. Some pass beneath her. Some arc, sudden mountains, about to break on steep shores and Click: she says, go see. Go see fast. Where did he go, what did he spend? Tie details in a neat cube and send it up the channels.

Several times a day, she does this.

Tells the blacksuits where. Says show up on their doorstep like you did on mine. Open your powerbadges. Put their heads in helmets, unpack their brains. Interrogate them with physics, with light. Unburden and unwind them.

Make them good or kill them trying.

■ ■ ■

On Connecticut Avenue in Washington D.C. it snows hard. Fred Upshaw slips in smooth-soled wing tips, socks soaked, and dodges into a noisy café filled with the usual lunch crowd.

"Someone's waiting for me—there, I see her."

Denise Upshaw's black hair shimmers with melted snowdrops beneath the dropped aluminum cone of light over her table. His phone vibrates; he takes it from his pocket. An unknown number. Disquieting. So many, lately.

Warm scents fill the air—baking bread, tomato soup. Brittle clink of glasses; he sees some lunch martinis on tables, wishes for one, forgoes the wish.

"Hi—sorry I'm late!"

"Hey! What about this weather? But I love snow!" Her smile is quick and lovely.

"I don't. It's messy. Have you decided?"

The waiter appears. "Take your order?"

Fred looks at him twice. "Are you new?"

"Did you see today's specials on the board? We have—"

"I'll have the soup. A bowl," she says, cutting in. "And hot chocolate. You have hot chocolate?"

"I'll check."

Denise dimples at Fred. "I have something to tell you."

■ ■ ■

Why do they want Lucy? Why is she better than Yoda? She is not sure. Hug-Woman mumbled something about "You pass the Turing Test" one time when she asked. She knows what that is. She just does not know why it is better than being a computer.

∎ ∎ ∎

Green: crackling/burning plastic. Sharp.

Blue: Oddly, hot. Like red for others. A moibus.

Yellow: Too far to ever go.

Purple: Taste of blood in her mouth. A cut on her finger when she was crawling and found a knife on the kitchen floor and her brain was defining sensory paths, the paths that were never pruned? Doesn't matter.

Red: A glimpse of trees overhead.

White: The Beatles: Love, Love, Love.

Orange: Play. Wild play. Sleek dogs run through gold autumn fields. Nothing better.

Black: Braincold.

These colors: so rudimentary.

But the beginnings of an infinite alphabet. And no one else will ever read the words.

∎ ∎ ∎

?

Why do you keep bothering me? All right. I was saying "with liberty and justice for all" with my hand over my heart when Mr. Thompson came to the classroom door.

Seriously.

That was the first time I rode in a limo. It was black inside; braincold. Mr. Burly Bumpnose sat next to me in the back and Ms. Painful Gamboge Yellow was in the front seat. All in all, they were sharp shouts mixed with bibble and they did not even move or smile or speak. I'm trying to be plain but it is hard. I really have to slow down and . . . No offense, but talking to other people is like talking to dogs or cats. I would rather showbrain with parrots. We are more alike. No one hears unless I talk in baby steps. Like, for instance, do you know what lake pigments sound like? Or even look like? Supreme Alternate Rainbow Ornette Coleman. Sure, sometimes I'm just pulling your leg. The plainest day for most people is my carnival, apparently. Sometimes it hurts.

What? Don't ask me about parrots again. I was just making that up. LOL. Parrots are cool, aren't they? Really, really smart. And they live a long time.

No, not really. I've never met one. Just read about them. Leave me alone.

Mouse click slows change. She tries to pinpoint. Interlocutor slips away.

Which surprises her: a limit to what she can do.

∎ ∎ ∎

Green song-couple. Her side blue, his yellow. Yearning a billisecond pause. She says "Fred, we're going to have a baby."

Brainyank. Burnvoice: "What?"

She skims the edge of intent, then drinks it; finds it good. She follows the trail of surmise and leaps backward and finds the false taste planted, rotten and retch-making as rotting meat.

She walks into a vortex and it is quiet in the middle. She hides from her handlers, realizing, They're okay. They are so okay it hurts, Fred and Denise Upshaw.

▪ ▪ ▪

She wakes in a cot in the sleeping room, and they know the instant she does so. How long has she been here? She doesn't remember leaving her cubicle.

"Sorry," says Hug-Woman, grabbing her hand and pulling her to the bathroom. "Orange alert." The color of resolution, when all is made right. The tonic chord. The perfect meal. Release; the path to truth; glory.

They shouldn't remind her of the possibility; should not give her the trumpet blare. They know this, but it seems too complicated for any one handler to remember.

Ice-arrows of shower barely wake her.

But the pill does.

▪ ▪ ▪

The wires jerk her to a traffic camera. Upshaw's car veers into a lamppost. She skids down the path to the remote computer controlling his steering wheel: the fleeting wisp of 0's and 1's that almost kill him. Denise. The baby she just told him about.

Why?

She tastes something and chases the taste like a gazelle.

The blue moibus pulls her onboard. It sears her, brings her back to her cubicle. "Hey!" Tight hands on her shoulders. Slaps. "Stop screaming! Stop it!" Blur eyes of MentorEnemyWoman. Pretend-black-sooth; inside swirl enemy colors. Fake blonde hair brushing Lucy's face. "You will report this as a satisfactory outcome. A success. You will redo your previous assessment."

"But I *told* you! They are not terrorists." Lucy shakes her head so violently that her dreads pelt the woman's face. "ItoldyouItoldyouItoldyou they are all right! They are . . ."

The woman pulls back. Stares at Lucy. Leaves the cubicle for a moment and returns with a glass in her hand. Grabs Lucy's cheeks, squeezes her mouth open in a Betty Boop pout. "Drink."

"Ow! Stop it!"

"Drink, damn you! You're wrong. They are terrorists." The woman yanks Lucy's head back with her hair, pours bitter night down her throat.

The flavor of knowing right, doing right, being punished for it.

"We can do this without you, you know."

■ ■ ■

Waking once more in her cubicle, Lucy wonders. Not for the first time, but more surely. This wonder is a cool breeze in her mind, a tang of snow, and white stars aglow on the back of her black arms and hands. She clasps star-hands in prayer, and they sing.

She knows there are no angels. They are from baby-time, Nanya's time.

Still, they sing.

Still, she listens.

A turquoise wave of Knowing, built on all the currents she tastes and sees, lifts her: Denise and Fred are not terrorists. This is iron-blood certainty. And further: she tastes, surely now, unpacking what she learned in a snip of time, the twist-reason for this, heavy and caustic. Upshaw knows something that, if revealed, could change a policy that is bringing floods of illegal money to various parties. their names, nearby on her spectrum, a dry taste, like sand, hidden in a crease she can unfold and shake out, like grains on a square of pure white paper.

She plans an intricate possible future: the blacksuits' own orange revenge, turned on them, blinking always in her upper right screen. To touch when it is Time. Not because she hates them. But yes, now. Because she hates them. All of them. They are using her. She sees that now.

Hug-Woman opens the door to her coffin space. She is sweet now. Another breakfast. More coffee, more French fries, more pills, more hugs. As if all is past, all is good, let's move on.

Back in her cubicle, Lucy's wonder now is very sharp: why? Do you not know what I know?

If so: sly delight.

Her mother: "They promised me I could always talk to you. Any time. I could see you. Any time. I could pull you out. Any time. But they keep—"

Silence.

■ ■ ■

They are in a hospital, Upshaw and his wife, on different floors. Machines beep. A disposition hovers. A turn of a valve, they live. A turn of the valve, they die.

Lucy does not know how to turn the valve.

She will gather knowing sidewise.

She does not have to infer anyone's intent this time.

She just needs the strength she knows is somewhere, past the flimsy pills, for she can smell it on the wind when helmeted. She walks up the street to home, cardamom and popped mustard-seed an abstract, repeating mirage she can dive into and swim to nearly remembered Somewhere, Someone. Anger trumps fear, mostly, but when anger congeals and shimmers, contained like mercury blobs that roll around the bottom of her mind, a poison that spatters when shaken, but apart from her, there is the flat desert certainty of them hurting her, her mother, with casual, chilling efficiency.

And that is fear.

■ ■ ■

Helmeted, Lucy follows one swooping, singing string and arrives sudden in a marketplace bursting with all her old signs, viridian on her tongue blending to tamarind turquoise. A flash of uprising gray, spurting machine curses, draws her down one bright aisle of chattering vendors. She takes a close look at a flapping scarf and sees a moving picture of Nanya staring at a deck of Cincinnati Bee Cards spread out on a small green table. The suits are new: Nanya flips up a parrot card. Looks straight at her. *I want to help* is a vase on the table with singing flowers swept by deep spring sun.

■ ■ ■

Offshift, a tired, big girl, asleep in jerk-dreams where she wonders: Now? Now? Now?

Still afraid to jump.

■ ■ ■

The thing is, she notices, they always believe her. She will have only one chance to use this knowledge. She can betray them only once.

Is it betrayal?

She wonders why she even thinks it may be. What is their pull on her?

■ ■ ■

Her mother, a brief call: "We are trying to get you out. I called—"

Then, silence.

It doesn't feel like a game any more.

■ ■ ■

Olu is in the market, gray as fog, large as her, hobbling alongside her and speaking in pictures, his claws splayed flat on pavement. Saying a picture of Nanya, a turquoise curse of springs and clicks.

What else would he say?

Can you hear that smell?

She does not have a phone any longer but she sees that does not matter. Of course, as the ruby slippers revealed, it never mattered.

She works on it in scattered spurts, less than a second each, keeping track of her progress in a pattern of cloth in the market. Finally, when the pattern is whole she reaches out and wraps it round her neck. A vendor holds up a wavy mirror, smiling, and she sees that she is older, thinner, much more beautiful. But she is also two years old and crying.

Tone of phone ringing. The answering voice a clash of machines, a gold infinity of Nanya.

"I knew you would call. Praise God! You did it. My small amazing girl.

"You need help. Your mother has told me. Hah! After so many years, she calls. Life is good, I swear it.

"I was so wrong, Lucy. I am healed now. Gamblers Anonymous, drugs, psychiatrists—but for years she would not talk to me. Like a stone, your mother. I was not a good parent to her.

"But—listen! There is probably not much time. I tell you this from my heart and from my life. Maybe you can understand now. Your mother never did.

"It is hard to know when you are making the choices that cage you.

"They do not always feel like choices. They are strong flavors, new roads, blurs of numbers. Is this not like you? Ah, yes, I thought so. When you were a baby, I knew. Your mother would not hear of it, would not have you tested, would not seek help. She didn't want you to be like me.

"But it is this.

"Cages can take many shapes and flavors. At first you might love them. Then you hear the wrong notes.

"Once you know you are in a cage, you can leave it.

"The cage itself holds the pathway. You always have the power to break loose.

"Use that power to leave or it will kill you."

Nanya's laugh before the connection severs is a clash of gears, and then a brief tonal song that pulses gold within her vision.

Lucy does not dare call her back.

But now she knows: she is a gambler too.

∎ ∎ ∎

No room for a single mistake. The sequence of events a complicated symphony.

A room she can enter, without legs. Majestic Yodas tall and everything. Truly, everything.

If she were a surgeon she would cut precise.

If she were a memory machine her screen would light in all of history.

If she were reading the memory machine she would see one line of type: a poem of many letters glowing.

If she were the letters glowing it would be a long-skip dance.

If she were a long-skip dance the stretch would almost kill her.

If she were almost dead she would bend the caging bands with skillful tools, a surgeon again.

Sewing, knot: tight and sure and fine.

In the hospital, the tide turns right. The valve is open to the life side. The Upshaws will live.

Lucy blocks the paths to the Upshaws. They and their history vanish, lost in infinite humanity. They are nothing to Yoda now, and can never be.

She releases what Upshaw knew, all that damage and more, to the Internet. No one will ever know where it came from. She makes sure of that.

She is human. Not machine. She can decide what is important because of the difference.

. . .

Kelly yanks off her helmet.

"You can save everyone in a city." Hug-Woman Kelly paces the tiny space. "You can save everyone in a plane. In a café. Look!" She takes Lucy's head, not gently, turns it toward a screen. "Open your eyes! Look at the horrible things they do! You could save so many people! You already *have*—"

"Let me out. Now." Instead of the screen, there is a sweep of ghostly parrot, a West African curse, a brain like hers, a vase of singing flowers.

She is a sport. The future is full of sports, like her.

The future *is* a sport.

She gathers the lovely wires of a million untold colors into her hands and this time they do not burn.

She looses them.

The rules of the game sweep skyward, a flock of gray parrots.

All the brains of living creatures are strange, and different.

As is Yoda, who will live and grow, but whose command codes she transmutes into patterns that will be difficult—perhaps impossible—for anyone to follow.

She sets the fuse that will dynamite the entrance to the mine with cadmium intent, with cardamom and ghost pepper and ginger, with that deep meal of dreams.

The specials, the Upshaws, all the friends and enemies in the world (depending how they slant the light of information), Yoda-that-is and Yoda-to-be— in fact, everyone! can do what they please. The blacksuits will not know this until it is over.

. . .

Two men come to get her. The men do not blink; their eyes are watered by machine. To blink is to lose the mark. They do not smile. So what else is new?

This is: they escort her to the entrance, past the guards, accompanied by a woman Lucy has never seen, who wears a black suit.

Then sunlight flashes off cars in the parking lot. Blue sky above. Wind. It is all so normal that it startles Lucy. Her mother is there. Waving, crying smiling hugging. Lucy: enfolded.

A woman in a green suit next to Lucy's mother leans against the car, holding a tablet. The bright wind wilds her hair.

Blacksuit woman, her hair unmoving as a helmet, writes on the tablet. The greensuit woman touches it.

Alone after so long, without the rainbow pathways, Lucy still feels the gold arrow strike deep into Yoda, behind her and beneath her, in that instant of consent, at her note of freeing.

Can you hear that smell?

A single parrot, with strange brain, swoops into the blue, clear sky.

Mostly, we'll adapt to changing times . . .
. . . except for our thundering dinosaurs.

ELEPHANT ON TABLE

BRUCE STERLING

Tullio and Irma had found peace in the Shadow House. Then the Chief arrived from his clinic and hid in the panic room.

Tullio and Irma heard shuddering moans from the HVAC system, the steely squeak of the hydraulic wheels, but not a human whisper. The Shadow House cat whined and yowled at the vault door.

▪ ▪ ▪

Three tense days passed, and the Chief tottered from his airtight chamber into summer daylight. Head bobbing, knees shaking, he reeled like an antique Sicilian puppet.

Blank-eyed yet stoic, the elderly statesman wobbled up the perforated stairs to the Shadow House veranda. This expanse was adroitly sheltered from a too-knowing world.

The panic rooms below ground were sheathed in Faraday copper, cast iron and lead, but the mansion's airy upper parts were a nested, multilayer labyrinth of sound baffles, absorbent membranes, metastructured foam, malleable ribbons, carbon filaments, vapor smoke and mirror chaff. Snakelike vines wreathed the trellises. The gardens abounded in spiky cactus. Tullio took pains to maintain the establishment as it deserved.

The Chief staggered into a rattan throne. He set his hairy hands flat on the cold marble tabletop.

He roared for food.

Tullio and Irma hastened to comply. The Chief promptly devoured three hard-boiled eggs, a jar of pickled artichoke hearts, a sugar-soaked grapefruit, and a jumbo-sized mango, skin and all.

Some human color returned to his famous, surgically amended face. The Chief still looked bad, like a reckless, drug-addict roué of fifty. However, the chief was actually 104 years old. The Chief had paid millions for the zealous medical care by his elite Swiss clinic. He'd even paid hundreds of thousands for the veterinary care of his house cat.

While Irma tidied the sloppy ruins of breakfast, Tullio queried Shadow House screens for any threats in the vicinity.

The Chief had many enemies: thousands of them. His four ex-wives were by far his worst foes. He was also much resented by various Italian nationalists, fringe leftist groups, volatile feminist cults, and a large sprinkling of mentally disturbed stalkers who had fixated on him for decades.

However, few of these fierce, gritty, unhappy people were on the island of Sardinia in August 2073. None of them knew that the Chief had secretly arrived on Sardinia from Switzerland. The Shadow House algorithms ranked their worst threat as the local gossip journalist Carlo Pizzi, a notorious little busybody who was harassing supermodels.

Reassured by this security check, Tullio carried the card table out to the beach. Using a clanking capstan and crank, Tullio erected a big, party-colored sun umbrella. In its slanting shade he arranged four plastic chairs, a stack of plastic cups, plastic cryptocoins, shrink-wrapped card decks, paper pads, and stubby pencils. Every object was anonymous and disposable: devoid of trademarks, codes or identities. No surface took fingerprints.

The Chief arrived to play, wearing wraparound mirrorshades and a brown, hooded beach robe. It was a Mediterranean August, hot, blue, and breezy. The murmuring surf was chased by a skittering horde of little shore birds.

Irma poured the chief a tall iced glass of his favorite vitamin sludge while Tullio shuffled and dealt.

The Chief disrobed and smeared his seamy, portly carcass with medicated suntan unguent. He gripped his waterproofed plastic cards.

"Anaconda," he commanded, and belched.

The empty fourth chair at their card table was meant to attract the public. The Chief was safe from surveillance inside his sumptuous Shadow House—that was the purpose of the house, its design motif, its reason for being. However, safety had never satisfied the Chief. He was an Italian politician, so it was his nature to flirt with disaster.

Whenever left to themselves, Tullio and Irma passed their pleasant days inside the Shadow House, discreet, unseen, unbothered and unbothering. But the two of them were still their chief's loyal retainers. The Chief was a man of scandal and turbulence—half-forgotten, half-ignored by a happier era. But the Chief still had his burning need to control the gaze of the little people.

The Chief's raw hunger for glory, which had often shaken the roots of Europe, had never granted him a moment's peace. During his long, rampaging life, he'd possessed wealth, fame, power, and the love of small armies of women. Serenity, though, still eluded him. Privacy was his obsession: fame was his compulsion.

Tullio played his cards badly, for it seemed to him that a violent host of invisible furies still circled the Chief's troubled, sweating head. The notorious secrecy. The covert scandals. The blatant vulgarity which was also a subtle opacity—for the Chief was an outsized statesman, a heroic figure of many perverse contradictions. His achievements and his crimes were like a herd of elephants: they could never stand still within a silent room.

Irma offered Tullio a glance over their dwindling poker hands. They both pitied their Chief, because they understood him. Tullio had once been an Italian political-party operative, and Irma, a deft Italian tax-avoidance expert. Nowadays they were reduced to the status of the house-repairman and the hostess, the butler and the cook. There was no more Italy. The Chief had outlived his nation.

Becoming ex-Italian meant a calmer life for Tullio and Irma, because the world was gentler without an Italy. It was their duty to keep this lonely, ill-starred old man out of any more trouble. The Chief would never behave decently—that was simply not in his character—but their discreet beach mansion could hush up his remaining excesses.

The first wandering stranger approached their open table. This fringe figure was one tiny fragment of the world's public, a remote demographic outlier, a man among the lowest of the low. He was poor, black, and a beach peddler. Many such émigrés haunted the edges of the huge Mediterranean summer beach crowds. These near-vagrants sold various forms of pretty rubbish.

The Chief was delighted to welcome this anonymous personage. He politely relieved the peddler of his miserable tray of fried fish, candy bars, and kid's plastic pinwheels, and insisted on seating him at the green poker table.

"Hey, I can't stay here, boss," complained the peddler, in bad Italian. "I have to work."

"We'll look after you," the Chief coaxed, surveilling the peddler, from head to foot, with covert glee. "My friend Tullio here will buy your fish. Tullio has a hungry cat over there, isn't that right, Tullio?"

The Chief waved his thick arm at the Shadow House, but the peddler simply couldn't see the place. The mansion's structure was visually broken up by active dazzle lines. Its silhouette faded like a cryptic mist into the island's calm palette of palms and citruses.

Tullio obediently played along. "Oh yes, that's true, we do have a big tomcat, he's always hungry." He offered the peddler some plastic coinage from the poker table.

Irma gathered up the reeking roast sardines. When Irma rounded a corner of the Shadow House, she vanished as if swallowed.

"It has been my experience," the Chief said sagely, scooping up and squaring the poker cards, "that the migrants of the world—men like yourself—are risk-takers. So, my friend: how'd you like to double your money in a quick hand of hi-lo with us?"

"I'm not a player, boss," said the peddler, though he was clearly tempted.

"So, saving up your capital, is that it? Do you want to live here in Italy—is that your plan?"

The peddler shrugged. "There is no Italy! In Europe, the people love elephants. So, I came here with the elephants. The people don't see me. The machines don't care."

Irma reappeared as if by magic. Seeing the tense looks on their faces, she said brightly, "So, do you tend those elephants, young man? People in town say they brought whales this year, too!"

"Oh no, no, signora!" cried the peddler. "See the elephants, but never look at the whales! You have to ride a boat out there, you get seasick, that's no good!"

"Tell us more about these elephants, they interest me," the Chief urged, scratching his oiled belly. "Have a prosecco, have a brandy." But the peddler was too streetwise: he had sensed that something was up. He gathered his tray and escaped them, hastening down the beach, toward the day's gathering crowds.

Tullio, Irma and the Chief ran through more hands of Anaconda poker. The Chief, an expert player, was too restless to lose, so he was absent-mindedly piling up all their coinage.

"My God, if only I, too, had no name!" he burst out. "No identity, like that African boy—what I could do in this world now! Elephants, here in Sardinia! When I was young, did I have any elephants? Not one! I had less than nothing, I suffered from huge debts! These days are such happy times, and the young people now, they just have no idea!"

Tullio and Irma knew every aspect of their Chief's hard-luck origin story, so they merely pretended attention.

The summer beach crowd was clustering down the coastline, a joyful human mass of tanned and salty arms and legs, ornamented with balloons and scraps of pop music.

A beachcombing group of Japanese tourists swanned by. Although they wore little, the Japanese were fantastically well-dressed. The Japanese had found their métier as the world's most elegant people. Even the jealous Milanese were content to admire their style.

Lacking any new victim to interrogate at his card table, the Chief began to reminisce. The Chief would loudly bluster about any topic, except for his true sorrows, which he never confessed aloud.

The Swiss had lavished many dark attentions on the Chief's crumbling brain. The Swiss had invaded his bony skull, that last refuge of humane privacy, like a horde of Swiss pikemen invading Renaissance Italy. They occupied it, but they couldn't govern it.

The Chief's upgraded brain, so closely surveilled by Swiss medical imaging, could no longer fully conceal his private chains of thought. The Chief had once been a political genius, but now his scorched neurons were like some huge database racked by a spy agency's analytics.

Deftly shuffling a fresh card deck, the Chief suddenly lost his composure. He commenced to leak and babble. His unsought theme was "elephants." Any memory, any anecdote that struck his mind, about elephants.

Hannibal had invaded Italy with elephants. The elephant had once been the symbol of an American political party. A houseplant named the elephant ear. The Chief recalled a pretty Swedish pop star with the unlikely name of Elliphant.

The Chief was still afraid of the surgically warped and sickening *Elephant Man*, a dark horror-movie figure from his remote childhood.

The Chief might not look terribly old—not to a surveillance camera—but he was senile. Those high-tech quacks in Switzerland took more and more of his wealth, but delivered less and less health. Life-extension technology was a rich man's gamble. The odds were always with the house.

Irma gently removed the cards from the Chief's erratic hands, and dealt them herself. The sea wind rose and loudly ruffled the beach umbrella. Windsurfers passed by, out to sea, with kites that might be aerial surveillance platforms. A group of black-clad divers on a big rubber boat looked scary, like spies, assassins or secret policemen.

The ever-swelling beach crowd, that gathering, multilimbed tide of relaxed and playful humanity, inspired a spiritual unease in Tullio. His years inside the Shadow House had made Tullio a retiring, modest man. He had never much enjoyed public oversight. Wherever there were people, there was also hardware and software. There was scanning and recording. Ubiquity and transparency.

That was progress, and the world was better for progress, but it was also a different world, and that hurt.

Some happy beachgoing children arrived, and improved the mood at the poker table. As a political leader, the Chief had always been an excellent performer around kids. He clowned with all his old practiced stagecraft, and the surprised little gang of five kids giggled like fifty.

But with the instinctive wisdom of the innocent, the kids didn't care to spend much time with a strange, fat, extremely old man wearing sunglasses and a too-tight swimsuit.

The card play transitioned from anaconda poker to seven-card stud. Tullio and Irma shared a reassuring glance. Lunch was approaching, and lunch would take two hours. After his lunch, the Chief would nap. After the summer siesta, he would put on his rubber cap, foot-fins and water wings, and swim. With his ritual exercise performed, dinner would be looming. After the ritual of dinner, with its many small and varied pleasures, the day would close quietly.

Tullio and Irma had their two weeks of duty every August, and then the demands of the Chief's wealth and health would call him elsewhere. Then Tullio and Irma could return to their customary peace and quiet. Just them and their eccentric house cat, in their fortress consecrated to solitude.

The Shadow House robot, a nameless flat plastic pancake, emerged from its hidden runway. The diligent machine fluffed the sand, trimmed the beach-herbage, and picked up and munched some driftwood bits of garbage electronics.

A beautiful woman arrived on the shore. Her extravagant curves were strapped into bright, clumsy American swimwear. Despite the gusting sea breeze, her salon updo was perfect.

The Chief noticed this beauty instantly. It was as if someone had ordered him a box of hot American donuts.

Tullio and Irma watched warily as the demimondaine strolled by. She tramped the wet edge of the foamy surf like a lingerie runway model. She clearly knew where the Shadow House was sited. She had deliberately wandered within range of its sensors.

The Chief threw on his beach robe and hurried over to chat her up.

The Chief returned with the air of synthetic triumph that he assumed around his synthetic girlfriends. "This is Monica," he announced in English. "Monica wants to play with us."

"What a pretty name," said Irma in English, her eyes narrowing. "Such glamorous lady as you, such beauty is hard to miss."

"Oh, I visit Sardinia every August," Monica lied sweetly. "But Herr Hentschel has gone back to Berlin. So it's been a bit lonely."

"Everyone knows your Herr Hentschel?" Irma probed.

Monica named a prominent European armaments firm with longstanding American national security ties.

The matter was simple. The Chief had been too visible, out on the beach, all morning. This was long enough for interested parties to notice him with scanners, scare up smart algorithms, and dispatch a working agent.

"Maybe we go inside the Shadow House now," Tullio suggested in English. "For lunch."

Monica agreed to join them. Tullio shut the rattling umbrella and stacked all the plastic chairs.

The microwave sensors of the Shadow House had a deep electromagnetic look at Monica, and objected loudly.

"A surveillance device," said Tullio.

Monica shrugged her bare, tanned shoulders. She wore nothing but her gaudy floral bikini and her flat zori sandals.

Tullio spread his hands. "Lady, most times, no one knows, no one cares— but this is Shadow House."

Monica plucked off her bikini top and shook it. Her swimwear unfolded with uncanny ease and became a writhing square of algorithmic fabric.

"So pretty," Irma remarked. She carried off the writhing interface to stuff it in a copper-lined box.

The Chief stared at Monica's bared torso as if she'd revealed two rocketships.

Tullio gave Monica a house robe. Women like Monica were common guests for Shadow House. Sometimes, commonly, one girl. Sometimes five girls, some-times ten or, when the Chief's need was truly unbearable, a popular mass of forty-five or fifty girls, girls of any class, color, creed or condition, girls from anywhere, anything female and human.

On those taut, packed, manic occasions, the Chief threw colossal, fully catered parties, with blasting music and wild dancing and fitful orgies in pri-vate VIP nooks. The Shadow House would be ablaze in glimmering witch lights, except for the pitch-black, bombproofed niche where the Chief retreated to spy on his guests.

Those events were legendary beach parties, for the less that young people saw of the Chief, the happier everybody was.

Lunch was modest, by the Chief's standards: fried zucchini, calamari with marinara sauce, flatbread drenched in molten cheese-and-olive spread, tender meatballs of mutton, clams, scampi and a finisher of mixed and salted nuts, which were good for the nervous system. The Chief fed choice table scraps to the tomcat.

Monica spoke, with an unfeigned good cheer, about her vocation, which was leading less fortunate children in hikes on the dikes of Miami.

When lunch ended, the Chief and the demimondaine retired together for a "nap."

After the necessary medical checks for any intimate encounter, the Chief's efforts in this line generally took him ten minutes. Once his covert romp was over, he would return to daylight with a lighter heart. Generally, he would turn his attention to some favorite topic in public policy, such as hotel construction or the proper maintenance of world-heritage sites.

His charisma would revive, then, for the Chief was truly wise about some things. Whenever he was pleased and appeased, one could see why he'd once led a nation, and how his dynamism and his optimistic gusto had encouraged people.

Italian men had voted for the Chief, because they had imagined that they would live like him, if they too were rich, and bold, and famous, and swash-buckling. Some Italian women also voted for the Chief because, with a man like him in power, at least you understood what you were getting.

But the Chief did not emerge into daylight. After two hours of gathering silence, the house cat yowled in a mystical animal anguish. The cat had no technical understanding about the Shadow House. Being a cat, he had not one scrap of an inkling about Faraday cages or nanocarbon camouflage. However, being a house cat, he knew how to exist in a house. He knew life as a cat knew life, and he knew death, too.

After an anxious struggle, Tullio found the software override, and opened the locked bedroom door. The cat quickly bounded inside, between Tullio's ankles.

The Chief was supine in bed, with a tender smile and an emptied, infinite stare. The pupils of his eyes were two pinpoints.

Tullio lifted the Chief's beefy, naked arm, felt its fluttering pulse, and re-leased it to flop limp on the mattress.

"We push the Big Red Button," Tullio announced to Irma.

"Oh, Tullio, we said we never would do that! What a mess!"

"This is an emergency. We must push the Big Red Button. We owe it to him. It's our duty to push the button."

"But the whole world will find out everything! All his enemies! And his friends are even worse!"

A voice came from under the bed. "Please don't push any button."

Tullio bent and gazed under the bedframe. "So, now you understand Ital-ian, miss?"

"A little." Monica stuck her tousled head from under the rumpled satin bed-coverlet. Her frightened face was streaked with tears.

"What did you do to our Chief?"

"Nothing! Well, just normal stuff. He was having a pretty good time of it, for such an old guy. So, I kind of turned it up, and I got busy. Next thing I knew, he was all limp!"

"Men," Irma sympathized.

"Can I have some clothes?" said Monica. "If you push that button, cops will show up for sure. I don't want to be in a station house naked."

Irma hastened to a nearby wardrobe. "Inside, you girls do as you please, but no girl leaves my Shadow House naked!"

Tullio rubbed his chin. "So, you've been to the station house before, Monica?"

"The oldest profession is a hard life." Monica crept out from under the Chief's huge bed, and slipped into the yellow satin house robe that Irma offered. She belted it firmly. "I can't believe I walked right in here in my second-best bikini. I just knew something bad would happen in this weird house."

Tullio recited: "Shadow House is the state of the art in confidential living and reputation management."

"Yeah, sure. I've done guys in worse dives," Monica agreed, "but a million bomb shelters couldn't hush up that guy's reputation. Every working girl knows about him. He's been buying our services for eighty years."

Stabbed by this remark, Tullio gazed on the stricken Chief.

The old man's body was breathing, and its heart was beating, because the Swiss had done much expensive work on the Chief's lungs and heart. But Tullio knew, with a henchman's instinctive certainty, that the Chief was, more or less, dead. The old rascal had simply blown his old brains out in a final erotic gallop. It was a massive, awful, fatal scandal. A tragedy.

When Tullio looked up, the two women were gone. Outside the catastrophic bedroom, Monica was wiping her tear-smudged mascara and confessing her all to Irma.

"So, I guess," Monica said, "maybe, I kinda showed up at the end of his chain here. But for a little Miami girl, like me, to join such a great European tradition—well, it seemed like such an honor!"

Tullio and Irma exchanged glances. "I wish more of these girls had such a positive attitude," said Irma.

Monica, sensing them weakening, looked eager. "Just let me take a hot shower. Okay? If I'm clean, no cop can prove anything! We played cards, that's all. He told me bedtime stories."

"Is there a money trail?" said Irma, who had worked in taxes.

"Oh, no, never! Cash for sex is so old-fashioned." Monica absently picked up the yammering tomcat by the scruff of the neck. She gathered the beast in her sleek arms and massaged him. The surprised cat accepted this treatment, and even seemed grateful.

"See, I have a personal relationship with a big German arms firm," Monica explained, as the cat purred like a small engine. "My sugar daddy is a big defense corporation. It's an artificial intelligence, because it tracks me. It knows all my personal habits, and it takes real good care of me. . . . So, sometimes I do a favor—I mean, just a small personal favor for my big AI boyfriend, the big corporation. Then the stockholders' return on investment feels much better."

Baffled by this English-language business jargon, Tullio scratched his head.

Monica lifted her chin. "That's how the vice racket beats a transparent surveillance society. Spies are the world's second oldest profession. Us working girls are still the first."

"We must take a chance," Tullio decided. "You, girl, quick, get clean. Irma, help her. Leave Shadow House, and forget you ever saw us."

"Oh, thank you, sir, thank you! I'll be grateful the rest of my life, if I live to be 150!" cried Monica. She tossed the purring tomcat to the floor.

Irma hustled her away. The Shadow House had decontamination showers. Its sewers had membranous firewalls. The cover-up had a good chance to work. The house had been built for just such reasons.

Tullio removed the telltale bedsheets. He did what he could to put the comatose Chief into better order. Tullio had put the Chief to bed, dead drunk, on more than one occasion. This experience was like those comic old times, except not funny, because the Chief was not drunk: just dead.

The lights of Shadow House were strobing. An intruder had arrived.

■ ■ ■

The hermit priest had rolled to the House perimeter within his smart mobile wheelchair. Father Simeon was a particularly old man—even older than the Chief. Father Simeon was the Chief's longtime spiritual guide and personal confessor.

"Did you push that Big Red Button?" said the supercentenarian cleric.

"No, Monsignor!"

"Good. I have arrived now, have I not? Where is my poor boy? Take me to him."

"The Chief is sick, Monsignor." Tullio suddenly burst into tears. "He had a fit. He collapsed, he's not conscious. What can we do?"

"The status of death is not a matter for a layman to decide," said the priest.

The Shadow House did not allow the cleric's wheelchair to enter its premises. The Vatican wheelchair was a rolling mass of embedded electronics. The Shadow House rejected this Catholic computational platform as if it were a car bomb.

Father Simeon—once a prominent Vatican figure—had retired to the island to end his days in a hermetic solitude. Paradoxically, his pursuit of holy seclusion made Father Simeon colossally popular. Since he didn't want to meet or talk to anybody, the whole world adored him. Archbishops and cardinals constantly pestered the hermit for counsel, and his wizened face featured on countless tourist coffee cups.

"I must rise and walk," said Father Simeon. "The soul of a sufferer needs me. Give me your arm, my son!"

Tullio placed his arm around the aged theologian, who clutched a heavy Bible and a precious vial of holy oil. Under his long, black, scarlet-buttoned cassock, the ancient hermit was a living skeleton. His bony legs rattled as his sandalled, blue-veined feet grazed the floor.

Tullio tripped over the housecat as they entered the Chief's bedroom. They reeled together and almost fell headlong onto the stricken Chief, but the devoted priest gave no thought to his own safety. Father Simeon checked the Chief's eyelids with his thumbs, then muttered a Latin prayer.

"I'm so glad for your help, Father," said Tullio. "How did you know that we needed you here?"

The old man shot him a dark look from under his spiky gray brows. "My son," he said, lifting his hand, "do you imagine that your mere technology—all these filters and window shades—can blind the divine awareness of the Living God? The Lord knows every sparrow that falls! God knows every hair of every human head! The good God has no need for any corporate AI's or cheap singularities!"

Tullio considered this. "Well, can I do anything to help? Shall I call a doctor?"

"What use are the doctors now, after their wretched excesses? Pray for him!" said the priest. "His body persists while his soul is in Limbo. The Church rules supreme in bioethics. We will defend our faithful from these secular intrusions. If this had happened to him in Switzerland, they would have plugged him into the wall like a cash machine!"

Tullio shuddered in pain.

"Be not afraid!" Father Simeon commanded. "This world has its wickedness—

but if the saints and angels stand with us, what machine can stand against us?" Father Simeon carefully gloved his bony hands. He uncapped his reeking vial of holy oil.

"I'm so sorry about all this, Monsignor. It's so embarrassing that we failed in this way. We always tried to protect him, here in the Shadow House."

The priest deftly rubbed the eyes, ears and temples of the stricken Chief with the sacramental ointment. "All men are sinners. Go to confession, my boy. God is all-seeing, and yet He is forgiving; whenever we open our heart to God, He always sees and understands."

Irma beckoned at Tullio from the doorway. Tullio excused himself and met her outside.

The emergency had provoked Irma's best cleverness. She had quickly dressed Monica in some fine clothes, left behind in Shadow House by the Chief's estranged daughter. These abandoned garments were out of style, of course, but they were of classic cut and fine fabric. The prostitute looked just like a Italian parliamentarian.

"I told you to run away," said Tullio.

"Oh sure, I wanted to run," Monica agreed, "but if I ran from the scene of a crime, then some algorithm might spot my guilty behavior. But now look at me! I look political, instead of like some lowlife. So I can be ten times as guilty, and nothing will happen to me."

Tullio looked at Irma, who shrugged, because of course it was true.

"Let the priest finish his holy business," Irma counseled. "Extreme Unction is a sacrament. We can't push the Big Red Button during this holy moment."

"Are you guys Catholics?" said Monica. At their surprised look, she raised both her hands. "Hey, I'm from Miami, we got lots!"

"Are you a believer?" said Irma.

"Well, I tried to believe," said Monica, blinking. "I read some of the Bible in a hotel room once. That book's pretty crazy. Full of begats."

A horrid shriek came from the Chief's bedroom.

The Chief was bolt upright in bed, moans and whispers bursting in anguish from his writhing lips. The anointment with sacred oil had aroused one last burst of his mortal vitality. His heart was pounding so powerfully that it was audible across the room.

This spectral deathbed fit dismayed Father Simeon not at all. With care, he performed his ministry.

A death rattle eclipsed the Chief's last words. His head plummeted into a pillow. He was as dead as a stone, although his heart continued to beat for over a minute.

The priest removed the rosary from around his shrunken neck and folded it into the Chief's hairy hands.

"He expressed his contrition," the priest announced. "At his mortal end, he was lucid and transparent. God knows all, sees all and forgives all. So do not be frightened. He has not left us. He has simply gone home."

"Wow," Monica said in the sudden silence. "That was awesome. Who is this old guy?"

"This is our world-famous hermit, Father Simeon," said Tullio.

"Our friend Father Simeon was the president of the Pontifical Council for Social Communications," Irma said proudly. "He also wrote the canon law for the Evangelization of Artificial Intelligences."

"That sounds pretty cool," said Monica. "Listen, padre, Holy Father, whatever . . ."

"'Holy Father' is a title reserved for our pope," Father Simeon told her, in a crisp Oxford English. "My machines call me 'Excellency'—but since you are human, please call me 'Father.'"

"Okay, 'Father,' sure. You forgave him, right? He's dead—but he's going to heaven, because he has no guilty secrets. That's how it works, right?"

"He confessed. He died in the arms of the Church."

"Okay, yeah, that's great—but how about me? Can I get forgiven, too? Because I'm a bad girl! I didn't want him to die! That was terrible! I'm really sorry."

Father Simeon was old and had been through a trial at the deathbed, but his faith sustained him. "Do not despair, my child. Yes, you may be weak and a sinner. Take courage: the power of the Church is great. You can break the chains of unrighteousness. Have faith that you can turn away from sin."

"But how, Father? I've got police records on three continents, and about a thousand johns have rated my services on hooker e-commerce sites."

Father Simeon winced at this bleak admission, but truth didn't daunt him. "My child, those data records are only software and hardware. You have a human soul, you possess free will. The Magdalen was a fallen woman whose conscience was awakened. She was a chosen companion of Christ. So do not bow your head to this pagan system of surveillance that confines you to a category, and seeks to entrap you there!"

Monica burst into tears. "What must I do to be saved from surveillance?"

"Take the catechism! Learn the meaning of life! We are placed on Earth to know, to love, and to serve our God! We are not here to cater to the whims of German arms corporations that build spy towers in the Mediterranean!"

Monica blinked. "Hey, wait a minute, Father—how do you know all that—about my German arms corporation and all those towers in the sea?"

"God is not mocked! There are some big data systems in this world that are little more than corrupt incubi, and there are other, better-programmed, sanctified data systems that are like protective saints and angels."

Monica looked to Tullio and Irma. "Is he kidding?"

Tullio and Irma silently shook their heads.

"Wow," breathed Monica. "I would really, truly love to have an AI guardian angel."

The lights began to strobe overhead.

"Something is happening outside," said Tullio hastily. "When I come back, we'll all press the Big Red Button together."

. . .

Behind the Shadow House, a group of bored teenagers had discovered Father Simeon's abandoned wheelchair. They had captured the vehicle and were giving one another joyrides.

Overwhelmed by the day's events, Tullio chased them off the Shadow House property, shouting in rage. The teens were foreign tourists, and knew not one word of Italian, so they fled his angry scolding in a panic, and ran off headlong to scramble up into the howdah of a waiting elephant.

"Teenage kids should never have elephants!" Tullio complained, wheeling the recaptured wheelchair back to Irma. "Elephants are huge beasts! Look at this mess."

"Elephants are better than cars," said Irma. "You can't even kiss a boy in a car, because the cars are tracked and they record everything. That's what the girls say in town."

"Delinquents. Hooligans! With elephants! What kind of world is this, outside our house?"

"Kissing boys has always been trouble." Irma closely examined the wheelchair, which had been tumbled, scratched and splattered with sandy dirt. "Oh dear, we can't possibly give it back to Father Simeon in this condition."

"I'll touch it up," Tullio promised.

"Should I push the Big Red Button now?"

"Not yet," Tullio said. "A time like this needs dignity. We should get the Chief's lawyer to fly in from Milan. If we have the Church and the law on our side, then we can still protect him, Irma, even after death. No one will know what happened here. There's still client-lawyer confidentiality. There's still the sacred silence of the confessional. And this house is radarproof."

"I'm sure the Chief would want to be buried in Rome. The city where he saw his best days."

"Of course you're right," said Tullio. "There will be riots at his funeral . . . but our Chief will finally find peace in Rome. Nobody will care about his private secrets any more. There are historical records, but the machines never bother to look at them. History is one of the humanities."

"Let's get the Vatican to publicly announce his passing. With no Italian government, the Church is what we have left."

"What a good idea." Tullio looked at his wife admiringly. Irma had always been at her best in handling scandalous emergencies. It was a pity that a woman of such skill had retired to a quiet life.

"I'll talk to Father Simeon about it. He'll know who to contact, behind the scenes." Irma left.

Tullio brushed sand from the wheelchair's ascetic leather upholstery, and polished the indicator lights with his sleeve. Since electronics were no longer tender or delicate devices—electronics were the bedrock of the modern world, basically—the wheelchair was not much disturbed by its mishap.

It was Tullio himself who felt tumbled and upset. Why were machines so hard to kill, and people so frail? The Shadow House had been built around the needs of one great man. The structure could grant him a physical privacy, but it couldn't stop his harsh compulsion to reveal himself.

The Shadow House functioned properly, but it was a Don Quixote windmill. The Chief was, finally, too mad in the head to care if his manias were noticed. What the Chief had liked best about his beach house was simply playing poker with two old friends. Relaxing informally, despite his colossal burdens of wealth and fame, sitting there in improbable poise, like an elephant perched on a card table.

The house cat curled around Tullio's ankles. Since the cat had never before left the confines of the Shadow House, this alarmed Tullio.

Inside, Father Simeon, Irma and Monica were sharing tea on a rattan couch, while surrounded by screens.

"People are querying the Shadow House address," Irma announced. "We're getting map queries from Washington and Berlin."

"I guess you can blame me for that, too," Monica moaned. "My Artificial Intelligence boyfriend is worried about me, since I dropped out of connectivity in here."

"I counsel against that arrangement," Father Simeon stated. "Although an AI network is not a man, he can still exploit a vulnerable woman. A machine with no soul can sin. Our Vatican theology-bots are explicit about this."

"I never thought of my sweet megacorporation as a pimp and an incubus—but you're right, Father Simeon. I guess I've got a lot to learn."

"Never fear to be righteous, my child. Mother Church knows how to welcome converts. Our convents and monasteries make this shadowy place look like a little boy's toy."

. . .

The priest and his new convert managed to escape discreetly. The wheelchair vanished into the orange groves. Moments later, Carlo Pizzi arrived at Shadow House on his motor scooter.

The short and rather pear-shaped Pizzi was wearing his customary, outsized, head-mounted display goggles, which connected him constantly to his cloudy network. The goggles made Pizzi look as awkward as a grounded aviator, but he enjoyed making entirely sure that other people knew all about his social-media capacities.

After some polite chitchat about the weather (which he deftly recited from a display inside his goggles), Pizzi got straight to the point. "I'm searching for a girl named Monica. Tall, pretty, red hair, American, height 175 centimeters, weight 54 kilograms."

"We haven't seen her in some time," Irma offered.

"Monica has vanished from the network. That activity doesn't fit her emotional profile. I've got an interested party that's concerned about her safety."

"You mean the German arms manufacturer?" said Irma.

Carlo Pizzi paused awkwardly as he read invisible cues from his goggles.

"In our modern transparent society," Pizzi ventured at last, "the three of us can all do well for ourselves by doing some social good. For instance: if you can reconnect Monica to the network, then my friend can see to it that pleasant things are said about this area to the German trade press. Then you'll see more German tourists on your nice beach here."

"You can tell your creepy AI friend to recalibrate his correlations, because Shadow House is a private home," said Tullio. His words were defiant, but Tullio's voice shook with grief. That was a bad idea when an AI was deftly listening for the emotional cues in human speech patterns.

"So, is Father Simeon dead?" Carlo Pizzi said. "Good heavens! If that famous hermit is dead, that would be huge news in Sardinia."

"No, Father Simeon is fine," said Irma. "Please don't disturb his seclusion. Publicity makes him angry."

"Then it's that old politician who has died. The last prime minister of Italy," said Carlo Pizzi, suddenly convinced. "Thanks for cuing up his bio for me! A man who lives for a hundred years sure can get into trouble!"

Tullio and Irma sidled away as Pizzi was distractedly talking to the empty air, but he noticed them and followed them like a dog. "The German system has figured out your boss is dead," Pizzi confided, "because the big-data correlations add up. Cloud AIs are superior at that sort of stuff. But can I get a physical confirmation on that?"

"What are you talking about?" said Tullio.

"I need the first post-mortem shot of the deceased. There were rumors before now that he had died. Because he had this strange habit of disappearing whenever things got hot for him. So, this could be another trick of his—but if I could see him with my goggles here, and zoom in on his exact proportions and scan his fingerprints and such, then our friend the German system would have a first-mover market advantage."

"We don't want to bargain with a big-data correlation system," said Tullio. "That's like trying to play chess with a computer. We can't possibly win, so it's not really fair."

"But you're the one being unfair! Think of the prosperity that big-data market capitalism has brought to the world! A corporation is just the legal and computational platform for its human stockholders, you know. My friend is a 'corporate person' with thousands of happy human stockholders. He has a fiduciary obligation to improve their situation. That's what we're doing right now."

"You own stock in this thing yourself?" said Irma.

"Well, sure, of course. Look, I know you think I want to leak this paparazzi photo to the public. But I don't, because that's obsolete! Our friend the German AI doesn't want this scandal revealed, any more than you do. I just pass him some encrypted photo evidence, and he gets ahead of the market game. Then I can take the rest of this year off and finish my new novel!"

There was a ponderous silence. "His novels are pretty good beach reading," Irma offered at last. "If you like roman-a-clef tell-all books."

"Look here, Signor Pizzi," said Tullio, "the wife and I are not against modern capitalism and big-data pattern recognition. But we can't just let you barge in here and disturb the peace of our dead patron. He was always good to us—in his way."

"Somebody has to find out he's dead. That's the way of the world," Pizzi coaxed. "Isn't it a better that it's just a big-data machine who knows? The guy has four surviving ex-wives, and every one of them is a hellion."

"That's all because of him," said Irma. "All those first ladies were very nice ladies once."

Pizzi read data at length from the inside of his goggles; one could tell because his body language froze while his lips moved slightly. "Speaking of patron-age," he said, "your son has a nice job in Milan that was arranged by your late boss in there."

"Luigi doesn't know about that," said Irma. "He thinks he got that job on merit."

"How would it be if Luigi suddenly got that big promotion he's been wait-ing for? Our AI friend can guarantee that. Your son deserves a boost. He works hard."

Irma gave Tullio a hopeful, beseeching glance.

"My God, no wonder national governments broke down," said Tullio, scowl-ing. "With these sly big-data engines running the world, political backroom deals don't stand a chance! Our poor old dead boss, he really is a relic of the past now. I don't know whether to laugh or cry."

"Can't we just go inside?" urged the paparazzo. "It won't take five minutes."

It took longer, because the Shadow House would not allow the gossip's head-mounted device inside the premises. They had to unscrew the goggles from his head—Pizzi, with his merely human eyes exposed to fresh air, looked utterly bewildered—and they smuggled the device to the deathbed inside a Faraday bag.

Carlo Pizzi swept the camera's gaze over the dead man from head to foot, as if sprinkling the corpse with holy water. They then hurried out of the radio silence, so that Carlo Pizzi could upload his captured images to the waiting AI.

"Our friend the German machine has another proposal for you now," said Carlo Pizzi. "There's nothing much in it for me, but I'd be happy to tell you about it, just to be neighborly."

"What is the proposal?" said Irma.

"Well, this Shadow House poses a problem."

"Why?"

"Because it's an opaque structure in a transparent world. Human beings shouldn't be concealing themselves from ubiquitous machine awareness. That's pessimistic and backward-looking. This failure to turn a clean face to the future does harm to our society."

"Go on."

"Also, the dead man stored some secrets in here. Something to do with his previous political dealings, as Italian head of state, with German arms suppliers."

"Maybe he stored secrets, and maybe he didn't," said Tullio stoutly. "It's none of your business.

"It would be good news for business if the house burned down," said Carlo Pizzi. "I know that sounds shocking to humans, but good advice from wise machines often does. Listen. There are other places like this house, but much better and bigger. They're a series of naval surveillance towers, built at great state expense, to protect the Mediterranean coasts of Italy from migrants and terrorists. Instead of being Shadow Houses, they're tall and powerful Light Houses, with radar, sonar, lidar, and drone landing strips. Real military castles, with all the trimmings."

"I always adored lighthouses," said Irma wonderingly. "They're so remote and romantic."

"If this Shadow House should happen to catch fire," said Carlo Pizzi, "our friend could have you both appointed caretakers of one of those Italian sea castles. The world is so peaceful and progressive now, that those castles don't meet any threats. However, there's a lot of profit involved in keeping them open and running. Your new job would be just like your old job here—just with a different patron."

"Yes, but that's arson."

"The dead man has no heirs for his Shadow House," said Carlo Pizzi. "Our friend has just checked thoroughly, and that old man was so egotistical, and so confident that he would live forever, that he died intestate? . . . No, correction." Pizzi tapped his earpiece, listening. "I mean having already settled with any and all potential heirs. They all signed quit-claims, years ago. So, if you burn the house down, no one will miss it."

"There's the cat," said Tullio. "The cat would miss the house."

"What?"

"A cat lives in this house," said Tullio. "Why don't you get your friend the AI to negotiate with our house cat? See if it can make the cat a convincing offer."

Carlo Pizzi mulled this over behind his face-mounted screens. "The German AI was entirely unaware of the existence of the house cat."

"That's because a house cat is a living being and your friend is just a bunch of code. It's morally wrong to burn down houses. Arson is illegal. What would the Church say? Obviously it's a sin."

"You're just emotionally upset now, because you can't think as quickly and efficiently as an Artificial Intelligence," said Carlo Pizzi. "However, think it over at your own slow speed. The offer stands. I'll be going now, because if I stand too long around here, some algorithm might notice me here, and draw unwelcome conclusions."

"Good luck with your new novel," said Irma. "I hope it's as funny as your early, good ones."

Carlo Pizzi left hastily on his small and silent electric scooter. Tullio and Irma retreated within the Shadow House.

"The brazen nerve of that smart machine, to carry on so 'deus ex machina,'" said Tullio. "We can't burn down this beautiful place! Shadow House is a monument to privacy—to a vanishing, but noble way of life! Besides, you'd need thermite grenades to take out those steel panic rooms."

Irma looked dreamy. "I remember when the government of Italy went broke building all those security lighthouses. There must be dozens of them, far out to sea. Maybe we could have our pick."

"But those paranoid towers will never be refined and airy and beautiful, like this beach house! It would be like living in a nuclear missile silo."

"All of those are empty now, as well," said Irma.

"Those nuclear silos had Big Red Buttons, too, now that you mention it. We're all here because they never got pressed." He pondered a long moment. "We're never going to push that button, are we, Irma? I always wondered what kind of noise it would make."

"We never make big elephant noises," Irma replied with an eloquent shrug. "You and me, that's not how we live."

A TSUNAMI OF LIGHT

DAVID BRIN

Light appears to be pouring across the planet. Young people log their lives with hourly True Confessions. Cops wear lapel-cams—and citizens stare back, uploading images to safe storage in the Cloud. Spy agencies peer at us—but suffer defections and whistleblowers. Bank and corporate records leak like a torn sponge and "uncrackable" firewalls topple. As we debate Internet privacy, revenge porn, the NSA and Edward Snowden, one technological trend propels all others. Cameras will keep getting cheaper, smaller, better, more mobile and more numerous—each year—at a rate much faster than Moore's Law. Soon they will be too small to detect—concealed in that woman's earring, or that fellow's shirt button. Then on the corner of every cheap pair of sunglasses.

Meanwhile, biometric scanners will detect who you are, using a myriad individual identifiers that you cannot help but emit, from iris or retinal patterns to your face structure or voiceprint or walking gait, to the ratios of bones in your hands . . . all the way to otto-accoustic tones that most people involuntarily and unconsciously emit from their own ears. The gas that you pass will carry samples of your micro-biome, laying a trail no less decipherable than any left by a snail.

Now throw in lie detectors and strongly predictive personality profiling—two technologies glimmering on the near horizon.

Is it the dawn of Big Brother? Either the old-fashioned kind—top-down oppression by all-seeing elites? Or else something equally scary but more lateral: scrutiny by a billion nosy neighbors and judgmental "little brothers"? Certainly, the press and airwaves and blogosphere surge with relentless jeremiads of imminent doom.

In fact, some trends defy the dystopian reflex—the tendency for our simplistic fears to focus only on downsides. For example, 2013 was the best year for U.S. civil liberties in three decades, when it became "settled law" that citizens may record their encounters with police. No single matter could have been more important because it established the most basic right of *sousveillance* or looking back at power. For in altercations with authority, what recourse can a citizen turn to, other than the Truth? A huge victory for the little guy . . . though making it stick will be another matter.

A balanced view would reveal both good and bad trends, more evenly distributed than you'll ever see told by the Fear and Anger Industry. In fact, the core issue of our time is mostly ignored by hand-wringing pundits and mass media.

Light is going to flow.

You may try to stand athwart history with your hand out, shouting "stop!" But it will do scant good against a river.

In which case, can we at least use light to enhance the things we cherish most, and to serve as—in the words of Justice Brandeis—a "great disinfectant" of the bad? I interrogated this topic in a nonfiction book—*The Transparent Society: Will Technology Make Us Choose Between Privacy and Freedom?* Also in two novels, *Earth* and *Existence*.

Others have also been exploring this territory. And if science fiction is (per James Gunn) the "R&D department of the future," then no topic is more fitting for SF examination than how we all, as individuals and societies, will deal with all this firehose—this tsunami—of illumination.

And hence this volume, offering a broader range of visions about our near future. Authors contributing stories and essays to *Chasing Shadows* were encouraged to explore their own notions of what might propel—or obstruct—a world civilization awash, for well or ill, in information. When soliciting stories, among many provocative questions that we posed were:

- Can citizens answer surveillance with *sousveillance*, or shining accountability upward? Is that how we got the freedom we already have? Is there an answer to the famous saying by Juvenal: "Quis custodiet ipsos custodes?" Who will watch the watchmen?
- Might light spread unevenly among countries, classes or genders? Even if it's fair, might effects vary? Will those with power find ways to keep it, even while being watched?
- In Damon Knight's famous "I See You," humans adapt blithely to an extreme case—all people seeing all things, all the time. In contrast, the Dave Eggers novel *The Circle* portrays privacy becoming a social crime. In classic cyberpunk, a skilled rat manages to stymie "the machine" by exploiting shadows invisible to others. What possibilities strike you?

- Will we spiral into busybody judgementalism? Or might people choose a habit of leaving each other alone? Will some privacy survive, if you can always catch voyeurs in the act, and tell their moms?

- John W. Campbell said "an armed society is a polite society." (Also attributed to Robert A. Heinlein, who followed Campbell.) Is that assertion true? History clearly says: not really. But might Campbell's riff come true if guns are replaced by cameras? The quickest draw may not always win!

- For generations, in the west, formerly pariah groups became more accepted, after public exposure. Take gays and lesbians and trans people, for example—to everyone's surprise, light became their best friend.

    Is this effect—tolerance via revelation—limited to a few cultures? Does it arise from eyewitnessing the pain of others? So far, so good, but might empathy reach limits in a much more transparent world?

- If cheap methods will soon let us detect both lies and psychopathy, will such tools make resistance to tyranny futile, locking in Big Brother forever?

    Or—if all citizens can apply such tools upward, aiming them at all elites—might those same tools ensure Big Brother happens never?

- Can we *own* our information? Will folks jealously guard it? Or buy and sell it in a web bazaar?

- What does openness do to Hollywood rhythms of drama? Tech-driven disasters—e.g. those of Michael Crichton—always happen amid and because of secrecy. Would transparency help? Or might too many staring critics stifle innovation?

- Will artificial intelligences be as open as Facebook teens? Or will they skulk, looking for the last remaining shadows? Will they hold each other accountable? Is transparency, then, our best defense against "Skynet"?

- "Cycling Stasi!" shouts the *London Daily Mail*: "Vigilantes in lycra are filming your every move!" The complaint? A trend for urban bicyclists to carry helmet-mounted cams and then upload anything they deem improper, from genuine misbehavior to a woman eating cereal in her car. Oh, each time something like this happens, handwringers never imagine ways that victims might fight back, as in the old song, "Harper Valley PTA." Can you, as a science-fiction writer or reader, envision this, so that even in an age of cameras, the meek will have the power to say (with some effectiveness) "MYOB!" (Mind Your Own Business)?

- About those tradeoffs—is there some missing element that could tip the balance, making light more effective for good and less threatening to eccentric individualism?

Authors and essayists who were invited to contribute to *Chasing Shadows* were asked to explore all these topics and more, in this anthology about a coming era when—for well and ill—we all step into the open. Into the light. But you, the reader, should judge. Was this challenge taken up successfully? Or else, scanning the list of topics above—plus your own concerns—do you feel there's more than enough unexamined ground for a sequel?

A word or two about how we got rolling on this project. It was sponsored, in part, by The Arthur C. Clarke Center for Human Imagination which—in cooperation with UCSD's Center for Design and CalIT2—plans to hold a two-day symposium to correlate with this anthology. The symposium may also produce an accompanying volume of academic papers. This kind of synergy among science-fiction authors, academics, civil servants and the corporate world has precedents, such as the successful 100 Year Starship conference of 2013, also sponsored by the Clarke Center. It is a template for combining and crossfertilizing various methods for exploring the ground ahead, a future filled with both dangers and opportunities.

LIBERTAS PERFUNDET OMNIA LUCE

The stories in this volume certainly span a range, with Nancy Fulda and Aliette de Bodard showing true science-fictional daring, as they portray far future worlds very different from ours, yet still realms where human beings struggle for self-discovery and growth. In contrast, Jack Skillingstead and Karl Schroeder depict very near tomorrows, revealing how the lives of normal people might change, if light flows in just the next few years.

We got political, in some places, with libertarian-leaning pieces by Gregory Benford and Robert Sawyer, who suggest that technologies of vision will enable free citizens to dispense with most government. Other authors, like Brenda Cooper and Vylar Kaftan, come from a more communitarian inclination, yet reach generally the same conclusion! How interesting that such a wide range of visionary authors—from liberal to libertarian and in wildly varied visions—nevertheless converge toward a shared ambition, reflecting how individuals may be empowered to hold each other accountable without (very much) coercion from above. (Who else but science-fiction authors would have the guts to transcend hobbling clichés like the shallow-silly left-right political axis?)

Oh but change won't come without poignancy or loss! Tales by Cat Rambo, Kathleen Goonan, David Ramirez, David Walton and Scott Sigler all show (in their own, uniquely vivid ways) how human beings will *remain* human—still wracked with doubts, worries and heartbreak, even when we're forced to admit that the world, as a whole, is getting better. Or even if it gets a lot better! Who wouldn't want to live in the future portrayed by Bruce Sterling? Well, his retired politician, for one. The kind of predatory user who thrived back in the dark ages of the twentieth and early twenty-first centuries.

Our reprints in *Chasing Shadows* are mostly classics of the genre, shining ageless light upon the problems and potential benefits of transparency, as well as revealing how far back great authors were thinking about such things. I'll leave it to our scholars—James Gunn and Stephen W. Potts—to comment on these treasures by Damon Knight, Robert Silverberg, R.C. Fitzpatrick and Neal Stephenson. Let me only comment that my own reprinted contribution to the volume, a story about crime and punishment in a tech-illuminated future, could be taken as an homage to Bob Silverberg's timeless tale . . . though I don't recall reading "To See the Invisible Man," before I wrote "Insistence of Vision." Sometimes great ideas . . .

Our essayists pursue truth more explicitly, offering perspective on how transparency might make us all more safe (Vinge), or help to keep us free (Gibson), or turn us into better citizens, or make government more effective at both protecting and serving us.

Of course, the treatises by Gunn and Potts remind us that one tool helps us to explore beyond the horizons of policy and even science. That tool is science fiction—truly the R&D department of human civilization, probing where other methods cannot peer, for dangers and opportunities. Beyond this horizon.

■ ■ ■

Speaking of valuable lessons from SF, we have all been taught, especially by George Orwell, to fret about threats to this narrow and recent renaissance of relative freedom. If we do succeed in extending this rare miracle, it will be in no small part owed to the self-preventing prophecy of *1984* and other dire warnings that girded millions to fight against Big Brother. Readers who self-identify with the "right" or the "left" may differ over which direction poses a more likely threat to liberty—bureaucracy or plutocracy—but most of us share the same general dread.

Alas, this excellent instinct all too often translates into a reflex to *hide*. To believe that we can stymie would-be tyrants by scurrying into shadows, by shrouding our communications in encryption, for example, or by passing noble-sounding laws that forbid elites to look at us. (Name one time when that prescription ever worked.) Or by using hackertech to scurry in hidden corners, as recommended by cyberpunk tales, the most romantic in all of Sci Fi.

Those who have read *The Transparent Society* know there is another possible approach, one that is more militant and aggressive than hiding, in every way. One that has the advantage of a track record, having actually worked somewhat . . . a bit, sometimes, barely enough . . . for two centuries or so. It is the answer to Juvenal's question about who will watch the watchmen, and it was the Latin title to this section:

"Freedom will flood all things with light."

Hence, let me conclude *Chasing Shadows* with a little lagniappe. Part polemic and part parable, it attempts to put our present dilemma in perspective. Not by looking ahead this time, but reaching back to a past era, when human beings first tried this great experiment. In openness. In enlightenment.

THE GARDEN OF OPENNESS

Ancient Greek myths tell of a farmer, Akademos, who did a favor for the sun god. In return, Apollo granted the mortal a garden wherein he could say whatever he liked, even about the mighty Olympians, without retribution. Inspired by this tale-—the earliest allegory about free speech—citizens of Periclean Athens used to gather at the Academy to openly debate issues of the day.

Now the fable of Akademos always puzzled me at one level. How could a mortal trust the storied Greek deities—notoriously mercurial, petty and vengeful—to keep their promise? Especially when impudent humans started telling bad Zeus jokes? Apollo might set up impenetrable barriers around the glade, so no god could peer in. That might work. But Akademos would have few visitors to join him, cowering under sunless walls.

The alternative was to empower Akademos with an equalizer, some way to enforce the gods' promise. And that equalizing factor could only be knowledge.

But more about that in a moment.

First though—how did the Athenians fare in their real-life experiment with free speech?

Alas, democracy and openness were new and difficult concepts. Outspoken Socrates eventually paid a stiff price for candor in the Academy. Whereupon his student, Plato, took paradoxical revenge by denouncing openness, calling instead for strict government by an elite. Plato's advice served to justify countless tyrants during the millennia since.

But humanity cannot be repressed forever. Right now the democratic vision is getting another trial run. Today's "academy" extends far beyond Earth's major universities. Throughout the world, millions have begun to accept the daring notion that disagreement isn't toxic. Free speech is increasingly seen as the best font of criticism—the only practical and effective antidote to error.

Let there be no mistake; this is a hard lesson, especially since each of us would be a tyrant if we could. (Some with the best intentions.) Very little in history—or human nature—prepared us for the task ahead, living in a tribe of six billion equal citizens, each guided by his or her own sovereign will, loosely administered by chiefs we elect, under just rules that we made through hard negotiation among ourselves. Any other generation would have thought it an impossible ambition—though countless ancestors strove, getting us to the point where we can try.

Even among those who profess allegiance to this new hope, there is bitter struggle over how best to resist the old gods of wrath, bigotry and oppression—spirits who reside not on some mountain peak, but in the heart of each man or woman who tries to gain power at the expense of others. Perhaps our descendants will be mature enough to curb these impulses all by themselves. Meanwhile, we must foil those who rationalize robbing freedom, claiming it's their right . . . or that it's for our own good. In other words, we still face the same dilemma that confronted Akademos.

According to some champions of liberty, shields of *secrecy* will put common folk on even ground with the mighty. Privacy must be defined by rules or tools that enhance concealment. One wing of this movement would create Eurostyle privacy commissions, pass a myriad laws and dispatch clerks to police what may be known by doctors, corporations and ultimately individuals. Another wing of strong privacy prefers libertarian technofixes—empowering individuals with encryption and cybernetic anonymity. Both wings claim we must build high walls to safeguard every private garden, each sanctum of the mind.

This widespread modern myth has intuitive appeal. And I can only reply that it's been tried, without even one example of a commonwealth that thrived based on this principle.

There is a better way—a method largely responsible for this renaissance we're living in. Instead of trying to blind the mighty—a futile goal, if ever there was one—we have emphasized the power of openness, giving free citizens knowledge and unprecedented ability to hold elites accountable. Every day we prove it works, rambunctiously demanding to know, rather than trying to stop others from knowing.

(Isn't it far easier to verify *that you know something* than to verify that someone else *doesn't*?)

It's called accountability—a light that can shine even on gods of authority. Whether they gather in the Olympian heights of government, amid the spuming currents of commerce, or in Hadean shadows of criminality, they cannot harm us while pinned by its glare.

Accountability is the only defense that truly protects free speech, in a garden that stands proudly, with no walls.

ACKNOWLEDGMENTS

Our appreciation goes to others who gave their time and talents to this project: Cheryl Brigham for her insightful reading and critique, Beverly F. Price for her office and technical support, and Robert Williamson, intern at The Arthur C. Clarke Center for Human Imagination, for eagerness to perform a variety of tasks. The Clarke Center's generous support included encouragement from Director Sheldon Brown and Program Manager Laura Martin. Also appreciated, vital engagement by Jennifer Gunnels and David Hartwell of Tor Books.

ABOUT THE AUTHORS

James Gunn, named Grand Master by the Science Fiction and Fantasy Writers of America, is a professor emeritus of English and the founding director of the Gunn Center for the Study of Science Fiction at the University of Kansas. His books include *Transcendental*, *The Magicians*, *The Immortals*, and *The Listeners*.

Nancy Fulda's stories have appeared in *Asimov's Science Fiction*, *Apex Magazine*, and *Daily Science Fiction*. She received the Jim Baen Memorial Award and has worked as an editor of *Jim Baen's Universe* and the SFWA website.

R. C. Fitzpatrick published several science-fiction stories in the 1960s, mostly in *Analog Science Fiction and Fact*. He was nominated for a 1966 Nebula Award for his novelette "Half a Loaf."

James Morrow's satiric novels *Only Begotten Daughter* and *Towing Jehovah* both received the World Fantasy Award. His shorter fiction has won the Theodore Sturgeon Memorial Award and, twice, the Nebula Award. In 2005 he was honored with the Prix Utopia. Morrow's latest novel, *Galápagos Regained*, celebrates the coming of the Darwinian worldview.

Damon Knight (1922–2002) was a Hugo Award–winning writer, best known for stories such as "To Serve Man" and "The Country of the Kind." A founder of the Science Fiction and Fantasy Writers of America and the Clarion Writers' Workshop, he was later named a SFWA Grand Master and inducted into the Science Fiction Hall of Fame.

David Walton's first novel, *Terminal Mind*, won the 2008 Philip K. Dick Award for best SF paperback of the year. His most recent books are the quantum-physics murder mysteries *Superposition* and *Supersymmetry*. By day he works as an engineer for Lockheed Martin and is the father of seven children.

Vylar Kaftan's stories have appeared in *Lightspeed, Strange Horizons, Asimov's Science Fiction*, and *Clarkesworld*. In 2013, she won a Nebula Award for her novella *The Weight of the Sunrise,* and in the same year a Sidewise Award for alternate history for the same work.

Jack McDevitt has won the Nebula, Philip K. Dick, Arthur C. Clarke, John W. Campbell, and Robert A. Heinlein Awards for his many short stories, novellas, and novels. His most recent novels include *Starhawk, Coming Home,* and *Thunderbird*.

Vernor Vinge is Emeritus Professor of Computer Science at San Diego State University. His science-fiction novels have won five Hugo Awards, including ones for *A Fire upon the Deep, A Deepness in the Sky,* and *Rainbows End*.

Aliette de Bodard has won two Nebula Awards, a Locus Award, and a British Science Fiction Award. Her novels include *The House of Shattered Wings, Obsidian and Blood,* and *On a Red Station, Drifting,* which was a finalist for the Nebula, Hugo, and Locus Awards.

David Ramirez was inspired by *Jurassic Park* into giving molecular biology a try and working on the Human Genome Project. Since then, he has realized that it was more the fiction part of science fiction that he loved. His novel *The Forever Watch* was published in 2014.

Neal Stephenson is the author of *Seveneves, Reamde, Anathem*, and the three-volume historical epic the Baroque Cycle (*Quicksilver, The Confusion,* and *The System of the World*), as well as *Cryptonomicon, The Diamond Age, Snow Crash,* and *Zodiac*. He lives in Seattle, Washington.

Jack Skillingstead's stories have been published in *Asimov's Science Fiction, Realms of Fantasy,* and *The Magazine of Fantasy and Science Fiction*. He has been a finalist for both the Philip K. Dick Award and the Theodore Sturgeon Award. His books include *Harbinger, Are You There and Other Stories*, and *Life on the Preservation*.

Gregory Benford is Emeritus Professor of Physics and Astronomy at the University of California at Irvine. He has published science fiction since the 1960s, won a Nebula Award for the novella *If Stars Are Gods,* coauthored with Gordon Eklund, and received multiple awards for his 1980 novel *Timescape,* including the Nebula, the John W. Campbell Award, and the British Science Fiction Association Award. His other novels include *In the Ocean of Night, Great Sky River,* and *In the Heart of the Comet,* written with David Brin.

Robert J. Sawyer has won the Hugo, Nebula, and John W. Campbell Memorial Awards, all for best science-fiction novel of the year, plus Canada's Aurora Award (a record-setting thirteen times), Spain's Premio UPC de Ciencia Ficción (three times), Japan's Seiun Award (three times), and China's Galaxy Award. He holds honorary doctorates from the University of Winnipeg and Laurentian University. The ABC TV series *FlashForward* was based on his novel of the same name. His twenty-third novel, *Quantum Night,* was published in March 2016.

Brenda Cooper is a technology professional and futurist. Her novels include *The Silver Ship and the Sea, Edge of Dark,* and *The Creative Fire,* the latter in the Ruby's Song series. She coauthored the novel *Building Harlequin's Moon* with Larry Niven. Her short stories have appeared in the collection *Cracking the Sky.*

Stephen W. Potts is a faculty member in the Department of Literature at the University of California, San Diego, where he specializes in modern fiction and popular culture. He has published books and articles on a range of subjects, especially science fiction and science studies, as well as editorials, reviews, and short fiction. In 1993, he won the Eaton Award for his monograph on Arkady and Boris Strugatsky.

Cat Rambo's short stories have appeared in *Asimov's Science Fiction, Weird Tales,* and *Strange Horizons.* Her collections include *Near+Far* and *Eyes Like Sky and Coal and Moonlight.* Her work has been short-listed for both the World Fantasy and Nebula Awards. She is the current (2016) president of the Science Fiction and Fantasy Writers of America.

Stephen Gaskell is a freelance video-game script consultant. His stories have appeared in *Interzone, Clarkesworld,* and anthologies such as *The Year's Best Military SF and Space Opera.* He coedited the anthology *Extreme Planets* with David Brin.

Scott Sigler is the creator of fifteen novels, six novellas, and dozens of short stories. His works are available from Crown Publishing and Del Rey Books. He is also a cofounder of Empty Set Entertainment, which publishes his young-adult Galactic Football League series. Scott lives in San Diego, California.

Robert Silverberg has won Hugo or Nebula Awards in every decade since the 1950s. Named a Grand Master by the Science Fiction Writers of America, he is the author of such novels as *Nightwings, A Time of Changes, Downward to the Earth, Dying Inside,* and *Lord Valentine's Castle,* as well as such shorter works as "Born with the Dead" and *Sailing to Byzantium.* When not engaged with science fiction, he has produced several books on archaeology and history.

Ramez Naam is a computer scientist, an entrepreneur, and the multiple award-winning author of five books, including the brain-hacking Nexus trilogy. He teaches at Singularity University on energy and environment. Follow him on twitter at @ramez or find him on the web at rameznaam.com.

Karl Schroeder is a Canadian science-fiction writer and futurist. Having published ten novels translated into as many languages, in 2011 Karl received a Masters in Strategic Foresight and Innovation from OCAD University, and consults on trends and opportunities for clients in government and industry. He lives in Toronto, Canada, with his wife and daughter.

Kathleen Ann Goonan is a visiting professor at the Georgia Institute of Technology. Her novels include *Queen City Jazz, This Shared Dream,* and *In War Times,* winner of the John W. Campbell Award.

Bruce Sterling, winner of Hugo, Clarke, and Campbell Awards, is a contributing editor of *WIRED* magazine. A central figure in the cyberpunk literary movement of the 1980s, he has produced such novels as *Islands in the Net, The Difference Engine* (with William Gibson), *The Caryatids,* and *Schismatrix Plus.*

David Brin is a scientist and futurist. His award-winning novels include *Earth* and *Existence,* as well as *The Postman* (loosely adapted into a movie by Kevin Costner), and the Uplift series. His nonfiction work *The Transparent Society: Will Technology Force Us to Choose Between Privacy and Freedom?* won the Freedom of Speech Award of the American Library Association.